FASHION

The Industry and Its Careers

Michele Granger
Missouri State University

Fairchild Publications, Inc.

New York

Director of Sales and Acquisitions: Dana Meltzer-Berkowitz

Executive Editor: Olga T. Kontzias

Senior Development Editor: Jennifer Crane

Development Editor: Sylvia L. Weber

Art Director: Adam B. Bohannon

Production Manager: Ginger Hillman

Senior Production Editor: Elizabeth Marotta

Cover Design: Adam B. Bohannon

Text Design: Nicola Ferguson

Library of Congress Catalog Card Number: 2006939042

ISBN: 978-1-56367-580-5

GST R 133004424

Printed in the United States of America

CH08, TP13

CONTENTS

Contents

EXTENDED CONTENTS

UNIT 3 THE ANCILLARY BUSINESSES

PREFACE

Fashion: The Industry and Its Careers is a text written for an introductory course that provides an overview or survey of the global fashion industry. It is based on three broad assumptions of education as they relate to the fashion industry.

▸ Students immerse themselves in studies they find personally and professionally relevant. They often view college as a means to an end, the end being a rewarding career. Most students who enroll in an introductory fashion, clothing and textiles, or interior design course possess a passion for fashion. A passion for lifelong learning, one hopes, becomes an integral part of the students' lives as it is clarified through the students' college journey.

▸ Fashion is a lifestyle that permeates many industry segments, from apparel and accessories to home fashions to beauty and wellness. We see it in films, books, leisure activities, travel destinations, and people.

▸ The careers within the sectors of the fashion industry provide an ideal way to define the industry and illustrate its various levels, from raw materials to ancillary services.

The first premise of this text is that the majority of students accurately perceive that an education is the gateway to a career, one in which they could not or would not be prepared to enter without a college education. Many students enroll in an introductory fashion course knowing that they love the world of fashion, yet wondering what careers exist in this world. They often recognize the careers of designer and buyer but what career tracks are available and where are those jobs found? Many students cannot imagine that they can spend a lifetime working in an area (fashion) they enjoy and in which they can apply their individual talents and skills. By examining the different levels or sectors of the fashion industry and exploring the career options that exist at each level, students will have the opportunity to see themselves on career paths and this will provide the students with goals for their educational experience. While there are numerous, excellent textbooks that provide an overview of the fashion industry, few, if any, provide overviews of employment opportunities within this industry and the qualifications needed to take part in those careers. Motivation and direction become critical factors in students' success.

The second premise of the text is that fashion is not limited to the world of apparel and accessories. It includes all products and services that are influenced by changing trends in form, materials, theme, and color. Form may range from modern, simple shapes to ornate Versailles influences. These forms can be revealed in a season's hairstyles, evening gowns, architecture, and bedroom suites. Alternately, the theme of a particular season may be based on a geographic location (e.g., Asia, Africa, or the Caribbean), a time period (e.g., the film stars of the 1940s or the "love children" of the 1960s), celebrities, movies and videos, visual arts, and more. Even more, new color palettes of dusty tones or bright primaries may be popular one season but not during another. Whether reflected in clothing, handbags, jewelry, shoes, cosmetics, fashion magazines, stationery, wall and floor coverings, as well as other home furnishings and accessories—for women, men, and children—fashion represents a lifestyle. Think of the artistic self-expressionist, the British gentleman, the retro teen, the glamour girl; all of them represent different fashion lifestyles by what they put on their bodies, the paper on which they write or print their letters, and the environments in which they live.

As people spend more time in their homes, either working, relaxing, or entertaining, they also spend more money on their homes, either renovating, decorating, or updating. As a result, fashion designers, textile producers, and retailers are paying more attention to the home furnishings and home accessories businesses. "Home fashion" is the umbrella term that refers to these two industries. The trend toward spending more leisure time at home, as well as more money on our homes, has increased the product life cycle of home fashions and has encouraged many well-known apparel designers to enter the field. Vera Wang, Donna Karan, Ralph Lauren, Nicole Miller, and Calvin Klein are just a few of the many top apparel designers who now design home fashion lines as well.

The third premise of this text is that the careers within the sectors of the fashion industry provide an ideal way to define and explain the industry and illustrate its various levels, from raw materials to ancillary services. Designers develop products for manufacturers, but retailers with private label lines also employ designers. A fashion stylist can be the person who modifies designs or the person who sets up a fashion shoot. Manufacturers hire people to buy, yet so do retailers. Some fashion products are not tangible; they are services. A career path may be titled one way by a manufacturer and another way by a producer in the same product area. If students understand what the jobs are and where they are located in the big picture of the fashion industry, then interpreting these position titles as actual careers is simpler. Exploring the industry by highlighting the careers in each industry segment provides a framework that allows students to see how the various levels work together because it can be confusing to the student beginning studies in a fashion-related program.

ORGANIZATION OF THE TEXT

Fashion: The Industry and Its Careers is organized in three parts, beginning with the creators and providers of raw materials and the manufacturers of products, followed by the retailers who create and/or sell the products to the consumer, and, finally, the auxiliary industries that support the work done by the product creators and product retailers. The text is organized in the following sequence: Unit 1, "Careers in Raw Materials and Manufacturing in the Fashion Industry;" Unit 2, "Careers in Product Development and Sales for the Fashion Retailer;" and Unit 3, "The Ancillary Businesses."

Unit 1: Careers in Raw Materials and Manufacturing in the Fashion Industry

The primary level begins with people responsible for the inspiration and conception of the fashion product's parts and raw materials (e.g., the forecasters, designers, and sourcing personnel). This section covers the manufacturers of fibers, fabrics, and products and features the promoters and sales personnel of the parts of the product. Finally, the "number crunchers," or accountants, and "people persons," or human resources managers, of the primary level of the industry are highlighted in this unit. In addition to the manufacturers of the parts of the product, the manufacturers of the completed fashion goods are examined, and the ways in which these manufacturers make and then market their products to retail buyers are explored.

Unit 2: Careers in Product Development and Sales for the Fashion Retailer

The secondary level of the fashion industry represents the retailers of fashion products, from apparel to home furnishings, and those involved with creating a desire in the consumer for the retailer's fashion goods. Design and product development for private label goods, promotion and sales of products, as well as merchandising and management in retailing, are also examined in Unit 2.

Unit 3: The Ancillary Businesses

A wide range of providers of fashion goods and services support the producers and retailers. These providers interconnect within the fashion industry, often offering services, and they are frequently structured as entrepreneurial ventures. Careers in fashion print, stage, and media are discussed, as are historical costume and education. Real estate and environments (e.g., contract interior design and website development) provide additional career opportunities, as does the beauty sector of the fashion industry. Cosmetics and wellness providers are key components of this sector.

FEATURES OF THE TEXT

Fashion: The Industry and Its Careers provides current visuals, discussion questions, and terminology used in the industry. These text features are included to help clarify concepts, stimulate class discussion, and encourage critical thinking with applications, illustrations, and industry buzzwords. Boxes feature help-wanted advertisements for key positions, profiles of individuals working in various aspects of the fashion industry, and readings from recently published articles. A glossary of key terms is included at the end of the text. Relevant education, work experience, salary ranges, personal characteristics, and challenges for different career paths are examined. Each of the 16 chapters concludes with a summary that highlights the content of each section. Finally, an instructor's guide is available to assist with course organization, class discussions, and teaching ideas.

ACKNOWLEDGMENTS

To Annie Wilson. How fortunate I am to be the mother of a beautiful ray of sunshine who is now in college. You have always shown me new ways to see the world. Now, I see my professional life through the student's eyes and my personal life as one of lifting off and letting go.

To Scott Axon. What a treasure I found in you. Thank you for working to make every day of my life better, for cherishing me always, and for flowers at the end of every chapter.

To Mom, Dad, Joe, and Patty Granger. Thank you for family dinners, a life of travel, and unconditional love.

To the Cool Girls. Thank you for love, support, and a dose of humility exactly when it is needed. You are there through fire and flood, and my life is enriched by all of you.

To Melody Edmondson. Only a lifelong friend can see into my head and my heart the way you do. You are my fashion consultant, secret sharer, and selected sister.

To Kirsty Buchanan and Sarah Riley. There are some people in your life with whom you never miss a beat. You two are my drummers.

To the women in my office, Nancy Asay, Sandy Bailey, Jeannie Ireland, Pat Juncos, Marciann Patton, and Jenifer Roberts. You have all contributed to this book through your friendship and expertise and for never saying I looked exhausted when I did. Jenifer, thank you for the original material included in the retail merchandising and management chapters.

To Jennifer McKelvie. Thank you for organizing, motivating, and selecting the visuals in the text. Fashion design consumers and students of the future will be influenced by your intelligence, energy, and talent.

Acknowledgments

To my students, past and present. You inspire me to do and be better. Most of you have become designers, buyers, and entrepreneurs; others will. Your career success stories are at the heart of this project.

To Olga Kontzias, executive editor at Fairchild Books. Paris, fashion, family, and great reads—these passions we share. Thank you for thinking of me when envisioning a need for this book. You are the model editor and *mon amie*.

To Jennifer Crane, senior development editor; Sylvia Weber, development editor; Elizabeth Marotta, senior production editor; Adam Bohannon, art director; Erin Fitzsimmons, photo researcher; and all of Fairchild Books. Much gratitude for your direction and assistance throughout the process.

To the reviewers. Your thorough and helpful recommendations made this product much better than it ever could have been as a solo project. The reviewers are Marie Aja-Herrera, Savannah College of Art and Design; Camille Aponte, Katherine Gibbs School, New York; Naomi Gross, Fashion Institute of Technology; Kathryn Jakes, The Ohio State University; Nicole Leinbach, Columbia College (Chicago); Pilar Saiki, International Academy of Design and Technology, Chicago; and Carolyn A. Thomas, International Academy of Design and Technology, Las Vegas.

FASHION

manu fact

raw fashion

ials

materials

raw

mater

fash

ash

raw

manufa

mate

ashion

UNIT 1

CAREERS IN RAW MATERIALS AND MANUFACTURING IN THE FASHION INDUSTRY

Unit 1 provides an overview of the firms that supply the information and components of fashion products to the producers that create the final products. Trend forecasters, those who interpret, inspire, and predict shifts in fashion preferences, have tremendous influence on both the raw materials and the actual outcomes of fashion production. Textile product developers and designers use colors, textures, patterns, and finishes to create the foundation on which fashion products are built. Sourcing personnel locate the components of products, constantly seeking unique, efficient, and value-appropriate fabrics and findings that become part of the fashion merchandise. Sourcing personnel may also find factories, particularly overseas, to produce the merchandise. Production employees work together to manufacture the final product, while promotion and sales personnel generate an interest and create a desire among the retail buyers who purchase the products for the ultimate consumer.

Unit 1 also discusses two aspects of products that are often overlooked by prospective fashion career professionals: accounting and human resources.

Accounting for the manufacturer begins with determining costs of goods and wholesale prices and ends with analyzing the bottom line, whether or not the company is generating a profit. Human resources focuses on the locating, hiring, training, motivating, and rewarding of all of the people who work within the companies that create fashion products.

CHAPTER 1

Trend Forecasting

When we, as consumers, walk into apparel, accessories, or home furnishings retail stores, we are introduced to the latest trends in fashion. Who decides what the latest themes, colors, or fabrics will be? From where do these concepts come? How far ahead of the retail season are these trends determined? What will next year's fashion trends be? No company has a crystal ball to foresee the future of fashion. The person responsible for making these predictions is the **trend forecaster**, or a **fashion forecaster**.

Customers are often unaware of the amount of lead time that fashion products require. **Lead time** refers to the number of days, weeks, or months needed for the intricate planning and production steps to be implemented before fashion products actually arrive at the retail store. Lead time includes the time fashion forecasters need to analyze and project colors, design themes, fabrications, and fabric patterns or prints, often years in advance of the actual manufacturing of the products. Without that proverbial crystal ball, trend forecasters must combine their knowledge of fashion design and history with consumer research and business information. If trend forecasters develop and market their visions of the fashion future effectively, designers, retailers, and manufacturers in the textiles, apparel, accessories, and home furnishings sectors who subscribe to the forecasters' ideas have an edge, and their lines will be on the mark for their specific target markets. They will have lower purchasing risks and greater opportunities to increase their customer following and, ultimately, their sales volume.

Many large corporations have research and development, or R and D, departments. In essence, trend forecasters are the *R* components of the R and D departments in the fashion business. They lead the research activities of the fashion industry and may also be involved in developmental functions. As researchers, trend forecasters provide new knowledge to designers, buyers, and product developers; assist in the development of new products; and look for ways to improve old products. Forecasters search for facts and then analyze the findings to predict trends that will positively affect the amount and types of fashion products consumers will buy.

Few career opportunities in fashion relate to all levels of the industry. Trend forecasting is one of the few. Population trends and interests, availability of raw materials, manufacturing capabilities, retail changes, merchandising and management developments, and entrepreneurial endeavors influence fashion forecasting. This chapter will introduce the career path of fashion forecasters, from those in color and textile forecasting to those in theme, form, and detail forecasting.

THE JOB OF A TREND FORECASTER

The position of trend forecaster is one of the most influential career options in the fashion industry. Many fashion consumers and most prospective fashion industry employees wonder where the latest and greatest fashion trends originate. Fashion forecasters continually monitor consumers and the industry through traveling, reading, networking, and, most important, observing. Fashion forecasters attend trade shows, where they analyze the wholesale end of the business by looking at new products and fresh designs from established and new designers. They gather information from the media on population, design, manufacturing, and retail trends to determine what the new looks, silhouettes, colors, and fabrics will be for upcoming seasons.

Types of Forecasters

There are four primary types of trend forecasters. First, there is the forecaster who works for a fiber or fabric house, such as Cotton Incorporated. Second, there is the forecaster who specializes in color trends and is employed by a firm such as *The color box*. This forecaster provides information on color preferences and palettes for a wide variety of clients, from automobile manufacturers to flooring producers to apparel designers. Next, there is the forecaster who projects population trends and explores the social, economic, geographic, technological, and demographic shifts in the population. The population trend forecaster tracks a population's age shifts; residential and geographic preferences; changes in family sizes and structures; entertainment preferences; spending patterns; and influences by celebrities, films, and art, as well as other people-related topics. Finally, there is the forecaster who is employed by a broad-spectrum firm, such as Promostyl and Trend Union. These companies provide information on all of the trend areas, including color, fabrications, silhouettes, fashion influences, design themes, and population trends. In essence, they offer a one-stop-shopping trend-forecasting service.

Sources of Information

Where do forecasters go for information? It depends on the forecasters' market sector in which they specialize (e.g., color, demographics, apparel, or home) or consumer segment they are investigating (e.g., contemporary women, preteens, or men). There is, however, a range of information sources that most trend forecasters find to be valuable. Following is a list of popular trend-forecasting resources:

Figure 1.1. An elaborate couture design by John Galliano for Dior.

▶ **Market research firms:** There are companies that, for a fee, provide specific information on consumer market segments, population changes by age and/or location, occupational shifts, income and spending patterns among consumer types, and related topics. Additionally, government data is available on similar subjects through resources such as the U.S. Census Bureau.

▶ **The couture collections:** Dior, Chanel, Celine, Gucci, Armani, Prada, Versace—the list of prominent and influential designers is a long one. The introductions of their seasonal collections are important times for fashion forecasters as these industry leaders have a great influence on future ready-to-wear and home trends (Figure 1.1).

Figure 1.2. Students can offer fresh interpretations of clothing and textile design, such as this manipulated Tyvek garment by Jennifer McKelvie at Missouri State University.

▶ **New designers:** Up-and-coming designers with fresh ideas and approaches to the fashion that we wear and live in and around are significant resources for trend information. Their collections are often viewed with as much enthusiasm and interest by trend forecasters as those of the established couturiers (Figure 1.2).

▶ **Other fashion services:** Apparel and accessories forecasters may subscribe to color forecasting services, for example. Some subscribe to competitors' services to stay on top of what the competition is doing.

▶ **Trade shows:** International fiber and fabric markets, such as Interstoff in Germany and Expofil in Paris (Figure 1.3), are primary information sources for forecasters who are researching color and textile trends. There are apparel and accessories trade shows at the markets in New York City, Dallas, Los Angeles, Las Vegas, and Chicago, to name a few. High Point, North Carolina, offers markets in home textiles and furnishings.

▶ **Communication with peers:** Networking is a key activity for trend forecasters. Updates from designers, buyers, and manufacturers can provide significant information on what is selling and what is not. Communication with representatives of key suppliers can assist the forecaster in identifying trends. Membership in professional organizations, such as the Fashion Group International, Inc., the International Textile and Apparel Association (ITAA), and the American Society of Interior Designers (ASID), also provides trend forecasters with the opportunity to network with others in the know in the fashion industry.

▶ **E-sources:** Websites, online music programs, chat rooms, news sites, and e-catalogs are valuable resources that are easily accessible to trend forecasters. Also, forecasters may subscribe to specific online trend-forecasting resources. A number of these sites are provided at the end of this chapter.

► **Design sources:** Reference books, historical costume collections and texts, vintage clothing shops, antique dealers, museums, bookstores, and libraries are excellent resources for forecasters who are exploring the influence of past eras on fashion, as in Figure 1.4. Videos and photographs of recent collections, designers' boutiques through mass merchandising stores, fashion shows, and home sewing stores are some examples of design resources that trend forecasters use for information on current designer and trend information.

► **Publications:** Trade journals and international consumer magazines are common, obvious sources for trend information. It is less apparent, however, that many apparel and accessories forecasters subscribe to shelter magazines to identify color, fabric, and theme trends in the home—and vice versa. New colors in automobiles are often gleaned from successful hues in home furnishings and apparel. Trend forecasters often read it all.

► **The arts:** Music venues, visual arts, dance, and theater can interrelate with fashion trends. For example, a Matisse exhibit that travels internationally, portrayed in Figure 1.5, can have an impact on textile patterns and color palettes of a particular season. Additionally, the wardrobes in a play, film, or television show can influence fashion trends. Think about *Sex and the City* and Carrie's much-imitated wardrobe or the costumes and accessories in *Marie Antoinette*.

► **Entertainment headliners:** Celebrities greatly influence fashion trends. People in the news, on the red carpet, in videos, on the radio, and on the big screen have the ability to set trends. For example, days after Oscars are

Figure 1.3. Expofil in Paris is among the world's premier international fabric trade shows.

Figure 1.4. Flea markets provide a visual smorgasbord of past decades of fashion, interiors, and cultural items.

Figure 1.5. Matisse's "Purple Robe and Anemones" from the Cone Collection at the Baltimore Museum of Art.

awarded, celebrity gowns are copied and made available to consumers (Figure 1.6). Forecasters often watch up-and-coming celebrities and project which newcomers have the star quality and visibility that will make them future stars. Forecasters observe what they wear, who their favorite designers are, how they style their hair, and where they hang out with friends. Since forecasters have to anticipate the actual trends before they happen, identifying the people who will influence future trends is a critical part of the forecaster's job.

▸ **Fabrics:** Cotton Incorporated is a company that represents the cotton industry and provides trend information to designers and retailers. Fabric mills may also develop trend information for current and prospective buyers.

▸ **Travel:** Vacation hot spots often are filled with people who influence fashion trends. Additionally, certain fashion trends develop in specific geographic locations. Brazil's low-cut jeans, Belgium's deconstruction techniques in apparel, and New York's retrospective exhibit of Chanel at the Metropolitan Museum of Art are examples of the travel destinations from which fashion trends have developed (Figure 1.7).

▸ **Lifestyle trends:** Think about the following lifestyle trends: an increasing interest in health and fitness, the baby boomers' desire to entertain at home, and couples deciding to have fewer children and start their families at a later age than previous generations. Next, ask yourself how these lifestyle changes influence fashion. Workout wear sales have increased. Patio furniture, cookware, and tabletop accessories have received a renewed interest in the home furnishings and accessories industries. The number of pieces sold in children's wear has decreased; however, sales in this merchandise classification have increased due to higher unit prices. Two working parents who have launched their careers and waited to have children often have the finances and desire to provide their children with more. Lifestyle shifts influence what the customer wants to buy (Figure 1.8).

Figure 1.6. Celebrities such as Michelle Williams, wearing a chiffon dress by Vera Wang, have a significant effect on fashion trends.

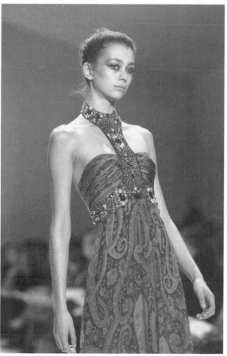

Figure 1.7. Monique Lauillier's India-inspired design is an example of a fashion trend inspired by travel.

Forecasters endeavor to become aware of these changes before they occur and identify the products that will meet consumer needs before customers know it.

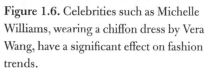

▸ **Places where people gather:** Airports, concert stadiums, street festivals, shopping malls, and Times Square on New Year's Eve are some of the locations where groups of people can be observed. Trend forecasters examine where these people are going, what they are wearing, and from whom and what they are buying.

▸ **Street scenes:** "I watch people anywhere and everywhere," one successful trend forecaster explains. "You never know where a trend will start." Worth Global Style Network (WGSN), a key forecasting resource, recruits people from colleges and other locations worldwide to submit trend information from their various locales. Every street, from WGSN's perspective, has the potential for fashion leadership (Figure 1.9).

Figure 1.8. Consumer preferences for organically grown products are manifest in fashion in organic cotton apparel.

Figure 1.9. Legwarmers and backpacks spotted on the streets of Tokyo.

▶ **Sports:** When a particular sport or activity gains consumer interest, its active sportswear is often imitated or modified for street wear. As Figure 1.10 depicts, high-top boxing boots, surfer shorts, golf shirts, and yoga capri pants illustrate the influence of sports trends on ready-to-wear.

THE CAREER PATH

Figure 1.10. Pilates and yoga dominate fitness and activewear trends.

Securing a position in trend forecasting does not happen quickly. Typically, many years of industry experience are required. A number of successful forecasters have previously worked as designers or buyers before moving into the fashion-forecasting career field. A few of the fortunate begin with internships or assistantship positions in forecasting firms to gain direct experience, exposure, and contacts in the forecasting world.

Qualifications

Successful trend forecasters often meet or exceed the following qualifications:

- **Education:** At the very least, a bachelor's degree in one of a wide range of disciplines is required. These disciplines most frequently include business administration (e.g., marketing or consumer behavior), visual arts, fashion design, or fashion merchandising.
- **Experience:** Forecasters often begin in entry-level positions in the areas of retail, product development, design, merchandising, or fashion coordination. A number of successful forecasters have held positions in several sectors of the industry, such as design, product development, and retailing.
- **Personal characteristics:** There are a few specific and unique qualities that trend forecasters display. Among them is an excellent understanding of people and human behavior, global population and industry shifts, and fashion trends. Successful trend forecasters have effective visual, written, and oral communication and presentation skills. They are often curious and creative people with superior networking abilities. Most important, they have an exceptional capability to analyze, synthesize, and organize observations into categories that are clearly communicated to clients. Think about viewing 15 couture collection presentations in a five-day period and then identifying the consistent trends among them. Fashion forecasters have the ability to find the common threads and, later, classify and describe these trends for designers, manufacturers, and retailers who use the trend services.

The Typical Forecaster's Career Path

While the majority of college graduates prefer to start at the top, it is an essential advantage for a fashion forecaster to understand all levels of the industry from a holistic perspective. Even the most entry-level retail sales positions provide valuable experience for future forecasters. As a sales associate, one is directly exposed to the customers' preferences and dislikes. Effective sales associates endeavor to understand who the customers are and identify their buying habits. As future fashion forecasters progress to higher positions within the industry (e.g., product development or merchandising), it is important that they keep in mind always who the customers are and how they are changing. The work experience fashion forecasters have acquired through the years is used on a daily basis when assisting designers, manufacturers, or merchandisers with future purchases for upcoming seasons.

The Job Market for Trend Forecasters

The fashion industry has a limited number of fashion-forecasting positions in the areas of color, textile design, apparel and accessories design, and home furnishings. Since fashion-forecasting positions are limited, successful fashion forecasters are well compensated for their knowledge and skills. A salary range for fashion forecasters begins at $40,000 for an assistantship in a smaller company and can reach more than $100,000 annually within larger firms. Sometimes, a commission will be paid to fashion forecasters based on how well their company performs with their assistance.

Career Challenges

The pros of a fashion-forecasting career have been discussed, but what about the challenges? Because there are a limited number of successful forecasting firms, there are only a few jobs for a few good men and women. The job of a fashion forecaster requires a tremendous amount of intelligence, skill, and exposure and, perhaps, a sixth sense. Forecasters must be aware of all of the external influences that may affect consumer behavior. The ability to observe, organize, and prioritize these outside influences is a rare skill. Fashion forecasters who consistently identify the right trends develop strong reputations. Many "wannabes" who provide the wrong information for a season or two are no longer hired by clients who depend on accurate fashion direction to make a profit. It can be stressful for fashion forecasters to identify significant fashion influences seasonally or annually. Additionally, fashion forecasters must be able to market their companies, their ideas, and themselves. The forecaster truly is the ultimate product.

EXAMPLES OF FASHION-FORECASTING COMPANIES

There are a number of successful fashion-forecasting companies, with new firms constantly entering the mix. Doneger Creative Services, based in New York City, is the trend and color forecasting and analysis division of The Doneger Group. According to their website, Doneger Creative Services offers a broad range of products and services, such as printed publications, online subscriptions, and live presentations. This division addresses the forecasting needs of retailers, manufacturers, and other style-related businesses. Doneger's **creative directors** cover the apparel, accessories, and lifestyle markets in the women's, men's, and youth merchandise classifications. Another forecasting company, FashionInformation.com, is an e-business service that publishes its fashion reports exclusively on the Internet. The company focuses primarily on women's wear trends.

Fashion Snoops is the creator of www.fashionsnoops.com, an online forecasting and fashion trend analysis service that covers the young men's, denim, junior women's, children's, and infant and toddler markets. Fashion Snoops was created in 2001 by a team of designers and merchandisers who have extensive industry experience. The company's goal in bringing professionals together from various sectors of the fashion and licensing industries was to bring practical experience to creative teams. Fashion Snoops has a creative services division that provides consulting and outsourced services in the areas of research, design, merchandising, styling, and graphic art. The company serves hundreds of leading fashion firms in the United States, Canada, Europe, Australia, Asia, and South America.

Founders Julian and Marc Worth launched WGSN, based in London, in 1998. It is one of the most successful online forecasting services to emerge. WGSN offers research, trend analysis, and news to the fashion, design, and style industries. Members of the 100-person staff travel extensively around the world. The WGSN team includes experienced writers, photographers, researchers, analysts, and trendspotters. **Trendspotters** are persons located at universities and other locations worldwide who provide information to the WGSN on the latest trends in each locale. The company tracks not only the latest fashion trends but also hot retail stores, new designers, emerging brands, and business innovations. WGSN maintains offices in London, New York City, Hong Kong, Seoul, Los Angeles, Melbourne, and Tokyo. Its client list is long and impressive and includes such designers and retailers as Giorgio Armani, Target, Mango, and Abercrombie & Fitch. The company's website is located at www.wgsn.com.

Based in New York City, the Zandl Group is a firm that provides trend analysis, consumer research, and marketing direction for businesses and advertising agencies. The company's area of specialization is a big one: 82 million young people between the ages of 8 and 24 in the United States. This market is segmented into the following classifications: young adults, teens, and preteens (also referred to as tweens). The Zandl Group publishes a bimonthly trend report on these market segments called "The Hot Sheet."

SnapFashun is a source for Los Angeles and European retail reporting, merchandising trends, and original design ideas. The firm monitors up-to-the-minute looks at top-selling items in trendsetting cities. To meet the needs of designers and manufacturers, SnapFashun offers a library of visual images that represents more than 25 years of fashion-reporting experience. The fashion library is updated with new details and silhouettes up to 14 times each year.

There are a number of trend-forecasting services and trade shows based in Paris, France. Carlin International is a forecasting firm dedicated to fashion trend information. The company's website, www.carlin-groupe.com, is available in English and French. Peclers Paris is a fashion trend-forecasting service that specializes in textile design, fashion, beauty, consumer goods, and retailing. Première Vision is the world's leading trade show in fabric forecasting, promoting fabric trends for designers and manufacturers in the fashion industry. Première Vision teams with the company Première Vision S.A., a subsidiary of the French Association for the Promotion of Textile Yarns (AFPFT), to produce the Expofil trade show near the Eiffel Tower. The world leader in yarn and fiber sectors, Expofil provides the whole textile industry with fashion information, colors, and materials. Another Paris-based forecasting agency, Nelly-Rodi, is featured in Box 1.1.

The color box researches and evaluates information gathered in the United States and Europe and then develops comprehensive color and design stories directed to the American market. Color forecasting is the company's primary service; they construct four forecasts per year. Additionally, *The color box* has a design studio that features a staff of artists and computer-aided design technicians who design, develop, and recolor fabrics for clients. Finally, the design studio produces graphics, original illustrations, and presentation boards as requested. Their website is www.thecolorbox.com.

The Color Association of the United States is another color-forecasting service. According to their website, www.colorassociation.com, it is the oldest color-forecasting company in the United States. Since 1915, The Color Association has been issuing color reports in fabric-swatched booklets. A committee panel of eight to 12 industry professionals selects seasonal color palettes. There are two younger players in the color-forecasting business: Color Portfolio, Inc., www.colorportfolio.com, and Cool Hunting, www.coolhunting.com. Started in 1986, Color Portfolio offers color and trend books to retailers, manufacturers, and related industries. The company provides recommendations for colors, trends, and textiles. Cool Hunting, featured in Box 1.2, employs a team of ten experienced editors and photographers, each based in a different city around the world. This firm works primarily with publishers, sending digital photos and text across the Internet to meet publishing deadlines.

Leading manufacturers of products for the environment, automotive, home, office, garden, textile, fashion, and beauty industries seek out advice and creative ideas from

BOX 1.1 • NELLYRODI

NellyRodi TrendLab, or NellyRodi, is a forecasting agency that has become renowned for its exceptional ability to provide designers with insight into future consumer trends. The agency specializes in publications designed to assist creative teams and manufacturers as they develop future product lines. Among the firm's key publications, **trend books** are invaluable design resources that include photos, fabric swatches, materials, color ranges, drawings of prints, product sketches, silhouettes, commentaries, and additional inspirational materials.

With expertise in the textile, packaging, automotive, and cosmetic industries, this France-based company has been helping design teams through their creative processes since 1985. NellyRodi agency features an in-house team of 28 people, experts in apparel, beauty, and the art of living. Team members represent a wide range of fashion- and art-related career areas, including fashion artists, designers, sketchers, scenographers, and model makers. Many travel around the world, detecting and interpreting signs that foreshadow changes in popular culture. By consulting with one another, sharing ideas, and envisioning the future of our world, all of these experts have a strong voice within the ongoing creative interaction of NellyRodi TrendLab. Additionally, the company regularly brings together researchers from such disciplines as sociology, philosophy, and linguistics to brainstorm on social and economic topics with marketing directors.

The Services

One of NellyRodi TrendLab's services is referred to as "made-to-measure consulting." These include individualized projects in the following areas:

- Presenting trends to fashion directors, buyers, and designers, including creating personalized trend books that cover color palettes, materials, and shapes
- Publishing trendsetters' guides to complement the trend books
- Collaborating with designers, manufacturers, and retailers on the development of product collections or taking charge of collection plan and product design
- Researching brand concepts
- Designing packaging
- Compiling buying guides for distributors
- Researching promotional venues, then creating and organizing press launches
- Developing trend presentations and exhibits for professional trade markets
- Designing visual merchandising projects, such as boutique and window designs

Beauty and Fragrance

With more than 15 years of experience and 70 clients in the cosmetics sector, NellyRodi TrendLab is an international leader of fashion information adapted for the beauty industry. Although for a long time they were limited to cosmetics,

(continued)

fashion influences have recently entered the domains of skin care, perfume, and packaging. NellyRodi assists brands in developing new perfumes and inspires perfumers by suggesting new olfactory directions. With its new division, Scent Factory, NellyRodi brought the company's expertise in perfume to the public. Scent Factory is the first perfume compilation, similar to a musical compilation in that it explores eight extreme olfactory creations conceived by eight perfumers under the direction of NellyRodi.

Source: www.nellyrodi.com

BOX 1.2 • JOSH RUBIN

Josh has been a designer and strategist for more than 10 years, creating mobile device interfaces, Web applications, embedded software, kiosks, installations, and a few T-shirts. When the Internet boom peaked, he was at Razorfish working as the director of mobile solutions. He oversaw the user experience for projects delivered to Vodafone, Citibank, and Adobe, among others. He then went to Motorola to be a lead user interface designer and was in charge of two new software platforms—one currently on handsets in the Asian market and the other to debut sometime this year. More recently, he was the vice president of product development at Upoc Networks, a software company that develops mobile-messaging applications.

In November 2004, Josh set out on his own to build a publishing and consulting business focused on design strategy, trend analysis, and mobile marketing for select clients.

Josh holds a bachelor's of arts degree in communications and cognitive science from Hampshire College and a master's in interactive telecommunications from New York University. He lives in New York City, drives a Mini Cooper, and obsesses over his two Sealyham Terriers—Otis and Logan.

Josh Rubin's Cool Hunting (www.coolhunting.com)

Since February 2003, Josh Rubin's Cool Hunting has been a daily update on happenings from the intersection of design, culture, and technology. Josh started the site as a way to catalog things that inspire him in his practice as a designer and strategist. Today, Cool Hunting has grown beyond a personal reference tool—designers, consumers, and marketers from around the world visit every day to get their dose.

As the site became increasingly fueled by contributions from readers, Josh realized Cool Hunting should be a collective. He now serves as editor of the site and wrangles contributions from a small gaggle of hand-picked writers who are out finding great things and looking at all the information readers are feeding them.

Trend Union when developing their own lines, services, and marketing strategies. Since 1985, Trend Union has developed a collection of biannual trend-forecasting books that set forth the colors, materials, shapes, and lifestyles for seasons to come. There are four major divisions of the company:

1. Edelkoort Etc. caters to the clients and projects of Li Edelkoort, who is featured in Box 1.3. This division is also responsible for the style presentations Edelkoort and her team of acclaimed speakers give for professionals all over the world. Located in Paris, Edelkoort Etc. can be contacted at studio@edelkoort.com.

2. Heartwear is a division of the company that was created by a group of stylist friends in 1993. They decided to sponsor a collection of garments utilizing native African skills and adapting the apparel to Western tastes. Profits from this project were returned to the country of Benin in Africa to be invested in educational projects. It was the beginning of a not-for-profit association that continues to help artisans in developing countries tailor their products for export without compromising the skill, knowledge, culture, and environment of the region involved. Heartwear is based in Paris and can be contacted at heartwear@edelkoort.com.

3. Studio Edelkoort is yet another division related to Trend Union. Founded in 1991, its purpose is to cater to the increased demand by major companies worldwide for private consulting, product development, brand identity, and strategic thinking. Also based in Paris, Studio Edelkoort can be reached at studio@edelkoort.com.

4. Finally, the magazine division of Trend Union is United Publishers. Li Edelkoort is the art director and copublisher of the magazines. United Publishers developed the lifestyle magazine *In View*, which outlines trends in interior decoration, design, and textiles in a conceptual way. In 1998, a magazine blossomed called *Bloom*, the first publication to discuss trends in terms of flowers, plants, and nature. *Bloom* is a biannual magazine that presents a horticultural view of trends in flowers, plants, and gardening for the public and professionals alike. The online contact address is info@united publishers.com.

Promostyl's mission is to pinpoint fashion, design, and lifestyle trends and help companies adapt to changing trends. The company bases its work on the currents of society, cultures, and lifestyles, believing that society makes fashion. The company creates trend books, develops visual presentations, consults with companies, and

BOX 1.3 · LI EDELKOORT

Dutch by birth, Parisian by choice, international in outlook, futurist Lidewij (Li) Edelkoort predicts what the needs, lifestyles, and choices of the global community will be two years from now and beyond. She is the founder and head of Trend Union, the Paris-based trend-forecasting service, and president of Edelkoort Inc., the American consulting corporation. Born in the Netherlands in 1950, Edelkoort is also the director of the renowned Design Academy Eindhoven. Beginning in 1991, she has announced the concepts, colors, and materials that will be in fashion two or more years in advance. She explains, "There is no creation without advanced knowledge, and with-

out design, a product cannot exist." In 2003, Edelkoort was named one of the world's 24 most influential people in fashion by *Time* magazine.

Where and how does she work? A converted factory on the Boulevard Saint Jacques in Montparnasse of Paris serves as headquarters for her four companies: Trend Union, Studio Edelkoort, United Publishers, and Heartwear (as described previously in this chapter). The environment— with its photo studio; open workrooms filled with drawing tables; storage areas filled with fabrics, toys, and treasures; and a family-style dining room—is intended to stimulate creativity and an exchange of ideas. When not in Paris, Li Edelkoort travels constantly, shopping and searching the world over for new ideas. She examines political, ethnological, artistic, literary, and consumer movements, interpreting them for the fashion world.

maintains an international network of subsidiaries and agents. Three main offices are located in New York City, Tokyo, and Paris.

Established in 1967, NPD Fashion World is a company that provides information about the apparel and footwear markets. It is a source of point-of-sale and consumer tracking information. **Point-of-sale** refers to the analyzing of transactions as they go through the retailers' cash registers or computer terminals. Point-of-sale tracking information is examined to see which colors and sizes sold, which fabrics and styles sold, who the top vendors were, and whether or not the merchandise was sold at full price or as a markdown. **Consumer tracking information** is more focused on demographics and psychographics. **Demographics** refer to consumer data that can be interpreted as numbers. Age, gender, income, education attained, and number of family members are examples of demographic data. **Psychographics**, however, refer to lifestyle choices, values, and feelings. NPD Fashion World's market information is delivered online and organized around key business issues, such as what is selling, to whom, and why. In addition to apparel and footwear, the firm offers market information for a wide range of other industries, such as food, toys and video games, consumer electronics, information technology, housewares, automotives, beauty, and music.

SUMMARY

Trend forecasters are central to the fashion industry. Accurate forecasting can make or break a company. Every designer and merchandiser must be aware of trend predictions to ensure their lines will appeal to their specific target market. Trend forecasters may be employed by broad-spectrum firms or fabric houses and specialize in color trends or project population trends. They gather information by examining market research firms, couture collections, new designers, trade shows, art, design, e-sources, travel trends, lifestyle trends, entertainment, and street styles. Fashion forecasting is one of the few careers that encompasses all of the aspects of the industry; therefore, it is essential for trend forecasters to possess a strong understanding of the fashion industry from creative product development to retail selling. Seldom does one gain a position in this field without a number of years of prior experience and education. As a trend forecaster, you may anticipate a challenging career that encourages you to be creative, observational, and highly receptive; travel often; and research always!

KEY TERMS

consumer tracking information
creative director
demographics
lead time
point-of-sale
psychographics
trend book
trend forecaster (fashion forecaster)
trendspotter

Discussion Questions

1. How conscious are you of current trends? Identify current color, design, art, textile, entertainment, and sociocultural trends for this season and the next.

2. Spot trends within the current season and trace their sources. Did these trends originate from the streets, art exhibitions, new technology, couture collections, or some other source?

3. Analyze the latest issues of fashion magazines and compare the contents with fashion six months ago. Describe three basic trend directions toward next year's fashion.

4. What are some examples of companies outside of the fashion industry that rely on trend forecasting? Why are trends important to these businesses?

CHAPTER 2

Textile Product Development and Design

Have you ever wondered who thought up the stripe pattern on your shirt or the crazy rubber ducky print on your bathrobe? Somebody has to be the creative force behind these designs, and that somebody is a **textile designer**. A textile designer creates original designs for the fabrics used in all sorts of industries. **Textile design** is a combination of visual arts and technical concerns. Pattern and print designs are evaluated in terms of how they can be combined with printing, knitting, weaving, embossing, and embroidery processes. Textile designers often collaborate with **textile colorists**. A textile colorist works with a design to determine **colorways**, color selections for a particular pattern or print. Figure 2.1 provides an example of a colorway for a woven floral print.

These two creative positions are just examples of the numerous career paths in the textile industry, which is a high-touch, high-tech industry. In the high-tech sector of the textile industry, there are a number of career options, including textile engineering and textile production. **Textile engineers** work with designers to determine how designs can be applied to a fabric while considering practical variables such as durability, washability, and colorfastness. **Textile technicians** work with the issues that are directly related to the production of textiles. Job opportunities in textile production have dramatically declined in recent years due to inexpensive labor costs overseas. United States fashion companies now, more than ever, outsource much of their production work to companies in foreign countries. **Outsourcing** refers to having an aspect of a company's work performed by nonemployees. Most outsourced jobs in the textile industry are low-paying production positions in countries with lower labor costs than those in the United States, such as those in the Pacific Rim, as well as South and Central America. The majority of American

Figure 2.1. Colorway.

companies design domestically, but they outsource goods internationally to take advantage of the free-trade agreements with low-wage countries. However, the loss in U.S. production jobs in the textile industry has been offset by creative and scientific tracks in design and product development.

In this chapter, the creative and scientific career tracks in textile design and textile technology will be examined. Whether one has a creative personality and an eye for pattern and color or a scientific mind that excels in engineering and production, there is a job path in the textiles field that can provide a fulfilling career.

FASHION DIRECTOR

A **fashion director** for a textile company is responsible for determining the trends, colors, themes, and textures for **piece goods**, or fabrics, that the firm will feature for a specific season. Fashion directors are primarily interested in identifying the most important fashion trends for their clients and communicating these trends to textile designers, production managers, and customers. Fashion directors often work with trend-forecasting firms to determine trend possibilities in color, form, theme, and, of course, fabric for each season.

Qualifications

The following is a list of qualifications for a career as fashion director:

▸ **Education:** A bachelor's degree in textiles, fashion design, fashion merchandising, visual arts, or a related field is a minimum requirement for employment as a fashion director.

▸ **Experience:** The majority of fashion directors moved up the ladder from within the ranks. Many of them were textile designers, product developers, or buyers before obtaining key positions as fashion directors.

▸ **Personal characteristics:** The fashion director often has similar characteristics to the trend forecaster: curiosity, strong communication skills, a strong visual sensibility, leadership abilities, a good understanding of who the customers actually are, and the ability to work with a variety of constituencies—from designers to production managers to technical assistants.

Career Challenges

The challenges of the fashion director's career relate to two primary areas: securing the job and keeping it. Fashion coordinators are expected to have a strong foundation of work experience in the industry. It takes time, skill, and effort to be promoted through a variety of positions, from technical textile designer to product developer to buyer. The best and the brightest climb smoothly up the career ladder. Once in the position of fashion director, there is a great deal of pressure to be *right*, meaning accurate about the color, pattern, style, and theme trends. If, for example, a fashion director determines that olive green is the color for a season and it bombs at the retail level, the company may lose a great deal of money from a high investment in olive green fabrics. As a result of this error, this fashion director may be searching for a new job. Additionally, the fashion director must collaborate successfully with a wide variety of people—designers, production personnel, and clients. It takes a person with a well-balanced personality to work effectively with so many different people.

TEXTILE DESIGNER

Textile designers create the designs for fabrics we wear and use, from our clothing to our interior decorations. They can be surface designers, knitters, weavers, or embroiderers for industries ranging from apparel to upholstery. To assist in textile design, there are **print services**, companies that sell print designs to mills, wholesalers, product developers, and retailers. Many textile designers utilize **computer-aided design (CAD),** which is the process of developing garments, prints, and patterns on a computer screen. This process has greatly influenced the field of textile design, as it provides faster, more varied, and more personalized design options in textiles than were possible in past years. Technological advances in CAD software, several of which will be presented later in this chapter, offer unlimited creative opportunities to designers. For instance, a customer can now have the photograph of her pet pug transferred to canvas, which will then be used to create a handbag. An image of a Parisian street scene can be scanned and printed on fabric that will later become bedroom curtains.

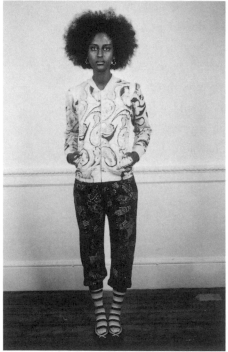

Figure 2.2. A print is interpreted in wallpaper (top) and knit pants by London-based artist and designer Zakee Shariff (bottom).

Figure 2.2 shows a textile design printed on a pair of pants and a roll of wallpaper.

A computer-aided textile designer knows how to paint and draw but works specifically on the computer to create designs. There are a number of specialized career paths that a textile designer can take; these include working with wovens, knits, or prints. For example, a textile designer may choose to focus on fibers and processes that are commonly used for knit goods such as sweaters, as illustrated in Figure 2.3. Another textile designer may decide to specialize in creating textile prints for woven fabrics by painting, as depicted in Figure 2.4, or using CAD to create **croquis** (renderings or miniature visuals of textile patterns or prints) for a garment or an accessory. The **assistant textile designer** works with the textile designer in accomplishing these tasks. What is the most important personal trait needed to be a successful textile designer? The key characteristic is to possess a mind that is simultaneously creative, business-oriented, and technically savvy.

TEXTILE STYLIST

A **textile stylist** is the creative person who modifies existing textile goods, altering patterns or prints that have been successful on the retail floor to turn them into fresh, new products. The textile stylist may develop color alternatives for the modified textile print or pattern or may work with a textile colorist to accomplish this task.

TEXTILE COLORIST

A textile colorist chooses the color combinations that will be used in creating each textile design. Colorists frequently travel to fashion markets and belong to color-forecasting organizations to stay on top of current and future color trends. There is a wide range of

Figure 2.3. The knit structure (left) and croquis of a sweater design (right), both developed using CAD software.

industries in which textile designers, stylists, and colorists are employed; they include the following:

▸ Knitted and woven textiles, used to make clothes and soft good products, as well as upholstered products, such as home furnishings and automotive seats
▸ Rugs and carpets
▸ Prints for wallpapers, paper goods, or tiles

The responsibilities of textile designers, stylists, and colorists are as follows:

▸ Interacting with customers to understand their needs and interpret their ideas accurately
▸ Collaborating with marketing, buying, and technical staff members, as well as design colleagues
▸ Understanding how textiles will be used, what properties textiles need to function optimally, and how the addition of color dyes or surface treatments will affect these properties
▸ Conducting research for ideas and inspiration, from antique embroidery to modern architecture to children's storybooks

Figure 2.4. Textile designer hand-painting a floral print on woven fabric.

- Experimenting with texture and pattern as it relates to color
- Producing design or color ideas, sketches, and samples and presenting them to customers
- Producing designs or color options for designs using CAD software
- Checking and approving samples of completed items
- Working to meet deadlines
- Working within budgets
- Keeping up-to-date with new fashions and population trends—current and projected
- Staying on top of new design and production processes
- Attending trade and fashion shows

Textile designers, stylists, and colorists need to consider such factors as how the designs will be produced, how the finished articles will be used, the quality of the materials used, and the budgets. They work standard hours, but they need to be flexible to meet deadlines. They are based in studios or offices. Their earnings range from $25,000 annually when newly qualified to $75,000 and above with experience. Prospective employers require a strong and relevant portfolio of work for review. Employers include large manufacturing companies and small, exclusive design houses. Some textile designers, stylists, and colorists are self-employed.

Qualifications

Requirements for employment in these positions include the following:

- **Education:** A bachelor's degree in textiles, visual arts, computer-aided design, graphic design, fashion design, or a related discipline is a minimal requirement.
- **Experience:** Entry-level design positions provide the ideal starting place for college graduates. Additional experience in technical design (CAD) and color will assist the candidate in moving up the career ladder. Box 2.1 describes a widely used CAD program for textile design.
- **Personal characteristics:** Flexible computer skills, a strong visual sense for color, texture, and pattern; a creative personality; knowledge of how textiles are produced; effective business skills; an awareness of fashion trends; a practical understanding of skills such as sewing, knitting, weaving, and embroidery; and knowledge of the target consumer help make the textile designer, stylist, and colorist successful.

BOX 2.1 • TEXTILE TECHNOLOGY PROGRAM: LECTRA U4IA

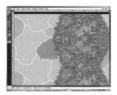

With 1,600 employees worldwide, Lectra is a leader in designing, developing, and supplying software and equipment to large-scale companies that work with textiles, leather, and other soft materials. Lectra's products and services are used in major global markets, including the manufacturing and retailing of fashion apparel, footwear, luggage and leather goods, furniture and home furnishings, automotive products, aerospace and marine products, as well as industrial fabrics.

U4ia is a software program by Lectra that can be used to develop textile design solutions, including prints, production, knits, or wovens. U4ia Graphic is resolution independent, meaning it is possible to work on images of any size with precision, clarity, and detail. U4ia Graphic assists textile designers in accomplishing the following tasks:

- Developing custom **color palettes**, groupings of color hues for fashion lines or products
- Reducing complex print designs into a specific number of colors and maintaining **color integrity**. Color integrity refers to a type of quality

control in which the original specified color of the design is the exact shade of the final product. The goal is to preserve identical colors from initial design to point of sale.
- Creating colorways, color variations of a specific pattern or print
- Painting original artwork with natural media tools
- Enhancing and modifying scanned artwork
- Creating catalog layouts

With this type of technology, companies can reduce the need for actual examples of fabrics. Additionally, with electronic communication between fabric design software and production tools (e.g., weaving and knitting looms or textile printers), textile producers can achieve a more efficient industrial process and continual communication with end-consumers.

Sapphire, a related product, is Lectra's digital fabric printing system. It was developed in partnership with Stork for short-run production of all types of natural and polyamide printed fabrics. **Short-run production** refers to the quick manufacture of limited yardage, allowing the designer to view print and pattern placements, different colorways, and **samples**, or prototypes, of the product. Sapphire makes it possible to rapidly produce a sample line of new styles and colors in a variety of fabrics for the design and sales teams to review before fabric is purchased and production begins.

Career Challenges

The challenges for textile designers, stylists, and colorists are similar. They must interpret the trends designated by the fashion director. Sometimes, converting the words of the fashion director into the images the director envisions can be difficult. Textile designers, stylists, and colorists also must be aware of the technical requirements of fabric development, such as the printing requirements, durability, and application of finishes. Most important, they are often under pressure to meet quick deadlines and work within budget constraints.

TEXTILE TECHNICIAN

A textile technician either oversees the production facilities of a company or supervises the production as it is done by a **contractor**, a firm that is hired to manufacture the product line, domestically or abroad. If a textile company owns its manufacturing facility, the textile technician is responsible for the smooth running of the equipment used in textile production to maximize production. If a textile company contracts its production out to another company, the textile technician works with the contractor to accomplish these goals. The primary responsibilities of the textile technician are as follows:

▶ Overseeing the regular routine maintenance of equipment, or the efficient production of the contractor
▶ Checking performance levels of equipment and/or contractors for optimal production
▶ Carrying out regular checks on production, spotting any difficulties and dealing with them before they become problematic

In a large textile factory, a technician may specialize in one type of production technique, such as knitting or weaving; however, in a smaller company, the responsibilities of the technician may be more wide-ranging. Technicians work approximately 40 hours a week, sometimes on shifts. Earnings for trained technicians range from $25,000 to $65,000 annually.

Qualifications

Requirements for employment as a textile technician include the following:

▶ **Education:** A bachelor's degree in textile technology, textile production, computer science, textile engineering, industrial technology, or a related field is required.

▶ **Experience:** A number of textile technicians begin in entry-level technical design positions. They may move up into management of a team of technical designers that covers specific merchandise classifications, such as men's wear or children's wear. Some technicians move into management or into specialized areas, such as quality control and research.

▶ **Personal characteristics:** High levels of technical knowledge and computer skills are extremely important personal qualifications in this career path. Strong practical and problem-solving skills are also essential. A thorough understanding of textile applications and usage assists the textile technician in making product-development decisions.

Career Challenges

Textile technicians face the challenge of understanding and anticipating the continually changing technologies in textile design and production. Deadlines are a constant challenge. Communicating and problem-solving with a variety of coworkers in different divisions, such as design and production, require a proactive approach, patience, and flexibility from textile technicians.

TEXTILE ENGINEER

Manufacturers are merging textiles with technology to create new products for the market. For instance, instead of being just wrinkle-resistant, fabrics have become truly wrinkle-free through a process patented by TAL Corporation of Hong Kong. The process involves baking a special coating onto the fabric, as well as innovative use of adhesives along the seams to prevent puckering. Other fabrics are coated

Figure 2.5. A crochet surgical patch (top) and a high-tech strong weave (bottom) are both examples of textile innovations.

with Teflon to resist stains. Materials have been developed to change color with body temperature changes, which is particularly appealing for hospital use. Figure 2.5 shows additional examples of innovative fiber technologies. The career path that directly relates to these new products is that of textile engineer. A textile engineer has a background in textile science that may include chemistry and manufacturing, in addition to textile analysis. A newly qualified textile engineer may earn $40,000 to $50,000 annually.

Qualifications

Requirements for employment as a textile engineer include the following:

- **Education:** A bachelor's degree in textiles, textile technology, textile production, computer science, textile engineering, industrial technology, or a related discipline is a minimal requirement.
- **Experience:** Many textile engineers working for companies that own and operate their own manufacturing facilities move up from the production line to this position. Textile engineers working with firms that contract out production may have a greater job emphasis on information technology in their positions. A number of textile engineers begin in apprentice positions as assistant textile engineers.
- **Personal characteristics:** A textile engineer has a broad knowledge of how textiles are produced. In addition, this position requires an understanding of technical considerations as they relate to textile applications, an awareness of consumer wants and needs, and a comprehension of textile science.

In addition to design, color, and technical positions in the textile industry, there are ancillary career paths. The resource room/reference librarian and the account executive are two career paths that relate to the textile industry, yet require different sets of skills and backgrounds from those of the creative and scientific positions.

RESOURCE ROOM DIRECTOR/ REFERENCE LIBRARIAN

Many large companies maintain a resource room or reference library of textile samples, reference books and magazines, Internet resources, print and pattern images, and possibly actual garments constructed from the companies' or competitors' fabrics.

These items are used by fashion directors, designers, technicians, and sales representatives for design inspiration and reference. The **resource room director** oversees the procurement, organization, and removal or replacement of these materials. Some companies, such as large apparel manufacturers, fashion publishers, and fiber/fabric houses, maintain reference libraries. The **reference librarian** is responsible for managing the inventory of books and resources and for procuring new ones.

Qualifications

Requirements for employment as a resource room director or reference librarian include the following:

- ▸ **Education:** A bachelor's degree in textiles, fashion merchandising, fashion design, or a related discipline is a minimal requirement.
- ▸ **Experience:** For recent graduates with work experience in fashion retailing and textiles, strong academic performances, and impressive references, these can be entry-level positions. Some resource room directors or reference librarians later move into the design divisions of firms. Exposure to the references of a particular firm helps build the potential designer's background.
- ▸ **Personal characteristics:** Strong organization skills, effective time management, first-rate communication skills, and an attention to detail are personal qualities that fit the position of resource room or reference librarian.

Career Challenges

Managing a resource room or reference library can be a daunting task. There is a constant flow of new acquisitions that need to be inventoried, labeled, and stored, often in a minimal space. There must be a high level of organization for the resource room director or reference librarian to be able to pull samples quickly for the fashion director or designer who needs them immediately.

ACCOUNT EXECUTIVE

Account executives, also referred to as *sales* or *manufacturer's representatives,* sell to and manage accounts for manufacturers. They are responsible for the sales of textiles and usually are assigned to specific territories. Account executives can be paid in several ways: a salary, commission, quota, or a combination of these. This is a great career for someone who prefers working independently and enjoys business, budgets, and sales, as well as the textile, fashion, and home furnishing markets.

Qualifications

Qualifications include the following:

- **Education:** A bachelor's degree in fashion merchandising, general business administration, or marketing is preferred.
- **Experience:** Retail or wholesale sales experience is most often required; however, working as an assistant to an account executive is an excellent way to open the door to this career path.
- **Personal characteristics:** A strong understanding of accounting, effective sales skills, good communication abilities, and excellent follow-up skills are important attributes of successful account executives.

EXAMPLES OF COMPANIES THAT EMPLOY OR ASSIST TEXTILE DESIGNERS AND PRODUCT DEVELOPERS

There are a number of large companies that employ textile personnel, from designers to resource room managers. Many of these firms are located in New York City; some have satellite offices in Dallas, San Diego, and Atlanta, as well as cities abroad. Next, nine of the top textile firms are examined, encompassing fur as a type of textile.

Cotton Incorporated

Cotton Incorporated is an information center for cotton and cotton-blend fibers and textiles. It provides fabric, color, and trend information for textile producers, soft goods and soft good products manufacturers, designers, and retailers. Working closely with Cotton Council International, Cotton Incorporated conducts research and promotion for cotton and cotton products with the primary goal of increasing the demand and profitability of U.S. cotton and its products. The company offers technical services, such as fiber processing, fabric development, dyeing and finishing, and cotton quality management assistance. Information services provide data on cotton supply and demand, fiber quality, and consumer research trends. To keep cotton on the runway, Cotton Incorporated's fashion services provide timely trend publications and conduct live trend presentations with leading forecasters, designers, and sourcing specialists, highlighting the company's trend research and supplier information. Cotton Incorporated World Headquarters is located in North Carolina. Offices are located worldwide, including New York, Los Angeles, Mexico City, Osaka, Singapore, and Shanghai. The company's website, www.cottoninc.com, provides corporate information, trend descriptions, and employment opportunity postings.

Australian Wool Services Limited (The Woolmark Company)

With over 60 years of expertise in the wool industry and textile innovation, Australian Wool Services Limited is the world's leading wool fiber textile organization. The company provides unique global endorsement through ownership and licensing of the Woolmark, Woolmark Blend, and Wool Blend brands. The Woolmark Company, a wholly owned subsidiary of Australian Wool Services, specializes in the commercialization of wool technologies and innovations, technical consulting, business information, and commercial testing of wool fabrics. If you check the label of any quality wool or blended wool item you own, you are likely to find one of the famous Woolmark symbols shown here.

These brands and their corresponding brandmarks are protected by strict and extensive control checks to ensure product quality. Australian Wool Services Limited operates globally, working with textile processors, designers, and retailers in both the apparel and interior textile markets.

PURE NEW WOOL

WOOLMARK

CONSEIL CANADIEN DE LA FOURRURE
FUR COUNCIL OF CANADA

Fur Council of Canada

The Fur Council of Canada is a national, nonprofit organization representing people working in every sector of the Canadian fur trade. This includes fur producers, auction houses, processors, designers, craftspeople, and retail furriers. Incorporated in 1964, the goals of the Fur Council programs include the following:

- Encouraging linkages between designers and other sectors of the fashion industry
- Sponsorship of competitions for both professional designers and students in Canadian fashion colleges
- Promotion of the work of innovative Canadian fur designers through advertising in top national and international fashion publications
- Providing accurate information about the Canadian fur trade to consumers, educators, and the public to counter criticisms that the industry's practices are cruel to animals. For example, in Canada, trappers must pass a mandatory course in which they learn how to use new humane trapping methods and how to apply the principles of sustainable use established by wildlife officials and biologists.

The Fur Council of Canada can be further investigated on its website at www.furcouncil.com.

North American Fur and Fashion Exposition

In addition to headquartering the Fur Council, Canada also is the site of a major, international fur market. The North American Fur and Fashion Exposition (NAFFEM) in Montreal is the largest fur and outerwear fashion fair of its type in North America and one of the most important fur fashion marketing events in the world. For over 20 years, NAFFEM has attracted thousands of professional buyers from the world's finest specialty boutiques and department stores with its wide array of luxury furs, boutique furs, shearlings, leathers, cashmere, and accessories. During the annual trade show, there are over 200 exhibitors representing designer labels and upscale women's and men's outerwear in fur and precious fabrics.

The lines range from formal looks to casual wear, sportswear, and streetwear. More than half of the buyers viewing the lines of these exhibitors come from across the United States and abroad. There is also an area of the trade show that features unique international accessory collections, including handbags, gloves, scarves, hats, wraps, and jewelry. NAFFEM is organized and managed by the Canadian Fur Trade Development Institute (CFTDI) and can be researched online at www.naffem.com.

Mohair Council

The Mohair Council is an organization exclusively dedicated to mohair, the fleece of the Angora goat. Established in 1966, the Mohair Council concentrates on marketing, education, and research as it relates to the mohair industry. The Mohair Council was created for mohair producers and is still primarily financially sustained by producers. It is a nonprofit organization funded by interest and dividend dollars from the now defunct Wool Act, a current voluntary producer mohair assessment program, and funds from the U.S. Department of Agriculture.

The council headquarters is located in San Angelo, Texas, on the edge of Edwards Plateau in southwest Texas. This rugged, ranching region is prime goat country and has long been home to many of the finest Angora goat breeding flocks in the world. Ninety percent of the U.S. Angora goat population grazes within a 150-mile radius of the Mohair Council's national headquarters. There, the mild, dry climate and hilly, brushy terrain are particularly well suited for raising Angora goats because of their dry mountain origin. The United States has developed into one of the three largest mohair-producing nations in the world with an annual production in excess of 2.4 million pounds. The other principal mohair sources are South Africa and Turkey. With over 220,000 goats, Texas is the primary mohair region of the United States.

The main function of the Mohair Council is to promote American mohair and to find viable worldwide markets for this unique commodity. To market its product, the Mohair Council has a team of 11 professionals who travel the world in search of profitable foreign markets for American mohair. These individuals meet one-on-one with prospective buyers, discover their needs, and then work to put the mohair buyer and supplier together. Another objective of the Mohair Council is to educate designers, manufacturers, retailers, and consumers about mohair and mohair products.

For example, did you know that as a decorating fabric, mohair is valued for its flame-resistance and high sound absorbency? It is ideal for public places such as symphony halls, theaters, hotel lobbies, and offices, as well as for homes. In addition, mohair draperies are effective insulators, keeping heat in during cold weather and serving as a barrier against outside hot temperatures in the summer. Mohair is also used for throws and blankets and for many clothing and accessory items, such as hats, scarves, and slippers; however, mohair is also used for carpeting and rugs, wigs, paint rollers, ink transfer pads, and children's toys. The Mohair Council's website is www.mohairusa.com.

Cone Mills

Cone Mills, LLC, is one of America's leading textile manufacturers. Cone Mills is a privately held company owned by W. L. Ross and Company as part of the International Textile Group. It is headquartered in Greensboro, North Carolina, with five manufacturing facilities located in North Carolina and Mexico. The company operates regional sales offices in Greensboro, New York, Dallas, Los Angeles, and San Francisco. Established in 1891, Cone Mills aims to be the largest producer of denim fabrics in the world. It has been selling denim and casual sportswear fabrics internationally for over 45 years, serves markets in over 35 countries, and is the largest U.S. exporter of denim and apparel fabrics.

Another component of Cone Mills's mission is a commitment to protecting the environment. Some of the strategies that Cone has implemented to assure sustainable resources include:

▶ Developing the technology used throughout the industry to treat textile wastewater. The company now operates four wastewater treatment plants.

▶ Being the first to recover and reuse indigo dye, the primary dye used in denim jeans

▶ Being a leader in water and solid waste recycling to reduce dependence on water resources and landfills

▶ Developing a system to recycle methane gas from a landfill by piping it to a nearby plant and using it for boiler fuel, a beneficial way to recycle material that could be harmful if released to the atmosphere

▸ Taking a leadership role in removing color from water that leaves its manufacturing plants

▸ Being the first denim manufacturer to apply biosolids to farmland as fertilizer (and making grass and crops greener at the same time)

For the prospective textile professional with a strong interest in environmental protection, Cone Industries provides internship opportunities. Further information about the company and its job opportunities can be found at its website, www.cone.com.

Springs Industries

Founded in 1887, Springs Industries supplies leading retailers with coordinated home furnishings. The company headquarters is located in Fort Mill, South Carolina. Springs Industries also produces and markets bed and bath products for institutional and hospitality customers, home sewing fabrics, as well as baby bedding and apparel products. This range of products is truly mind-boggling. Springs's bedding products include sheets and pillowcases, comforters and comforter accessories, bedspreads, blankets, bed skirts, quilts, duvet covers, pillow shams, decorative and bed pillows, and mattress pads. Its bath products include  towels, bath and accent rugs, shower curtains, and ceramic and other bath accessories. Its window products include window hardware and decorative rods, horizontal blinds in a range of widths and materials, motorized blinds, pleated and cellular shades, and soft window treatments such as drapes, valances, and balloon shades.

Through licensing agreements, Springs Industries has extended its product lines to include kitchen and table linen items, decorative napkin rings, flannel and knit sheets, toilet seat covers, blankets and throws, and fabric-covered lampshades. These licensed brands include Burlington House, American Lifestyle, Kate Spade, Liz At Home, Harry Potter, Mary-Kate and Ashley, Coca-Cola, Serta, and NASCAR.

With such a vast array of product classifications, it is no surprise that Springs Industries has approximately 30 manufacturing facilities in the United States, Canada, and Mexico and employs about 15,000 people. Five generations of the Springs family have led this private company. Major brands of Springs Industries include Wamsutta,

Springmaid, Regal, Beaulieu, Graber, Bali, Nanik, Dundee, Wabasso, and Texmade. The company's website address is www.springs.com.

DuPont

When it was founded in 1802, E. I. du Ponte de Nemours was primarily an explosives company. Today, it is a company that has shown explosive growth. DuPont offers a wide range of innovative products and services for numerous markets, including agri-

culture, nutrition, electronics, communications, safety and protection, home and construction, transportation, and apparel. DuPont operates in more than 70 countries and employs over 60,000 people worldwide. It is a Fortune 500 company with revenues of $27.3 billion in 2004.

DuPont's mission includes research and development as high priorities. The company has more than 40 research, development, and customer service labs in the United States, and more than 35 labs in 11 other countries. The productive results of DuPont's research are illustrated by its products. DuPont's brands include Teflon fluoropolymers, films, fabric protectors, fibers, and dispersions; Corian solid surfaces; Kevlar high-strength material; and Tyvek protective material; DuPont's innovative fabrics run the gamut of uses from hospital and medical care applications to firefighters' gear and sportswear. The company can be located online at www.DuPont.com.

SUMMARY

As fashion companies in the United States now, more than ever, outsource much of their production work to companies in foreign countries, job opportunities in textile production have dramatically declined domestically. The majority of American companies design domestically but outsource goods internationally to take advantage of the free-trade agreements with low-wage countries. However, the loss in U.S. production jobs in the textile industry has been offset by creative and scientific tracks in design and product development, in addition to textile technology. Some of the key career tracks in the creative sector of textiles include fashion director, textile designer, textile colorist, and textile stylist. In the scientific and manufacturing areas of textiles, career options include textile engineer and textile technician. Additionally, there are ancillary career paths in textiles in a variety of areas such as reference libraries and sales. The director of a resource room or reference library for a fiber association, such as Cotton Incorporated, maintains the fabric samples, garments, books, and trade journals that company employees use for inspiration and reference. The account executive is the sales representative for a fabric producer, selling piece goods to clients, such as the designers and manufacturers of apparel, accessories, or home furnishings. Whether you are interested in sales, technology, or design, there are career opportunities in the primary level of the fashion industry, fiber and fabrics.

KEY TERMS

account executive
assistant textile designer
color integrity
color palettes
colorway
computer-aided design
contractor
croquis
fashion director
outsourcing
piece goods
print services
reference librarian
resource room director
samples
short-run production
textile colorist
textile design
textile designer
textile engineer
textile stylist
textile technician

Discussion Questions

1. In light of the trend toward outsourcing in textile production, what new career options do you believe will develop in the fiber and fabric sector of the fashion industry? What types of knowledge, training, and skills will best equip a job candidate to succeed in this industry over the next decade?

2. What are the differences between the textile designer, stylist, and colorist? The similarities?

3. Using the Internet, locate and describe two new CAD programs, one that assists with textile design tasks and another that facilitates textile production.

CHAPTER 3

Sourcing

There is a person whose job is to buy the materials that make up your favorite jean jacket, your great leather belt, or your comfortable sofa. There is yet another person who locates the manufacturing facility that produces the jacket, belt, or sofa. Both of these people are involved in the work of sourcing. **Sourcing** refers to one of two activities. It may refer to the process of locating the suppliers, or vendors, of components needed to make a final product. A **vendor** is any firm, such as a manufacturer or a distributor, from whom a company purchases products or production processes. Sourcing includes the activities of determining the amount of product needed, negotiating the best possible price and discounts, scheduling deliveries, and following up on actual shipments to make certain that due dates are met and that quality control is maintained. Sourcing may also refer to the job of locating manufacturers to produce end products and then collaborating with those manufacturers while the products are being created. Either way, sourcing results in taking products from their conception stages to sales floors.

Let's say a designer of an apparel line comes up with several amazing **collections**, or groupings of related styles. According to the designer's sketches, to actually make the illustrations a reality, the company will need several tapestry fabrics for jackets, silk chiffons for blouses, and colored denim for bottoms. Additionally, there will be the need for faux fur for the detachable collars, buttons for the jackets and tops, lining fabrics, interfacing, belting, and zippers; the list goes on and on. In some companies, the designer and an assistant will locate the places from which to purchase these items. In larger companies, there may be buyers who source fabrics and related products for the items in the designer's line. The sourcing manager takes the designer's vision and helps turn it into reality.

SOURCING THE PRODUCT

How do design companies locate the fabrics and other product parts necessary for producing their lines? There are career options that focus on sourcing fabrics and other product components. Fashion production planners, piece goods buyers, and findings buyers are three examples of these career paths. Sourcing may encompass buying goods domestically or abroad. If products are purchased from an overseas vendor and shipped to the United States, they are referred to as **imports**. In contrast, products that are bought by an overseas company from a vendor in the United States and sent out of the country are referred to as **exports**. Imports and exports are examined in further detail in the following discussion of sourcing careers.

FASHION PRODUCTION PLANNER

Fashion production planners are sometimes referred to as "raw materials buyers." Their main task is material planning, anticipating all of the parts needed to make the final product. In the United States, the average salary reported for this position is $44,000 per year. The primary responsibilities of fashion production planners include the following:

- Reviewing forecasts of sales generated by the manufacturers' representatives and/or by analyzing past sales performance of line items
- Planning fabric production based on current orders and projected reorders
- Scheduling and monitoring works in progress
- Working with material manufacturers to determine the availability of goods
- Collaborating with key departments, such as design and product development, to anticipate future needs
- Meeting strict deadlines to keep line shipments on time

Qualifications

A career as a fashion production planner requires the following qualifications:

- **Education:** A bachelor's degree in fashion merchandising, fashion design, business administration, marketing, international marketing, or a related field is a requirement.

- **Experience:** Skills in a similar role within the fashion manufacturing sector of the industry is a hiring plus. Knowledge of offshore raw materials planning and purchasing as it relates to sales forecasts is essential. Experience in a large and varied manufacturing fashion company would be highly regarded. An internship during college is an added bonus to post-graduate employment.
- **Personal characteristics:** The ability to communicate clearly is essential. Often, fabrics and findings are sourced overseas; therefore, a multilingual background may be extremely valuable. A few of the languages that are currently important in the sourcing field are Mandarin, Cantonese, Taiwanese, and Spanish.

PIECE GOODS BUYER

The **piece goods buyer** works for a company that uses textiles in the production of its final products. This can be an apparel company, a home furnishings firm, an automotive manufacturer, or an accessories producer. The responsibilities of a piece goods buyer include the following:

- Shopping for textile supplies at trade markets and through textile manufacturers' representatives (Figure 3.1).
- Planning the amount of fabric, referred to as **yardage**, to purchase in various colors and styles.

Figures 3.1. Leather wholesaling: Leather drying in a wholesale warehouse (left); leather wholesaler showing a skin (right).

- Sourcing or determining from which vendors the piece goods will be purchased and communicating with these vendors.
- Coordinating with **production managers** who advise on the delivery status of purchase orders; a **purchase order (PO)** is a contract for merchandise between buyers, as representatives of their firms, and vendors.
- Communicating with accounts payable on payments and financing, to include proof of payments, wire transfers, and letters of credit; a **letter of credit** is a document issued by a bank authorizing the bearer to draw a specific amount of money from the issuing bank, its branches, or associated banks and agencies. It allows importers to offer secure terms to exporters.
- Working with warehouse managers on inventory management, such as availability and accessibility of fabrics.
- Monitoring quality control by inspecting shipments and dealing with **chargebacks**, credits for damaged merchandise, and returns on defective goods.

An **assistant piece goods buyer** often works with the piece goods buyer to accomplish this long list of responsibilities and as training for a similar position in the future.

Qualifications

A career as a piece goods buyer requires the following qualifications:

- **Education:** A bachelor's degree in fashion merchandising, fashion design, textiles, or a related field is a minimum requirement.
- **Experience:** A great number of piece goods buyers are promoted from the position of assistant piece goods buyer; others move into piece goods buying from the textile design track.
- **Personal characteristics:** A piece goods buyer has excellent quantitative skills, which are needed for calculating cost of goods, delivery expenses, and yardage amounts. This person must be able to work effectively under pressure, have excellent follow-up and communication skills, and be a successful negotiator.

FINDINGS AND/OR TRIMMINGS BUYER

The **findings buyer** is responsible for ordering findings and trimmings. **Findings** include such product components as zippers, thread, linings, and interfacings. Findings are functional and may not be visible when viewing the final product.

Trimmings, however, are decorative components designed to be seen as part of the final product. Trimmings include buttons, appliqués, and beltings. The **trimmings buyer** is responsible for ordering these product components. Locating findings and trimmings is an important job in which timing is critical. Think about the production line, quality control, and the end product. If the findings buyer orders zippers that are too short, either the zippers will be installed and the customers won't be able to get into the skirts or production on the skirts will be halted until the correct zippers are received. If a button shipment is late, the trimmings buyer is held accountable as the entire production has to be held until it arrives. Figure 3.2 shows a photo of Tender Buttons, a famous trimmings shop in New York City.

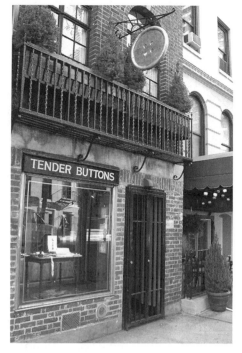

Figure 3.2. Tender Buttons shop in New York City.

Qualifications

The education, experience, and personal characteristics required for findings and/or trimmings buyers are as follows.

- ▶ **Education:** A bachelor's degree in fashion design, fashion merchandising, product development, or a related discipline is a minimal requirement.
- ▶ **Experience:** Most findings and trimmings buyers work as assistants to the buyers before moving into this position. Internship experience and employment in either the manufacturing or design sector of the fashion industry are beneficial to securing these positions.
- ▶ **Personal characteristics:** High attention to detail is a critical asset to findings and trimmings buyers. Understanding product construction, sewing techniques, and product quality are essential skills. The abilities to locate vendors and negotiate with them are critical, as is following up on deliveries.

Career Challenges

Planners and buyers of raw materials, piece goods, and findings and trimmings share similar job struggles. It can continually be a source of stress to follow up on shipments needed to meet deadlines. Negotiating with vendors for priority shipping and competitive pricing can be a challenge. Written and oral communication skills may be tested when the buyer is putting together a deal with an overseas supplier. Currency exchanges, shipping costs, language barriers, and cultural differences can contribute to communication breakdowns. Attention to detail and written agreements are critical to minimizing these challenges. Finally, the buyer in sourcing is faced with constantly recalculating costs of goods. Shipping prices can change overnight. Handling fees may be added. Taxes may change. The dollar may fluctuate in currency exchange. Reviewing costs is a task that must be reexamined from the time an order is placed until the products reach the receiving dock. Fortunately, most buyers in sourcing enjoy quantitative work that demands a high attention to detail.

SOURCING MANAGER

In addition to sourcing materials needed to create the end product, some large companies have a position available entitled **sourcing manager** in which an individual is responsible for sourcing production. The sourcing manager communicates with the company manufacturing the product, referred to as the contractor. Sourcing managers work with overseas or domestic producers, discuss product specifications with them, and negotiate contracts. Next, controls need to be put into place to make certain that production is executed correctly by the outside vendor. After production begins, the sourcing manager monitors quality control and delivery schedules. Throughout the process, there are, more often than not, problems to be resolved. The successful sourcing manager may earn $65,000–$75,000 annually.

Qualifications

Sourcing managers should possess the following qualifications:

- ▸ **Education:** A bachelor's degree in fashion merchandising, fashion design, product development, business administration, or a related field is a requirement.
- ▸ **Experience:** Strong knowledge of sewing and product construction is necessary for sourcing production, fabric, and findings. Also, a general technical knowledge of fabric use and construction is required. This is a position that requires prior work experience. Two to three years as a retail buyer or several years as a wholesale merchandiser provide a good background.

> ## BOX 3.1 • SAMPLE CLASSIFIED ADVERTISEMENT: SOURCING AND LOGISTICS MANAGER
>
> TexGlobal, Inc., is an international leader and innovator in the fiber, fabric, and fashion industry. We are currently seeking to fill the following position:
>
> ### Sourcing and Logistics Manager
>
> - Five-plus years of experience sourcing in China
>
> - Background in source selection, vendor quality, and logistics
> - Must come from a manufacturing background
> - All candidates must be able to provide work-related references
>
> Salary: $70,000–$85,000 + bonus; excellent employee benefits.
> Location: Denver, Colorado

> ▶ **Personal characteristics:** Flexibility is often cited as the number one quality for the successful sourcing manager. One has to see far enough down the road to anticipate changes and potential problems and then be flexible enough to keep the work on track. Top sourcing managers are proactive, rather than reactive. Stamina is also a critical characteristic, as there are long hours that require tremendous focus and effort. Frequent travel may be required. Particularly for overseas travel, sensitivity to cultural differences is an asset. The abilities to handle stress, learn from experience, negotiate effectively, and maintain a sense of humor are additional helpful characteristics.

Box 3.1 is a sample of an online classified advertisement for a sourcing manager.

IMPORT PRODUCTION COORDINATOR

An **import production coordinator** is the apparel or home furnishings company's liaison with the manufacturer or contractor. The import production coordinator is involved in all aspects of the production process, works closely with the design team, and is the link between overseas factories (in China, Japan, Taiwan, India, and South America, to name a few locations) and the company's design and buying teams. The import production coordinator's main goal is to ensure on-time delivery and quality of production. This person must have strong analytical skills and materials-planning knowledge to review product forecasts and plan raw materials to manufacture domestically and internationally. Good communication, effective negotiating, and time-management abilities are key attributes, as problems often need to be resolved quickly and with consensus. Import production coordinators negotiate quality, price, and delivery dates of products and track the supply chain from sample production to bulk delivery. A more detailed listing of the main responsibilities of an import production coordinator follows.

▸ Scheduling sample and line production in collaboration with design team
▸ Coordinating sample production and communicating any changes to the factory
▸ Establishing and maintaining strong relationships with offshore suppliers
▸ Anticipating the length of time it will take goods to be shipped and received from factories abroad
▸ Knowing import and export laws and how to complete the necessary documents to ship and receive goods and understanding how to work with customs
▸ Completing final sign-off on samples to begin production
▸ Managing critical time to ensure on-time deliveries
▸ Updating in-house computer systems on styling information
▸ Monitoring the production process and updating management on any changes or needs to create quality products
▸ Having an eye for detail and quality
▸ Identifying and resolving issues quickly and with cost efficiency
▸ Having the accounting knowledge needed to determine **landed costs,** the actual price of goods after taxes, tariffs, handling, and shipping fees are added to the cost of goods

Assistant importers work for the import production coordinator and follow up on orders with overseas suppliers. They also communicate with freight companies and customs agents, process documents, and check pricing agreements. They may also be responsible for arranging payments to overseas suppliers and liaising with internal customers to ensure goods arrive as expected. They can usually earn annual salaries of $28,000–$35,000.

Qualifications

The required qualifications for the import production coordinator follow.

- **Education:** A bachelor's degree in fashion design, fashion merchandising, product development, business administration, or a related field is essential.
- **Experience:** To secure this position, a prospective employee will need a number of years in previous import production experience within the apparel or home furnishings industry. Often, the position of import production coordinator requires fluency in a foreign language (Cantonese, Japanese, Spanish, or Mandarin, to name a few). Import production coordinators will also need to have intermediate to advanced Microsoft Office skills; strong candidates are competent in Microsoft Word and Excel. This experience may be obtained in the position of assistant importer. This position often requires someone who is willing and able to travel extensively. A proven background in importing, shipping, and client relationships is helpful.
- **Personal characteristics:** To be successful, import production coordinators need a keen attention to detail, self-motivation, and the ability to work on a team. Excellent written, visual, and oral communication skills are required. They must be highly organized and able to work in a fast-paced environment.

Career Challenges

The sourcing manager, import production coordinator, and assistant importer are faced with the primary challenge of effective communication to assure on-time deliveries, the best prices, and top-quality products. They are often juggling many balls, working with the numerous vendors, production managers, and designers simultaneously. While global travel may be an exciting adventure in the beginning of these careers, it can become a burden to pack a suitcase, jump on a plane to put out a production "fire," and return to the office, ready to work the next day. It takes a great deal of flexibility, stamina, and organizational skills to rise above the potential stress of a worldwide business operation.

SOURCING CAREER OPTIONS IN THE GLOBAL COMMUNITY

The world has become one huge global market. Because many countries no longer produce all of the goods and services that they need and/or want, they have come to rely on one another to obtain what they cannot or choose not to produce. As this movement has evolved, the world's nations have become more economically interdependent.

Figure 3.3. Vendors and buyers at Hanoi Trade Fair.

Globalization, the process of interlinking nations of the world with one another, is a growing trend in the fashion industry. **Global sourcing** refers to the process of locating, purchasing, and importing or exporting goods and services (Figure 3.3). When a retail buyer for a United States store, for example, buys leather handbags from Milan and has them shipped to the United States, his or her company imports them. The country that provides and ships out the goods—in this case, Italy—exports them. There are international trade guidelines for importing and exporting that professionals in the sourcing field must understand.

Buyer for a Store-Owned Foreign Buying Office

There are two types of retail organizations that operate company-owned foreign buying offices: retailers that are large enough to use and pay for this ancillary operation and stores with very special images, such as exclusive boutiques and designer emporiums. Buyers who work in store-owned foreign buying offices support and advise other buyers of their respective stores. (In Chapter 11, the career track of the retail buyer is examined.) The buyers for a store-owned buying office survey the market looking for new trends. They recommend vendors and styles, develop catalogs and mailing pieces, and follow up on deliveries. Because they are employed by the retail store, they are, in essence, an extension of it. Buyers in many foreign buying offices are authorized to make purchases from vendors for the company, just as the domestic store buyers are when they shop the local markets. In some situations, the store buyers place purchase orders on the lots procured by the buyers of the foreign buying office. In other companies, the buyers of the foreign buying office place the orders and break down the merchandise to be shipped to the individual retail stores. The **breakdown** of merchandise refers to the segmentation of a purchase order into quantities by sizes and colors to prepare for shipping to specific store branches.

Companies with foreign buying offices generally locate these offices in major fashion capitals such as Paris, London, Rome, Hong Kong, and Tokyo. Saks Fifth Avenue and Neiman Marcus are two examples of major retail operations that maintain store-owned foreign buying offices. Some large mass-merchandise chains also own foreign buying offices; Wal-Mart and JCPenney are two examples. Smaller stores cannot afford to own and operate their own foreign buying offices. Instead, they may choose to subscribe to the services of independently owned resident buying offices with foreign buying divisions. Independent buying offices do not represent retail store competitors in the same city or local area. Examples of these companies include the Donegar Group and Associated Merchandising Corporation.

Foreign Commissionaire or Agent

Foreign commissionaires, or foreign-owned independent agents, usually have offices located in key buying cities overseas. Commissionaires often represent both retailers and manufacturers. They are paid on a fee basis rather than at a monthly or annual rate. Usually, commissionaires receive a percent of the **first cost**, or wholesale price, in the country of origin. The **country of origin** refers to the nation in which the goods were located and purchased. While commissionaires provide many of the same services as store-owned foreign buying offices, their offices are often smaller than store-owned offices. They often have **market representatives**, or specialized buyers of individual merchandise classifications (for example, junior sportswear, children's wear, or men's wear), who work closely with their client stores, keeping them up-to-date on new product offerings in the marketplace, recommending new vendors, and assisting them in locating new goods. A great amount of the market representative's time is spent following up on the client's purchase orders to make sure they are shipped on time and as ordered.

Qualifications

The following are qualifications foreign commissionaires should possess to obtain employment:

- ▶ **Education:** A bachelor's degree in fashion design or fashion merchandising, business administration, marketing, international marketing, or a similar field is a minimal requirement.
- ▶ **Experience:** Many commissionaires begin working for a manufacturer, resident buying office, or a retail operation. Experience in wholesale and retail sales, as well as buying, provides a strong background for this career path. The position of market representative is one that requires a candidate with buying experience.
- ▶ **Personal characteristics:** The commissionaire must work with people all over

the world. The ability and desire to travel extensively and work with persons from a wide range of cultures are important. Strong negotiation skills are valuable. Comprehension of product construction, quality, and design is a necessity. An understanding of import and export laws, shipping options, and finances is critical to this career path.

Importer—Company-Owned

Some retail store buyers may elect to purchase imported goods from United States–owned importing firms. Importers based in the United States shop international markets to purchase goods that will come together as their own "lines." The merchandise is purchased with themes, colors, and styling in mind to create cohesive collections that are displayed and presented to the retail store buyers. Shopping the collections of importers, such as the textile markets in Pakistan and Bangkok depicted in Figure 3.4, allows store buyers in the United States to purchase foreign fashion merchandise that would not be available to them for one or more of the following reasons: the cost of traveling abroad, the high minimum quantities often required to place purchase orders overseas, and the costs and time requirements of shipping merchandise into the country.

Figure 3.4. Buyers often source quality imports from textile markets in Pakistan (top) and Bangkok (bottom).

Qualifications

The fashion importer is required to meet the following qualifications:

- **Education:** A bachelor's degree in fashion design or merchandising, business administration, entrepreneurship, marketing, international marketing, or a similar field is a minimal requirement.
- **Experience:** Many fashion importers begin working for a manufacturer, either in sourcing or sales. Others have work experience as a retail store buyer. Retail sales experience during college provides an entry to retail buying or manufacturer's sales. Importers are responsible for their businesses.

As a result, knowledge of business planning, finances, personnel, marketing, and operations is essential.

▶ **Personal characteristics:** Fashion importers must be leaders, people who can manage businesses and position them for growth. The abilities to manage time and stress, sell themselves and their product lines, and monitor finances are critical. Effective negotiation and follow-up skills are necessary. The ability to put a line together each season is a necessity. An understanding of import and export laws, shipping alternatives, landed costs, and different cultures is also critical to this career.

Career Challenges

The career challenges for professionals involved in fashion imports (e.g., a buyer from a store-owned foreign buying office, a foreign commissionaire/agent, and an importer for a company-owned office) include staying abreast of the restrictions and regulations of international trade, managing transactions with overseas suppliers, and planning for extended lead times to accommodate overseas deliveries. Many importers will agree that the best and easiest part of the job is locating great fashion products around the world. Instead, importers spend a large amount of time investigating the limitations on export quantities, communicating any needed modifications to the manufacturer, and getting the merchandise to their warehouses in the United States in a timely fashion. Building relationships with overseas vendors takes time, and it can make or break the success of an importer.

LICENSING AND SOURCING

Global sourcing has created a new fashion career path in licensing. Think of European designer names like Christian Dior, Chanel, Versace, and Gucci; American designers such as Donna Karan, Calvin Klein, and Ralph Lauren; American characters like Mickey Mouse, Care Bears, and Barbie; or manufacturers such as Harley Davidson, Nike, and Hershey's. All of these companies offer product lines that are not central to their primary product lines. For example, in addition to a Fat Boy motorcycle, you can purchase Harley Davidson belts, apparel, and sunglasses. Another example of international appeal for character product lines can be found at EuroDisney SCA in Paris, which features a range of Disney character products. The

Disney boutique on the Champs Elysées is a prime retail location for the French and tourists alike.

Many well-known fashion companies offer alternative product lines by working with manufacturers to produce goods under their names. For example, Fossil Inc. produces a line of watches for Donna Karan International Inc. The timepiece line fits the Donna Karan image, coordinates with her DKNY clothing and accessories, and features her name; however, Donna Karan International Inc. does not own the watch company. Fossil Inc., owner of the line, is the timepiece company that manufactures this product classification for and pays a fee and/or royalties to Donna Karan International Inc. This arrangement is referred to as a **license**, an agreement in which a manufacturer, the **licensee**, is given exclusive rights to produce and market goods that carry the registered name and brandmark of a designer (e.g., Ralph Lauren), celebrity (e.g., Michael Jordan), character (e.g., Mickey Mouse), or product line (e.g., Hershey's). The owner of the name or brandmark is called the **licensor**. The licensor receives a percent of wholesale sales or some other compensation for the arrangement. Figure 3.5 provides an example of a DKNY watch licensed under Fossil Inc.

Figure 3.5. The name on the watch is DKNY, but manufacturing of this brand is licensed by Fossil Inc, which also manufactures watches under its own name and for several other licensors.

Today, many companies combine sourcing merchandise from overseas with importing and licensing. Additionally, a large number of these firms have finished products delivered from overseas manufacturers to retail operations abroad rather than solely importing the merchandise to the United States. It is truly a global market for many licensed products, one that can establish and strengthen brand identity. As international distribution continues to develop, particularly in Asia, manufacturers in the United States need specialists with knowledge of sourcing, importing, exporting, and licensing regulations. These specialists are referred to as **licensing directors**.

LICENSING DIRECTOR

Licensing directors are responsible for overseeing the look, quality, labeling, delivery, and distribution of their companies' product lines. Sourcing is an integral part of this job. They work with the foreign and domestic manufacturers of various product lines, the licensees, to make certain that the products are branded correctly. The style, placement, size, and color of the brandmark and labels must be consistent across all product lines. Additionally, licensing directors make sure product lines meet quality expectations and fit within the design concepts of their company's primary line, whether it be Donna Karan Collection dresses or Kate Spade handbags. For example, if the Kate Spade handbag line for a particular season features petite floral print totes with striped linings, designs of the licensed sunglass line should coordinate with similar colors and patterns. The results the sunglass manufacturer and designer desire are multiple sales to the consumers and a greater presence on retail floors.

Qualifications

The job requirements for licensing directors are as follows:

- ▸ **Education:** A bachelor's degree in fashion design or merchandising, business administration, marketing, international marketing, or a similar field is a minimal requirement.
- ▸ **Experience:** Many licensing directors begin on the showroom floor of a manufacturer or as account representatives. Prior to this, retail sales experience during college provides a solid foundation in working with various product lines and customers. The position of licensing director is one that a candidate is promoted into after showing knowledge and skills in the business.
- ▸ **Personal characteristics:** The licensing director must juggle many tasks at one time. The abilities to manage time, stay calm under pressure, and prioritize tasks are significant. Strong negotiation skills are a plus. Comprehension of product construction, quality, and design is a necessity. An understanding of import and export laws, branding regulations, and different cultures is critical to this career path.

Career Challenges

One of the greatest challenges in a licensing career is the need to clearly understand and stay up-to-date in a wide range of areas. The licensing professional must have thorough knowledge of design and product development, branding specifications, import and export legislation and regulations, and manufacturing processes—all for a variety of products, such as sunglasses, gloves, sportswear, and footwear. If a product of poor quality that does not reflect the licensor's vision slips out from under the licensing director's radar, the image and sales of the licensor can be negatively affected. Therefore, coordinating the work of many manufacturers located around the world that produce a range of product types is a tremendous task and responsibility.

SUMMARY

From locating vendors to collaborating with manufacturers, sourcing is the process of taking a product from its conception stage to the sales floor. In some companies, designers and their assistants locate the places from which to purchase piece goods. Larger companies may employ buyers to source fabrics and related products for the items in the designer's line. The career options that focus on sourcing fabrics and findings necessary for producing collections include fashion production planner, or raw goods buyer, and piece goods buyer. Production managers, contacts between buyers and vendors, advise on the delivery status of purchase orders. Sourcing managers work with overseas or domestic producers to figure out product specifications and negotiate contracts. An import production coordinator is involved in all aspects of the production process and is often the link between the overseas factories and the design and buying teams.

Today's global market has inspired many companies to combine sourcing merchandise from overseas with importing and licensing. Foreign commissionaires, or foreign-owned independent agents, often employ market representatives, or specialized buyers of individual merchandise classifications. As international distribution continues to develop, manufacturers employ licensing directors, specialists with knowledge of sourcing, importing, exporting, and licensing regulations.

While education and field experience are important qualifications for a career path in sourcing, the qualifications key to success are flexibility, organization, and communication. Knowledge of import and export laws, branding regulations, foreign languages, and different cultures is important to those working within all aspects of the global industry. If you are interested in sourcing as a future career, you must have the ability to work effectively when under pressure and possess excellent negotiation skills. Sourcing is an ideal profession for the curious, creative, and detail-oriented person. It is an exciting and satisfying journey to take a design from dream to reality.

KEY TERMS

assistant importer

assistant piece goods buyer

breakdown

chargeback

collection

contractor

country of origin

export

fashion production planner (raw materials buyer)

findings

findings buyer

first cost

foreign commissionaires (foreign-owned independent agents)

globalization

global sourcing

import

importers

import production coordinator

landed cost

letter of credit

licensee

licensing

licensing director

licensor

market representative

piece goods buyer

production manager

purchase order (PO)

sourcing

sourcing manager

trimmings

trimmings buyer

vendor

yardage

Discussion Questions

1. How many different components, or parts, make up the clothes and accessories you are wearing today? Determine the fabrics, trimmings, and findings that were sourced to assemble each garment. How likely is it that all of these parts have come from the same producer or even the same country?

2. Research to discover how many licensing agreements your favorite designer shares with manufacturers. Do the manufacturers produce similar lines for other fashion companies?

3. Why do piece goods buyers rarely source fabrics and findings from the United States?

4. Which countries host the largest manufacturing companies for fashion products? In what specific merchandise classifications, fabrics, or production processes does each country specialize? What are some reasons for specialization?

CHAPTER 4

Production

Some fashion students find raw materials, such as fabrics and trims, to be one of the most interesting areas of the industry. Others are drawn to the more quantitative tasks, such as buying, costing, and production planning. Many are fascinated with the technical and computer-oriented aspects of the fashion business. Whether materials, numbers, or computers are one's preference, there are career paths in production that relate directly to each area. For almost every fashion product-manufacturing firm, a global perspective is necessary for career success.

As emphasized in the first three chapters, effective career preparation for the apparel, accessories, soft goods, and home furnishings industries requires across-the-board understanding of the following concepts:

▸ The apparel and textile industry operates in a global market, making an understanding of cultural diversity and the world economy essential.
▸ Activities of product development, manufacturing, and retailing are interrelated, from fiber and textiles to design and production to sourcing and merchandising.
▸ Successful companies recognize that product decisions are consumer-driven.

The manufacturing sector of the fashion industry exemplifies all of these concepts. The basic stages of the production process can be mapped as follows:

Sourcing and sales → Piece goods/Findings and trimmings bids → Product costing → Ordering of product components → Production scheduling → Creation of production pattern → Grading → Marker making → Spreading and cutting → Product construction/assembly → Quality control → Packing and shipping → Reorder production and shipping.

Production or manufacturing of **end products**, the products that will actually be purchased by the customer, is an area that offers a number of career opportunities. Several technological and management concepts relative to the fashion industry have created or affected career tracks in this area. These include computer-integrated manufacturing, quick response, electronic data interchange, and mass customization. In this chapter, an exploration of career options relating to these concepts, in both domestic and overseas production, includes employment opportunities in the following positions: product manager, production planner, production manager, traffic manager, production efficiency manager, quality control manager, pattern production (e.g., pattern maker, pattern grader, and marker maker), and spreader and cutter.

PRODUCT MANAGER

A **product manager** can be responsible for all of the products within a company's product lines or for a specific product category within a line. Product managers monitor market and fashion trends related to their assigned product lines. They work to integrate the product into the whole of the company for a consistent and total fashion look, and they investigate the lines of other manufacturers, making certain that their company's lines will blend with the color, form, and fabric trends being shown for the season in the departments carrying their company's product lines and those of their competitors, as well as related departments of retail operations. For example, the product manager of a handbag manufacturer, Annie Bags, will review the new line for trend representation and look for a variety of fabrics, the key colors for the season, and a clear image for Annie Bags. The product manager will also review competitive lines, looking for similarities and product voids. **Product voids** refer to merchandise categories in which there are few, if any, items to fill consumer needs and desires. Finally, the product manager will examine related product lines that appeal to the Annie Bags' target market, such as footwear, sportswear, and outerwear lines that target customers buy. The project manager's goal is to guide the product line to higher sales by creating a timely fashion presence that fits with trends while filling a product niche.

Box 4.1 is an interview with a product design manager.

BOX 4.1 • INTERVIEW WITH A PRODUCT DESIGN MANAGER

Interviewee: Jillian Lemaster

Job title: Product Design Manager—Ladies Cut and Sew Hats, Bags, and Fleece

Education and experience to move into this career track: I graduated with a double major in fashion merchandising and design, a bachelor of science degree, from Missouri State University in May 2003. In the summer between my junior and senior years, I studied in London through American Intercontinental University, taking a trend-forecasting class and interning at the Profile Group on the publication *Fashion Monitor*. I moved to New York City late summer after graduation. There I did a short internship with Catherine Malendrino during Fashion Week, and soon after, I landed my first job at Capelli New York as an assistant in product and design.

If you were hiring someone to work for you, these are the personal characteristics that you would look for in a job candidate: When interviewing, the qualities we look for are a unique sense of passion, motivation, ambition, enthusiasm, organizational skills, good communication skills, and a positive attitude.

What do you enjoy most about your job: I enjoy the constant mix of business and creativity, managing a small team, and seeing my products' development from beginning to end. The results in the sales percentages in store are a constant challenge and a daily reward. Product development is the perfect mix for someone with a design and merchandising-based mind to be a part of the always-evolving fashion industry.

What do you like the least: In this industry, you work hard and long, and everything is urgent. So I believe you have to have passion about what you are doing; otherwise, it is not worth it.

Industry trends that you believe will affect what you are doing or will be doing in the next five to ten years: The knowledge and experience you gain working in the New York fashion industry are incomparable and things you can carry with you forever. Whether I am still here in New York in the next five to 10 years or have moved on to the slower suburban life I grew up with, I believe people will always desire to accessorize themselves in one way or another, and fashion will always have an influence on the way people feel in their lives. So no matter where you are or where you work in the world, these two constants and trends will always need to be fulfilled.

Advice to people interested in entering this career field: My advice for those entering this career field is to have a clear and direct sense of motivation regarding where you are going. Acknowledge and accept gracefully the fact that you need to start at the bottom and work your way up. Have a positive attitude no matter what task you are performing. Let every day build your character into a stronger and more valuable asset to your company. Be assertive, not aggressive; always respect the chain of command; and, most of all, never stop learning.

Qualifications

Successful product managers may earn annual salaries ranging from $75,000 to $100,000, depending on the size of the company for which they work and their employment credentials. A list of qualifications for this career follows.

▸ **Education:** A bachelor's degree in fashion merchandising, fashion design, product development, production, apparel manufacturing, or a related field is commonly a requirement.

▸ **Experience:** A sales representative for a manufacturing company may climb the career ladder into the position of product manager. An assistant in a trend-forecasting firm may leave that sector of the industry to move up to a product manager position. Large firms have assistant product manager positions for which product manager positions are the next step up the career ladder.

▸ **Personal Characteristics:** Successful product managers have the ability to analyze their firm's market for opportunities and threats. Assessing competition, communicating fashion trends, and investigating retail trends require the personal attributes of curiosity, observation, and creativity, as well as strong skills in communication, organization, and presentation.

Career Challenges

Many small companies do not employ product managers; instead, designers are responsible for evaluating competitors and determining fashion trends for the line. As a result, the number of positions in this area is limited to mid- and large-sized firms. Product managers are "under the gun" when it comes to being correct on the fashion colors, forms, and themes their companies will feature in product lines. If, for example, purple turns out to be a color a company's target market does not buy, its product manager may be job hunting. Since there is much at stake when a company features the wrong products, product managers must conduct detailed research to make accurate decisions, which makes this position exciting, fun, and an ongoing challenge.

PRODUCTION PLANNER

The majority of large manufacturing firms have production planners on staff. **Production planners** estimate the amounts and types of products a company will manufacture, based either on previous seasonal sales or on orders being received by sales representatives on the road and in the showroom. There are two primary methods of production planning: cut-to-order and cut-to-stock. **Cut-to-order** is considered the safest method of projecting manufacturing needs. It entails waiting until orders are received from buyers and then working within tight timelines to order product parts, construct product lines as ordered, and ship them to the retail accounts on time. Which types of fashion companies prefer the cut-to-order option? This technique is most often used by designer firms that feature higher-priced, high-fashion merchandise. For these companies, forecasting the sales of products that reflect new fashion trends is more difficult. Also, the costs of being wrong may be much higher than for less expensive, less fashion-forward merchandise because of the more expensive fabrics and, often, more detailed workmanship these high-fashion companies include in their products.

Cut-to-stock involves purchasing fabrics and other product components before orders are acquired. Production planners using the cut-to-stock method examine a number of variables before projecting manufacturing needs. They look at the economy and how, when, and on what consumers are spending their money. They investigate what the competition, including new companies entering the market and targeting their customers, is doing. They study sales histories of products in the line, focusing on sales for each season. They analyze the strength of new lines by discussing sales potential with the design staff and sales representatives.

What are the advantages of the cut-to-stock option? It enables production to be spread out over a longer period of time. This permits the manufacturer to keep factories in production mode throughout the year, rather than working around "peaks and valleys." Cut-to-stock also allows for a longer lead time, the amount of time needed between placing a production order and receiving a shipment of the products. With international production gaining importance, lead times have become longer for manufacturers using overseas factories. Which types of firms find the cut-to-stock alternative to be most efficient and cost-effective? Manufacturing companies that produce a significant number of basic products, such as a T-shirt company, have the ability to project sales more closely than do producers of more expensive, fashion-sensitive goods.

Qualifications

Whether the production planner uses the cut-to-order or cut-to-stock option, the education, work experience, and personal characteristics needed for successful employment in this career track are similar, including the following:

▸ **Education:** A bachelor's degree in fashion merchandising, fashion design, product development, apparel manufacturing, or a related field is commonly required.

▸ **Experience:** Work experience with a manufacturer is needed, possibly beginning in the showroom and later moving into product development or purchasing. An understanding of how products are constructed, the materials they are made from, and the manufacturing processes required to bring them to fruition is critical. Average earnings for production planners range from $30,000 to $50,000 annually.

▸ **Personal characteristics:** The successful product planner has strong quantitative abilities, effective communication skills, a good sense of time management, and top organizational skills.

PRODUCTION MANAGER

Production managers, also referred to as *plant managers*, are responsible for all of the operations at plants, whether domestic or overseas locations, contracted or company-owned. The job responsibilities of production managers include supervising or completing the estimation of production costs, scheduling work flow in factories, and hiring and training production employees. Production managers are also ultimately responsible for quality control of the products. Think about the number of employees, tasks, and potential problems associated with cutting, constructing, pressing, and shipping a product line. This is a challenging career track, but one that pays well and is critical to the success of a company. Plant managers may earn $80,000 to $125,000 annually. Box 4.2 is an example of a classified ad for an open plant manager position.

Production assistants often support production managers with detail work and record keeping. Assistants may track fabric, trim, and findings deliveries; help with developing production schedules; and communicate the work flow of the factory to production managers. They also follow up on outgoing shipments, often keeping customers informed on the progress of their orders and expediting deliveries when needed. A typical annual salary for this position ranges from $20,000 to $30,000.

Additionally, production managers may have the assistance of traffic managers. **Traffic managers** supervise work flow on factory floors, monitoring products from start to finish. They anticipate problems that may stall production, whether in materials, personnel, or equipment. The goal of the traffic manager is to make certain that the factory employees have all they need to manufacture products with efficiency and in good quality. Successful traffic managers may earn $60,000 to $80,000 annually.

BOX 4.2 · SAMPLE CLASSIFIED ADVERTISEMENT: PLANT MANAGER

**Plant Manager—Textile manufacturing and pro-
duction**
Company: Twist Manufacturing, Inc.
Location: Dallas, Texas
Base Pay: $50,000–$80,000/year
Industry: Fashion, Apparel, Textile, Manufactur-
ing, Industrial
Required Education: Two-year degree
Required Experience: More than five years
Relocation Covered: Yes

Job Responsibilities

- Manage production facility of
  approximately 15 employees, consisting of
  supervisors, drivers, and production crew
- Manage day-to-day operations of the
  production process, including quality
  control and productions checks
- Hire, train, review, promote, and discharge
  employees as required
- Manage service technicians and
  maintenance crews as necessary
- Meet operational efficiencies by
  implementing process improvement and
  monitoring work flow and production
- Create and continuously promote a safe
  work environment by ensuring all staff
  understands and adheres to safety-related
  policies and procedures
- Maintain appropriate safety and waste
  disposal records / logs
- Resolve day-to-day issues for production
  facility
- Monitor and order supplies
- Develop and maintain operational budget

Job Requirements

- Management experience within a
  production / manufacturing facility
  environment
- Excellent management skills with the
  ability to delegate responsibilities and
  tasks
- Solid understanding of budgeting and
  plant operations
- Associate's degree or higher

We offer a competitive salary, a comprehensive
benefits package, incredible growth potential,
and learning opportunities. So, if you have more
than five years of management experience within
a production/manufacturing facility environment,
please apply for immediate consideration. We
look forward to speaking with you soon.

Qualifications

The qualifications for a production manager, production assistant, and traffic manager
are similar. The production assistant and traffic manager positions usually precede that
of production manager.

▸ **Education:** A bachelor's degree in fashion merchandising, fashion design, product development, apparel manufacturing, or a related field is commonly required.

▸ **Experience:** Hands-on experience in the industry, which may include work experience in computer-aided pattern design, grading and marker making, product costing, and quality control, is required for this position. The ability to produce flat sketches and specification drawings using a computer is helpful. A Production assistant position is often posted as an entry-level position with the potential of moving into a production manager opening. Larger manufacturers offer assistant traffic manager positions as a starting place.

▸ **Personal characteristics:** Knowledge of raw materials and manufactured products, design and product development, and production technology is required. An understanding of textiles, product construction, the capabilities and limitations of production equipment, and the principles of pattern making is essential. The ability to work as part of a team, as well as independently with little supervision, is critical to success. Good communication skills, both oral and written, are also required. Because apparel production workers represent many nationalities, the ability to speak Mandarin, Cantonese, other Asian languages, or Spanish is an asset. An appreciation of cultural diversity is essential.

Career Challenges

What are the challenges for production managers, assistant production managers, and traffic managers? All of them face the obstacles of tight deadlines, sometimes worsened by external factors that are difficult to foresee. Manufacturing equipment breakdowns, delayed textile shipments, defective zippers, or thread in the wrong color are types of problems that can halt the work flow of the manufacturing facility and cause the manufacturer to miss shipping commitments. This can be a high-stress area in which to work. Effective communication and excellent follow-up skills are essential to making it in this career path.

PRODUCTION EFFICIENCY MANAGER

Some manufacturing firms offer the positions of production efficiency managers and traffic managers. These companies are usually quite large and conduct global manufacturing activities. **Production efficiency managers** are responsible for monitoring the speed and output of the manufacturing facilities and for managing waste (Figure 4.1). Often, production efficiency managers work closely with quality control managers to assure products meet quality standards while costs are under control. For example, the production efficiency manager of a handbag company may find an accessory firm to purchase leather scraps left over from the cutting tables to use for belts. The annual salary range for this position usually falls within the $65,000–$90,000 range.

Figure 4.1. The production efficiency manager oversees speed and output of the manufacturing employees and equipment.

QUALITY CONTROL MANAGER

Quality control managers, or *quality control engineers*, develop specifications for the products that will be manufactured. They are responsible to see that those standards are met during all of the phases of production, identifying quality problems and working with manufacturing personnel to correct them. The quality control manager works with such issues as fit, fabric performance, construction difficulties, packaging and shipping needs, and production pace.

In large companies, a manufacturer's factories may be located worldwide. The quality control manager frequently travels to a number of manufacturing sites, coordinating production and deliveries, while checking to be certain that quality standards are being met at all locations. Because quality problems can run the gamut from the original product specifications to a defective button-holer machine, the quality control manager collaborates with personnel in a number of the company's divisions—from the design staff to plant employees. The salary of the quality control manager is comparable to that of the production efficiency manager.

Qualifications

The qualifications for production efficiency managers and quality control managers are related with similar requirements in education, work experience, and personal characteristics.

- ▸ **Education:** A bachelor's degree in fashion design, fashion merchandising, textiles, production, or a related discipline is needed.
- ▸ **Experience:** Knowledge of product construction, textile technology, and manufacturing capabilities is required. A number of quality control managers enter the field from design, merchandising, production, and/or human resources backgrounds.
- ▸ **Personal characteristics:** Personal characteristics that enhance the work of quality control managers include organizational abilities, effective time-management skills, and communication skills. Effective quality control managers are strong problem-solvers with good follow-up skills and are detail oriented. This position requires human resources skills to gain the commitment of factory workers to produce high-quality products.

Career Challenges

Production efficiency managers and quality control managers face the challenge of working with a wide range of constituencies, from designers and patternmakers to plant workers located in the United States and abroad. It is a significant challenge to communicate with so many people on such diverse levels in, possibly, a number of global locations in different time zones. Strong communication skills and superior organizational abilities are key to being successful in these two career tracks.

PATTERN PRODUCTION

There are a number of career paths in the area of pattern production. They include pattern maker, pattern grader, and marker maker. Pattern production employees earn an average income of $30,000–$55,000, depending on the location and size of the company.

Pattern makers, marker makers, and pattern graders share common characteristics: a superior level of accuracy, an understanding of how textiles perform, and an ability to adjust to increasing technological advances in pattern production. Pattern production requires a single focus and a strong attention to detail. If a single pattern piece is one-quarter of an inch too large, the apparel or home furnishing product will likely not flow through the production process. If, by chance, it does, the consumer will likely not purchase a product that does not fit correctly or look attractive. If details and accuracy are in your realm of expertise, pattern production offers a number of career options for you.

Pattern Maker

Pattern Makers play a key role in the production process: They translate the design concept into a pattern for the actual garment. Pattern makers develop a **first pattern,** which is used to cut and sew the **prototype,** or first sample garment. The first pattern is made in a **sample size,** the one used for testing fit and appearance in addition to selling purposes. For juniors, sample sizes are 7 or 9; for misses, they are 6, 8, or 10, depending on the line and its target market. For men's wear, sample sizes are 34 for trousers and 38 for tailored suits. For toddlers' apparel, size 2 is often the sample size; in children's wear, it is usually a size 7.

Pattern makers can use three techniques to develop the first pattern: draping, flat pattern, or computer-aided pattern making (Figure 4.2). With the **draping** method, pattern makers shape and cut muslin or the garment fabric on a dress form to create a pattern. Draping is the preferred strategy for soft, flowing designs. It allows the pattern maker to adjust the design as it evolves three-dimensionally as with a piece of sculpture. When the designer approves the look, the pattern maker removes the muslin from the form and then draws the pattern on heavy paper. Alternately, the **flat pattern** method uses angles, rulers, and curves to alter existing basic patterns, referred to as **blocks** or **slopers.** Finally, **computer-aided pattern making** is utilized by many large firms that can afford the expense of the equipment and software programs. With computer-aided pattern making, pattern makers can work one of two ways. They can manipulate graphics of pattern pieces on a computer screen or make patterns manually using a **stylis,** a computerized pen. Whether draped, created by flat pattern, or developed on a computer, the first pattern must accurately reflect the style, proportion, and fit the designer had in mind when conceiving the product.

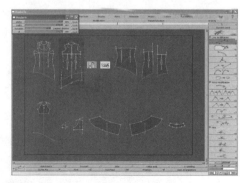

Figure 4.2. Three techniques for developing the first pattern: draping (top), flat pattern (middle), and computer-aided pattern making (bottom).

Qualifications

Following are the qualifications for a pattern maker:

- ▸ **Education:** A bachelor's degree in fashion design, product development, apparel manufacturing, or a related field is commonly required.
- ▸ **Experience:** Preparation for the career of pattern maker includes knowledge of draping, flat pattern making, and computer-aided design. Most pattern makers begin their careers as an assistant pattern maker or a pattern grader. Later in this chapter, these entry-level positions are discussed.
- ▸ **Personal characteristics:** Pattern makers must have an understanding of mathematical calculations as they pertain to sizing and fit. They must have keen eyes for proportion and line, as well as the ability to achieve perfect fits. The successful pattern maker is a technician with a critical eye for detail.

Pattern Grader

Working from the **master pattern**, which often evolves from adjusting and perfecting the sample pattern, **pattern graders** cut in the full range of sizes offered by the manufacturer. For example, the master pattern may be graded in misses' dress sizes 12 to 20 or sizes 6 to 14, depending on the garment style, the company, and its target market. By enlarging or reducing the pattern within a figure-type category, all of the pattern pieces of a particular design are developed for each size. Pattern grading is technical and precise work. It is often work that must be done at a fast pace under the pressure of production deadlines. While the majority of large manufacturing companies use computers to do grading work quickly, many smaller companies cannot initially afford this technology and/or prefer the hands-on skills of a grader. Figure 4.3 depicts a pattern that has been graded using CAD software.

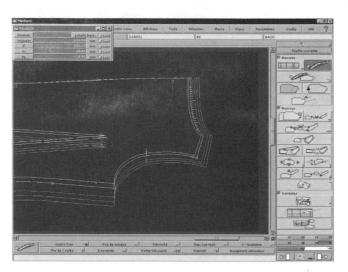

Figure 4.3. Bodice pattern piece graded using CAD software.

Qualifications

Pattern graders should have the following background in terms of education, experience, and personal characteristics:

- ▶ **Education:** A bachelor's degree in fashion design, apparel production, or a related field is a minimal requirement.
- ▶ **Experience:** Effective skills in pattern making, drafting, and product construction are necessary. Experience in pattern draping is a plus. An understanding of and work experience with pattern grading technology are needed.
- ▶ **Personal characteristics:** Strong attention to detail, the ability to work independently and under tight deadlines, and quantitative skills are job requirements for successful pattern graders.

Marker Maker

After the pattern is graded, it is time to develop a marker. A **marker** is the layout of pattern pieces on the fabrication from which the pieces will be cut, as illustrated in Figure 4.4. There are two main purposes of a marker. First, a good marker minimizes fabric waste; secondly, it generates an accurate end design. Fabric prints and patterns, textures and naps, and sheens and matte finishes must be taken into consideration when creating a marker. Think, for example, about a corduroy jacket. If the fabric in the back of the jacket is cut in a different direction from the front, the front and the back will appear to be two different colors. **Marker makers** trace the pattern pieces, by hand or by computer, into the tightest possible layout, while keeping the integrity of the design in mind. In some cases, a marker is generated in hard copy, or print; in other cases, it is stored in the computer.

Qualifications

The qualifications required for a marker maker follow:

- ▶ **Education:** A bachelor's degree in fashion design, apparel production, or a related field is a minimal requirement.
- ▶ **Experience:** Effective skills in pattern making,

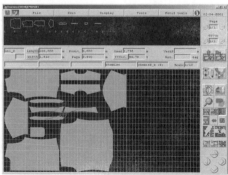

Figure 4.4. Skilled marker makers minimize fabric waste.

drafting, and product construction are necessary. Experience with marker making technology is often required.

► **Personal characteristics:** Like pattern graders, marker makers must have a strong attention to detail, the ability to work independently and under tight deadlines, and strong quantitative skills. Additionally, marker makers must have the ability to "see" the product in its final form when determining pattern piece layout.

SPREADER AND CUTTER

After the marker is developed, it is ready to be placed on the fabric as preparation for cutting the pattern pieces. A **spreader** lays out the selected fabric for cutting. The spreader guides bolts of material on a machine that lays the fabric smooth and straight, layer over layer. In mid- to large-sized companies, a machine as shown in Figure 4.5 does this function. In smaller companies or computerized factories that require fewer employees, this job may be done by cutters. A **cutter** uses electronic cutting machines to cut precisely around the pattern pieces through layers of fabric, often several inches in thickness, as shown in Figure 4.6. While firms with advanced technology may use water jets or lasers to cut out garments quickly and accurately, some companies specialize in merchandise classifications that require hand cutting. A bridal wear manufacturer, a firm that produces beaded eveningwear, or a couture design house may choose to have fabrications manually spread and cut in consideration of the delicate nature and high cost of the fabrics. For the spreader and the cutter, vocational training or training with the manufacturer are usually considered adequate experience. Salary depends on the level of skill and responsibility; experienced cutters earn between $18,000 and $20,000 annually. In addition to these positions, there are a number of skilled or semi-skilled workers on the production assembly line. These employees run the sewing machines, press or steam the final products, and package them for shipping, among

Figure 4.5. A mechanized spreader.

Figure 4.6. Electronic cutting technology enables several layers of pattern pieces to be cut accurately and simultaneously.

other tasks. The production picture is a broad one with a variety of personnel opportunities.

EXAMPLE PROFILES: TRENDS AFFECTING CAREERS IN PRODUCTION

At the start of this chapter, four trends in the production of apparel and home soft goods products were mentioned: computer-integrated manufacturing, quick response, electronic data interchange, and mass customization. As these trends will undeniably shape the requirements for production careers in the fashion industry of the future, a brief discussion of them follows.

Computer-Integrated Manufacturing

In many firms, computer-aided manufacturing exists in such forms as computer-aided pattern making, marker making, cutting, and programmable sewing equipment. As technology develops at a rapid pace globally, the ability to link computers together has introduced amazing advances in production. Computers are being tied together, referred to as **computer-integrated manufacturing (CIM)**, to communicate throughout the entire product development and manufacturing processes, from design to distribution. Computer-aided design and computer-aided manufacturing are linked to a CIM system so that design and product development activities move smoothly into pattern making, grading, marker making, cutting, and product construction activities. Concurrently, computerized information systems develop costing reports and specification sheets; later, shipping and sales data are analyzed. Examples of manufacturers and retailers using CIM include H&M (Figure 4.7), Talbots, and Zara.

Quick Response

Quick response (QR) refers to decreasing the amount of time required from design and the purchase of raw materials to production and distribution of the final

Figure 4.7. H&M utilizes a CIM system to coordinate production activities.

product. In essence, QR requires a partnership among the supplier, manufacturer, retailer, and consumer in which open and honest communication is the key to success. Once these players have developed a relationship that facilitates a constant exchange of accurate information, the results often include increased sales for all. Top-selling products can be reordered and received faster. Modifications of these products give the consumer more options through preferred merchandise assortments. For example, when the retailer reports to the manufacturer that the shipment of a pair of brown leather slacks sold out within a week, the manufacturer can quickly contract with the supplier to buy the slacks in other colors, to change the topstitching or pocket detailing, or to add a jacket to the mix.

Electronic Data Interchange

Electronic data interchange (EDI) has been a critical factor in the growth of QR. EDI refers to the electronic exchange of computer-generated information between one company's computer system and another's. Through EDI, manufacturers and retailers share data about the styles, colors, sizes, and price points that consumers are buying or those that are not selling and require markdowns. For example, retail buyers may peruse manufacturer's selling reports and purchase styles that they did not in initial orders.

Mass Customization

Mass customization is a strategy that allows manufacturers or retailers to provide individualized products to consumers. Products may be personalized through fit preferences, color selection, fabric choices, or design characteristics. **Body scanning** is a method used by some fashion firms, such as Custom Footwear, to provide mass customization. This type of customization is limited to a select customer with a large budget. For a broader customer base, Nike provides a website that allows the consumer to select from a variety of athletic shoe styles, then choose its colors and add design details from an assortment. Levi Strauss has a similar program through which customers provide inseam, hip, and waist measurements; they are then shipped a pair of "better-fitting" jeans within a two-week period. Figure 4.8 depicts the body-scanning process utilized by Brooks Brothers Company.

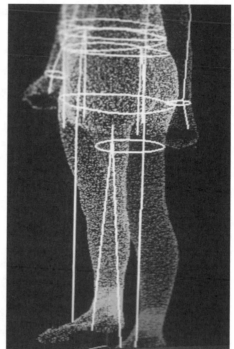

Figure 4.8. "Digital Tailoring" at Brooks Brothers Clothing Store on Madison Avenue. In the privacy of a felt-lined chamber, the body scanner (top left) takes 200,000 measurements in 15 seconds (top right) and then converts them into a virtual mannequin for a perfect fit (bottom).

SUMMARY

Within fashion firms, large and small, there is a vast range of employment opportunities in the production sector, whether the firms manufacture their lines domestically, overseas, or both. Career tracks exist in production for those interested in fabrics, numbers, or technology. Careers that relate directly to manufacturing include product manager, traffic manager, production planner, production manager, quality control manager, and production efficiency manager. After the designer has created the line, development of the actual product before it goes into production is facilitated by the pattern maker and marker maker. Computers are quickly affecting the job responsibilities and requirements in these positions. Additionally, there are a number of technological trends that will undeniably shape the requirements for production careers in the fashion industry of the future. These include computer-integrated manufacturing, quick response, electronic data interchange, and mass customization.

KEY TERMS

block
body scanning
computer-aided pattern making
computer-integrated manufacturing
cutter
cut-to-order
cut-to-stock
digitizer
draping
electronic data interchange
end products
first pattern
flat pattern
lead time
marker
marker maker
mass customization
master pattern
pattern grader
pattern maker
product manager
product void
production assistant
production efficiency manager
production manager
production planner
prototype
quality control manager

quick response
sample size
sloper
spreader
stylis
traffic manager

Discussion Questions

1. Select a well-known apparel manufacturer that would likely require a pattern maker to have exceptional abilities in each of the following skill areas: draping, flat pattern making, and computer-aided pattern making. Why did you choose this manufacturer?

2. Consider apparel and home soft goods production a decade from now. What will be the education, experience, and personal qualities the production manager of a large domestic manufacturer in home furnishings will need? Develop a classified advertisement to recruit a qualified candidate for this position.

3. The introduction to this chapter states that career success requires an understanding that the fashion industry operates in a global market; product development, manufacturing, and retailing are interrelated; and product decisions are consumer-driven. Select a benchmark company that is of interest to you and that has implemented these concepts; next, provide illustrations of how the company has accomplished these objectives.

CHAPTER 5

Promotion

Promotion refers to the endorsement of a person, a product, a cause, an idea, or an organization. The ultimate goal of promotion is to encourage the growth, exposure, and development of an image by advancing it to a higher position. Think about a new designer who has recently been featured in newspapers, fashion magazines, on television, and on the Internet. As if it happens overnight, the former Mr. Unknown becomes a significant name and face in the fashion industry and to fashion followers. When perusing a fashion magazine, such as *In Style* or *W*, the reader is inundated by promotion in the forms of glossy and eyebrow-raising advertisements of fashion brands such as Versace, Gucci, and Dior. Readers will also see editorial pieces on celebrities who wear these designs (Figure 5.1) or the designers themselves. For example, John Galliano made the editorial pages when he made a controversial political statement about the homeless with one of his couture collections. Other examples include a home decor story about Donna Karan's seaside residence and a listing of where the consumer can buy Angelina Jolie's Seven jeans. In a major television show, the main character is in search of a specific brand of beaded high-heel sandals to wear for her first date with Mr. Right. Pop-up advertisements on the Internet direct you to some new website. These are all forms of promotion.

Someone wrote the press release, hired the photographer, shipped the shoes to the television stylist, planned the seasonal advertising expenditures for the company, contacted the magazine's editor and pitched his or her story, located the retailers and verified the retail prices, and worked with the models and photographer to shoot the ads. This someone is in the field of promotion. The major components of promotion involve an understanding of the costs and uses of various advertising vehicles, the significance of public relations, the value of sales promotions, the importance of selling, and the recent impact of sponsorships and partnerships on fashion and businesses and events. The interrelationship between these promotional areas illustrates the teamwork and versatility required by the industry: from glossy magazines through advertising and feature stories to pop media with its backstage administration for shows and events and front-of-house press dossiers and seating plans. Promotion can refer to an item, such as a press release or an advertisement, or an event, such as a fashion show or music video.

In this chapter, the promotional career tracks within the primary level of the fashion industry will be explored. The **primary level** of the industry includes fiber and fabric producers and trade organizations, designers and product developers who create for manufacturers, and the manufacturers with their brand names and images. Career opportunities in fashion promotion exist in the industry sectors of apparel and accessories; home furnishings and accessories; publishing, art, and music; image and style consultancy; photography, illustration, and digital visual imagery; and styling of all kinds, from music groups to television and theater celebrities, broadcast media, and DVDs to the Internet.

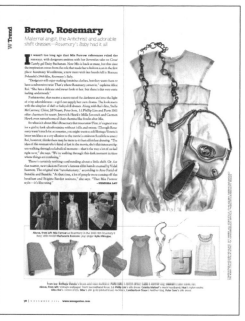

Figure 5.1. Fashion magazines feature articles about celebrities and how their lifestyles are reflected in their wardrobes.

There are general areas of study that provide a strong foundation for future employees in all career tracks within the fashion promotion industry. An understanding of buying, merchandising, and marketing will be used consistently in all fashion promotion career options. Knowledge of computer-aided design provides an employee in this area of the industry with the skills to communicate a design concept through drawings and board presentations. Fashion forecasting and trend analysis allow the employee to look ahead to cutting-edge fashion, while the study of historical costume enables one to look back and identify fashion cycles and looks that are inspired by past decades or centuries. Public relations knowledge is a key component of all promotional careers. For some, studies in photography, display, and fashion show production are needed. Journalism skills prepare the fashion promotion candidate for fashion writing, whether in commentary scripts, advertising copy, press releases, or editorial features in consumer or trade publications.

Figure 5.2. Consumer publications.

CONSUMER AND TRADE PUBLICATIONS

What is the difference between a consumer and a trade publication? A **consumer publication** is one that is readily available to the layperson, the general customer. One may subscribe to the periodical or purchase it at a bookstore, grocery store, convenience store, drugstore, mass merchandiser, or newsstand. Nearly all consumer publications feature some type of fashion content (e.g., *People*, *Town and Country*, and *Travel*); some are devoted exclusively to fashion and interior design. Examples of these publications include *Vogue, In Style, House & Garden, W, Dwell,* and *Elle*; the list goes on and on (Figure 5.2). Most magazines with a nationwide readership are headquartered in New York City.

In contrast, **trade publications** are periodicals that are designed for specific professions or vocations. These magazines and newspapers are made available to people in a specific career field. Table 5.1 lists a few major trade journals and the segments of the fashion industry to which they most appeal. There are also publications that provide information about a wide range of merchandise classifications to retailers, designers, manufacturers, and buyers. The top publication in women's wear is *Women's Wear Daily*, which focuses on different merchandise types each day of the week and often features broader fashion news such as general retail trends in sales or mergers and acquisitions in the fashion industry. (Figure 5.3).

Table 5.1

Top Trade Publications in the Fashion Industry

Industry Segment	Trade Publications
Accessories	*Accessories, Footwear News*
Beauty	*Beauty Biz, Beauty Report*
Interior Design	*Home Furnishing News, InFurniture*
Men's Wear	*DNR*
Retailing	*Stores*
Women's Wear	*Women's Wear Daily*

FASHION STYLIST

A **fashion stylist** is the person who does most of the work before the cameras start shooting. A fashion photostylist must be aware of the latest trends and driven to bring great resources and a strong personal style to every photo shoot. Fashion shoots are a team effort, and the stylist's role is critical to its success. Stylists are responsible for assembling the items and preparing the people involved in the shoot, such as apparel and accessories to be worn by models or a bedroom suite and linens to be featured. Stylists make quick decisions, determining in minutes, for example, how various items of apparel are to be combined and accessorized to show each off to their best features. They also handle a myriad of details, ensuring that the right sizes and colors are available for each model. If the models are celebrities, the appropriateness of the ensembles to each of their images becomes an additional factor. Stylists must be diplomats to win the cooperation of everyone involved in a shoot. In addition to magazine work, stylists may find employment with advertising agencies, working on print ads or television commercials. Entry-level pay may range from $150 to $200 per day, while top stylists may earn thousands of dollars per photo shoot. Figure 5.4 features a fashion stylist working with a model in a photography studio.

Figure 5.3. *Women's Wear Daily* is the top trade publication in the fashion industry.

Figure 5.4. A fashion stylist directs a model and pug for a photo shoot.

Qualifications

Do you have what it takes to pursue a career in fashion styling? Following is a list of qualifications for fashion stylists:

- ▸ **Education:** A bachelor's degree in fashion design, fashion merchandising, fashion journalism, fashion communication, photography, visual arts, or a related field is preferred.
- ▸ **Experience:** An internship with a photographer or stylist is an excellent way to build one's resume for employment in this industry. Some fashion stylists

begin in visual merchandising or as an assistant to a stylist. Fashion stylists are often chosen based on the look of their "books," large volumes of tear sheets from published magazine or newspaper work, as well as Polaroid or digital images that illustrate work they have done with different photographers and/or models. Digital portfolios and computer-aided design skills are beneficial.

▶ **Personal characteristics:** The attributes of successful fashion stylists include a network of professionals in photography, hair and makeup design, and the modeling industry; a keen eye for detail; the ability to apply visual art principles to advertisements and photographs; effective verbal, written, and visual communication skills; strong time-management skills; and the ability to work well under pressure, whether with deadlines or uncontrollable factors, such as poor lighting during an outdoor shoot or models who miss their flights.

Career Challenges

Fashion stylist positions are often only available with large companies or as freelance work. While it is an exciting and potentially profitable career track, there are not as many job opportunities in this field as in other fashion career areas. Fashion stylists face a number of challenges, including quick decision making and coordinating a multitude of details. Since stylists must ensure that the correct apparel is available for the right models, they must do a great deal of preplanning for the expected and the unexpected, such as broken zippers, poor lighting, and models with attitude. "Be prepared" is a motto for successful fashion stylists. Stylists must also work with all types of people and be able to motivate everyone involved in the shoot. It is not enough to have the vision; it is as important to have the skills to implement the vision. Box 5.1 features a *Wall Street Journal* article about the increasing demand for stylists.

PUBLIC RELATIONS DIRECTOR

Public relations directors are responsible for finding cost-effective ways to promote the company they represent. They develop proposals that will put their company in a favorable spotlight and persuade the media to feature press about the company. Public relations directors work with all types of media representatives, from television and radio producers to newspaper and magazine publishers. There are a number of public

BOX 5.1 • WHO'S THE COOLEST KID AT FASHION WEEK? SOME SAY THE STYLIST

by Teri Agins

Inspired by the 1999 movie *The Talented Mr. Ripley*, designer Vera Wang wanted to capture the mood of American expatriates in 1950s Italy for her fall 2006 collection.

For advice, she called in a freelance stylist named Lori Goldstein.

Ms. Goldstein, whose job it is to anticipate which way fashion's winds are blowing, was immediately alarmed by a jacket and a skirt that had big buttons. "As soon as I saw them I said, 'We can't show that,'" says Ms. Goldstein. "All those buttons felt like the period, but they don't look modern, and no one is going to wear it with all those buttons."

Ms. Wang sent the garments back to be made with two buttons instead of six.

Operating in the background, stylists are becoming necessary accouterments for fashion designers. Top stylists—many of whom put together editorial photo shoots for the pages of such magazines as *Vogue*, *Harper's Bazaar*, *W*, and *Elle*—are called in before fashion shows to help choose pieces for the runway, coordinate handbags and shoes, and generally, decide what looks good. For designers, they act as sounding boards and sometimes cheerleaders.

Ms. Goldstein first looked in on Ms. Wang's collection in October, helping to select fabrics. When the first sample garments arrived in December, she dropped in again to see how things were going. In the past five days, she has been editing down the 70 outfits in the collection to about 45, discarding, among other things, two ball gowns and several full skirts that "looked too much like last season." She also helped choose 20 models and zeroed in on details like the shade of lipstick they will wear and a soft hairdo "hinting at the 1950s, without being too literal." Yesterday, she was shuffling stacks of Polaroid shots to determine the order and pace of the show. As with all stylists, Ms. Goldstein's greatest contribution to the fall collection is much more subtle: She knows what is cutting edge and what isn't.

"Designers want the cool person," explains Sally Singer, fashion news-features director at *Vogue*. "Part of a designer's cool can be validated by the stylist they use."

In the past few years, as the job of fashion designer has gotten more complicated, stylists have been in more demand. The best, who can earn as much as $8,000 a day, help designers create an image for product lines that now include handbags, shoes, and watches.

Beyond their own good taste, many star stylists, with their ties to photographers, starlets, socialites, and journalists, are big-time networkers. Much as lobbyists wield influence in Washington, stylists can curry favor with the magazines they work for and the fashion crowd with which they run.

"Having somebody who is out and about and doing shoots to be the devil's advocate here is great," Ms. Wang says.

Ms. Goldstein, 49, has always been obsessed by fashion. After high school, she began as a saleswoman in boutiques, first in her hometown of Cincinnati, and then at Fred Segal in Los Angeles and Fiorucci in New York. In the 1980s, she began

(continued)

styling clothes for catalogs and advertising shoots, before becoming a stylist for *Vanity Fair* photographer Annie Leibowitz and fashion photographer Steven Meisel.

Ms. Goldstein's signature styling flourish is "the unexpected way I put clothes together. I refused to do that full looks from one designer, and I started using a lot of jewelry and mixing things up," she says. "I can't stand when anything matches."

A big part of [Ms. Goldstein's] job is saying no. Last year, [she] nixed a crocheted necklace of silver lace balls that Ms. Wang planned to use. As soon as she saw them, Ms. Goldstein recognized that they were similar to the necklace by Marc Jacobs that Ms. Goldstein herself had used in photo shoots. Ms. Wang relented. "I took them out of the show," the designer recalls.

Source: *The Wall Street Journal*, 247, no. 33 February 9, 2006.

relations companies that specialize in fashion and represent a number of designer and manufacturer clients. In addition, many of the designer houses, such as Gucci, Salvatore Ferragamo, and Tod's, have their own in-house public relations staffs. Public relations directors for large companies may earn $90,000–$110,000 per year.

Some of the activities that public relations directors develop include charity events, such as fashion shows and parties; marathons that raise awareness and money for specific causes; press coverage for well-known designers who are presenting new collections in top specialty stores across the nation; and competitions for fashion students to submit original designs that will be produced by major manufacturers.

Public relations directors attempt to find themes or topics that the media will want to cover and to tie these into the businesses of their clients. For example, a public relations director may work for a major apparel manufacturer/designer, such as Nicole Miller. When Nicole Miller introduces her new home accessories lines of bed linens, pillows, photograph frames, and dinnerware, the public relations director may schedule her to appear at a number of key retail stores around the country. In conjunction with these retail partner arrangements, the public relations director will contact the media and fashion organizations in each city to generate news coverage of the designer's appearances in the retail stores.

Qualifications

Public relations directors should meet the following criteria:

- ▶ **Education:** A bachelor's degree in marketing, public relations, advertising, business administration, fashion merchandising, or a related field is a minimal requirement.

- **Experience:** To move into the director position, one usually needs a minimum of eight to ten years of fashion public relations experience and must have an array of excellent contacts within the fashion and lifestyle media. Additionally, a public relations director must compile a portfolio of proposals.
- **Personal characteristics:** Public relations directors must have exceptional writing skills and be confident team players. Successful public relations directors are described as possessing "excellent pitching skills," the ability to sell one's ideas in a persuasive and articulate manner. Budget management skills are also essential.

Career Challenges

A public relations director is a salesperson, frequently selling an image, a company, or an idea. This person must have the ability to stay positive and enthusiastic in a world of repeated rejection. With so much going on in the fashion world, the public relations director is one of many vying for the attention of newspaper and magazine publishers. Finding creative ways to pitch stories and building relationships with ever-changing media contacts are challenges public relations directors face. This career path is not all about selling, creating, and networking. Public relations directors must have a head for numbers to meet the responsibility for finding cost-effective ways to promote the company. At some point in their careers, many public relations directors are confronted with countering negative publicity. Under the pressures of time and stress, quickly developing plans that will put the company in a favorable spotlight and persuading the media to feature positive press about the company are necessary skills to respond to negative publicity.

ADVERTISING RESEARCH AND PROMOTION POSITIONS

The major source of revenue for a publication is generated from the sale of advertising space. Those who like to sell may find their niche in selling advertising for fashion publications, such as *Vogue*, *Women's Wear Daily*, or *Lucky*. There are a number of other positions in fashion publications, among them are those in advertising research and promotion. Many publications offer positions for those who prefer research. An **advertising research assistant** helps sell advertising space in a publication by supplying facts that advertisers will want to know, such as the number of issues sold and top locations in terms of sales volume, and

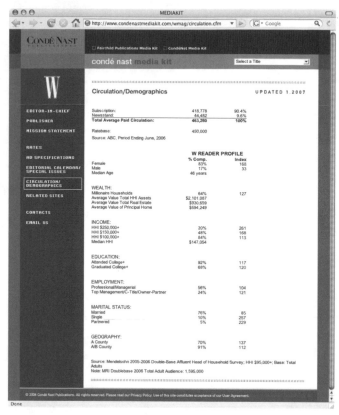

Figure 5.5. Demographics tearsheet.

the profile and buying power of the publication's readers. These facts indicate the publication's ability to enlist retail cooperation. Figure 5.5 provides an example of a publication's facts being used to entice advertisers. The **advertising promotion staff**, yet another source of job opportunities, develops presentations to help sell advertising space to new and existing accounts. These people often have skills in persuasive writing and creative projects. A related job option in advertising is that of **media planner**. Media planning is a statistical and mathematical process through which planners determine prices, including quantity discounts, for a media buy that may include several venues, such as radio, television, and newspaper. They determine how advertising budgets are best spent to generate the most exposure and sales. The annual salary range for media planners employed in the United States is $39,000–$50,000.

Qualifications

Following is a list of qualifications for a career in advertising research and promotion:

- ▶ **Education:** A bachelor's degree in advertising, journalism, business administration, marketing, fashion merchandising, or a related field is required.
- ▶ **Experience:** Working in retail sales is a great way to get started while still in school. Selling is selling, whether it's apparel or newspapers. Some students gain more direct experience selling advertisements for college publications, such as the yearbook and programs for athletic events and theatrical performances. Some enter the advertising industry through copywriting and/or research jobs with newspapers or publishing firms and then move into the advertising sales representative position. Others gain experience at the retail

level through a position in a store's advertising department, writing copy for advertised items or laying out the actual advertisement.

▶ **Personal characteristics:** The ability to sell one's ideas is key to success in advertising. An understanding of budgets and accounting is helpful. With a high attention to detail, successful advertising professionals are focused on accuracy and fact-checking.

Career Challenges

Advertising research and promotion personnel must gather data from all types of sources and then compile this research to tell a story—why their media vehicle is the best choice for advertisers to spend promotional dollars. This job is not an easy one as it combines the abilities of acquiring and interpreting data with strong writing skills. It is a number-crunching and fast-paced field. Advertising research and promotion staff members need to stay up-to-date on all facets of the competition: their target markets, companies that advertise in their publications, and their advertising rates. As competition in this industry is constantly evolving, this is a time-consuming task.

FASHION EVENT PLANNER

Have you ever seen a fashion show production? Attended a trunk show? Participated in a bridal show extravaganza? If so, you have seen the handiwork of a **fashion event planner**, also referred to as a **special events coordinator** fashion event planners increase the visibility of design houses, brands, products, or fabrics by coordinating fashion events that provide exposure. Special events coordinators are likely to earn $30,000 to $45,000 per year.

Fashion Events

There are many types of events that fashion event planners can coordinate to promote an image, an idea, an organization, or a product. As illustrated by Figure 5.6, trunk shows in the designer salon of a department store, for example, may spotlight a new designer line.

Figure 5.6. Derek Lam trunk show at Barneys.

Figure 5.7. Bridal event for prospective brides and their wedding parties.

(Trunk shows are further explained on page 89). Another way to create exposure is through tearoom modeling for a women's club or church group at a country club or café. Some of the fashion events that fashion event planners develop and participate in follow.

Bridal Shows

Through **bridal shows**, bridal wear manufacturers and retailers get together with auxiliary organizations, such as wedding planners, caterers, florists, and travel agents, to present the season's offerings for brides-to-be and their friends and families. As Figure 5.7 illustrates, the bridal extravaganza is often organized in a convention center with booths that feature each of the vendors and with a fashion show as the main event. These are usually staged in January and July for the spring and fall wedding seasons.

Mannequin Modeling

A promotional event of the 1960s, this entertainment and promotion activity is back. Mannequin modeling involves live models who are hired to stand motionless in the place of regular mannequins in windows or on showroom or retail floors. People often stop to stare, waiting for the models to blink, move, and flinch.

Tearoom Modeling

Tearoom modeling is an informal fashion show that often takes place in a hotel or restaurant in which models circulate among the tables as the meal is being served. A women's group or other organization may use this activity as a drawing card for a meeting. Instead of commentary, printed programs are often left at the place settings to enable guests to read descriptions, prices, and size ranges of the featured garments and accessories so that commentary will not interrupt the meal or speakers.

Trunk Shows

Through a **trunk show**, a fashion event planner or a manufacturer's representative brings a manufacturer's full seasonal line to a retail store that carries this manufacturer. The planner or representative works with individual customers, educating them about the line and providing personal fashion consultation. The customers can then place special orders. Sometimes, a trunk show in an upscale department or specialty store may feature a well-known designer as well as the designer's latest collection. The trunk show ad for Bergdorf Goodman featured in Figure 5.8 promotes a sample sale for Versace's collection.

Party Planning

In some instances, fashion event planners are literally paid to party. **Party planning** involves a manufacturer, a designer, a retailer, or an organization hiring a fashion event planner to put together a party event. For example, Cone Mills, a textile producer, may employ a fashion event planner to coordinate such an event for

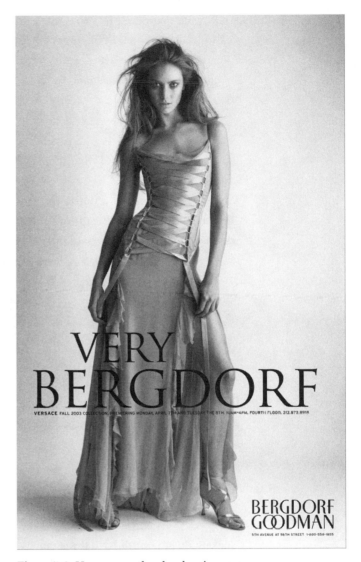

Figure 5.8. Versace sample sale advertisement.

one of the Fashion Group International, Inc., chapters. The planner arranges to have the showroom open after-hours for the party and sends out invitations to the Fashion Group members, offering them a private showing of the new product line during the party. He or she works with the sales manager to schedule sales associates for this evening event and locates a new restaurant and wine shop to serve complimentary appetizers and wine in exchange for publicity. The planner decorates the entrance of the showroom with Fashion Group banners and locates a desk at the entrance of the showroom to greet and sign in guests, to secure their addresses for future mailings. Door prizes from manufacturers that use Cone Mills's textiles are incentives for guests to stay for the entire length of the party. The cost of the event is minimal; the visibility is sensational as Cone Mills is able to expose its business to the fashion executives in the community. The freelance fashion event planner is then paid well for a job well done.

Educational Events

A fashion event planner, a manufacturer's representative, or an employee hired by a planner may stage an **educational event** to inform an audience about a product. For example, in apparel, the presenter may demonstrate different ways to wear scarves, separates, or eveningwear. In home furnishings, a demonstrator may educate an audience by showing how to configure a new sectional sofa for a number of different looks and space needs.

Book Signings

The fashion event planner may organize **book signings**, in which well-known beauty or fashion writers agree to sign copies of their latest books in a book, specialty, or department store.

Complimentary Services

An example of **complimentary services** may proceed as follows: A fashion event planner may work with a diamond vendor and offer free jewelry cleaning at a major jewelry showroom. The service is intended to draw customers into the business. Wardrobe planning services are another activity an apparel manufacturer may hire a fashion event planner to do within the manufacturer's department of a retail store.

Charity Group Fashion Shows

A fashion event planner might execute a fashion show with ticket sales that benefit a nonprofit or charitable organization, which is referred to as a **charity group fashion**

show. Often, community leaders, local celebrities, or executives of the philanthropic organization model the apparel and accessories as a drawing card for the show (Figure 5.9). The fashion event planner may also solicit door prizes or auction items from benefactors to generate additional funds for the cause.

Duties of Fashion Event Planners

There are many ways to generate interest through fashion events. Because there is much work involved and, in many cases, a great deal of expertise needed, many manufacturers and designers hire fashion event planners to execute them. So, what kinds of activities do fashion event planners do? Here is a sampling:

- Locate, reserve a place, and negotiate terms and dates for the event
- Determine lighting, music, sound system, and staging needs
- Assemble merchandise to be featured
- Hire and fit models, arrange lineup, and supervise rehearsals
- Compile commentary, if appropriate, and recruit commentator
- Arrange for printing needs (e.g., tickets, signage, invitations, and programs)
- Arrange for seating, to include setup and breakdown of seats
- Recruit backstage help, such as hairstylists, makeup artists, and dressers
- Recruit front-of-stage help, such as ticket sales, concessions, and ushers
- Locate caterers or sponsors for refreshments, if needed

Figure 5.9. A model displays an outfit during Alexander McQueen's "Black" fashion show at Earl's Court, London, June 3, 2004. The show and auction included art and black-themed objects donated by celebrities to raise money for the HIV and AIDS charity Lighthouse Services.

▸ Handle publicity, which may include invitations, press releases, advertisements, television and/or radio interviews, and other media-related activities

The job of fashion event planner is one of those "chief cook and bottle washer" positions that may have the planner initially doing a little bit of everything to pull the event together. Once more established in the industry, the fashion event planner is able to hire others to handle parts of the larger projects.

Qualifications

This career requires the following qualifications:

▸ **Education:** A bachelor's degree in fashion merchandising, fashion design, promotion, special events planning, or a related field is required.
▸ **Experience:** Fashion event planners come from a wide range of industry sectors: retail, design, and manufacturing. Many work as an assistant to a fashion director or coordinator in a retail operation or manufacturer's showroom before branching out on their own. Others initially work as assistants to established fashion event planners. Some large retail stores have special events departments through which future fashion event planners can learn the ropes of fashion show production and event planning. Through the positions leading up to becoming a fashion event planner, one develops a large and useful network of contacts related to the fashion industry.
▸ **Personal characteristics:** Successful fashion event planners have the following skills and knowledge: an enthusiastic and creative personality, the ability to sell one's ideas and vision, accounting skills to develop and manage budgets, strong organizational and communication skills, and effective time-management abilities.

Career Challenges

The job tasks of fashion event planning require endless attention to detail to ensure trouble-free events. Fashion event planners need a strong sense of fashion, organizational skills, the ability to work well in stressful situations, and the communication skills to work with a wide range of people. Managing a major fashion event can be compared to coordinating a three-ring circus. Frequently, there is a large number of people involved and a myriad of details to consider. When combining these stresses with the need to keep events on budget and on time, fashion event planners must have the skills to remain calm and collected under pressure.

SUMMARY

Promotion refers to the endorsement of a person, a product, a cause, an idea, or an organization. The ultimate goal of promotion is to encourage the growth, exposure, and development of an image by advancing it to a higher position. Promotion career opportunities in the primary level of the fashion industry include fashion stylist, public relations director, advertising director, advertising sales representative and related positions, and fashion event planner. While the public relations director and advertising representative are usually employed by a large firm, the fashion stylist and fashion events planner may choose a freelance career or decide to open their own companies. In all of these promotion careers, the goal is to sell an idea, an image, or a product—directly or indirectly. It is marketing in its truest form; it is creative, thought provoking, and profitable at its best.

KEY TERMS

advertising promotion staff
advertising research assistant
book signing
bridal show
charity group fashion show
complimentary service
consumer publication
educational event
fashion event planner
fashion stylist
mannequin modeling
media planner
party planning
primary level
promotion

public relations director
tearoom modeling
trade publication
trunk show

Discussion Questions

1. How does your favorite designer promote his or her products? Determine the promotional activities coordinated by the company's public relations director. Is the public relations director contracted from an outside firm? If so, what other companies does this firm promote? Are there similarities among its clients?

2. Which do you read more regularly—consumer or trade publications? Read an article from each type of publication and analyze the value of each in relation to your future career goals.

3. Locate and review an advertisement, invitation, or news article for a fashion event that benefited a charitable cause. Next, ask yourself in which places the fashion event planner could have saved money on implementing the event to increase proceeds for the event. Develop a list of the possibilities for contributions, or buy-ins, from outside companies and designate what these companies would receive in return.

CHAPTER 6

Sales

You likely know people who are natural-born salespersons. You probably have worked with this type of person, or you may be one of these people. They have the enthusiasm, drive, and persuasive skills to sell a product, service, concept, or idea. They enjoy the thrill of the chase and the excitement of the closing. The best salespersons are skilled at gaining the attention of customers and, almost instantly, building a rapport with them. Through keen observation and active listening, sales gurus can determine the customers' needs and desires and then, by emphasizing their benefits, effectively explain how particular products will fit those needs. The finish line is in sight when the customer's concerns are alleviated and the sale is closed. As a grand finale, additional products or services are offered to build the sale. If you have ever purchased an automobile, a cellular phone, a sofa, or a dress from a sales pro, then you know the feeling of a smooth sale (Figure 6.1). Some of the top fashion companies are also the employers of the top salespeople. Every manufacturing firm has a person or staff of employees whose primary job is to sell the product line. The product line can be the best in the world; however, if it is not effectively marketed and sold, it will not be manufactured for long. Designer Tom Ford describes the sales potential within the fashion industry: "As a fashion designer, I was always aware that I was not an artist because I was creating something that was made to be sold, marketed, used, and ultimately discarded."[1]

In this chapter, sales careers in the wholesale businesses of apparel, accessories, soft goods, and home furnishings and accessories will be explored. These include employment opportunities in the following positions: manufacturer's representative, company salesperson, merchandise coordinator, and showroom salesperson.

Figure 6.1. Salespeople can make or break a shopping experience.

MANUFACTURER'S REPRESENTATIVE

A manufacturer's representative, also referred to as a *manufacturer's rep* or *sales rep*, is a wholesale salesperson who is often independent; in essence, the sales rep is often a business owner. Manufacturer's reps sell the product line of one or several manufacturers to retail store buyers. Reps who choose to sell a number of lines usually work with noncompetitive product lines and manufacturers. This type of manufacturer's representative is classified as a **multiline**, or *multiple line,* **rep**. For example, the manufacturer's rep may represent a handbag line from one manufacturer, a jewelry line from another vendor, and a glove line from yet another manufacturer. Such a rep can call, for instance, on the accessories buyers of retail stores and offer a selection of products that the specialty or department store carries. If the manufacturer's rep elected to represent several lines in the same merchandise classification, the lines could be competing against one another for the same department's dollars. Occasionally, manufacturer's representatives decide to sell lines that are seasonally opposite, such as swimwear and outerwear. This way, the reps have better opportunities to generate sales volume and, subsequently, income year-round. The manufacturer's rep who prefers to sell solely one manufacturer's line as an independent rather than as a company employee is a **single-line rep**.

The manufacturer's representative usually works within a given territory, as negotiated with the manufacturer, such as the East Coast, Florida and Georgia, or Europe. Manufacturer's reps will travel to the buying offices of retail companies, the locations of small store operations, or **apparel marts** and **trade marts** to sell their lines to retail buyers. These marts house temporary sales booths and permanent showrooms leased by either the sales representatives or the manufacturers. **Market weeks**, also called **trade shows,** are scheduled at apparel and trade marts throughout the year in conjunction with the introduction of the new, seasonal lines presented by manufacturers.

The main seasons of the apparel industry are Fall I, Fall II, Holiday, Cruise, Spring, and Summer. While apparel marts are located across the United States, some of the larger ones are situated in New York City, Dallas, Los Angeles, Chicago, and Atlanta. In Figure 6.2, manufacturers' product lines are featured on the runway at MAGIC, the premier men's wear trade show in Las Vegas. Manufacturer's representatives arrive at the apparel marts that cater to buyers in their territory a day or two ahead of the market opening. At this time, the reps set up booths or showrooms, as in Figure 6.3, with the new lines and other materials, such as purchase orders, line brochures, and displays, that will help sell the line. When the market opens, it is showtime. The manufacturer's reps show the line to buyers with whom prearranged appointments have been set or to buyers who stop by hoping to find new lines that customers will purchase. Market weeks are key times for representatives to gain new retail clients, meet with current accounts, and secure a part of the retailers' buying dollars.

Figure 6.2. Will.I.Am of Black Eyed Peas launches I.Am Streetwear at MAGIC men's apparel market in Las Vegas.

Compensation

A manufacturer's representative may be paid in a number of ways: commission, quota or a base salary plus commission, or salary. Through **commission**, manufacturer's reps are paid a percentage of the sales volume on merchandise that they have sold that is shipped and accepted by the retailers. For instance, if a rep sells a product line but the manufacturer ships it late, the retailer may refuse it. In this case, the manufacturer's rep will not receive a

Figure 6.3. Visual merchandising display at Showroom Seven in New York.

commission for the sale. Therefore, a key task for a manufacturer's representative is to follow up on deliveries and to communicate with the retail buyers about orders that may contain style substitutions or arrive a bit late. Commission percents are often negotiable and range greatly, from 7 to 20 percent. **Quota plus commission** refers to a form of remuneration in which manufacturer's representatives are paid commission on sales procured over a specific amount, or baseline, called a quota. **Salaried** manufacturer's representatives are paid set amounts every month. **Base salary plus commission** refers to paying reps a set amount each month and commission payments periodically. Some salaried reps receive bonuses for exceptional sales.

There are a number of expenses that manufacturer's reps can incur in the process of doing business. Some manufacturer's representatives are required to purchase their **sample lines**, often at a discounted price, from manufacturers. A sample line includes a prototype of every style within the line. Each prototype is tagged with fabric swatches, color options, sizes available, and its wholesale price, also referred to as **cost price** or *cost*. Depending on the size of the product line, a sample line can cost a manufacturer's representative thousands of dollars. Some manufacturers buy back the sample lines, possibly to sell at factory outlets. In other cases, reps may sell sample lines independently. Additionally, there are costs associated with showing lines during market weeks. There are rental fees for booths, showrooms, and fixtures, as well as trade organization dues. Some manufacturer's representatives contribute to retailers' advertising costs by marketing the rep's product lines. There is also the cost of travel: airfares, automobile costs, lodging expenses, and meals must be paid for while traveling. Manufacturer's representatives who have large businesses may employ assistants and secretaries. As independent contractors, manufacturer's representatives are business owners who share the risk, potential, and challenges associated with being their own bosses.

The Career Path

The salary range for manufacturer's reps and for company salespeople, discussed next, starts at about $18,000 and goes up to $30,000 annually for entry-level candidates. Experienced salespeople may earn from $40,000 to over $75,000 per year. Top-level pay may range from $80,000 to more than $100,000. The outlook for employment in this sector is strong as there is higher than average projected growth within the United States, with additional positions available overseas.

Qualifications

Most important, the ability to sell is key. An understanding of accounting is also necessary. Often, the way to secure this job is to be willing and flexible to travel.

- **Education:** A bachelor's degree in fashion merchandising, product development, business administration, marketing, or a related field is most often a minimal requirement.
- **Experience:** Sales, sales, and more sales are the key experiences needed for a manufacturer's representative career. Many students gain work experience in retail sales. Working as an assistant to a manufacturer's representative is an excellent route to understanding the responsibilities of this career and to building a network of industry contacts.
- **Personal characteristics:** Self-discipline, self-motivation, good follow-through skills, perseverance, organizational abilities, and the ability to handle rejection are key attributes of top manufacturer's representatives. Successful reps are highly competitive, believe in the products they sell, and have the ability to maintain enthusiasm for them. They need excellent communication skills, both written and oral. Successful reps are able to establish trust, and, subsequently, good relationships with customers. Knowledge of fashion industry trends and manufacturers' competitors is critical.

Career Challenges

Many manufacturers' reps are faced with the uncertainty of not knowing how much their next paycheck will be. In this career, income is primarily based on sales performance. Sometimes, there are external factors beyond a rep's control that may decrease the amount of money the rep receives. Unshipped orders, late deliveries, and incorrect shipments can reduce the remuneration reps expect based on merchandise they have sold. Also, for some people, extensive travel can be a burden. Traveling to trade markets, sales meetings, and retail accounts costs money. Manufacturer's reps need many of the skills of successful entrepreneurs, as they must manage their budgets to accommodate their costs of doing business.

COMPANY SALESPERSON

The majority of large manufacturing firms hire company salespeople. The **company salesperson** is a sales representative employed directly by a particular firm who carries just one line, that of the employer. Often, company salespeople have broader territories than manufacturers' representatives may cover. Like manufacturers' representatives, company salespeople travel to retail buying offices, retail stores, or trade markets to show and sell their company's line. Remuneration is often base salary plus commission rather than entirely commission-based. Often, they receive employee benefits, such as health insurance and vacation pay. Employers of company salespeople may also cover some of the expenses that manufacturers' representatives must incur. More often than not, the manufacturer pays for trade show fees, the cost of sample lines, and advertising expenses for company salespeople.

When the manufacturer contributes to the cost of advertisements paid for by the retailer, the arrangement is referred to as **cooperative** (or *co-op*) **advertising**. While each manufacturing company develops its own cooperative advertising agreement, there are a number of consistent requirements. An example of a cooperative advertising agreement is presented in Box 6.1. Most cooperative advertising agreements designate whether or not the retailer must feature the manufacturer's products in an advertisement exclusively, rather than in conjunction with other product lines. Most manufacturers calculate the amount of money that will be contributed to retailers' advertising efforts as a percent of the dollar amount in orders that the buyer places with the company. Most manufacturers request that the company, line, or designer name be included in the advertisement once or twice, and, sometimes, in the headline of print advertisements. The majority of manufacturers who offer cooperative advertising funds also require proof of advertising, such as a CD-ROM of a television commercial or a tearsheet of a newspaper advertisement. A **tearsheet** is a print page that features the retailer's advertisements, provided by the newspaper's advertising department. Refer to Figure 6.4 for an example of a tearsheet.

Why do some companies invest in hiring an exclusive and salaried company salesperson rather than a commissioned manufacturer's representative? While increased sales are at the top of the list, advertising is another important reason for hiring company salespeople. Company salespeople work closely with their retail clients to promote the product line and build the company's name and image through effective and brand-oriented marketing. They also plan consistent deliveries with buyers, creating a flow of new merchandise that keeps the line looking fresh and its customers coming back. Since many of the firms that employ company salespeople are very large, company salespeople may be working with retailers that have a separate department, and subsequently, an immense investment, for the line in the store. They may assist buyers with fixture selections, signage, and layout of departments. Additionally, company salespeople are often called on by retail clients to educate the store sales and management staff about the product line. If it is a home furnishing line, for example, a company salesperson may be enlisted as a guest presenter at a breakfast meeting. During this meeting, the company salesperson will show the fabrics featured in the new season; discuss durability and care factors; and provide information about new sofa and chair forms, design themes, and

BOX 6.1 • COOL GAL LINGERIE COOPERATIVE ADVERTISING AGREEMENT

As we recognize the importance of print, television, radio, and Internet advertising as a valuable means of promoting increased sales of all Cool Gal Lingerie (CGL) products, we offer to our esteemed customers the cooperative advertising plan set forth below. We believe that it will assist our retail clients, our consumers, and CGL in maintaining the very highest standards with regard to the public's perception and awareness of the quality and image of the CGL lines. This plan is in effect until further notice for all ads run on or after June 1, 2007.

1. **CGL and Customer Share.** CGL will share 50 percent of the cost in preapproved advertising vehicles based on the retailer's earned CGL advertising budget, up to an amount not to exceed 5 percent of first-quality, branded net purchases at wholesale for each season. This plan only covers first-quality branded net purchases (applied to all CGL lines).
2. **Charges.** Net cost is limited to actual advertising costs. This agreement shall not include the cost of special preparation, filming, artwork, graphic design, or any other preparatory advertising and/or production costs. We do not share in the cost of agency fees or special service charges. We do not share in mechanical or production costs for color reproduction.
3. **Enclosure Advertising**. Each season CGL will make statement enclosures available to be included in charge statement mailings. Enclosures are to be ordered on the special forms provided by our advertising department. Minimum quantity orders are necessary to qualify to receive these enclosures. Check with your sales representative for the minimum quantity necessary. A fraction of the actual cost of enclosures will be charged, and this amount will be applied against the 5 percent CGL cooperative advertising limit as set forth in the agreement.
4. **Media.** This plan covers media advertising with those providers that have recognized audited circulation and published rates. Final approval of the content of ads and the CGL dollar amount for share of costs are contingent on our approval. To receive approval, contact your sales representative. After receiving approval, a copy of the approval form, receipt of payment from the advertising provider, and sample of the advertisement must accompany your invoice.
5. **Copy Requirements.**
   a. The CGL product-logotype must appear prominently in the advertisement. For print advertisements, the Cool Gal Lingerie name must also appear in the heading or subheading. The use of the CGL product-logotype in the graphics only will not meet our requirements. The name must be as large as the largest type in the advertisement exclusive of the retailer's own logotype. We will supply the Cool Gal logotype as requested.
   b. Competitive merchandise cannot appear in the same advertisement with the CGL

(*continued*)

name or product-logotype. If the advertisement shows other merchandise, this other merchandise must be goods other than lingerie, innerwear, robes, loungewear, or sleepwear. In addition to this requirement, the CGL portion of the advertisement must be separate and clearly defined. If any other merchandise is shown in the advertisement, we reserve the right to final approval on such advertisement.

c. No advertisement in any media shall show a sale price or markdown price on any CGL product. If a price is listed, it must be the full list price, given in an even dollar amount (e.g., $100, $148, and $65). In addition to this requirement, any advertised sale that shows or presents any CGL product or that uses the CGL or the

Cool Gal Lingerie name must obtain approval from our advertising department.

6. **Payment.** Invoices must be submitted within 45 days of placement of the advertising effort. An advertising credit will be issued for the Cool Gal Lingerie share. No deductions are to be made for advertising prior to receiving the credit memo authorizing the amount to be deducted.

Please submit invoices accompanied by required documentation for each advertisement to:

CGL Advertising Department
Cool Gal Lingerie Products, Inc.
P.O. Box 22688
New York, NY 10109
1-888-555-1215
coolgal_lingerie.com

color palettes. The retailer's sales staff leaves the meeting informed, excited, and appreciated, ready to sell the products to the customer. Company salespeople do more than sell the line to retail buyers. They represent the manufacturer in the areas of advertising, marketing, merchandise planning, visual merchandising, and retail sales staff education.

Qualifications

The education, work experience, and personal characteristics needed for successful employment as a company salesperson are similar to those of the manufacturer's representative.

▸ **Education:** A bachelor's degree in fashion merchandising, fashion design, product development, business administration, marketing, or a related field is commonly required.

▸ **Experience:** All types of sales experience provide a foundation for future employment as a company salesperson. Working on a retail sales floor or selling advertisements for the campus newspaper provides important knowledge and skills in sales. Work experience with a manufacturer is a plus; one could possibly begin in a showroom as a receptionist and then move into sales.

▶ **Personal characteristics:** Successful company salespeople are self-disciplined, internally motivated, and excited about their business. Exceptional communication skills, a contagious enthusiasm, and top organizational skills are also necessary characteristics. Understanding how products are constructed, the materials from which they are made, and the manufacturing processes required to bring them to completion helps company salespeople educate their clients, retail buyers in this case, about the product.

Figure 6.4. This tearsheet features an advertisement for Lacoste.

Career Challenges

Company salespeople must work under the guidelines of their employer. In some cases, new accounts, trade market participation, and travel plans must be approved by the administration. This position is not as autonomous as that of the manufacturer's representative. When working with a single company, if the product line for a certain season is not strong, the company salesperson does not have another line to rely on for income. If competitive lines become stronger in terms of securing the retail buyers' orders, the company salesperson faces the challenge of staying afloat during a tough sell period or securing a position with a new employer.

MERCHANDISE COORDINATOR

In the early 1990s, the number of specialty stores began declining, and large department stores began increasing in size and number of units. Many of these massive department stores did not offer the customer service that most specialty stores provided. In the department stores, there were fewer sales associates. The few sales staff members in the department stores were often part-time or moved from department to department, leaving little time to get to know the customers and provide personal service. As a result, some of the large manufacturers were compelled to find a way to assist the department stores and, ultimately, help their firms to higher sales volume. These manufacturers, among them Liz Claiborne, Ralph Lauren Polo, and Fossil, developed a new career path in the fashion industry, that of merchandise coordinator.

Merchandise coordinators are employed by manufacturers and work in retail stores. Merchandise coordinators are hired to service a number of key accounts in a specific area. **Key accounts** are the large retailers, in terms of sales volume, carrying the manufacturer's line. Today, specialty stores have made a comeback as customers seek personalized service. Key accounts can include boutiques, specialty stores, Internet websites, and large department stores, depending on the amount of inventory they carry of a particular manufacturer's product line. Merchandise coordinators travel to the retail sites to work with the owners, buyers, management personnel, sales staff, and customers. Most of these retail sites can be visited by car, as they are frequently in large metropolitan areas.

In most cases, it is not the merchandise coordinator's primary responsibility to sell the line to the buyer or customer; coordinators may write **reorders**, fill-ins on merchandise that is selling well. Another service merchandise coordinators may perform is moving merchandise that has been shipped and is waiting in the stockroom to the sales floor. Reorders and stock placement on the floor are commonly referred to as **inventory replenishment**. **Visual merchandising** is another job responsibility of merchandise coordinators. This activity may include changing displays, straightening racks, and resizing and folding stacked goods to present the best possible visual image to the customer. In essence, merchandise coordinators are somewhat like dedicated store owners, except the "stores" are that of the manufacturers' departments in the manufacturers' key accounts. Some retailers collaborate with merchandise coordinators on promotional events. For example, the merchandise coordinator may be featured in an advertisement as the line's representative, and customers are invited to meet the coordinator for personal assistance with line purchases. A merchandise coordinator is likely to earn $40,000–$50,000 a year.

Career Outlook

The future for merchandise coordinators is bright. This career track has been so successful for manufacturers that many large companies have added merchandise coordinator positions. Ralph Lauren Polo employs merchandise coordinators for children's wear, misses' sportswear, and men's wear, among other divisions, in New York City, St. Louis, Chicago, Atlanta, and other large cities. Box 6.2 features a Ralph Lauren Polo advertisement seeking a college student for an internship with a children's wear merchandise coordinator.

As another example, Jones Apparel Group, Inc., employs more than 70 merchandise coordinators who are trained by their apparel designers to make appropriate recommendations to meet customers' tastes. Karla Viola, retail development representative for Jones Apparel Group, explained the benefits of the merchandise coordinator program to shoppers: "We've had tremendous success with this program. The merchandise coordinators are our link between the showroom and the stores, and they provide us with invaluable feedback regarding customer preferences." According to Viola, merchandise coordinators work with the company's more than 1,000 designated sellers to build clientele.[2] The growth in merchandise coordinator positions is not limited to the traditional retail specialty and department stores; online companies are offering these positions as well. Box 6.3 is a sample classified advertisement for a merchandise coordinator with an online retailer.

Qualifications

Successful merchandise coordinators may meet or exceed the following criteria:

- ▸ **Education:** A bachelor's degree in fashion merchandising, fashion design, product development, business administration, marketing, sales, or a related field is commonly required.
- ▸ **Experience:** Hands-on experience in the industry, which may include work experience in retail or wholesale selling, is required for this position. Many companies hire college graduates with strong selling skills and an enthusiasm for the manufacturer's line.
- ▸ **Personal characteristics:** Knowledge of the product line and marketing is required. An understanding of sales, visual merchandising, textiles, and product construction is helpful. The ability to work independently with little supervision and guidance is critical to success. Strong communication skills, both oral and written, are also required.

BOX 6.2 · SAMPLE CLASSIFIED ADVERTISEMENT: INTERNSHIP WITH A MERCHANDISE COORDINATOR

Ralph Lauren Children's Wear
New York, NY
Ralph Lauren Children's Wear currently has openings available to become part of our Retail Merchandising Internship Program.

Benefits

- Gain insight to what is expected of a full-time merchandise coordinator
- Expand your knowledge of the fashion industry
- Receive hands-on experience
- Network through contact with professionals

The intern will be responsible for the following:

- Maintaining and merchandising the Ralph Lauren Infants, Toddlers, Girls, and Boys in-store shop presentations with the guidance and supervision of a merchandise coordinator
- Educating store management and personnel about the Ralph Lauren Children's Wear lines from information given by assigned lead merchandise coordinator and the internship manager
- Completing store visit reports, which highlight key issues and potential opportunities within our shops, and submitting to assigned lead merchandise coordinator
- Working with a Ralph Lauren merchandise coordinator to recognize and address any outstanding issues, problems, and opportunities

Ralph Lauren is looking for interns with the following skills and traits:

- Willingness to take on responsibility and complete assigned job duties
- Well-spoken individual with a professional appearance
- Good organizational skills for assigned paperwork and projects
- Ability to take initiative and action to resolve a problem
- Good communication skills for developing relationships within the store
- Motivation to work on own without constant supervision and guidance

This is a nonpaid internship. Intern **must** be able to receive academic credit. Internships are available each fall, summer, and spring throughout the United States. Schedules are individualized for each intern. Great opportunity and experience in a growing children's wear company. Upon successful completion of an internship, we offer interns the opportunity to submit their resumes for possible consideration for prospective employment.

BOX 6.3 • SAMPLE CLASSIFIED ADVERTISEMENT: MERCHANDISE COORDINATOR WITH AN ONLINE RETAILER

Company: Skinshop.com

Description: SkinShop.com is a leading retailer for skin care products online. This position requires a highly organized individual who will work in conjunction with the merchandising manager and is responsible for all aspects of writing, editing, and maintaining our product database, including product descriptions, images, and specifications for our e-commerce retail site. Excellent communication skills, both written and oral, are required for communication with both internal personnel and external clients.

Responsibilities

* Secure product information and images from manufacturers
* Write and edit product descriptions
* Launch new products in a timely and efficient manner
* Coordinate graphics both with graphic designer and IT team
* Write online educational copy and other online promotional copy

Qualifications

* Advanced knowledge of Microsoft Office (Word, Excel, Outlook). Basic HTML and Photoshop skills are desirable.
* Familiarity with Internet technology. Candidate should have background and directly relevant experience in e-commerce. Advertising, copywriting, or catalog merchandising background a plus.
* Excellent written, grammar, editorial, and verbal communication skills with the ability to create product descriptions that are both technically correct and capture the essence of the product to drive sales
* Ability to work well independently
* Ability to adapt well to changing priorities

Physical Demands/Work Environment

This position requires working in an office environment. Must be able to sit for extended periods of time and use hands and fingers. Work is performed in dry, temperature-controlled environment.

Career Challenges

Merchandise coordinators walk a fine line between two key parties—the employer (the manufacturer) and the clients (the retailers). This career requires strong attention to the goals of both parties. They are constantly challenged to find ways to help retailers generate profits, while keeping their focus on their employer's line. There may be many client stores in a merchandise coordinator's territory, requiring carefully scheduled travel plans and exceptional time management. Additionally, they have a large number of tasks to complete in each retail location. It is a fast-paced job with a moderate salary, in most cases. It is, however, an excellent starting place and the ideal place for someone who enjoys crossing the lines between retailers' and manufacturers' worlds.

SHOWROOM SALESPERSON

As depicted in Figure 6.5, the majority of large manufacturers in the apparel and accessories industry have **showrooms** in New York City, Dallas, Chicago, Atlanta, and Los Angeles, as these are the major metropolitan areas featuring large fashion trade markets. Pacific Design Center in Los Angeles and the New York Design Center in Manhattan house showrooms in the home interior design industry. These design showrooms usually cater only "to the trade," designers with a resale certificate and the clients for whom they shop. Showrooms, unlike typical apparel, accessories, furniture, and fabric retail stores, rarely sell merchandise from the floor. Items are generally for display only to allow the buyers to see pieces that would otherwise be visible only in a catalog or online. The buyers then order the items they believe their customers will purchase.

Showrooms come in all types. In the home interiors industry, they showcase kitchen and bath fixtures, hardware and cabinetry, fabrics and wallpapers, interior and exterior furnishings, flooring materials, lighting, antiques, paintings, and other accessories. Some interior design showrooms offer only one type of item, while others may have fabrics, furnishings, lighting, and accessories, all together under one roof. This type of showroom is similar in the wholesale level of the apparel and accessories industry. Merchandise is displayed for ordering. Some showrooms carry a variety of merchandise classifications, and others feature a single product type or manufacturer's line.

Showroom salespeople, also called **showroom representatives,** work at a manufacturer's or designer's showroom, where they meet with visiting retail buyers and present the latest product line to them. Once buyers agree to purchase the manufacturer's products, the showroom sales representatives

Figure 6.5. In the Lee Joffa fabric showroom, interior designers can view fabrics both on wings and in samples of upholstered furniture. A designer can request memos of selected fabrics from a showroom salesperson to share with clients before placing an order.

are responsible for accurately taking the buyers' purchase orders. They must then make sure that the right quantity of the right product reaches clients' stores at the right time and in saleable condition. A typical entry-level wage for a showroom representative is $26,000–$30,000 per year.

In the home and interior design industry, showroom sales representatives are located on-site and are usually assigned to specific designers. They are responsible for helping clients find fabrics, providing suggestions, inputting orders, checking stock, and supplying price quotes. Once designers have decided on a certain fabric, they will call showroom reps with the quantity of fabric needed and the dye lot, if applicable. The sales reps will check the inventory or call the factory, then let the designers know whether the fabric is available, and if so, determine the lead time (that is, time from when payment is received until the fabric is expected to arrive) and which **cuts**, or yardage amounts, are available. On occasion, only a group of small cuts are available at a given time. If those are not adequate because a designer needs one large length for a window treatment, as an example, the designer must decide whether to wait for the next supply of new goods or to select an alternate fabric. Fabric yardage may also be needed to match a certain dye lot. If a designer has previously used a fabric on a sofa, for instance, and now needs more of the same fabric for a new chair in the same room, it is important to ensure the fabric comes from the same dye lot or is similar enough in color to ensure continuity. Showroom salespeople are responsible for making sure that designers receive written quotes with shipping charges and a **cutting for approval** (**CFA**), a fabric sample also called a *memo*, if requested. Maintaining a good relationship with each client through efficient follow-up and a positive personality is imperative to ensure ongoing sales.

Showroom salespeople should expect to work additional long hours during the fashion market weeks each year. The annual salary range for a showroom sales representative is broad, from an entry-level pay range of $20,000–$30,000 to about $60,000 for experienced showroom salespeople to a top-level salary of more than $100,000. Showroom salespeople often have the opportunity to increase their pay through commissions on orders and bonuses based on their sales performance.

Qualifications

A career as showroom salesperson may be achieved with the following qualifications:

▸ **Education:** A bachelor's degree in interior design, textiles, fashion merchandising, fashion design, business, or marketing is preferred, but not always required. Graduates with good communication skills and the right personality have a good chance of being hired right out of college, particularly if they have interned in this area.

▸ **Experience:** Previous retail sales experience is helpful. The traditional career path for showroom sales assistants is to move up to the position of showroom sales representative to showroom sales manager.

▸ **Personal characteristics:** Successful showroom salespeople are enthusiastic, friendly, and outgoing. Effective listening skills, excellent communication and presentation abilities, knowledge of the manufacturing and retail sectors of the fashion industry, as well as good organizational and computer skills, are all assets.

Career Challenges

The showroom salesperson often works long hours, crisscrossing the showroom floor, writing orders for buyers, and contacting suppliers. When not selling the line, the showroom representative is following up on product availability, ordering shipments, and checking delivery options. It is a highly detailed business in which products are often expected and needed quickly. If, for example, the incorrect color number of a tile is posted on an order, a kitchen renovation can be delayed for weeks by the arrival of the wrong product. Or, for example, if a carpet style cannot be delivered within two weeks, the showroom salesperson may lose the order (and the commission that comes with it). For some, it can be stressful to work under such details and deadlines in a fast-paced environment. For others, it can be exhilarating.

SUMMARY

Manufacturing firms, possibly titled under a designer's name, are prevalent in the apparel, accessories, soft goods, home furnishings, and home accessories industries. The designer's name, the company's name, or the brandmark may be well-known, but if it is not effectively marketed and sold, it will not be manufactured for long. These companies employ or contract a person or a staff of employees for whom their primary job is to sell the manufacturer's product line. Within this wholesale level of the fashion industry, the main career paths include the manufacturer's representative, the company salesperson, the merchandise coordinator, and the showroom salesperson.

A manufacturer's representative, or sales rep, is an independent salesperson who may represent the lines of several manufacturers, often working exclusively on commission or commission with a salary component. The company salesperson is a sales representative employed directly by a particular firm who carries one product line, that of the employer, and usually works on a salary plus commission or bonus basis. The merchandise coordinator is employed by the manufacturer and works in the retail stores, servicing key accounts in a specific territory. Merchandise coordinators travel to the retail sites to work with the owner, buyer, management personnel, sales staff, and/or customers in the areas of visual merchandising, inventory replenishment, retail sales staff training, and promotional events. Finally, the showroom salesperson works at a manufacturer's or designer's showroom, meeting with visiting retail buyers to present and sell the latest product lines to them.

Sales are key to a fashion company's success. No matter how exceptional the product line is, there has to be a sales force behind it. With each season, with every trend, and with the ever-changing customer, there is a new opportunity to sell fashion.

KEY TERMS

apparel mart
base salary plus commission
commission
company salesperson
cooperative advertising
cost price (cost)
cut
cutting for approval (CFA)(memo)
inventory replenishment
key account
market week
manufacturer's representative (manufacturer's or sales rep)
merchandise coordinator
multiline rep
quota plus commission
reorder
salaried
sample lines
showroom

showroom salesperson (showroom representative)
single-line rep
tearsheet
to the trade
trade mart
trade show

Discussion Questions

1. Visit a large department store and find a national brand sold within the store. Are these products merchandised differently from other products within the store? Is the department store staff knowledgeable about this national brand's merchandise?

2. In what types of sales environments are commissions, quota plus commissions, or salaried methods of payment most effective? Why? Provide examples.

3. What constitutes a successful sale? Recall your sales experiences as a customer or salesperson and determine why each was positive or negative and why.

ENDNOTES

1. www.brainyquote.com/quotes/t/tomford209396.html
2. Cotton Incorporated, 2006. "Are You a Specialty Store Shopaholic?" www.cottoninc.com *Womenswear Articles.*

CHAPTER 7

Accounting at the Manufacturer's Level

You may wonder, "Why would anyone choose an accounting career in the fashion industry, rather than any other business profession in the field?" When many people think fashion, they envision color and style trends, flamboyant designers, and action-packed runway shows. When they think about accounting, two words may come to mind: *boring* and *tedious*. Add to this the image of a bespectacled person wearing a pocket protector and crunching numbers in a sparse, little room (Figure 7.1). It is a fact—accounting has had an image problem; however, that is the past. While the geek stereotype may have dominated, it no longer represents an accurate picture of this career track. Accounting functions are increasingly becoming automated through technological advances. Accountants are focusing more on analysis, interpretation, and business strategy. Many designers have learned through tough times that a focus on the accounting side of the business could save a company.

Isaac Mizrahi's career is a prime example of the importance of accounting in the fashion industry. You may know him as a designer for Target, an author, and a talk show host, but did you know that, in 1988, he formed his own company and presented his first collection of women's wear? In 1990, Isaac Mizrahi was presented with his first of four Council of Fashion Designers of America (CFDA) Designer of the Year awards. In 1995, he starred in his own fashion documentary, *Unzipped*, made by his friend Douglas Keeve. That same year, a bright red gown he designed was worn by Cindy Crawford on the December cover of *Vogue* (United Kingdom). He was well-known for his gregarious personality and his fashion sense, particularly his use of color and the clean flattering lines of his designs. It was not enough, however, because the

Figure 7.1. Accounting is not just for geeks.

bottom line was as red as Cindy Crawford's gown. Chanel, the firm that was financing him, pulled the plug in 1998, causing Mizrahi to close his fashion house and file for bankruptcy. Box 7.1 presents a news article by Teri Agins on Mizrahi's revised fashion focus.

What are the strengths of a career in accounting? Accounting is a field that provides adaptability to many functions (e.g., purchasing, manufacturing, wholesaling, retailing, marketing, and finance). As a

BOX 7.1 • CLASS TO MASS

by Teri Agins

When he ran his own fashion house in New York from 1988 to 1998, Isaac Mizrahi had little patience for the minutiae of business.

In the mid-1990s, retail buyers begged him to repeat his popular "paper bag waist" pants—cotton trousers with a cinched waist—to meet strong demand. But the designer refused. "I just got bored with them," Mr. Mizrahi said at the time.

Today, Mr. Mizrahi is no longer oblivious to the machinations of retail. After almost two years of designing $19.99 tops and $29.99 dresses for Target Stores Inc., he's gone through a midlife, bottom-line epiphany.

Mr. Mizrahi learned the importance of profits the hard way. After launching his fashion house in 1988, he quickly became famous for his colorful, original take on classic clothes.

Yet despite his fame, the Isaac Mizrahi business remained small. When Parisian fashion house Chanel SA stepped in to become Mr.

Mizrahi's financial backer in 1994, fashion insiders hoped the brand would finally reach a critical mass with the launch of Isaac, a line of $150 dresses and sportswear.

But Isaac didn't catch on, and Chanel pulled the plug in 1998, forcing the business to close.

After a period of artistic experimentation, Mr. Mizrahi got a call from Target with an offer for a licensing agreement in 2002.

Target's high-volume production has brought unexpected creative opportunities, he says. Target's ability to produce thousands and sometimes tens of thousands of an item allows [Mizrahi] to make products he wouldn't otherwise attempt.

While some in haute fashion circles have criticized his commercial turn, Mr. Mizrahi is sanguine about his creative efforts, considering himself both an artist and an entrepreneur. "Target has an image—a humor and a freedom that is more cutting edge than anywhere," he says enthusiastically. "You're not selling out, you're reaching out."

Source: *The Wall Street Journal*, February 7, 2005.

result, networking opportunities are abundant in the business of accounting. This area provides a base from which to build broad knowledge about virtually all business functions and industries. As the collectors and interpreters of financial information, accountants develop comprehensive knowledge about what is occurring and close relationships with key decision makers, and they are increasingly being called on to offer strategic advice. The accounting field also provides great appeal for women. Women represent an increasing segment of the accountants in the United States. The profession has taken great strides to implement flexible work arrangements and other initiatives to provide lifestyle choices for women (Figure 7.2). The hours and travel required by accountants in the fashion industry are much less stressful and more predictable than those found in investment banking and consulting.

In this chapter, accounting careers in the wholesale businesses of apparel, accessories, soft goods, as well as home furnishings and accessories, will be explored. These include employment opportunities in the following positions:

Figure 7.2. There are a great variety of career opportunities for accountants in the United States.

- ▶ chief financial officer
- ▶ controller
- ▶ senior, intermediate, and entry-level accountants
- ▶ accounts receivable personnel
- ▶ bookkeeper
- ▶ accounts payable personnel

CHIEF FINANCIAL OFFICER

A **chief financial officer (CFO)** directs the overall financial plans and accounting practices of an organization. These executives oversee finances, accounting, budget, and tax and audit activities of the organization and its subsidiaries and are responsible for determining the financial and accounting system controls and standards. This includes ensuring timely financial and statistical reports used by management and the board of trustees. This is the top finance and accounting position within an organization.

Qualifications

Following are qualifications for a chief financial officer:

- ▸ **Education:** A bachelor's degree in accounting, finance, or a related field is a minimum requirement. In some companies, a master's degree in business -administration, accounting, or finance is required. Most firms require that the CFO have a certified public accounting (CPA) or equivalent certification.
- ▸ **Experience:** A minimum of ten years of administrative experience in finance and accounting is often required.
- ▸ **Personal characteristics:** Successful CFOs have strong managerial abilities, effective oral and written communication skills, a quantitative aptitude, and organizational expertise. They have the ability to synthesize and summarize financial data for constituencies of the company, from management to stockholders. They are skilled at making strategic projections for the company based on an in-depth knowledge of the company's financial transactions.

A CFO located in the Midwest earns approximately $236,000 annually; in New York City, the average CFO annual salary is about $300,000.

Career Challenges

The CFO commonly works long hours, often more than 60 per week. CFOs are generally required to travel extensively to attend meetings of financial and economic associations and visit subsidiary firms or divisions of the corporation. They work in a leadership position of high visibility, one that requires a broad range of business and people skills. Interpersonal skills are important because this position involves managing people and working as part of a team to solve problems. A broad overview of the business is also essential. Being able to shift from problem solving in financial issues to concerns with personnel in moments takes practice, focus, and skill. Financial operations are increasingly being affected by the global economy, so CFOs must continually update their knowledge of international finance.

CONTROLLER

A **controller,** also referred to as *comptroller*, is responsible for a company's financial plans and policies, its accounting practices, its relationships with lending institutions and the financial community, the maintenance of its fiscal records, and the preparation of its financial reports. This position may be the top level in a mid-size company or report to the CFO in a very large company. If there is no CFO, the controller is, in essence, the top gun in accounting. Controllers direct the financial affairs of organizations by preparing financial analyses of the companies' operations for management's guidance. In some companies, they have the final responsibility for providing effective financial controls for the organization. In others, the CFO has this responsibility.

While most people recognize that the controller works with the company's finances, many do not realize that the position requires working effectively with people, too. In large firms, controllers may supervise a staff of accountants in several accounting divisions, from general accounting and property accounting to internal auditing and budgetary controls. They are responsible for evaluating the performance of personnel in the accounting divisions, determining training requirements, and, in some firms, recommending that personnel be hired, promoted, or removed from the accounting divisions. Overall, they have the duty to keep staffs at the highest level of skill necessary to meet the company's needs and objectives.

The essential functions of the controller are as follows:

▶ Develop, analyze, and interpret statistical and accounting information to evaluate profitability, performance against budget, and other matters that affect the fiscal health and operating effectiveness of the organization.

▸ Maintain the company's system of accounts to include books and records on all company transactions and assets; consolidate all budgets within the company.

▸ Establish major economic objectives for the company and prepare reports that outline the company's financial position in the areas of income, expenses, and earnings based on past, present, and future operations. Read industry news for current trends and ideas on how to better the company. (Figure 7.3).

▸ Coordinate and direct development of the budget and financial forecasts, develop policies and procedures for financial planning and control, and analyze and report variances to ensure budget compliance and improve company efficiencies.

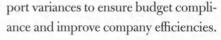

▸ Oversee tax planning and compliance with all federal, state, local, corporate, payroll, and other applicable taxes.

▸ Revise and update useful and efficient internal reports and furnish external reports as necessary.

▸ Evaluate and recommend insurance coverage for protection against property losses and potential liabilities.

▸ Allocate funding to support management decisions on projects with the highest priorities.

▸ Ensure the adequate allocation of funding to the various business departments.

Qualifications

The necessary education, experience, and personal characteristics for employment as a controller may include the following:

▸ **Education:** A bachelor's degree in business administration (e.g., accounting, finance, control,

Figure 7.3. Financial controllers must keep up-to-date with financial news.

or marketing) or a related field is a minimal requirement. Some firms require a master's degree in one of these disciplines. Often, major companies will also require the controller to complete one to two years of post-graduate studies in a finance or controlling area and CPA certification or an equivalent licensure.

▶ **Experience:** For this executive position, many corporations require a minimum of five to seven years of relevant experience in financial management.

▶ **Personal characteristics:** The person in this key financial position must have very strong analytical skills, effective computer skills, and excellent communication abilities, both oral and written. In an international company, skills in a foreign language may be required. For example, Adidas requires fluent written and spoken English and German language abilities for its company's controller candidates.

The controller at a senior vice president level for a New York firm earns between $165,000 and $240,000 annually. The career challenges for the controller are similar to those of the CFO. In large firms, there may be a position for an assistant controller. The **assistant controller** supports the company's controller in directing budget and cost controls, financial analysis, and accounting procedures. This person may be called on to manage financial statement preparation, organize and plan auditing schedules, and develop policy and procedure manuals for the accounting department. This position requires a bachelor's degree in accounting, finance, or a related field and four to six years of relevant experience. The assistant controller earns an average annual salary of $60,000 to $80,000.

SENIOR ACCOUNTANT

The **senior accountant** has extensive experience and depth of knowledge in the accounting field. Some senior accountants in large firms directly supervise accounting associates who may be responsible for a variety of functions. They are responsible for establishing, interpreting, and analyzing complex accounting records of financial statements for management, which may include general accounting, costing, or budget data. They also analyze variances in monthly financial reports, forecast finances, and reconcile budgets. Preparation of tax and audit schedules quarterly is often part of the senior accountant's tasks. The median salary for a senior accountant in Illinois is $55,000.

Qualifications

The following list of qualifications is applicable to the senior accountant position:

- ▸ **Education:** A bachelor's degree is required, preferably in accounting or finance.
- ▸ **Experience:** Work experience, such as an internship with an accounting firm or in the accounting department of a company, is a door-opener to the accounting profession. Experience in fashion, whether in retail sales or merchandising, provides an advantage to the accountant interested in employment with a fashion firm. Three to five years of general accounting experience is usually required to obtain a senior accountant position. Proficiency with computer programs, such as Microsoft Excel and Word, is required. General ledger experience is expected. Supervisory experience is a plus.
- ▸ **Personal characteristics:** Strong communication (both written and oral) and analytical skills are needed. Senior accountants must be detail oriented, organized, and capable of prioritizing their own workloads, as well as the workloads of other accounting staff, to complete multiple tasks and meet deadlines.

The **intermediate** or **mid-level accountant** prepares and maintains accounting records that may include general accounting, costing, or budget data. Mid-level accountants analyze and interpret accounting records for the purpose of giving advice or preparing statements. They have completed a bachelor's degree in accounting, finance, or business, followed by two to four years of relevant accounting experience. Often, this previous experience may be as entry-level accountants. The typical annual salary range for mid-level accountants is $30,000–$45,000.

An **entry-level accountant** maintains records of routine accounting transactions and assists in the preparation of financial and operating reports. This involves helping with the analysis and interpretation of accounting records for use by management. This position is a great starting place for college graduates with a bachelor's degree in accounting, finance, business, or a related field.

Career Challenges

Most accountants generally work a standard 40-hour week, but many work longer hours, particularly if they work for a large company with many divisions. Tax specialists often work long hours during the tax season. People planning a successful career in accounting must be able to analyze, compare, and interpret facts and figures quickly. Accountants must stay up-to-date on accounting software. Because financial decisions are made on the basis of their statements and services, accountants should have high standards of integrity. They carry a legal responsibility for their reports.

ACCOUNTS RECEIVABLE PERSONNEL

What does the term **accounts receivable** mean? It refers to the amount of money owed to a business that it expects to receive for goods furnished and services rendered, including sales made on credit, reimbursements earned, and refunds due. It is imperative for a business to monitor accounts receivable and collect funds due to stay in business. There are a number of career opportunities related to this accounting department. An **accounts receivable manager** supervises the accounts receivable division within an organization's established policies. Job responsibilities include arranging and overseeing the completion of all accounts receivable work, including posting, processing, and verifying receipts, credit claims, refunds, interest charges, or other similar records (Figure 7.4). In addition to producing regular or special written reports, the accounts receivable manager suggests improvements to increase effectiveness of units. The **accounts receivable supervisor** oversees recordkeeping in this department. This person ensures that cash receipts, claims, or unpaid invoices are accounted for properly and calculates and enters charges for interest, refunds, or related items, then produces account statements or other related reports. The **accounts receivable clerk** verifies and posts accounts receivable transactions to journals, ledgers, and other records. The clerk is responsible for sorting and filing documents after posting and preparing bank deposits.

Qualifications

The qualifications for personnel in the accounts receivable department of an accounting division are as follows:

▶ **Education:** To secure a position as an accounts receivable manager or supervisor, a bachelor's degree

Figure 7.4. The accounts receivable clerk verifies financial transactions.

in accounting or finance is a minimal requirement. Some firms will hire a candidate with an associate's degree as an accounts receivable clerk.

▸ **Experience:** The accounts receivable manager position usually requires four to six years of relevant accounting work experience. Two to four years of relevant work is expected for the position of accounts receivable supervisor. Accounts receivable clerk is an entry-level position. This position requires an understanding of bookkeeping procedures and one to two years of relevant work experience. Work experience should be in general accounting procedures and related computer programs; however, those interested in obtaining employment in the accounting division of a fashion firm should gain work experience in retail or merchandising.

▸ **Personal characteristics:** A strong attention to detail, strong organizational skills, and a high-quantitative aptitude are critical to success in this position.

An accounts receivable supervisor working in the Midwest now earns an average annual salary of approximately $48,000, including benefits.

Career Challenges

Accounts receivable personnel deal with a continuing cycle of financial analyses that must be accurate and completed within tight deadlines. There are several times of the year, such as preparing for a board meeting or preparing tax returns, when the accounts receivable staff works many hours of overtime. To some, the work is never ending, as it is difficult to see the end of a project when many are ongoing every year.

BOOKKEEPER

A **bookkeeper** records an organization's business transactions and maintains all of its accounting records. Bookkeepers' responsibilities include posting, verifying, and reconciling accounts payable, accounts receivable, expenses, payroll, or other ledger accounts. They also prepare statements, invoices, and vouchers and submit reports of business financial operations.

Qualifications

Gaining employment within this career track requires the following criteria:

- **Education:** Some firms will hire bookkeepers who have associate's degrees.
- **Experience:** Employment in this position usually requires two to four years of work experience in general accounting procedures. Computer knowledge is important, particularly knowledge of Microsoft Excel. Some large firms employ **bookkeeping managers** to supervise teams of bookkeepers.
- **Personal characteristics:** A strong attention to detail, good organizational skills, and a quantitative ability are critical to one's success in this position.

Career Challenges

A bookkeeper's work is highly detailed and requires accurate posting and calculations. The job can be tedious and repetitive, as a bookkeeper works exclusively with posting financial numbers and developing business reports (see Figure 7.5). It is, however, a doorway to greater opportunities in the accounting department, such as the position of an accounts receivable or accounts payable clerk. A bookkeeping manager working in Iowa now earns an average annual salary of about $43,000.

ACCOUNTS PAYABLE PERSONNEL

Accounts payable is defined as the monies owed to creditors for goods and services; often, it is the amount owed by a business to its suppliers or vendors. Analysts look at a company's relationship of accounts payable to purchases as an indication of sound financial management. An **accounts payable manager** directs the accounts payable division of a company under the organization's established policies. This person arranges and oversees the completion of all accounts payable work by examining records of amounts due

Figure 7.5. A bookkeeper's work can be repetitive, as statements are received daily.

and making sure invoices are paid and discounts taken on time. The accounts payable manager directs invoice processing and verification, expense coding, and the drafting of payment checks or vouchers. Developing written reports and suggesting improvements in processes to increase effectiveness of the accounts payable unit are key responsibilities of this position. Working under an accounts payable manager, an **accounts payable supervisor** oversees accounts payable record keeping by looking after the recording of amounts due, verification of invoices, and calculation of discounts. The entry-level position in this division is that of the accounts payable clerk, or officer. The **accounts payable clerk** reviews invoices for accuracy and completeness, sorts documents by account name or number, and processes the invoices for payment. The clerk may also be responsible for posting transactions to journals, ledgers, and other records.

Qualifications

The qualifications for personnel in the accounts payable department of an accounting division are as follows:

- ▶ **Education:** To secure a position as an accounts payable manager or supervisor, a bachelor's degree in accounting or finance is a minimal requirement. For an accounts payable clerk position, some firms will hire a candidate with an associate's degree.
- ▶ **Experience:** The accounts payable manager position usually requires four to six years of relevant accounting experience. For the accounts payable supervisor position, two to four years of relevant work is expected before hiring. Since the accounts payable clerk is an entry-level position, work experience should be in general accounting procedures; however, for people interested in securing employment in the accounting division of a fashion firm, work experience in retail or merchandising is a plus. Computer knowledge is important, particularly knowledge of Microsoft Excel.
- ▶ **Personal characteristics:** A strong attention to detail, good organizational skills, and a strong quantitative aptitude are critical to success in these positions.

An accountant working in Arizona now earns an average annual salary of approximately $38,000. Career challenges for accounts payable personnel are similar to those for accounts receivable personnel, as discussed previously in this chapter. A classified advertisement for an accounts payable clerk is presented in Box 7.2.

BOX 7.2 • SAMPLE CLASSIFIED ADVERTISEMENT: ACCOUNTS PAYABLE CLERK

Accounts Payable

- Excellent data-entry speed
- More than one year accounts payable experience
- 1-year assignment with opportunities

Working in a supportive environment, you will work as part of an accounts payable team responsible for a large number of nationwide accounts. Duties will include such things as writing checks, answering queries, dealing with creditors, and reconciling journals. To apply, it is vital that you have at least one year of accounts payable experience and an excellent data-entry speed. Excellent communication skills will be crucial for this role. Any other accounts system skills will be looked on favorably.

SUMMARY

While a career in accounting has had a mundane image in the past, today's accountants focus more on analysis, interpretation, and business strategy and spend less time crunching numbers in a cubicle than accountants have in the past. As the collectors and interpreters of financial information, accountants develop comprehensive knowledge about what is occurring within a company and close relationships with key decision makers and are increasingly being called on to offer strategic advice.

Accounting employment opportunities in the wholesale businesses of apparel, accessories, soft goods, as well as home furnishings, include the positions of chief financial officer; controller; senior, intermediate, and entry-level accountants; accounts receivable personnel; accounts payable personnel; and bookkeeper. The chief financial officer holds the top accounting position in a large company, directing its overall financial plans and accounting practices. In smaller companies, the controller may hold the top position in addition to being responsible for the company's financial plans and policies, accounting practices, relations with lending institutions, fiscal maintenance, and financial reports. Senior, intermediate, and entry-level accountants may be responsible for a number of functions ranging from analyzing and interpreting complex accounting documents to maintaining records of routine transactions, dependent on their education background and relevant work experience. Accounts receivable, the amount of money owed to a business that it expects to receive, and accounts payable, the amount owed to creditors, are accounting departments that offer manager, supervisor, clerk, and bookkeeping career opportunities.

Every business needs good accounting personnel and practices to succeed in its industry, and fashion companies are no exception. Rated as one of the most desirable professions available, the accounting job track offers low stress, high compensation, great autonomy, and significant employment demand. If you are quantitative and analytical, adept with computers, organized, and detail oriented, you may enjoy a future along the accounting career path.

KEY TERMS

accounts receivable
accounts receivable clerk
accounts receivable manager
accounts receivable supervisor
accounts payable
accounts payable clerk
accounts payable manager
accounts payable supervisor
assistant controller
bookkeeper
bookkeeping manager
chief financial officer
controller (comptroller)
entry-level accountant
intermediate/mid-level accountant
senior accountant

Discussion Questions

1. Major fashion companies may require their accountants to have worked for one of the "Big Four" accounting firms in the United States. Research to find the names and backgrounds of these firms and determine why this experience is important. Which of the "Big Four" is most appealing to you? Why?

2. Consider your personal accounting and bookkeeping experience. Do you keep accurate records of your debts and credits? Why is this type of record keeping crucial to the success of a company?

CHAPTER 8

Human Resources

uman resources development (HRD) professionals work in the field of business that is concerned with recruiting, training, maintaining, motivating, and managing the people who work for a business or organization. Viewed as a group, all of the employees or staff of a company are known as **personnel**. Sometimes, the human resources (HR) division of a company is called personnel or, for example in reference to a modeling agency, talent management. If you are a people person, a natural teacher, and someone who also enjoys working with numbers, a career in human resources may be just the place for you. The HR division is often considered the most valuable asset of a company. A graduate with strong interpersonal skills and a drive to help others grow and prosper will find a wealth of job opportunities in this area of fashion industry businesses.

Human resources refers to the department in charge of an organization's employees, which includes finding and hiring employees (Figure 8.1), helping them grow and learn within the organization, and managing the process when employees either leave or are fired (Figure 8.2). The HR staff takes care of people from the time they are interested in an organization to, often, long after they leave. **Human resources management (HRM)** includes a variety of responsibilities. Key among them is gauging the staffing needs a company has and will have and deciding whether to use independent contractors or hire employees to fill these needs. HRM is also responsible for recruiting and training the best employees, supporting them to be high performers, dealing with performance issues, and ensuring that personnel and management practices conform to various regulations. Tasks also include overseeing the management of employee benefits and compensation, as well as employee records and personnel policies. Effective human

Figure 8.1. A human resources manager interviews a prospective employee.

resources offices always ensure that employees are aware of personnel policies that conform to current regulations.

Some people distinguish between HRM as a major management activity and HRD as a profession. Those people may include HRM in HRD, explaining that HRD includes the broader range of activities to develop personnel inside of organizations, including, for example, career development, training, and organizational development. The HRM function and HRD profession have undergone tremendous change over the past 20–30 years. Many years ago, large organizations expected the personnel department to manage the paperwork required for hiring and paying people. More recently, organizations look to the HR department to play a major role in staffing, training, and managing employees so that people and the organization are performing at maximum efficiency in a satisfying environment. HRD includes employment opportunities in the following positions:

- ▶ human resources manager
- ▶ hiring manager
- ▶ recruiter
- ▶ trainer
- ▶ benefits manager
- ▶ payroll manager

HUMAN RESOURCES MANAGER

Human resources managers, or human resources directors, play a leadership role in all aspects of a company's business strategy and legal compliance, as well as the business and people issues of the company. They identify the human relations and work-related issues in the workplace and meet with supervisors and managers to determine effective solutions. They also provide guidance and counsel to managers, supervisors, and employees on a variety of issues, including human relations, conflict resolution, interpersonal communications, and effective group interaction. Another responsibility is negotiating contracts with vendors for programs, such as health insurance, and then managing the relationship between the vendor and the company. HR managers prepare annual operating budgets and monitor costs to ensure compliance with budgetary guidelines. They represent the organization at personnel-related hearings and investigations, providing information and coordinating responses for legal issues and interpreting changes in laws, guidelines, and policies as representatives of the firm. An HR manager working for a large firm in New York City may earn $85,000–$110,000 annually.

In small to midsize companies, HR managers recruit, interview, and select employees to fill vacant positions. They may administer tests to applicants when appropriate and plan employee orienta-

Figure 8.2. HR managers are responsible for firing employees whose work doesn't meet company standards.

tion seminars to help new employees meet company goals. HR managers recommend procedural changes to adjust to the changing needs of the organization. They work with other departments to make certain that there is a consistent application of policies and procedures and access to available training and development opportunities. HR managers are ultimately responsible for ensuring a safe and comfortable work environment for all employees. A list of job descriptions for an HR manager follows:

- ▸ Promotes the ongoing role of HR and operations
- ▸ Creates development opportunities for HR consultants and provides coaching

- Establishes department goals and action plans
- Monitors and reports on progress in the HR division
- Provides coaching and training opportunities for HRD staff and personnel
- Identifies and proactively raises organizational issues and trends; diagnoses processes, structures, and approaches; recommends alternatives for improved effectiveness
- Clarifies present and future skills and competencies needed by employees. May act as "external search" consultant in skills and talents to be brought to the company

Assistant human resources managers often are responsible for maintaining records and files on all injuries, illnesses, and safety programs within a company. They ensure that all reports are maintained to meet regulatory requirements and corporate policies, and they maintain records of hired employee characteristics for governmental reporting, such as the number of minority employees. Responsibilities also include preparing employee separation notices and related documentation and conducting exit interviews to determine the reasons for separations. Box 8.1 provides an example of a classified advertisement for a human resources assistant manager.

Qualifications

The following is a list of qualifications for human resources managers:

- **Education:** A bachelor's degree in organizational development, human resources, or a related field is a minimal requirement. Some firms specify a master's degree as a preferred qualification.
- **Experience:** Seven to 10 years of related experience in HRD is usually required. On-the-job experience in interviewing, hiring, and training employees; planning, assigning, and directing work; appraising performance; rewarding and disciplining employees; and addressing complaints and resolving problems is required for this supervisory position.
- **Personal characteristics:** Successful HR managers have the ability to maintain a high level of confidentiality when dealing with highly sensitive issues or information. They must be able to present information effectively and respond to questions from groups of employees, administrators, customers, and the general public. Strong leadership skills, effective interpersonal relationship skills, and conflict resolution abilities are important characteristics. HR

BOX 8.1 • SAMPLE CLASSIFIED ADVERTISEMENT: HUMAN RESOURCES ASSISTANT MANAGER

Company Name: Jones Apparel Group, Inc.

Job Position: HRD/HR

Job Description: Jones Apparel Group, Inc. (www.jny.com), a Fortune 500 company, is a leading designer and marketer of branded apparel, footwear, and accessories. The company seeks a human resources assistant manager.

Responsibilities: Responsible to support site human resources by performing related duties at the professional level, with emphasis on employee relations. Partners with management and employees to communicate/monitor various HR policies, procedures, laws, standards, and regulations. Responds to employee relations issues, such as employee complaints, management concerns, and harassment allegations in accordance with policies, procedures, laws, standards, and regulations. Assists in the evaluation of reports, decisions, and results of individuals and departments in relation to established goals. Recommends new approaches and procedures to affect continual improvement and efficiency. Recruits, screens, and interviews job applicants for positions. Conducts exit interviews and analyzes data to make recommendations to the management team for correction and continuous improvement. Performs benefit administration, including resolving claims, change reporting, assisting employees with benefit enrollment, and communicating benefit information to employees. Performs compensation administration, including monitoring performance evaluations and compensation for job changes/promotional increases. Facilitates various training programs within the site, including new hire orientation, benefit orientation, and sexual harassment prevention.

Requirements: The candidate should have a bachelor's degree (BA or BS) from a four-year college or university. Should have minimum four years of related experience and/or training. Previous experience specializing in employee relations in a distribution center environment preferred. Strong understanding of state and federal employment laws and other compliance regulations. Effective oral and written communication skills. Excellent interpersonal skills. Ability to interact effectively with employees on all levels. Ability to effectively coach employees through complex, difficult, and emotional issues. Ability to make recommendations to resolve problems effectively or issues by using judgment that is consistent with company policy, procedures, laws, standards, and regulations. Able to research and analyze various types of information. Must be organized and able to prioritize work.

Job Location: West Deptford, New Jersey

Experience: Four to six years

managers must also have excellent written and oral communication skills, the ability to manage multiple projects simultaneously, excellent decision-making and analytical skills, strategic design and change management experience, and strong coaching and consulting skills.

Career Challenges

The HR manager has the big responsibility of overseeing all of the personnel needs for a company. It is challenging to stay on top of all of the government hiring regulations, the firm's current and future employment requirements, internal company conflicts, employee satisfaction, and personnel budgets. The HR manager is a budget manager, a negotiator, an evaluator, a communicator, and a motivator. It is a huge task to manage and respond to all of the employees in a company; yet, ultimately, this is the HR manager's job.

HIRING MANAGER

In some companies, the HR manager is responsible for recruiting and hiring employees. In larger firms, there may also be a hiring manager and a recruiter or a team of recruiters. The **hiring manager** is responsible for making the decisions on whether or not a job opening will be filled and who will fill it. A job opening comes about one of two ways: either someone has left the position or a new position has been created. If an existing position needs to be filled and has been proven over time to be an essential role within an organization, the hiring process can go relatively smoothly. The hiring manager reviews the job description and the budget for it and then posts the job on internal and external listings, such as help-wanted classified advertisements in newspapers and trade publications and on websites that feature job listings. The hiring manager or recruiter is the first company representative to review the applications of potential candidates. Once applications are reviewed, or screened, the hiring manager will schedule interviews with select applicants. The applicants may need to interview with several other people in the organization. It is the hiring manager's job to determine with whom these interviews will be and then to schedule them. Additionally, it is the hiring manager's responsibility to know which types of interview questions are appropriate and legal to ask.

If a new position needs to be filled, hiring managers will work with others in the organization to develop a job description and salary package for their ideal candidate. Since they have never hired anyone for this position before, hiring managers have no way of knowing if there will be many, if any, candidates who actually meet their set of criteria. In some cases, the hiring manager will have to start over. Once job candidates are located and interviewed, it is the hiring manager's responsibilities to recommend the top applicant for the position, to offer the position and negotiate its terms to the applicant, and then to follow up on the hire.

Qualifications

What does a hiring manager need in terms of education, experience, and personal characteristics to succeed in this career track? A list of qualifications follows:

- ▸ **Education:** A bachelor's degree in organizational development, business administration, human resources, or a related field is a minimal requirement. Some firms specify a master's degree as a preferred qualification.
- ▸ **Experience:** Five to seven years of experience in HR is usually required. On-the-job experience in interviewing and hiring employees is required for this position. Some hiring managers begin as an assistant to the HR manager. If interested in a hiring manager position with a fashion-related firm, then work experience in a fashion company at almost any level is a bonus. For example, candidates who worked part-time during college for manufacturers are likely to have insight on the skills needed for various positions in this type of company.
- ▸ **Personal characteristics:** Successful hiring managers are good at reading people and ask the right questions to discern whether or not a person is prepared and able to handle a specific job. Strong communication skills, the ability to manage multiple projects simultaneously, and excellent decision-making skills are necessary qualifications to be successful in this position.

Career Challenges

The hiring manager is held accountable for finding the right people for the positions the company needs to fill. If poor job and personnel matches are made and if there is excessive employee turnover, management turns to the hiring manager. It can be difficult to find excellent employees, particularly in certain geographic locations and if the positions require specialized skills or the organization is offering less than competitive salary ranges.

RECRUITER

Recruiters generally work for a specific employer or are in business for themselves and have several companies as clients. Companies such as Ralph Lauren, Jones Apparel Group, and Levi's, to name a few, all have recruiters that they employ directly. **Recruiters** seek out job candidates at college campuses, job fairs, other companies, and online to apply for positions the company is seeking to fill. On average, a recruiter earns $30,000–$45,000 a year.

The duties of a recruiter include:

- Understanding the employer's staffing needs in terms of open positions and the types of candidates that will fit with the employer's with corporate strategy and culture
- Developing sources for locating the best applicants, including **cold calling** (contacting businesses or people without a personal contact), developing leads, and networking
- Locating and implementing tools (e.g., interview strategies or tests) that reveal an applicant's strengths and weaknesses
- Screening candidates
- Keeping up-to-date on workforce trends

Qualifications

What backgrounds and personal characteristics fit the career track of a recruiter? Following is a list of qualifications:

- **Education:** A bachelor's degree in human resources, business administration, or a related field is a minimal requirement.
- **Experience:** Some companies hire recent college graduates as recruiters, particularly if the companies send recruiters to college campuses to recruit job candidates for them. On-the-job experience in some facet of HR, such as an internship, is a plus.
- **Personal characteristics:** The recruiter is a cheerleader for the company, selling the firm and its opportunities for professional and personal growth to top candidates. This person also has a knack for identifying which candidates would best fit the company culture and the specific job openings. The ability

to effectively present information and respond to questions is a key attribute. Strong interpersonal skills, a high energy level, and a love of travel are important traits for recruiters.

Career Challenges

The recruiter often has strong competition for the top job candidates. At job fairs, there are often a large number of recruiters, some working for more widely recognized companies and companies offering more attractive salary and benefit packages. The recruiter is challenged with marketing the company and its positions, selling the firm to prospective employees. Once the recruiter has identified and persuaded top candidates to apply for openings, the hiring manager takes over. If there is not a quick response by the hiring manager, the recruiter is back to square one.

The Hiring Manager and the Recruiter as Partners

In most successful companies, a recruiter and hiring manager spend time together researching and crafting job descriptions for open positions. Through this process, it is likely that their efforts will result in quicker and better-quality hires. Smart recruiters understand that their key objective is to bring hiring managers the right candidates, and good job descriptions help accomplish this goal. When developing a job description, three questions are key:

▸ What are the specific skills required for the position?
▸ What are the goals to be accomplished by the person in the position?
▸ Is there something unique and exciting about the job that can be presented to the candidate as a compelling selling point?

A recruiter may want to ask a hiring manager one specific question: "Can you tell me about someone who works for you and is particularly great?" In those named, both the recruiter and hiring manager will identify the attributes of the ideal candidate by noting the behaviors and characteristics of the valued people in the company. In addition to the laundry list of desired qualifications, such as education level, employment background, and certification, there are qualifications or personal characteristics that tend to be a better fit for the company.

TRAINER

A **trainer** either directs or recruits an expert to work with employees on certain areas of knowledge or skills to improve employees' performances in their current jobs. Training sessions, or seminars, are designed to develop the company's workforce (Figure 8.3). **Development** is a broad, ongoing multifaceted set of activities created to bring an employee or an organization up to another threshold of performance, often to perform some job or new role in the future. Training and development for an employee or a group of employees can be initiated for a variety of reasons:

- When a performance appraisal indicates performance improvement is needed
- As part of an overall professional development program
- As part of succession planning to help an employee be eligible for a planned change in role within the organization
- To pilot, or test, the operation of a new performance management system
- To educate employees about a specific topic

Current topics of employee training that have resulted from a global marketplace include diversity, human relations, communications, and ethics. **Diversity training** usually includes an explanation about how people of different cultures, races, and religions, for example, can have different perspectives and views. It includes techniques to value and expand diversity in the workplace. **Human relations training** focuses on helping people get along with one another in the workplace. Conflict management is often part of this training seminar. **Communications training** has become a need as a result of the increasing diversity of today's workforce, which has introduced a wide variety of languages, ethics, customs, values, and morals to the workplace.

Other current trends in training topics include sexual harassment, safety, customer service, quality initiatives, and technology. **Sexual harassment training** usually includes careful description of the organization's policies concerning

Figure 8.3. Employee training seminars are designed to develop a company's workforce.

sexual harassment, what are inappropriate behaviors and what to do about them (Figure 8.4). **Safety training** (Figure 8.5) is critical in situations where there are employees working with heavy equipment, hazardous chemicals, and repetitive activities, such as in an apparel factory or textile mill. Increased competition in today's marketplace makes it critical for employees to understand and meet the needs of customers; therefore, an emphasis on **customer service training** is significant. **Computer skills training** (Figure 8.6) is becoming an ongoing necessity for conducting administrative and office tasks and for communicating with other departments in a company. **Quality initiatives training** examines such programs as total quality management (TQM), quality circles, and **benchmarking**, the activity of identifying competitors and organizations in other industries with features or skills in areas

Figure 8.4. Sexual harassment training equips employees with the knowledge of which behaviors are and are not appropriate for the working environment.

Figure 8.5. Safety training is critical where there are employees working with heavy equipment, hazardous chemicals, and repetitive activities, such as an apparel factory or textile mill.

Figure 8.6. Computer skills training is becoming an ongoing necessity for conducting administrative and office tasks and for communicating with other departments in a company.

that the company does not currently have and would like to have. Once benchmark organizations are identified, managers of the HRD division analyze how the company compares in terms of such variables as number of employees, salaries and benefits, employee retention, job descriptions, and other factors. Benchmarking allows HRD administrators and trainers to see how their company compares to firms that they believe are strong competitors.

What are the goals of the trainer in developing and coordinating these training seminars? Increased job satisfaction, motivation, and morale among employees are prime objectives that often result in reduced employee turnover. Internally and externally, an effective training program can enhance the company's image. Effective training can also produce increased efficiencies in processes, resulting in financial gain for the company, as well as greater innovation in strategies and products. For example, the capacity to adopt new technologies and methods is a common result of an ongoing computer training program for employees at all levels.

Qualifications

A trainer is expected to have the following qualifications:

- ▸ **Education:** A bachelor's degree in human resources, psychology, education, or a related field is a job prerequisite.
- ▸ **Experience:** An internship in the human resources department of a major company is an excellent way to open the door to a trainer's position. Most companies expect two to four years of experience in human resources as background for this career path.
- ▸ **Personal characteristics:** The trainer is, first and foremost, an excellent communicator in all areas: writing, speaking, and listening. Teaching abilities, presentation skills, and enthusiasm for the subject matter characterize the successful trainer. Additionally, the trainer is an effective networker, able to recruit experts for the various programs that the employees will need.

Career Challenges

The trainer must motivate, inform, and educate employees from all levels of the company on an ever-changing range of subjects. The wide range of audiences and training topics require trainers to find continually new ways to present information effectively and to educate themselves constantly. Developing alternative methods of training delivery (e.g., online training, video productions, and guest speaker presentations) can be a full-time job in itself. There can be a great deal of pressure to get the job done in a timely and entertaining fashion.

BENEFITS MANAGER

When prospective employers describe the "fringes" their company will provide, they typically list retirement plans, health insurance, life insurance, disability insurance, vacation and leave, employee stock ownership plans, and, possibly, **flexible compensation**, which is also called a **cafeteria plan**. When most job seekers speak of **fringe benefits**, they are usually referring to tangible employee benefits. **Employee benefits** are forms of value, other than financial compensation, that are provided to employees in return for their contribution to the organization, that is, for doing their jobs. Some benefits, such as unemployment insurance and workers' compensation, are federally required; others are employer provided. Prominent examples of these benefits include insurance (e.g., medical, life, dental, and disability), vacation pay, holiday pay, maternity or family leave, contributions to retirement (pensions), profit sharing, stock options, and bonuses. There are several objectives of an employee benefit plan.

- ▸ Protects employees and their families from economic hardship brought about by sickness, disability, death, or unemployment
- ▸ Provides retirement income to employees and their families
- ▸ Structures a system of leave or time off from work
- ▸ Makes the company competitive when hiring and maintaining top employees.

Benefits can be classified as company paid and employee paid. While the company usually pays for most types of benefits (e.g., holiday pay or vacation pay), some benefits, such as medical insurance, are often paid in part by employees to alleviate the high costs for the employer. Benefit plans can also include other items such as bonuses, service awards, and reimbursement of employee educational expenses. The absence of a good benefits program can seriously hinder a company's ability to attract and keep good employees.

A **benefits manager**, or **coordinator**, of the HR division has to consider many issues, including tax and legal aspects of and the funding and finding of the right vendors or administrators for benefits. The benefits manager is responsible for implementing **mandated benefits,** those that the employer must pay in whole or in part for certain legally required benefits. Mandated benefits and insurance coverage include Social Security, unemployment insurance, and workers' compensation. Funding for Social Security comes from payments by employers, employees, and self-employed persons into an insurance fund that provides income during retirement years. Other aspects of Social Security deal with survivor, dependent, and disability benefits, plus Medicare, Supplemental Security Income (SSI), and Medicaid. Unemployment insurance benefits are payable under the laws of individual states from the Federal-State Unemployment Compensation Program. Employer payments, based on the total payroll of the company, contribute to the program. Workers' compensation provides benefits to workers disabled by illness or injury suffered while being on the job. Each state mandates coverage and provides benefits for workers. In most states, private insurance or an employer self-insurance arrangement provides the coverage. Some states mandate short-term disability benefits as well.

Why does a company offer employee benefits? Benefits help attract and hold capable people; foster good morale; and provide opportunities for advancement. In essence, they help the company keep up with the competition by attracting and keeping employees who can make the business a success. The benefits manager is critical in locating, securing, and managing benefits that appeal to the top job candidates. In the United States, a benefits manager earns an average salary of $50,000–$65,000.

Qualifications

Following are some requirements for the position of benefits manager:

- ▶ **Education:** A bachelor's degree in human resources, psychology, accounting, or a related field is commonly required.
- ▶ **Experience:** Work experience with an HR department or company is a plus. Many employers will hire a college graduate who has on-the-job experience, even part-time, for this position.
- ▶ **Personal characteristics:** Successful benefits managers have effective oral and written communication skills, strong managerial abilities, and top organizational skills.

Career Challenges

The benefits manager is part accountant, part investigator, and part communicator. It is a challenge to analyze and calculate benefits for all employees while constantly updating one's knowledge of changing legal requirements and evolving benefits coordinators and providers, such as government agencies and insurance firms.

PAYROLL MANAGER

A **payroll manager** is responsible for **employee compensation**, the amount of money paid to employees in exchange for the work they do for the company. Unless you are the president or owner of a small company, others deal with compensation issues, such as the HR department or, specifically, the payroll manager. Compensation literally includes many things beyond straight salary, such as benefits, bonuses, and stock options; however, the payroll manager is responsible for monetary pay. The most common forms of compensation are wages, salaries, and tips.

Compensation is usually provided as base pay or variable pay. **Base pay** is dependent on the employee's role in the organization and the market for the expertise required to perform that role. **Variable pay** is based on the performance of employees in their roles, for example, how well they achieved their goals for the year. **Incentive plans**, such as a **bonus** for exceptional work submitted early, are a form of variable pay. (Some people consider bonuses a benefit, rather than a form of compensation.)

In collaboration with the HR manager, the payroll manager determines salary ranges for existing positions and adjusts those periodically to take into account economic factors (e.g., cost of living changes or inflation) and competitive pressures (e.g., industry demand for employees in specific positions and profit margins). Equitable salaries need to be calculated for new positions or promotions of employees to positions with new responsibilities. The payroll manager is also responsible for complying with government regulations regarding discrimination. Each job must have the same pay range for all employees performing that job. One person cannot receive a higher maximum pay than someone else doing the same job. The payroll manager may also determine whether to contract out a job or use current employees to complete the job. Additionally, the payroll manager works with the HR director on merit-based, bonus-based, and commission-based programs.

The payroll manager is responsible for withholding certain monies withheld from employees' payroll checks, including federal income tax, state income tax, FICA

(Social Security) contributions, and employee contributions to the costs of certain benefits (e.g., medical insurance and retirement). Organizations have two job classifications: exempt and nonexempt. Professional, management, and other types of skilled jobs are classified as **exempt**. Employees in exempt jobs receive a **salary**, that is, a fixed amount of money per time interval. Employees in **nonexempt** jobs usually earn a **wage**, or an amount of money per hour. Nonexempt employees also receive payment for **overtime**, that is, extra pay for hours worked over 40 hours a week or on certain days of the week, usually weekends or holidays.

Qualifications

The payroll manager earns an average salary of $44,000–$60,000 and may possess the following qualifications:

- ▸ **Education:** A bachelor's degree in human resources, accounting, business administration, or a related field is commonly required.
- ▸ **Experience:** This position requires a thorough knowledge of HR-related programs, policies, benefits, and services and a clear understanding of regulatory requirements related to employment, payment of wages, and hours worked. An internship or summer work experience in accounting or HR is a good starting place. A year or two of employment in the payroll department of a firm provides a solid foundation for this position.
- ▸ **Personal characteristics:** A keen attention to detail, quantitative abilities, and organizational skills are attributes of successful payroll managers.

Career Challenges

A payroll manager must accurately calculate financial compensation and benefits for each of a company's employees. As soon as one round of payroll is completed, another is ready to begin. The job may be redundant to some and requires careful attention to detail. As changes in financial compensation (e.g., an increase in salary resulting from a promotion) or in benefits (e.g., an individual to family insurance policy) require immediate revisions, there are constant deadlines to meet.

SUMMARY

Human resources development (HRD) professionals work in the field of business focused on recruiting, training, maintaining, motivating, and managing personnel. Human resources management (HRM) tasks include determining current and future staffing needs and deciding whether or not to use independent contractors or hire employees to fill these needs; recruiting and training the best employees while supporting them to be top performers; dealing with performance issues; ensuring that personnel and management practices conform to various regulations; and overseeing the management of employee benefits and compensation, as well as employee records and personnel policies. Some people distinguish HRM as a major management activity and HRD as a profession. Those people incorporate HRM into HRD, explaining that HRD represents the broader range of activities to develop personnel inside organizations, including career development, training, and organizational development. In most organizations, the HR department plays a major role in staffing, training, and managing employees so that workers and the organization are performing at maximum efficiency in a satisfying environment. The HR department provides employment opportunities in the following areas: human resources manager, hiring manager, recruiter, trainer, benefits manager, and payroll manager.

Human resources managers play a leadership role in all aspects of a company's business strategy and legal compliance to employment laws. They identify the human relations and work-related issues in the workplace and meet with supervisors and managers to determine effective solutions. Hiring managers screen job applicants, conduct interviews, and recommend preferred candidates. Recruiters travel to locate favorable job candidates to apply for the positions the company is working to fill. Trainers either direct or recruit experts to work with employees on certain areas of knowledge or skills to improve the employees' performance in their current jobs or prepare them for advancement. Benefits managers of the HR division examine the tax and legal aspects of HRD and oversee the funding and finding of the right vendors or administrators for benefits, such as health and dental insurance and retirement plans. Payroll managers are responsible for employee compensation, the amount of money paid to employees in exchange for their work for the company.

HRD is a field that is gaining importance in businesses around the world. Most will agree that employees are a company's greatest resource. Building and maintaining a strong workforce are key to the success of every fashion organization. If supporting people to be their best in an optimal environment is your dream job, then HRD offers a range of opportunities to fulfill this dream.

KEY TERMS

assistant human resources manager

base pay

benchmarking

benefits coordinator

benefits manager

bonus

cafeteria plan

cold calling

communications training

computer skills training

customer service training

development

diversity training

employee benefits

employee compensation

exempt

flexible compensation

fringe benefits

hiring manager

human relations training

human resources (HR)

human resources development (HRD)

human resources director

human resources manager

human resources management (HRM)

incentive plan

mandated benefits

nonexempt

overtime

payroll manager

personnel

quality initiatives training

recruiter

safety training

salary

sexual harassment training
trainer
variable pay
wage

Discussion Questions

1. Compare and contrast the areas of HRD and HRM. Locate several classified advertisements for major fashion businesses to illustrate the differences.

2. What employment trends do you anticipate will affect hiring in the next ten years of the fashion industry? Which skills do you believe will be essential for managerial employees in the fashion industry? Which skills do you believe will be essential for managers in HRD within this field?

3. Research the legal issues for which HRD personnel are responsible for training employees (e.g., sexual harassment, diversity, and ethics). Assuming you are an HRD director for a firm with more than 10,000 employees and a number of global locations, what techniques would you implement to educate your company's employees about these topics?

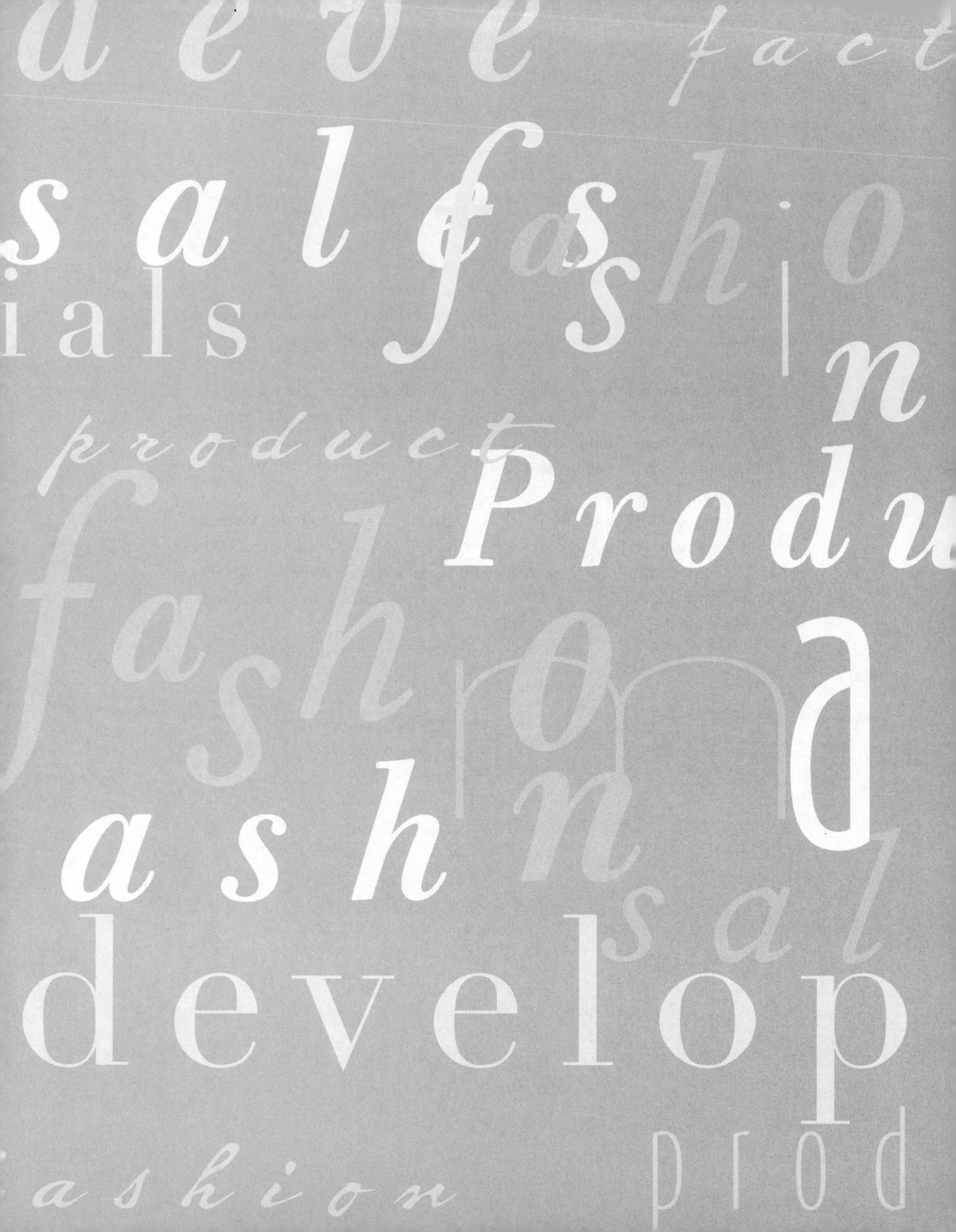
fact
ials
product
Produ
ash
develop
prod
ashion

UNIT 2

CAREERS IN
PRODUCT DEVELOPMENT
AND SALES FOR
THE FASHION RETAILER

Some retailers purchase finished fashion merchandise from manufacturers or wholesalers. Others also develop and manufacture products specifically for their clientele. As a result, Unit 2 begins with a discussion of product development and design by and for the fashion retailer. A number of large retail operations own a product development division that functions as a design and production source exclusively for them. Whether the fashion product is created and manufactured by the retailer or purchased from a manufacturer or wholesaler, it must be marketed to appeal to the consumer. The promotion division of a retail operation does just that through such professionals as the advertising director, visual merchandiser, and personal shopper. Merchandising refers to the buying and marketing of products by a retail operation. Merchandise managers, buyers, allocaters, and planners work on the selection, pricing, and placement of merchandise on retail sales floors. Management careers in the retail sector include administration of the store, its departments, its distribution center, its database, and its personnel. Finally, there are the all-in-one retail specialists, the entrepreneurs who own and operate their retail organizations, whether brick-and-mortar, mail-order, brick-and-click, or online only.

CHAPTER 9

Product Development and Design by the Retailer

What is product development? **Product development** is the creation and making of a product, such as a dress, belt, or chair, from start to finish. This is not a new process. Manufacturers in every industry, from fashion to automobiles to household appliances, have always engaged in product development. In the 1980s, it became very popular for retailers to develop products of their own instead of simply selling the lines of manufacturers' brands. The Gap, for example, used to carry a variety of national brands, such as Levi's. Now it carries only Gap-branded merchandise that is designed and developed in-house.

Product development may be the function of one department in a retail operation or a division within an organization. For example, Federated Department Stores, Inc., acquired the May Department Stores Company in 2005 and announced plans to convert about 400 May Company locations to Macy's or Bloomingdale's stores in 2006. That year, Federated realigned its stores into eight retail operating divisions, seven Macy's and one Bloomingdale's. Two new Macy's divisions, St. Louis-based Macy's Midwest and Minneapolis-based Macy's North, were created. Concurrently, five existing Macy's divisions were expanded to incorporate new stores and geographic markets, serving millions of new customers. Federated introduced Macy's private brands throughout all of the former May Company stores in 2006, offering more exclusive and differentiated merchandise. In 2007, Federated Department Stores, Inc., announced that its Board of Directors will ask shareholders to change the company's name to Macy's Group, Inc., effective June 2007.[1]

Within the corporation, there is a division called Macy's Merchandising Group (MMG). MMG is responsible for conceptualizing, designing, sourcing, and marketing private label and private branded goods sold at Macy's and, in some cases, at Bloomingdale's. Some of MMG's highly successful private brands are I N C, Charter Club and Club Room, Alfani, Style & Co., Tasso Elba, Tools of the Trade, Hotel Collection, The Cellar, Greendog, and First Impressions. MMG's private brand merchandise represents about 17.4 percent of Macy's total sales, about $2.5 billion a year at retail.[2]

Whether it is for a single department or a division of a retail firm, a number of steps are taken when developing a line, though the details may change depending on the type of product, on whether the line is to be produced overseas or domestically, or if the company has an in-house sample department. The general steps for each season are as follows.[3]

1. Inspiration sources (e.g., fabrics, art and museum exhibitions, travel destinations, films, color palettes, and so on) are reviewed. Market research is conducted. The previous year's sales and markdowns are analyzed. Product categories are decided.

2. Trend forecasts are discussed. The preliminary line is planned. The company decides "what it believes in." Color stories are selected.

3. Fabrics and trims are researched, then selections are made. Prints are designed.

4. Concepts are developed, storyboards are created, and designs are sketched. Sample fabrics and trims are ordered. **Labdips,** colored samples of selected fabrics, are requested.

5. Merchandising meetings are held. The line may be edited from sketches.

6. Specifications are written, and technical packages are compiled.

7. Sourcing is completed. Samples, or prototypes, are constructed, and preliminary costing is requested.

8. Patterns and first samples are produced by a sample room or contractors. Often 20–50 percent more designs are made than those that actually will be manufactured. Factories advise on costs.

9. Samples are fitted, edited, and adopted into the line during a line review. The fitting process continues until the sample is approved or dropped. Costs are negotiated. Quantity may be an integral part of cost negotiations, or it may be determined when orders are generated. Quantities may be finalized and orders may be placed at this time, depending on factory lead time.

10. Samples, or prototypes, are produced. Private label goods may require only a meeting sample. Costs are finalized. Photo and production samples are requested.

11. For a private brand in a retail operation with decentralized buying, the styles will be "sold" internally to buyers who quantify the purchase.

    Decentralized buying refers to individual stores or groups of stores within a retail chain that have a buyer who selects from the company's primary buyer's purchases.

12. Production fabric and trim are ordered as soon as the factories receive orders.

13. Production goods are manufactured, and quality control is completed.

14. Goods are packed and shipped to the retailer.

15. Merchandise is received by the retailer and delivered to the warehouse or selling floors.

In the fashion industry, there are three key types of businesses that produce merchandise: manufacturers, contractors, and retailers. As discussed in Unit 1, manufacturers are companies that create, produce, market, and distribute product lines on a continual basis. This may be a designer who owns a company or a company that employs designers. Manufacturers may own their own factories or use contractors to construct their products. Contractors, factories that make and finish goods as shown in Figure 9.1, may be domestic, meaning in the United States, or offshore, as in China, India, or Taiwan. **Retailers** are businesses that sell products to the ultimate consumer and may include the vast range of **brick-and-mortar stores** (e.g., department stores, mass merchants, specialty stores, boutiques, discount stores, and outlet stores), as well as catalogs, **brick-and-click stores**, and online stores. *Brick-and-mortar* is a term that refers to retail operations in a facility, such as a building or a store in a mall. *Brick-and-click* refers to a retail operation that offers products through actual stores and online. Some retailers sell through all or several of these channels. JCPenney, Saks Fifth Avenue, and Nordstrom's, for example, sell their product lines through brick-and-click stores and catalogs. Figure 9.2 shows examples of brick-and-mortar, catalog, and online retailers. Nearly all of the large retailers are currently engaging in some form of product development. In this chapter, the focus is on the product development and design activities of retail operations.

Figure 9.1. Contractors are factories that make and finish goods.

WHY RETAILERS BECAME DESIGNERS

Figure 9.2. Brick-and-mortar stores such as Lord & Taylor (top), catalogs such as L.L.Bean (middle), and online retailers such as Yoox (bottom) are examples of retailers that sell finished products to the ultimate consumer.

There are three main reasons why retailers moved into the business of developing their own products or lines of products. First, retailers wanted to be able to satisfy specific customer demands. Sometimes the retail buyers were unable to locate the products, looks, prices, or fit that their customers sought. The second reason retailers went into the business of creating products is fashion exclusivity. **Fashion exclusivity** refers to merchandise that is unique to a particular company. You may have remarked or may have overheard a customer saying, "Everything in the mall looks the same. I cannot find anything unique." Retailers that wanted to project fashion images unique to their particular companies established product development departments or divisions. Finally, and most important, product development provided new profit margins. Retailers reasoned that by producing directly through contracted or company-owned factories instead of buying from manufacturers, they could make more money on each item, even while charging the customers less than they charged for nationally branded merchandise.

Initially, retailers who developed their own product lines ran into a few problems. There is a long tradition in the fashion business of knocking off the hot or successful designs offered by top designers, rather than creating new looks. A **knockoff** is a copy of another style, often with minor modifications and of lesser quality. Knockoffs (Figure 9.3) of the Hermès Birkin and Kelly bags, carried by Naomi Campbell and Sarah Jessica Parker, can be found in midpriced retail stores. **Counterfeit merchandise**, however, is an imitation of a product, usually one with a designer name, that is intended to fool the customer into thinking it is the real deal. While it is less common today, retailers were historically known for creating private label lines that were collections of knockoffs. **Private label** refers to a line name or brand that the retailer develops and assigns to a collection of products. Since many of the retailers were knocking off products that were already on the market, the majority of the private label products lacked fashion newness. Retailers also had to take responsibility for securing fabrics, avoiding fit problems, and shipping goods. Another obstacle was that many overseas factories required retailers to open letters-of-credit to pay for goods. As a result, retailers were faced with tying up large amounts of their operations' dollars in advance of shipping, rather than paying for merchandise 30 days after they received shipment.

Figure 9.3. Counterfeit handbags are among the most widely sold types of merchandise illegally trading on the names of prominent designers.

As retail-driven product development matured, retailers began to build highly skilled design and merchandising teams to forestall some of the previously mentioned problems. Some major retailers do not attempt to develop products in certain specialized apparel categories because these areas are too precarious or too dependent on major brand names. A few of the product categories that retailers place in product development are: basic apparel because of ease of fit, jeans because of the low risk and ease of entry into the market as a price-point alternative (lower and higher) to major brands, and product categories that have a lower level of competition from major brands. Many retail operations prefer to leave development of highly specialized apparel, such as swimwear and hosiery, or categories that require major advertising investments, such as cosmetics and fragrances, to the major brand manufacturers. As styling in basic products makes it difficult to distinguish a major brand from a private label, some retailers have found that they are safer developing this type of merchandise. Other retailers choose private label lines to create unique and exclusive products that are not available in the market. Most retailers take a big risk when trying to develop trendy, high-priced merchandise because customers often prefer a designer name attached to investment purchases.

TYPES OF PRODUCT DEVELOPMENT BUSINESSES

A number of product development classifications have evolved as retailers engage more and more in the customizing of product lines. These classifications include retail label, private label, private brand, direct market brand, and licenses. A **retail label** is a brand with the retailer's name on it, such as Neiman Marcus, Custom Interiors, or Saks Fifth Avenue. A retailer may negotiate with a manufacturer to put its label on a group of items instead of or in addition to the manufacturer's label, though the retailer may not have had anything to do with the design or development of the items. Some of the items carrying a retail label may be **exclusives**, or items that only one retailer carries. In some cases, a retailer may negotiate to be the only one in a geographic region to carry a particular item or the only one in the country to carry a particular color. For example, the label may read, "Burberry exclusively for Neiman Marcus."

Similar to a private label, yet with a greater level of market penetration primarily through advertising, a **private brand** is a name owned exclusively by a particular store that is extensively marketed with a definite image, such as Target's Mossimo and Isaac Mizrahi brands; Macy's brand I.N.C. (Figure 9.4), and JCPenney's brand Stafford. A **direct market brand** describes a brand that is the name of the retailer. Often, this is a specialty store chain, such as Ann Taylor, IKEA, or Gap (Figure 9.5). A license agreement, discussed in Chapter 3, is a contract with a company that owns the rights to the name of a designer, a celebrity, a sports star, an animated or storybook character, or a distinctive design. Retailers pay royalties to develop lines under those names. Licensees typically must receive approval from the licensor on the design direction of the line, but they are responsible for financing all of the line development, marketing, and sales of the products.

Today, large retail companies are major employers of product development staffs. The career paths in this field include the following: director of product

Figure 9.4. Macy's displays clothing from I.N.C., International Concepts Collection, which is a private brand.

Figure 9.5. Gap is a specialty chain that is both the name of the retailer and its product labels.

development, merchandiser, sourcing staff, designer, retail trend forecaster, colorist, textile technical designer, pattern maker, and quality control manager.

DIRECTOR OF PRODUCT DEVELOPMENT

A **director of product development** is ultimately responsible for the strategic planning of the division, specifying exactly what it is the company will make and market, as well as when it will do this. After selecting a general product category, such as junior T-shirts, the director of product development must narrow the focus. The fashion market is extremely segmented, with each brand filling its particular niche. It is not enough simply to decide to create a line of junior T-shirts because that is far too broad a category to allow for effective line development. Instead, the director of product development will decide, for example, to create vintage-inspired T-shirts for fashion-forward, young female customers in junior sizes extra-small (XS) to large (L). A key product segmentation decision is specifying the target market niche, and that can be accomplished only by knowing the customer well—who she is, what she likes, and where she lives, works, and plays. Other product segmentation decisions that product development directors must make relate to the product, price, size, and taste level. Next, they will work to create a brand by creating an image or personality for the line. An **image** is the way the product developer wants the brand to be perceived, the way that will best attract the target customer. With the abundance of fashion products on the market, image may be the only means of product differentiation. Carefully defined target customers will allow brands to develop images and product lines that will appeal to them.

There are two main approaches the director of product development may take toward the branding of a line: a design-driven brand or a merchandising-driven brand. A **design-driven brand** is one that is led by a designer who is expressing a personal artistic vision and sense of taste. This type of brand appeals to customers who relate to the designer's particular style and flair and includes most brands with designer names. These apparel brands tend to be more original and creative. Design-driven brands also have the peculiar distinction of representing both a particular designer's viewpoint and a line of products. In the case of a manufacturer's line, such as Ralph Lauren's home accessories, the brand has several faces: English gentleman, East Coast aristocrat, and Western individualist, shown in Figures 9.6.

Merchandising-driven brands, or "void-filling" brands, do just that. These market-based brands search for a void in the market or an underserved customer and create a product to fill that void and appeal to that distinct customer. Styling decisions

Figure 9.6. Two of the many faces of designer Ralph Lauren: rugged individualist (left) and British gentleman (right).

are based on careful monitoring of past sales successes and failures in conjunction with customer wants. Customer comfort and competitive pricing are of utmost importance to merchandising-driven brands. Many private labels are merchandising-driven brands. The director of product development has an important overall task. Retailers' brands must have a fashion image consistent with that of the customer the operation attracts. It is the responsibility of the director of product development to make certain that the designed products add up to a marketable line that matches the image of the retail operation. If, for example, a retailer of women's conservative career wear brings in a private label line of Indian cotton bohemian blouses and skirts, the customer may be turned off by the confusing look of the inventory.

Market knowledge is as critical to the success of a fashion brand as is customer knowledge. The director of product development must examine the competition. The **competition** is any other brand producing a similar product at roughly the same price point, targeted toward the same customer or market niche. It is important for product developers to be attentive to what direct competitors are doing, if only to refrain from duplicating their products or visual image. These direct competitors are fighting to be the consumer's choice. Ideally, a company wishing to grow a brand will have such a great product and know its customers so well that customers feel they must buy it. In a broader sense, competition is any other brand vying for consumers' retail dollars.

Types of competition change as retailing venues change. Think about the Internet as a shopping mall of new competitors. As the face of retail changes, a brand's product line may be competing with brands online, at different price ranges and from global companies. Consumers are less loyal to retailers today as there is no stigma attached to cross-shopping. **Cross-shopping** refers to the customer's inclination to purchase a wide variety of products in an array of brands from any number of providers—directly from the manufacturer, in a resale store, at a flea market, or through a couturier (Figure 9.7). It is cool to buy smart. The new consumer mentality puts added pressure on the director of product development, who must now be aware of price, quality, and look of products in all categories, not just one narrow market niche.

Figure 9.7. Cross-shopping is when a customer purchases a wide variety of products in an array of brands.

Qualifications

The qualifications for the position of director of product development include the following:

▶ **Education:** A bachelor's degree in fashion merchandising, fashion design, product development, or a related field is required.

▶ **Experience:** The director of product development holds an executive position that often requires five to seven years of successful work experience as a merchandiser or designer.

▶ **Personal characteristics:** Creativity, a strong marketing sense, and an understanding of consumers, quantitative skills, and networking abilities are key attributes for directors of product development. They are excellent communicators—orally, in writing, and visually. Also, the director of product development has other diverse characteristics: curiosity, leadership abilities, and the ability to work with a variety of constituencies, from designers to merchandisers to colorists.

A classified advertisement for a director of product development is featured as Box 9.1.

BOX 9.1 • SAMPLE CLASSIFIED ADVERTISEMENT: PRODUCT DESIGN AND DEVELOPMENT DIRECTOR

Position Detail: Director of Product Design and Development

Location: New York, New York

Responsibilities

- Develop full pattern, spec, and wash development
- Monitor and plan accordingly to meet calendar milestones and deadlines
- Lead fittings and meetings
- Communicate with vendors and factories and with design, merchant, and production teams
- Ensure timely completion of garments for line review and stock approval
- Proactively identify and solve potential development and production issues
- Organize department work flow and staff and restructure department as needed
- Comprehensively understand esthetic and sensibility and be able to design within those parameters
- Demonstrate ability to take initiative on projects, concepts, and new ideas
- Attend design meetings, giving creative concept and development direction

Job Requirements:

- Bachelor's degree required. Education in apparel studies preferred but not required
- More than 10 years' experience in the apparel industry
- Proficiency in WEB PDM, Excel, Micrografx, Outlook
- Ability to fit and analyze appropriate fit corrections
- Knowledge of pattern making and grading, garment construction and washing processes, and production/manufacturing processes and capabilities
- Ability to multitask and problem solve, plan and organize long-term goals, and manage and mentor personnel
- Strong leadership skills
- Overseas travel experience and knowledge

This company is an equal opportunity employer. We offer dynamic career opportunities with growth potential and a generous company discount.

Career Challenges

Earning $90,000–$150,000 annually, the director of product development is the leader of the pack. It is a high-pressure job in which one must be a motivator, guide, and, sometimes, the "take charge" person. It takes a strong person with vision to manage a team of executives.

MERCHANDISER

A merchandiser's responsibilities vary widely depending on company requirements. A **merchandiser** collaborates with the director of product development in deciding what to produce and then organizes and manages the entire product development process. Merchandisers are responsible for the development of a balanced, marketable, profitable, and timely line. In some companies, merchandisers oversee the design function and may serve as liaisons between design and sales. They will create the initial line plan and project target wholesale costs by analyzing sales from previous seasons, fashion trends, and customer wants. As Figure 9.8 illustrates, merchandisers work closely with designers on seasonal themes and guide designers on the development of cost-effective and marketable styles. In some companies, merchandisers may also have responsibilities in sourcing and marketing functions. In other companies, there is a sourcing staff to locate the suppliers and manufacturers for the product.

Figure 9.8. A merchandiser discusses designs with a product developer.

The merchandiser is responsible for constructing the **merchandising calendar**, the product development team's schedule. The goal of the calendar is to deliver the right product (e.g., style, quality, and price) at the right time. When creating a new line, developers carefully plan how often they want goods to flow into the stores. Once they complete the delivery schedule, merchandisers create a calendar by working backward from in-store delivery dates, listing all of the tasks in the product development cycle, with deadlines for each. Next, merchandisers develop detailed line plans. The **line plan** shows the number of styles in the line, the number and general types of fabrics and yarns to be used, the colors per style, the anticipated stock-keeping units (SKU), and the approximate preferred costs. The line plan not only gives product developers guidelines from which to work and focuses their efforts in a distinct direction but also it takes into account fabric and yarn minimums and lead times. Merchandisers often work on different phases of several seasons at once.

Typical responsibilities of the merchandiser include the following:

▸ Researching the market, including tracking market trends and attending trade shows

▸ Fashion forecasting

▸ Attending consumer focus groups

▸ Shopping the competition

▸ Scouting fabric and trim markets

▸ Analyzing past sales, markdowns, and market trends within the retail operation

▸ Developing the merchandising calendar and line plan

▸ Creating design concepts with the product developers

▸ Calculating cost estimates for new products

▸ Directing and participating in line presentations

▸ Choosing and quantifying which styles will actually be produced, sometimes prior to sales (referred to as **production authorization**)

▸ Sourcing, in some cases

▸ Fostering a creative environment so technical design and sourcing staffs can do their best work

Qualifications

The experienced and educated merchandiser may earn a pay range from $50,000 to more than $80,000 annually. To achieve a career as a retail merchandiser, consider obtaining the following qualifications:

▸ **Education:** A bachelor's degree in fashion merchandising, fashion design, retailing, or a related field is required.

▸ **Experience:** The merchandiser is sometimes promoted from within the product development department or division, having worked on the sourcing or technical design staff, for example. Three to five years of on-the-job experience in product development is preferred. In some cases, highly skilled people from the retail side of the business may be trained for this position. After all, who knows the customer better than someone who has worked successfully with the retail operation's clientele on a daily basis?

▸ **Personal characteristics:** The merchandiser is an excellent communicator, orally and in writing. Thorough market knowledge, a keen fashion sense, strong analytical skills, creativity, and an astute marketing instinct are essential characteristics. Successful merchandisers are continually cognizant of the market environment and the target customer and make well-informed decisions quickly and confidently. In companies that manufacture the majority of their product lines overseas, fluency in the languages of the countries where production takes place can be very helpful.

Career Challenges

The merchandiser is a planner. You know—or perhaps you are—this type of person, with your schedule drafted months in advance, telephone numbers and addresses at your fingertips, and a to-do list in a constant state of addition and completion. The merchandiser thinks creatively and quantitatively. The product lines are viewed from many perspectives—what will be in fashion, how much will it cost to manufacture a product, which items will the customer purchase or not, and what is the competition doing. The successful merchandiser must be a sponge, soaking up all of the variables that affect whether a product will sell or not.

SOURCING STAFF

Sourcing, locating components and producers of the final product, was discussed in Chapter 3 as it relates to the primary level of the industry, manufacturers of fashion merchandise. Sourcing in product development for the retailer is much the same as it is for the manufacturer. The primary difference, in most cases, is that the retailer often finds and hires contractors to produce private label lines, rather than building or purchasing factories to manufacture the lines. The sourcing staff of a product development team is responsible for finding the best possible fabrics, findings, trims, and manufacturers to make the designers' lines reality. Members of the sourcing staff may specialize in specific categories, such as belting or trims. They may also travel extensively to locate parts of the product or a manufacturer for the product. Earnings may range from $45,000–$90,000 annually, depending on the staff member's experience and the size and location of the company.

The sourcing staff often works with a sales forecast to determine the amount of product components needed. A **sales forecast** is created by the product development director and merchandiser, in conjunction with the sourcing staff. It includes projections of sales by category, style, color, and size based on historical data and statistical analysis. This information may be used to place preliminary fabric and trim orders and block out production time in factories. As the sourcing staff must often place orders early, an accurate sales forecast is critical to deliveries made at the right time and in the right amount.

Qualifications

To become a member of a company's sourcing staff, one should fulfill the following qualifications:

- ► **Education:** Usually employers require a bachelor's degree in fashion design, fashion merchandising, product development, or a related field.
- ► **Experience:** In many corporations, sourcing personnel are promoted from the technical design staff or are hired with assistant designer experience from outside of the company.
- ► **Personal characteristics:** Sourcing personnel pay attention to detail and have efficient organizational skills and strong written and oral communication abilities. They are "born to shop," comparing quality, price, and availability in product parts and production requirements.

Career Challenges

Sourcing staff personnel face the task of finding the best product or product parts at the best price, in the right quantity, and in a timely fashion. Many are required to travel globally and frequently. Negotiations can be tough when working with people from different cultures, with or without an interpreter. The abilities to shop until you drop and then communicate effectively and negotiate successfully take a great deal of flexibility and stamina.

PRODUCT DEVELOPMENT AND PRIVATE LABEL DESIGNER FOR A RETAILER

Product development, or *private label*, **designers** are the creators of the product line for the retailer; they are trend forecasters in their own right by determining what the customer will be ready for next. They go through the design process with each new season. Table 9.1 shows monthly activities for product development by season. The **design process** refers to the conception of a style to include its inspiration or theme, color palette, fabric selection, form, and fit. Private label designers must be adept at synthesizing a variety of fashion influences while acknowledging marketability and

Table 9.1

Product Development Activity Calendar

Activity	Fall	Holiday/Resort	Spring	Summer
Design/Development	Jan/Feb	Apr/May	July/Aug	Nov/Dec
Selling and Show Dates	Feb/Mar	June/Aug	Sept/Oct	Jan
Producing Orders Begins	May 1	Aug 1	Nov 1	Feb 15
Shipping Starts	June 30	Oct 1	Jan 30	Apr 15
Shipping Completed	Sept 30	Dec 15	Mar 31	May 31

Adapted from Gary, Susan P. and Connie Ulasewicz. *The Business of Apparel and Sewn Products Manufacturing* (Sebastopol, CA: GarmentoSpeak), 1998.

fulfilling customer wants and needs. An important designer trait is the art of compromise. These designers must balance the desired fashion look of a product and the highest possible quality standards with a price tag that is desirable to the target customer.

After determining the style, color, fabric, and trend concepts, designers begin sketching individual styles, usually with a particular form, or silhouette, in mind that epitomizes the fashion trends for the upcoming season. They may repeat versions of this silhouette throughout the line. Some styles may be completely original, but sometimes designers will adapt a style from an actual garment found on a shopping expedition or in a magazine. Most lines include at least a few **carryovers**, best sellers from a previous season. The designers will be careful to include important basics and to balance each group with the help of the merchandiser. Many companies ask for estimated costs from factories before samples are made so that styles can either be dropped or adjusted when the line is still in sketch form. Oversampling is quite expensive, so the merchandiser will generally try to keep it under control. When a complete group of styles is finalized, all of the sketches are placed on a line sheet so the group may be seen at a glance.

Typical tasks of the designer may include the following:

▶ Shopping the retail market, sometimes with merchandisers or a member of the sourcing staff, for design ideas and knowledge of the competition; buying samples
▶ Shopping the fabric, yarn, and trim markets
▶ Attending trend-forecasting meetings
▶ Developing color palettes, groups of colors, and colorways, combinations or pairings of colors

- Determining the styling direction of the line and creating concept boards or storyboards
- Shopping the print market and buying print paintings
- Developing styles through sketching garments by hand or on a computer
- Recoloring garments or prints
- Designing embroideries, screen prints, and appliqués
- Writing specification sheets
- Corresponding with factories or in-house sample departments regarding drapes, patterns, and garment construction
- Attending fit meetings

These tasks, of course, vary, often depending on the size of the company for which the designer works. Some of the larger companies may assign some of these tasks, such as writing specifications or developing color palettes, to more specialized personnel, such as technical designers or colorists. Salary ranges also vary for similar reasons, although the average annual earnings are $40,000–$80,000.

Qualifications

Designers on product development teams of retailers are likely to have the following qualifications:

- **Education:** A bachelor's degree in fashion design, product development, fashion merchandising, or a related field is a minimal requirement.
- **Experience:** Employment as an assistant designer or technical designer is an excellent stepping-stone to the position of designer. These entry-level positions provide knowledge of fabrics, construction, and fit. Additionally, the designer needs prior experience in PC software, such as spreadsheets, databases, and word processing. Many employers require designers to have CAD experience.
- **Personal characteristics:** Successful designers have excellent organizational skills and pay attention to detail. They can create an image of the final product, either on a drawing pad or on the computer. Because much business is conducted in Asian countries, foreign language skills in languages such as Cantonese, Mandarin, or Japanese are a plus.

PRODUCT DEVELOPMENT AND DESIGN BY THE RETAILER

Career Challenges

The successful designer must know the retailer's customer well because knowing the customer's likes and dislikes minimizes the designer's fashion risks. Designers must be able to multitask with the best, often working on two or more collections at one time. Working with color, silhouettes or forms, fabric, and trend themes, they are challenged to create collections. It may be difficult to find new sources of inspiration and find a common theme to weave among the items in a collection.

RETAIL TREND FORECASTER

Retailers must continually research their customers, products, and markets through consumer, product, and market research. In Chapter 1, the trend forecaster employed in the primary level of the industry was discussed. In this chapter, the career track of the retail trend forecaster is examined. The **retail trend forecaster** researches many sources to create formal reports that summarize important fashion trends in a particular season that will appeal to the retailer's clientele. These reports are presented to the product development team members to ensure the development of consistent looks across all departments. Trend forecasters in the product development divisions of retailers identify the fashion trends and then interpret them for the retailers' particular customers, or markets. Additionally, they project looks for the retail operations' customers for upcoming seasons. The experienced retail trend forecaster has the potential to earn an annual salary of $100,000 or more.

Qualifications

The following are education and experience goals, as well as personal characteristics, of the successful retail trend forecaster:

- ▶ **Education:** A bachelor's degree in product development, fashion design, fashion merchandising, visual arts, or a related field is a minimum requirement.
- ▶ **Experience:** The majority of retail trend forecasters move up the ladder from within the ranks. Many are textile designers, product developers, or buyers before obtaining the key position of retail trend forecaster.

▶ **Personal characteristics:** Curiosity, an awareness of global population shifts and consumer interests, and a fascination with fashion trends are important characteristics of a retail trend forecaster. Additionally, the abilities to synthesize, categorize, and prioritize key fashion trends are critical attributes. Most important, an understanding of the retailer's customers in terms of fashion taste is required.

Career Challenges

Predicting fashion trends of color, form, and theme is just one of the challenges facing the retail trend forecaster. An equally significant challenge is determining which fashion trends the retailer's customers will actually buy. One's personal tastes have to be set aside in this career track. The retail trend forecaster must know where in the fashion life cycle the customer is most comfortable, how much the customer will spend, and what will entice the customer to buy. Trend forecasting is simply one part of the job; customer forecasting is another. Box 9.2 is an article related to the challenges of retail trend forecasting.

COLORIST

A **colorist** in product development chooses the color combinations that will be used in creating the product lines. Colorists frequently travel to trade and fashion markets and subscribe to color-forecasting publications to stay on top of current and future color trends. They observe what the customers purchase, or do not buy, to understand their needs and interpret their color preferences accurately. Colorists collaborate with marketing, buying, and technical staff members, as well as design colleagues, on color trends and preferences. They often conduct research for ideas and inspiration, with topics ranging from historical costume to modern architecture. After determining a color palette for the season, the colorist produces boards, swatches, or other visuals to present the color ideas to the product development team. Finally, the colorist is responsible for checking and approving samples of completed items.

Colors and patterns are constantly changing in the fashion industry. There is a special language to describe this area of product development: labdips and strikeoffs. As soon as colors and fabrics have been determined, a company must decide whether any of the colors will be custom dyed in any of the fabrics. If so, original color standards must be sent to the dyeing mills or fabric companies so that dye formulations may be created. The mills will send labdips to the product development team for color approval

BOX 9.2 • A SLIP ON CUTTING EDGE OF FASHION

by Jayne O'Donnell

There's such a thing as being painfully hip, as the folks at Urban Outfitters (URBN) know all too well.

The company, which owns the stores Urban Outfitters, Anthropologie, and Free People, prides itself on being on fashion's cutting edge. Last fall, that became a tough place to be as it filled its often-quirky stores with the latest styles, and many buyers bolted.

The company makes no apologies for staying on top of the trends. "We should be fashion forward," says Urban Outfitters CFO John Kyees. "That's who we are."

[The] "French flea market approach" Anthropologie takes to home furnishings in its 81 stores is able to catch that shopper who has a real need to spend money on clothing items and also is interested in doing things for her home.

Urban Outfitters, which caters to teenage and twentysomething men and women, has 18 of its 89 stores in the [United States] near college campuses. Like Anthropologie, it combines offbeat home (well, dorm) decor with trendy fashions. Urban Outfitters acknowledged the stores have been slower to recover because many of their accessories didn't keep up with new trends.

Free People, the name of the original store that later became Urban Outfitters, is now a sophisticated clothing line for twentysomething women and six stand-alone boutiques. Same-store sales increased 14 percent in the first quarter, a marked contrast with Urban Outfitters and Anthropologie.

Kyees isn't apologizing. "This is the first quarter in the last five years that we've had a problem with our earnings."

Kyees says the merchandise mix is far more appealing to shoppers than it was at the start of the year.

"The consumer is starting to understand the fashion a bit better," Kyees says. "But you can never blame the consumer for not accepting your fashion, because our job is to satisfy them."

Source: www.usatoday.com/money/industries/retail/2006-06-21-urban-outfitters-usat, June 21, 2006.

---

prior to dyeing large yardages of fabric. Organizing and approving labdips may consume a significant amount of a colorist's time. Printed fabric may be purchased from a number of companies, but sometimes, a designer will want to include a print on the line that is exclusive to the company. This requires that the company buy a croquis, a painting of the print, have it printed into repeat, and decide colorways or the color composition. When these projects are finalized, the painting is sent to a printing mill. The mill will print a few yards of fabric, called a **strikeoff**, and send them to the product developer (e.g., colorist, designer, and sample maker) to be made into a sample.

Colorists need to consider such factors as how the design will be produced, how the finished article will be used, how good the quality of materials is, and how big or limited the budget is. They work standard hours but need to be flexible to meet deadlines. They are based in studios or offices. Earnings range from $25,000 annually when newly qualified to $75,000 and above with experience. Prospective employers require a strong and relevant portfolio of work for review.

Qualifications

Following are the qualifications for a successful colorist:

- ▸ **Education:** A bachelor's degree in visual arts, fine arts, computer-aided design, graphic design, fashion design, textiles, or a related discipline is a minimal requirement.
- ▸ **Experience:** Technical designers, particularly those with experience in textiles, may move into the position of colorist. An understanding of how a textile will be used, what properties it needs to function optimally, and how the addition of color dyes or surface treatments will affect these properties is critical to the colorist's work. Two to five years' experience in design is often a prerequisite for this position. One of the paths to move into the position of colorist is to work as an assistant to the colorist. Some fortunate college students are able to secure internships in the color department of a product development division.
- ▸ **Personal characteristics:** The colorist must keep up-to-date with fashion and population trends—current and projected—while staying on top of new design and production processes. Flexible computer skills, the ability to meet deadlines, and effective business skills make colorists successful. They have an exceptional eye for discerning and recalling colors. A strong network of color expertise, from trade organizations to publications to peers, supports the colorist's own expertise. The successful colorist has the ability to identify color trends that evolve from such external influences as major art exhibitions, timely couturiers, and popular travel destinations.

Career Challenges

The colorist is part chemist, part artist, and part fashion forecaster. It takes a wealth of skills in many areas. This person must maintain extremely high standards and pay careful attention to detail. It is critical that the colorist be an effective communicator. Think about describing a specific color to someone and explaining it so effectively that this person can actually mix the paint for the exact color. It is not an easy task.

TEXTILE TECHNICAL DESIGNER

A **textile technical designer** creates new textile designs or modifies existing textile goods, altering patterns or prints that have been successful on the retail floor to turn them into fresh, new products. The textile technical designer will develop color alternatives for a modified fabric print or pattern or work with a colorist to accomplish this task. Most technical textile designers work on computers to create or modify designs. There are a number of specialized areas in which they can work; among these are wovens, knits, or prints. For example, a technical textile designer may work primarily with sweater knits or shirtings. The technical designer who specializes in prints will often use a computer-aided design program to create a croquis. Technical designers are likely to earn $40,000–$80,000 per year.

Qualifications

The following is a list of qualifications for the career path of a textile technical designer:

- **Education:** A bachelor's degree in textiles, textile technology, fashion design, computer-aided design, graphic design, or a related discipline is a minimal requirement.
- **Experience:** Many textile technical designers begin in this position after college graduation. An internship in the technical design division of a retail corporation is an ideal way to open the door to this field.
- **Personal characteristics:** A textile technical designer has knowledge of computer-aided design and an understanding of technical considerations as they relate to textile applications. An awareness of consumer wants and needs and an eye for color and patterns are essentials. The successful technical textile designer is simultaneously creative and technologically savvy.

Career Challenges

Technical textile designers live in a high-touch, high-tech world. They must understand the technical features of CAD and the production aspects of knit, woven, print, and textured fabrics. In addition, they must understand the feel, or hand, of a diverse array of fabrics and the application of each. Which types of fabrics are best suited for which products? How do these fabrics wear? What are the care factors for each? There

BOX 9.3 • SAMPLE CLASSIFIED ADVERTISEMENT: ASSISTANT TECHNICAL DESIGNER

Position Detail: Assistant Technical Designer, Women's Active Wear

Location: Chicago, Illinois

Purpose and Scope: Participate in and support the technical development of product from initial design concept through development.

Responsibilities

- Maintain and update tech packs in WebPDM
- Maintain updated proto status chart
- Coordinate and monitor pattern work and cut work flow
- Prepare garments and paperwork for fitting
- Take concise fit notes
- Communicate with vendors and factories
- Communicate with design, merchant, and production teams
- Assist in preparation for line review

Job Requirements and Preferences

- One to two years of industry experience
- College degree preferred
- Knowledge of WebPDM preferred
- Pattern making knowledge
- Knowledge of sewing/construction of garment and/or pattern making a plus

This company is an equal opportunity employer. We offer dynamic career opportunities with growth potential and a generous company discount.

is much to know in this field, in which new fabrics, computer technology, and manufacturing techniques arrive daily.

Box 9.3 features a classified advertisement for an assistant technical designer.

PRODUCT DEVELOPMENT PATTERN MAKER

Technical design and follow-up are parts of a pattern maker's responsibilities on a product development team. The **product development pattern maker** takes accurate measurements and develops a pattern, using either draping or flat pattern methods that, if correctly written, ensure the designer's vision will be implemented. Specification lists, commonly referred to as **spec sheets**, typically provide detailed measurements and construction guidelines. Designers may give pattern makers sketches and a few measurement specifications for guidance or may actually drape a garment to get the exact form they envisioned. Following the designers' approval, pattern makers will develop detailed spec sheets. A spec sheet includes a technical sketch, all of the measurements and tolerances, type and yardage of fabrication, and trim information. Different companies have their own spec sheet formats; however, all of them have similar components. Each item on the spec sheet can have a critical impact on cost and on production of the item. The components of a spec sheet are illustrated in Figure 9.9.

Some retail product developers have additional challenges. They often do not employ in-house pattern makers and do much of the manufacturing in faraway factories where the factories' pattern makers do the work. They frequently have to complete whole spec packages to send overseas that tell factories every detail of what will be required when engineering a style. Many times spec sheets are used to calculate estimated costing so that items can be adjusted or canceled before a costly sample is made. If the company does not employ the technical staff to write specifications, it can contract with pattern making and CAD companies that will write specs and prepare detailed spec sheets.

Qualifications

The average salary for a pattern maker in the United States is around $45,000. Following are the qualifications for a pattern maker of a product development team:

- ▶ **Education:** A bachelor's degree in fashion design, product development, or a related field is often required.
- ▶ **Experience:** If the pattern maker has an assistant, this position is often an entry for college graduates. Some technical designers and sample makers move into the pattern maker slot. Two to five years' experience is usually required for a key pattern maker position. Effective skills in draping, flat pattern, and CAD are necessary.
- ▶ **Personal characteristics:** The pattern maker is, in essence, an engineer. A keen attention to detail, the ability to construct almost every type of garment, and a focus on accuracy are necessary characteristics of successful pattern makers.

Career Challenges

Pattern makers must work with accuracy and speed on details. If a pattern piece is one-eighth inch smaller than it should be, the entire garment may not be able to be

		S	M	L	XL	1X	2X	3X	TOLERANCE
CUSTOMER:							SEASON:		
DESC. OF SAMPLE:	WOMEN'S SS KNIT SHIRT POLO						DATE:		
STYLE : KN21							MODIFY:		
QTY : (PCS)							VENDOR:		
DESC.									
CHEST (1" BELOW ARMHOLE)		38	41	44	47	52	55	58	+/-1/4
SWEEP		38	41	44	47	52	55	58	+/-1/2
BACK LENGTH (FROM COLLAR SEAM DOWN)		25.5	26	26.5	27	27.75	28.5	29.25	+/-1/4
FRONT BODY LENGTH (FROM HIGH POINT)		26	26.5	27	27.5	28.25	29	29.75	+/-1/4
ACROSS SHOULDER		16	16.5	17	17.5	19	19.5	20	+/-1/4
ARMHOLE (CURVE)-HALF		9	9.5	10	10.5	11	11.75	12.5	+/-1/4
SLEEVE LENGTH (FROM CENTER BACK)		17	17.5	18	18.5	20	21	22	+/-1/4
SLEEVE OPENING (ON THE HALF)		5.5	6	6.5	7	7.25	7.5	7.75	+/-1/4
NECK OPENING		19.25	20	20.75	21.5	23	23.75	24.5	+/-1/4
COLLAR HEIGHT (CENTER BACK)		2.5	2.5	2.5	2.5	2.5	2.5	2.5	+/-1/8
FRONT NECK DROP		3.25	3.5	3.75	4	4.25	4.5	4.75	+/-1/8
BACK NECK DROP		1	1	1	1	1	1	1	+/-1/8
FRONT PLACKET WIDTH		1	1	1	1	1	1	1	+/-1/8
FRONT PLACKET LENGTH		4.5	4.5	4.5	4.5	4.5	4.5	4.5	+/-1/8
SLIT HEIGHT AT BOTTOM		2	2	2	2	2	2	2	+/-1/8
HEM HEIGHT		1	1	1	1	1	1	1	+/-1/8

Figure 9.9. Example of a spec sheet.

produced. Even if it can be manufactured, it may not fit or it may have a design flaw. That is a large responsibility to bear. Many of the people who are interested in pattern making enjoy methodical and detailed work—engineering of sorts. What they often do not enjoy is the pressure of deadlines.

QUALITY CONTROL MANAGER

A quality control manager of a retail product development team is responsible for the final inspection of garments from the manufacturer, checking fabric, fit, and construction for quality and adherence to product specification guidelines. This person is responsible for training new and existing quality control employees and for developing specific guidelines and standards for the department. The typical quality control manager may earn $65,000 annually.

Qualifications

The background and characteristics of a successful quality control manager in the retail setting are as follows:

- **Education:** An associate of arts degree in fashion design, product development, or a similar field is required. A bachelor's degree is preferred.
- **Experience:** Two to four years of experience in quality control are expected as a prerequisite for this supervisory position. The quality control manager must have a solid understanding of garment construction, garment specifications, and spec sheets.
- **Personal characteristics:** The quality control manager should possess an excellent eye for detail and a commitment to high standards. Bilingual skills may be necessary, depending on the location of the manufacturing facilities. Excellent communication and people skills are important.

Career Challenges

The quality control manager must maintain excellent standards and oversee every detail of production from beginning to conclusion. It can be a high-pressure job with little recognition. The product development team, the retail personnel, and the customers assume that products will be made correctly and will perform well. When this is not the case, the white-hot spotlight shines on the quality control manager.

SUMMARY

Product development describes the processes needed to make a product, from conception to manufacturing. In this chapter, product development conducted by the retailer is examined. The three main reasons retailers moved into the business of developing their own product lines included satisfying specific merchandise needs of their customers, creating exclusive products unique to their particular companies, and generating new profit margins. The result is private label merchandise, lines for which the retailer develops brands that are assigned to collections of products. A number of product development classifications have evolved as retailers engage more and more in the customizing of product lines. These classifications include retail label, private label, private brand, direct market brand, and licenses.

As a result of this move into product development, large retail companies are major employers of product development staffs. The careers in this field include director of product development, merchandiser, sourcing staff, designer, retail trend forecaster, colorist, textile technical designer, pattern maker, and quality control manager. The director of product development is ultimately responsible for the strategic planning of the division, specifying exactly what it is the company will make and market, as well as when it will do this. The merchandiser collaborates with the director of product development in deciding what to produce and then organizes and manages the entire product development process. The sourcing staff of a product development team is responsible for finding the best possible fabrics, findings, trims, and manufacturers to make the designers' lines a reality. The product development designer is the creator of the merchandise lines for the retailer. The retail trend forecaster creates formal reports that summarize important fashion trends with seasonal themes. The colorist chooses the color combinations that will be used in creating the product lines. Using this color direction, the textile technical designer creates new fabric designs or modifies existing textile goods by altering patterns or prints that have been successful on the retail floor to turn them into fresh, new products. The pattern maker uses draping or flat pattern methods to develop a pattern that uses these textile options and implements the designers' vision. The quality control manager reviews the final product for fit, durability, and overall quality. Together, the product development team brings exclusive merchandise developed specifically to appeal to the retailer's target market from conception to reality.

KEY TERMS

brick-and-click store

brick-and-mortar store

carryover

color palette

colorist

colorway

competition

counterfeit merchandise

cross-shopping

decentralized buying

design-driven brand

design process

direct market brand

director of product development

exclusive

fashion exclusivity

image

knockoff

labdip

line plan

merchandiser

merchandising calendar

merchandising-driven brand

private brand

private label

production authorization

product development

product development designer

product development pattern maker

quality control manager

retail label

retail trend forecaster
retailer
sales forecast
spec sheet
strikeoff
textile technical designer

Discussion Questions

1. What are your predictions for the future of private label merchandise by retailers? Will it increase or decrease and why?

2. This chapter mentions that a few of the product categories retailers place in product development include basic apparel, jeans, and product categories that have a lower level of competition from major brands. Provide examples of the latter product category, those with less competition from national brands, and identify retailers that have succeeded in these merchandise classifications.

3. Develop a line plan for a small private label jean line. Specify the season of the line, then identify the number of styles, colors, size ranges, and price points that are in your line. Provide visuals for the line—magazine clippings, sketches, and word descriptions.

ENDNOTES

1. www.fds.com/pressroom/releases.asp, "Federated Plans Corporate Name Change." February 27, 2007.
2. www.retailology.com/macysmerchandisinggroup/index, "Get to Know Us."
3. Kirsteen Buchanan, Stephens College, Columbia, Missouri, 2006.

CHAPTER 10

Promotion in Retailing

This chapter examines the fashion careers in retailing that relate to the promotion of the retail operation, internally and externally, whether as a whole, for its individual products, or complete product lines. *Promotion* refers to the activities that communicate the company's or product's attributes to target consumers. Promotion for a large national or regional chain store organization is often a fast-paced career track for a full-time staff. In contrast, promotion for a small, local retailer may be conducted by the store owner or an advertising agency hired for this purpose.

Promotion consists of two primary channels: publicity and advertising. **Publicity** is, in essence, free press; it refers to the mention of a company or its merchandise in the media for which the company does not pay a fee. For example, when a retailer hosts a well-known guest designer and receives television, radio, and newspaper coverage because of the designer's visit to the store, the result is publicity. The event or news will likely involve some expenditures, but the retailer does not pay for the media coverage; the store's image is enhanced by the recognition. In contrast, **advertising** is paid, nonpersonal communication. Examples of advertisements are abundant in newspapers, magazines, online, and on the radio. Think about how many advertisements interrupt your favorite television shows. Whether it is publicity or advertising, the primary goal of any promotional campaign is to raise visibility in a positive fashion and, ultimately, to increase sales volume. Figure 10.1 is an example of a fashion advertisement.

To promote effectively, a retail business first needs to determine the message it will like to convey and to whom that message will be sent. The first question the organization should ask when developing a promotional activity is, "What does this business

Figure 10.1. In high-fashion advertising, campaigns often make a bold, artistic statement that do not necessarily reveal the company's name or product, as in this Pirelli ad.

want or need to communicate?" A young and trendy fashion image? Community involvement? Exclusive merchandise and superior service? The answer to these questions will help ensure that the company is using its promotional efforts effectively. A company knows its promotions are effective when increases in consumer traffic and sales volume are significant, such as experiencing an increase in orders placed through the company website or by tracking sales of the specific product promoted through an advertising campaign.

A successful promotional message accomplishes the following:

▶ Generates attention
▶ Stimulates an interest
▶ Promotes a desire
▶ Induces action

Think about the parts of a promotional message and how they relate to retailing career tracks in promotion. If you are looking for a field of action, then promotion may be your fast track to success in the fashion industry. The following careers in retail promotion are explored within this chapter: promotion director; publicity/public relations director; special events coordinator; advertising director; art staff (illustrator, photographer, art director, and website developer); store-planning director; visual merchandiser; and personal shopper.

PROMOTION DIRECTOR

A **promotion director** guides the marketing activities of the retail operation. Have you ever thought about how you learned that a new product or fashion line was available in your town? Did you watch television, peruse a magazine or newspaper, or read a billboard on your way to class or work today? If so, you were exposed to marketing that was designed to persuade you to enter a store, view a website, or buy a product or service. Think about a specialty retailer, such as Eddie Bauer. In an Eddie Bauer store, there is signage throughout the store that promotes new products. These signs may be designed to create a mood for new products, such as a floral-bordered strawcloth board announcing the arrival of new tank tops. There are also silent promotions at Eddie Bauer in the forms of displays, hangtags, labels, and shopping bags, as well as fliers promoting the store's credit cards. You may also be one of those customers who receive a mail-order sale catalog from Eddie Bauer, which is another form of promotion. Ultimately, if the promotion for the store and its products is a success, the retailer sees an increase in the number of customers shopping at the retail operation, often resulting in higher profits.

There are many types of promotional campaigns: television commercials, radio spots, print publications (e.g., magazine ads, fliers, and catalogs), billboards, and the Internet. Because there are so many options, many retail companies seek the guidance and expertise of an advertising agency. An **advertising agency** is an outside firm that may be contracted by the retail organization to help choose the right promotional vehicles that will reach the company's target market and maximize its advertising budget. The advertising agency may also be contracted to create the advertisements. The promotion director may collaborate with an advertising agency or may make the media and budget decisions independently.

The promotion director is expected to know which media types are most effective for different types of promotions. For example, television and radio are considered best suited for institutional advertising. In many retail operations, promotion directors, with their overview of the organization, focus on institutional advertising. **Institutional advertisements** are promotional activities that sell an organization as a whole, as a fashion leader, community supporter, or provider of the best value for the dollar, among other images.

Qualifications

What are the personal characteristics, skills, education, and experiences that would best support a candidate in climbing the career ladder to the position of promotion director? Following is a description of the preferred backgrounds and characteristics for successful promotion directors:

- ▸ **Education:** A bachelor's degree in promotion, advertising, fashion communication, fashion merchandising, or a similar field is a minimal requirement.
- ▸ **Experience:** Becoming a promotion director does not happen overnight; usually, many years of industry experience are required. A few candidates start at the most entry-level position, sales associate. Others begin in an advertising department, then move to the promotion department.

▸ **Personal characteristics:** An excellent understanding of fashion marketing, the ability to communicate fashion trends, an understanding of consumer behavior, strong communication and presentation skills, and a great networking ability are key personal characteristics of the successful promotion director.

Career Challenges

The promotion director has the difficult challenge of differentiating the retail organization from its competitors. Meeting this challenge requires a keen understanding of the market, its customers, and the media—not a small task. Promotion directors are challenged with creating cost-effective and eye-catching marketing activities that communicate an organization's personality and generate sales. Throughout these activities, the bottom line is always in sight, as they must generate more profit than the activities cost. As a result, promotion directors are constantly under the pressure of coming up with innovative ideas that fit within their budgets. Additionally, they coordinate all of the marketing efforts of their company to communicate clear, consistent company images. There are many people involved in this collaboration and many days when creative ideas are not forthcoming.

PUBLICITY AND THE PUBLIC RELATIONS DIRECTOR

Publicity refers to the dissemination of information about people, places, special events, or other newsworthy topics through a variety of communications media. As previously noted, there are no media costs for publicity, which is why it is often difficult to obtain. Media editors choose the topics they publicize based on information they believe will be of most interest to the public. Publicity helps sell fashion merchandise by making a style, trend, designer, or retailer better known to the consumer. A **publicity director** is responsible for securing publicity for the retail operation and may collaborate with other departments to create events, such as fashion show productions or celebrity personal appearances.

The publicity director provides the media with information about such events or people with the goal that the media will publicize them. Summaries of the important facts relating to these events, called **press**, or *news releases,* are formatted specifically for the media and sent directly to them by the publicity director. If photographs and related information, such as news articles from similar events in other cities or background information, are included with the press release, the parcel is referred to as a **press package,** or *press kit*. The publicity director is responsible for directing the press package to the media whose audience would be most interested in its message. The press release and press packages may be intentionally designed to provide different perspectives to ensure that each medium has a different angle on the story.

Qualifications

Following are the qualifications for the publicity director of a large company:

- ▶ **Education:** A bachelor's degree in promotion, advertising, fashion communication, journalism, fashion merchandising, or a similar field is a minimal requirement.
- ▶ **Experience:** A number of publicity directors began in the advertising department, then transfered to assistant positions in the public relations department. Others gain experience working in one of the media fields before moving into retailing.
- ▶ **Personal characteristics:** An excellent understanding of media alternatives, journalism, and marketing provides a solid foundation for public relations work. Exceptional communication and presentation skills, attention to detail, and a strong networking ability are common personal characteristics of successful public relations directors.

Box 10.1 is a classified advertisement for a public relations director or manager. The salary range for this position is $60,000–$100,000 annually, depending on the size of the company and the experience of the candidate.

Career Challenges

The publicity director is always searching for a "free ride." The "ride" is publicity, positive mention of the company in the press. It takes a great spin master to create a new way of looking at something old. Take, for example, the in-store visit of a designer. The publicity director must find a way to make this event appear new and fresh by tying it to a fashion show that benefits a charitable cause or a model search for an in-store informal show. It is challenging to create new perspectives, find publicity opportunities, and communicate effectively with the various media contacts.

BOX 10.1 • SAMPLE CLASSIFIED ADVERTISEMENT: PUBLIC RELATIONS MANAGER

Reporting to the senior director, the public relations manager is responsible for creating awareness for the retailer by developing and executing public relations strategies and programs. In this highly visible role, the public relations manager will work directly with key executives and the corporate communications department to develop strategic corporate, store, and product messaging to generate regular press coverage. The public relations manager is the primary daily contact for the retailer's outside public relations agency and manages all media inquiries pertaining to the brand. The ideal candidate will possess a passion for retailing, an interest in fashion, strong communication skills, and a desire to leverage business momentum through communications.

Job Requirements

- Four to six years' public relations experience, with a strong preference given to candidates with prior experience working for retail, fashion, or lifestyle brands or with a leading public relations agency
- Excellent verbal and written communication skills
- Outgoing, positive personality
- Strategic thinker—strong planning, priority-setting, and time-management skills
- Enjoys and understands the creative process and comfortable translating strategic goals into creative solutions
- Accepts personal and team accountability and drives toward these goals
- Must have strong presentation skills and be comfortable presenting in front of large audiences
- College degree required
- Moderate travel required

SPECIAL EVENTS COORDINATOR

Special events refer to designed occurrences that are intended to communicate particular messages to a target audience. A **special events coordinator** develops and executes events that are fashion related, such as fashion and trunk shows, as well as fashion presentations at clubs and for organizations. Additionally, the special events coordinator creates and directs activities that are not fashion related, but put the company in a favorable light in the public eye. A company's participation in Habitat for Humanity, its sponsorship of a sporting event to raise money for a local school, or a fund-raising drive among company employees for survivors of hurricanes or other natural disasters are illustrations of special events that may be coordinated as public affairs activities to support the community, locally, regionally, or nationally.

Special events coordinators collaborate with the promotion and public relations directors to develop events that will either feature merchandise or enhance the company's image. They are effective at finding opportunities to accomplish both. They may work with promotion directors and retail buyers on sales promotion events. **Sales promotions** often feature short-term incentives that encourage the sale of particular products or categories of merchandise. Examples of sales promotion techniques include free samples, coupons, gift-with-purchase giveaways, point-of-purchase displays, contests, sweepstakes, and games. An example of an externally sponsored sales promotion is *Seventeen*'s back-to-school fashion show. *Seventeen* provides funding for the retailer to sponsor the event, such as advertising monies and door prizes, as well as gifts for students who audition as models. In exchange, the retailer features merchandise advertised in *Seventeen* in the fashion show.

The special events coordinator is adept at planning activities, recruiting partners (e.g., country clubs, community clubs, and philanthropic organizations), finding assistance for events, working within budgets and schedules, and recruiting press coverage. It is not an easy job, but it can be exhilarating and fulfilling. The average salary for a special events coordinator is $35,000–$60,000 annually.

Qualifications

What does it take to be a special events coordinator? Following is a list of qualifications:

- ▶ **Education:** A bachelor's degree in public relations, fashion merchandising, fashion communication, or a related discipline is a common requirement.
- ▶ **Experience:** Between two and five years of experience in advertising, public relations, or fashion coordination is required. Retail or sales experience can be obtained during the educational years to help open a door to this field.
- ▶ **Personal characteristics:** The special events coordinator has the ability to create enthusiasm and drama for a product, line, or activity. A person in this position is creative in finding new and exciting venues to introduce the retail operation and its products to consumers. The successful special events coordinator remains well organized and detail oriented while working effectively with others and staying calm under pressure.

Career Challenges

The special events coordinator must be a jack-of-all-trades, for instance, while direct-ing a fashion show to introduce a new season's merchandise, coordinating a marathon that raises funds for a charity, and hosting a luncheon for women executives—all in the same month. Time-management ability, attention to detail, and organizational skills required for this position are essential but are not the only necessary personal traits. Additionally, special events coordinators must be able to motivate all of the people involved in the events. It can be a huge task to juggle several events and a large number of employees at one time; yet, the best special events coordinators do so with grace.

ADVERTISING DIRECTOR

An **advertising director** of a retail operation develops and implements the company's advertising strategy for the purpose of increasing sales. Designed to serve different pur-poses, there are five primary types of advertising: institutional, brand, sales, classified, and advocacy. As mentioned previously, institutional advertising is intended to build the organization's image and create community goodwill. **Brand advertising** promotes a particular label or manufacturer, while **sales advertising** announces specific value items. **Classified advertising** disseminates information about a sale, service, or event. These advertisements are usually presented as small ads in specific sections of print publications. **Advocacy advertising** supports a particular cause. For example, a home-building retailer may run a newspaper advertisement that entirely features green design merchandise, all composed of sustainable resources or recyclable prod-ucts, in support of environmental awareness. Figure 10.2 provides an example of a controversial advocacy campaign advertisement.

In addition to determining which type of advertis-ing best suits a product, line, or event, the advertising director also selects the venue for the advertisement, called media forms. Advertising **media forms**, or sim-ply **media**, include magazines and newspapers, televi-sion and radio, outdoor displays, direct mail, novelties (e.g., calendars, pencils, and memo tablets), catalogs, directories, and circulars. After deciding the

Figure 10.2. United Colors of Benetton, notorious for controversial ad campaigns that convey social messages, posted this HIV positive print ad in the London Underground.

media form of an advertisement, advertising directors work to position their companies relative to the competition. They first determine the goal of the advertisement. Is the objective to get consumers to make buying decisions in the near future? Is the goal to introduce a new product or service? The goals of advertising campaigns influence which media forms advertising directors will choose to convey messages.

The advertising director will likely work with support departments to develop a promotional campaign that is within the company's advertising funds. Support departments can include media sales, graphic design, illustration, photography, and printing. For example, an advertising director may work with an illustrator to develop drawings depicting a promotional concept for television, magazine, or newspaper ads. The ideas would then be evaluated by looking at concept boards to determine whether the promotion is likely to be successful. The selected concept would then be implemented using whatever resources necessary to complete the project. In a print ad, for example, a fashion photographer may be hired to shoot the necessary pictures. Finally, the advertising director measures the outcome of advertising efforts, in terms of sales volume, customer traffic generated, and units sold, to determine the success of the advertisement. The most common form of advertising evaluation is an analysis of sales and profit impact before, during, and after the promotion effort occurs.

Qualifications

Here is what you need to know and do to become an advertising director for a retail organization.

- ▶ **Education:** A bachelor's degree in advertising, fashion merchandising, fashion communication, or a similar field is frequently a minimum requirement.
- ▶ **Experience:** An entry-level position in advertising, such as sales associate or copywriter, is an excellent starting place. The advertising director has completed a minimum of between three and five years' experience in promotion and retailing.
- ▶ **Personal characteristics:** An excellent understanding of fashion trends, customers, and retail competition is extremely helpful. The ability to sell is a critical skill. The advertising director has mastered the skills of persuasion and communication.

The salary range for an advertising director begins at about $22,000 annually for an entry-level position with a small retail company and can go up to $100,000 a year for an executive-level position with a large retail operation.

Career Challenges

Advertising directors of large companies must develop expertise in a wide range of media sources, from print advertising in magazines and newspapers to television and radio commercials to Internet advertisements. Each media type requires different strategies and skills. Maintaining a strong attention to detail while managing quick deadlines can be a challenging task.

ART STAFF

Art directors, illustrators, photographers, and website developers are categorized as members of an art staff. Large companies usually employ a full art staff, while small retailers hire an advertising agency or freelance personnel to do these jobs. As an **art director** develops and implements the creative concepts for advertisements, catalogs, mailers, and so on, the goal is providing an overall and consistent visual view with regard to the retailer's graphic design execution, including signage, photography, direct mail, packaging, and advertising illustrations. **Illustrators** often work within the advertising departments of major retailers to sketch garments for print advertisements. Illustrations can show more detail than photographs, may be less expensive to create, and can take less time to execute than a photography session. Many illustrators begin in a freelance capacity, with the hope of future full-time employment with a large retailer. Today, a number of them work with computers to develop or finalize drawings. Adobe Photoshop and Illustrator are important CAD programs for illustrators. Many large retailers also employ **photographers** in their promotion division. Figure 10.3 is of photographer Oliviero Toscani working with children to create a United Colors of Benetton advertisement. Retailers with a major Internet presence will hire **website developers**, or **designers,** to construct, maintain, and grow the company's website. Box 10.2 provides a classified advertisement for an art director of a major retailer, while the ad in Box 10.3 solicits a website designer.

Figure 10.3. Benetton photographer Oliviero Toscani is known for shooting interesting images for the Italian retailer's advertisements.

BOX 10.2 • SAMPLE CLASSIFIED ADVERTISEMENT: ART DIRECTOR

Our company aims to be a world-class brand for the tween (ages 7–14) girl. To accomplish this, we operate two divisions that create magical places for the tween girl. We sell apparel, swimwear, sleepwear, underwear, footwear, and lifestyle and personal care products for active, fashion-aware tween girls. The company publishes a catalog coinciding with key tween shopping times throughout the year and conducts e-commerce on its website.

The primary responsibilities of the art director include, but are not limited to

- Developing and implementing brand building, conceptually creative for retail catalog, signage, and collateral
- Providing overall point of view with regard to in-store graphic design execution, including permanent and promotional signage, photography art direction, direct mail, and packaging
- Working within a multidisciplinary team to ensure successful execution of campaigns

Required Qualifications

- College graduate with a Bachelor's of Fine Arts

- Five to 10 years agency or in-house marketing experience
- Highly creative designer/thinker
- High quality of craft in design execution and layout
- Experience working with creative teams—creative management
- Computer skills in Adobe InDesign, Photoshop, Freehand, and Illustrator
- Effective communication skills, demonstrated ability to interface well with various groups and outside contacts
- Strong organizational skills
- Portfolio of work required

Desired Qualifications

- Experience in retail or catalog industry
- Illustration skills
- Photo shoot experience
- Copywriting skills

We offer highly competitive salaries, excellent benefits, and an environment that encourages professional growth. We are an equal opportunity employer.

Qualifications

If you are interested in an art-related position with a retailer, here are an employer's expectations in terms of education, experience, and personal characteristics.

▶ **Education:** A two-to-four-year college degree in fashion illustration, fashion design, fine arts, photography, or computer science is often a minimal requirement.

BOX 10.3 · SAMPLE CLASSIFIED ADVERTISEMENT: WEB DESIGNER

Web Designer

Job Category: Advertising/Marketing/Public Relations

Career Level: Experienced (Nonmanager)

Relevant Work Experience: Two to five years

Status: Full-time employee

Position Summary:

The Web designer, under the supervision of the Web manager, is responsible for the concept, creation, development, and design of Web promotions/campaigns for an assigned brand(s). These include e-mails, landing pages, home page refreshes, virtual catalogs, and other promotional materials utilizing a Macintosh-based desktop publishing system. The timely upkeep includes, but is not limited to, updating the website and Web promotions in a timely fashion with market reactions such as fashion news/trends. Excellent design skills and the ability to be a leader as well as part of a team. Ability to meet deadlines, communicate effectively, and manage many projects at one time is a must. Must be able to design based on a solid knowledge of the branding requirements/standards for brand(s) assigned by the manager.

Duties/Responsibilities

- Concept, create, develop, design, and produce Web promotions using graphic design software (QuarkXpress, InDesign, Dreamweaver, Photoshop, Illustrator, and so on) on a Mac-based computer system
- Attend brand meetings to ensure creative elements are in line with brand requirements and brainstorm creative concepts with an eye on the feasibility of requests from a design perspective
- Attend internal meetings with departmental groups to ensure timely approval process
- Independently, or in conjunction with creative director or art director, interpret creative "looks" of each promotion and build/develop layouts of those materials assigned
- Provide creative direction and guidance to image processors
- Ensure all work, both creative and technical, is reviewed for accuracy before deployment
- Deploy site designs/redesigns and work with outside vendors to ensure redesign launches are on a timely basis
- Work on special creative projects for brands as assigned by manager

Minimum Qualifications

- Strong creative skills in layout, typography, shape, and color work are a must. The ability to conceptualize several creative comps for presentation is also a must.
- Expertise in current Internet standards, including Web browsers and browser specifications
- Experience in managing website content
- Very strong organizational skills a must. Attention to detail and the ability to multitask are also required.

- Dedication to developing and implementing effective methods for meeting project deadlines
- Evidence of strong inclination toward collaborative work style coupled with leadership skills
- Any combination of relevant and equivalent education, experience, or training that provides the necessary skills, abilities, or knowledge will be considered.
- Direct-mail marketing knowledge a plus
- Working knowledge of networking technologies, including security and encryption on the Internet, and basic networking concepts, is a plus.

Redcats USA, formerly Brylane, is "America's Specialty Catalog Leader," with ten catalogs and ten e-commerce websites. Our three divisions include value-priced misses' fashions, women's, and men's plus-size apparel as well as home fashions, gifts, and lifestyle products. In 2003, Redcats USA mailed over half a billion catalogs in the United States alone. Redcats USA is a subsidiary of Redcats, the home-shopping division of Pinault-Printemps-Redoute (PPR). With 26 mail-order catalogs and 51 websites in 18 countries, Redcats services customers on three continents, making PPR a global powerhouse in home shopping. Redcats' merchandise includes up-to-the-minute women's and men's fashions, plus size apparel, giftware, recorded music, videos, and home furnishings.

Redcats USA's corporate office is located in New York City and has merchandising, fulfillment, and call center operations in West Bridgewater, Massachusetts; Indianapolis, Indiana; Plainfield, Indiana; El Paso, Texas; and Universal City, Texas.

- ▶ **Experience:** An outstanding portfolio should be developed to show one's ability to work with a variety of products in a range of styles. Two to five years of experience in freelance work can open the door to these positions. Most companies expect candidates to have skills in computer-aided design applications.
- ▶ **Personal characteristics:** A solid background in visual design is necessary. The abilities to work quickly, adapt to different viewpoints, and work with a range of mediums are important. Members of an art staff must be able to work independently and meet deadlines.

The salary range for a fashion illustrator, photographer, or website developer is approximately $24,000–$60,000 annually. An art director can expect to earn $35,000–$80,000 a year.

Career Challenges

Members of the art staff, whether they are illustrators, photographers, or website developers, are confronted with the challenges of acquiring and understanding new technology on a regular basis. Most illustrators work on computers, even if simply to finalize hand-drawings. Computers have become vital instruments in the photographer's world. The website developer is likely the most comfortable with technology; however, the influx of new innovations in website retailing keeps the developer in constant training as well.

STORE-PLANNING DIRECTOR

A **store-planning director** develops a plan that details fixture placement, lighting, dressing rooms, restrooms, windows, aisles, and cash and wrap areas of a store. Store-planning directors keep several goals in mind when laying out store floor plans. Esthetic appeal, image consistency, visibility and security of merchandise, comfort and ease of staff and consumers, and merchandising flexibility are among these objectives. Once a floor plan is finalized, all of the **supplies** (e.g., hangers, bags, and tissue) will be purchased along with the **equipment** (e.g., four-way fixtures, T-stands, slat walls, mirrors, and computer registers), to set up the retail floor. All of this must be accomplished within a predetermined budget.

The store-planning director often works with the visual merchandising director to design the store layout. Window and interior display areas and cases to exhibit small goods, fixtures, and mannequins are of interest to both. The store planner who has work experience in visual merchandising often has an edge over one who does not.

Qualifications

What else does it take to have a successful career in store planning? The qualifications are the following:

- ▸ **Education:** A bachelor's degree in fashion merchandising, interior design, retailing, or a related field is minimally required.
- ▸ **Experience:** Between two and five years of experience in retail management, visual merchandising, interior design, or buying is preferred.

▸ **Personal characteristics:** Store planners are detail oriented, computer-literate (CAD), and task oriented. They have effective communication skills—oral, written, and visual. Additionally, they have strong quantitative skills, as space allocation and budgeting are core responsibilities of this career path.

The job outlook for this field is good. Most large retail operations rely on store-planning directors for updating facilities, setting up new departments or stores, and keeping the equipment and supplies for the retail floor in-stock, up-to-date, and safe. Salaries range from $24,000 to more than $80,000 a year.

Career Challenges

The store planner has a great deal to consider when designing or remodeling a retail operation. Store managers, buyers, sales associates, customers, receiving clerks, and maintenance staff have specific space needs and desires. While working under the control of a budget, the store planner must consider the comfort and safety of all constituencies while keeping in mind the main goal of the retailer—selling merchandise. Designing a space to meet all of these objectives takes observation, patience, and perseverance.

VISUAL MERCHANDISER

Promotions are not limited to print ads, television commercials, and billboards. Promoting the image of the store through visual merchandising is another way retailers market their products to perspective customers.

What is visual merchandising? Often called the "silent salesperson," **visual merchandising** refers to the design, development, procurement, and installation of merchandise displays that enhance the ambiance of the environment in which the displays are shown. Effective visual merchandising aims to create an image that reflects the company and sells the company's product lines. Some visual merchandising efforts are institutional, such as Macy's large boulevard windows that feature holiday extravaganzas of mechanical dolls and a twelve-foot tree made of glass lollipops. Others are product-driven, such as Tiffany's shadow-box windows that highlight new jewelry pieces.

Visual merchandisers are the people responsible for window installations, in-store displays (Figure 10.4), signage, fixtures, mannequins, and decorations that give a retail operation esthetic appeal and a distinct image. Visual merchandisers have the ability to look at the merchandise selected by the buyers and, through their creativity and expertise, create an image of the store that entices customers to enter the store and purchase merchandise. Think about an outfit displayed in a retail window or on a mannequin. As a result of seeing the presentation of the garment and accessories, you may have decided to buy the items on display. This purchase is due to the successful work of a visual merchandiser.

The visual merchandiser is responsible for a number of key tasks:

Figure 10.4. The Impulse department in Macy's displays one of this retailer's private labels.

▶ Designing an esthetically appealing environment that reflects the company's image, sometimes including floor, wall, and furnishing selections

▶ Creating exciting visual displays to educate customers and to sell merchandise

▶ Presenting the merchandise in ways that will maximize sales, such as displaying the full range of colors of a new handbag and matching footwear

Most often, the visual merchandiser consults with the retail operation's buyers to determine which merchandise should be featured. Since one of the main goals of visual merchandising is to increase revenue, merchandisers will ask the visual merchandiser to create displays for new, key items that have been purchased in depth, as in Figure 10.5. Alternatively, the buyer may ask the visual merchandiser to feature products that are not selling well to increase sales on the items so that the merchandiser will not have to mark them down, thereby decreasing the retailer's profit. Some visual merchandisers have numerous job responsibilities in addition to designing and installing window displays. They also place inventory of the sales floor stock and set up new stores for openings. They locate and purchase props and fixtures for installations and create signage for display windows and the sales floor.

Figure 10.5. A visual merchandiser features Ugly Dolls as a key item in a display at Phorm, a retail boutique.

Qualifications

Are you a person who is artistic, resourceful, and loves creating visual displays? This may be the career path for you if you have the following qualifications:

▶ **Education:** A two- or four-year college degree in fashion merchandising, fashion design, interior design, retail planning and design, fine arts, or visual merchandising is often a minimal requirement.

▶ **Experience:** Many visual display directors begin as members of a visual merchandising crew, installing windows and interior displays. Others may come from the field of fashion stylist. One of the best ways to prepare for the job search is to build a portfolio of work: photographs of displays created for local merchants, class projects, or internships in visual merchandising. Most visual merchandisers have experience in drafting, allowing them to sketch concepts before executing them.

▶ **Personal characteristics:** The successful visual merchandiser requires a breadth of skills and knowledge: an understanding of fashion marketing and merchandising; an eye for color, line, balance, and proportion; a theatrical esthetic sense; a strong sense of fashion; the ability to develop and follow time and budget schedules; computer-aided design skills to develop schematics of displays; and the ability to rethink and reuse props, mannequins, and other display components. The effective visual merchandiser is not only self-motivated but also able to take directions to execute concepts and work as a member of a team. This position requires one to be able to work well under pressure.

Career opportunities in this field are increasing (Box 10.4). Because the retail industry understands how important visual image is to the consumer, retailers are focusing more funding in this area of promotion. Remuneration ranges from a starting wage of $8.00–$10.00 per hour for an assistant to an annual salary of $60,000–$80,000 for director positions. It is significant to note that the job of visual display is one that can be accomplished at the primary level of the fashion industry. There are a number of companies outside of the retail industry that hire visual merchandisers as part of their staffs. These include home furnishings and accessories manufacturers, beauty and cosmetics firms, apparel and accessories manufacturers, trend-forecasting firms, and fabric and notions representatives or suppliers. In addition to employment with a primary level firm, there are also opportunities to work as a freelance visual merchandiser in all levels of the fashion industry.

BOX 10.4 • SAMPLE CLASSIFIED ADVERTISEMENT: VISUAL MERCHANDISER

Industry: Apparel/Clothing/Fashion/Retail/ Stores

Title: Visual Merchandiser

Experience: Two to four years

Our company is the premier sporting goods store. We carry the best brands, but that's not all. We offer unparalleled customer service and dozens of value-added services, from rentals to repairs. With 17 specialty shops all under one roof, our full array of products and services will thrill any sports lover. The company seeks a visual merchandiser.

Job Responsibilities

- Maintain all merchandising within store, including business analysis, window changes, holiday installations, lighting, housekeeping, and any store decor-related maintenance or enhancement

- Assist with training clinics, executing all signage and stock placement for advertisements, and other selling activities
- Communicate with store supervisors and management regarding stock issues and merchandising directives
- Assist with new store openings and remodels

Qualification Requirements

Minimum of two years' visual merchandising experience with soft goods. Hard goods merchandising experience preferred. Understanding of visual concepts, square footage, and space relationships. Understanding of color and composition. Able to read architectural floor plans and draw grid map. Excellent communication skills. Computer skills required. Time-management skills, ability to multitask, and ability to meet multiple deadlines are required.

Career Challenges

People interested in pursuing a visual merchandising career often start at the first rung of the career ladder as a display associate, or **window trimmer**, paid a fairly low hourly wage. The job does not solely consist of selecting beautiful merchandise and designing attractive displays. It includes vacuuming the floors of the store windows, cleaning the glass, refurbishing props to stay within budget, and working evenings to install displays when customers are not in the store. After paying their dues in this position, display associates may move into assistant visual merchandising director positions and upward to the position of director.

PERSONAL SHOPPER

Imagine a retail apparel company paying you a high salary for shopping for its customers—pulling together wardrobes for their cruises, weddings, or new career positions. Perhaps you want to work in the home interior industry. Here again, retailers hire personal shoppers to help their customers select home furnishings, wall coverings, flooring, and home accessories. Yes, there is actually a fashion career in shopping—that of **personal shopper** (see Figure 10.6). The stereotype of the personal shopper is of a person who works part-time for the rich and famous; however, this career track is rapidly changing. Today's society places great demands on family life. More often than not, both parents are working full-time jobs, and their children are participating in extracurricular activities. This leaves little time for the parent/professional to shop, whether it is for food, clothing, or home furnishings. Personal shoppers of a retail operation free up time for the family.

They may freelance or work for a boutique, an upscale department store, or a specialty store. These personal shoppers assist customers with individualized attention and service. They maintain a log of sizes, preferred brands and styles, and special occasion dates for each client. Personal shoppers may assist customers in selecting an entire season's wardrobe or an outfit for a specific occasion, based on the needs of the customers, including their budgets, activities, and personal styles.

An additional impetus for the increase in personal shopper positions is the fact that we are an aging society. Today, senior citizens have more disposable income than ever before. Because they often choose to live in their own residences instead of assisted-living facilities, they welcome assistance with the constraints of shopping, which involves time and traveling. Personal shoppers can assist with buying groceries, clothing, and gift items for family members because it may be difficult for older customers to get around physically, and they may no longer have the ability or desire to drive a car. Yet another reason for the increase in the number of personal shoppers is the increase in the number of retailers' corporate clientele. Executives who work for large companies may hire

Figure 10.6. *Queer Eye for the Straight Guy*, a Bravo television series, features fashion expert Carson as personal shopper for "fashion-deficient" men.

personal shoppers to find the perfect gifts for important clients, holiday gift giving, special events, and conferences.

Qualifications

If you love to shop, understand a customer's needs, work well with people, and enjoy attention to detail, then the personal shopper position may be designed for you. Following are the requirements to secure this position:

- ▸ **Education:** A two- to four-year college degree in fashion merchandising, fashion design, retailing, or a similar field is preferred.
- ▸ **Experience:** Successful retail sales experience in a variety of departments is key to securing a personal shopper position. The top sales associates in a retail operation are usually recruited for these openings.
- ▸ **Personal characteristics:** Personal shoppers are effective communicators, active listeners, and strong record keepers. They are strong at networking, poised and tactful, and up-to-date on fashion trends.

This career path is wide open. The customer's preference for more individualized attention while shopping and more personal, or free, time has made this a career choice in demand. The salary range for a personal shopper is approximately from $24,000 to more than $100,000 annually. Most personal shoppers are paid on commission, a percent of the merchandise sold; some are paid a salary; and a few receive a base salary plus commission.

Career Challenges

The successful personal shopper needs to combine the skills of a top-notch salesperson with the abilities of a retail promoter. This person is required not only to sell the store's merchandise but also to sell the store as the place for the customer to make all fashion purchases. This skill enables the personal shopper to build a customer base of repeat patrons. It is challenging to maintain detailed customer records, contact customers when new merchandise arrives without appearing overly aggressive, and continually add new customers to the clientele list. Additionally, the successful personal shopper knows how to effectively collaborate with the retail buyer to secure the products the clientele desires.

SUMMARY

Promotion refers to advertising and publicity efforts that communicate the company's or product's attributes to the target consumers. The promotion director guides the marketing activities of a retail operation. Working with the promotion director, the publicity director solicits publicity, or free press, for the company. The special events coordinator develops and executes events that are fashion related, such as fashion shows, and those that are not fashion related, such as a company's participation in Habitat for Humanity. It is the advertising director who develops and implements the company's advertising strategy. Advertising differs from publicity in that it is paid-for, nonpersonal communication delivered through mass media. Working with the advertising director, the illustrator creates sketches used in print and electronic advertising. Some companies also employ in-house photographers for promotional activities; others also have positions for an art director and a website developer.

Promotion also occurs within the retail store. A store-planning director develops the layout that details fixture placement, lighting, dressing rooms, restrooms, windows, aisles, and cash and wrap areas of a store or department. Once the store layout is constructed, the visual merchandiser is responsible for the window installations, in-store displays, signage, fixtures, mannequins, and decorations that give a retail operation esthetic appeal and a distinct image. Many large retailers promote products through the assistance of personal shoppers who select merchandise to meet the needs of personal clients.

Promotion is successful when the customer is affected by the communication and then purchases merchandise from the retailer. The customer walks out of the store with a smile, shopping bag in hand, and a good feeling about both the purchase and the source of the purchase, the retailer.

KEY TERMS

advertising
advertising agency
advertising director
advocacy advertising
art director
brand advertising

classified advertising

equipment

illustrator

institutional advertisement

media form

personal shopper

photographer

press package (press kit)

press release (news release)

promotion director

publicity

publicity director

sales advertising

sales promotion

store-planning director

special event

special events coordinator

supplies

visual merchandising

visual merchandiser (visual merchandising director)

website developer

window trimmer

Discussion Questions

1. Using a print source, such as a newspaper or magazine, or the Internet, locate and copy an example of an institutional advertisement for a retail operation. Attach to the ad a one-page summary of the retailer's image the advertisement conveys. How does the image differentiate this retailer from its competitors?

2. Locate a print source, such as a newspaper or magazine, or the Internet that provides an example of publicity for a retail operation. Copy the publicity illustration and develop a one-page press release that could have been used to solicit the publicity among media sources.

3. Assume that you are the promotion director for an Internet retailer. How would you promote your company? Construct a list of promotional activities that you would implement to market your website.

4. Develop a list of special events that could be used to introduce a new brick-and-mortar home accessories store to your community. Include partnership promotions, externally funded events, and activities that would likely attract publicity.

5. Consider a variety of retailers and note those that excel in visual merchandising. Which visual elements are used to strengthen their company image? Provide examples of current visual merchandising trends implemented by these retailers.

CHAPTER 11

Merchandising for the Retailer

How simple is it to find a new pair of jeans to buy? All you have to do is go down to the nearest department store or specialty shop. You may even decide to order the jeans online at your favorite apparel website. Have you ever wondered how the dozens or even hundreds of blue jeans ended up at the retail store or website in the first place? Who decided which brands and styles of jeans the retailer would sell and which ones it would not? Chances are, a buyer indirectly influenced your wardrobe. The merchandise found in a fashion retail operation has been purchased either by the business owner, a buyer who is employed by the company, or a resident buyer who represents the retailer (Figure 11.1). In large operations, the buying tasks are performed by specialists who have acquired in-depth knowledge of the merchandising function of a specific department or a group of related departments. In small operations, the buying function may be one of many carried out by the company's owner.

As discussed previously, merchandising refers to all of the activities involved in the buying and selling of the retailer's products. The major responsibilities of merchandising personnel are to locate and purchase products, with the preferences of the consumer in mind, and then to sell these products at a profit. The selection of products available for sale in a fashion operation is commonly called its **inventory**, or *merchandise assortment*. Who are the people involved in selecting the merchandise assortment, and how do they do it?

In this chapter, merchandising positions for the retailer are explored. The career options that are discussed include general merchandising manager, divisional merchandise manager, buyer/fashion merchandiser, assistant buyer, planner, distribution manager/allocator, and merchandising executive trainee.

GENERAL MERCHANDISING MANAGER

A **general merchandising manager (GMM)** is the boss of the buyers' boss. The GMM leads and manages the buyers of all divisions in a retail operation. This key administrator is responsible for setting the overall strategy and merchandise direction of the retail operation. GMMs develop the buying and selling strategies that will, hopefully, maximize business performance and profitability. They ensure that pricing decisions, promotional strategies, and marketing activities support the financial objectives of the merchandising team. To accomplish this, they must understand not only the competitors' strengths, weaknesses, and strategies, but also the customers' demographics, wants, and needs.

GMMs set the merchandise direction to ensure a focused continuity on the selling floor. They work with the divisional merchandise managers and buyers to develop competitive merchandise assortments that appeal to customers at

Figure 11.1. A customer reviews the brands, sizes, and styles of jeans purchased for the specialty store by a buyer.

the right prices and at the right fashion level. They also assist the buying staff with securing the best merchandise exclusives, product launches, and deliveries available in the market. They collaborate on which manufacturers or designers, fashion items, and merchandise categories will be carried in depth by the retail organization.

GMMs manage, coach, and develop the buying staff, creating an environment that promotes the professional development of the divisional merchandise managers and buyers and enhancing morale among the entire buying team. While collaborating with the divisional merchandise managers in developing merchandise assortments that support the needs of the customers and the financial objectives of each merchandise division, GMMs

BOX 11.1 • SAMPLE CLASSIFIED ADVERTISEMENT: GENERAL MERCHANDISING MANAGER

Function: Senior Management/CEO/President
Industry: Retail
Locale: San Antonio, Texas

Job Responsibilites:

General Merchandising Manager (GMM)—Junior's Apparel

The general merchandise manager is a senior position with a private, regional, midsize retailer of junior apparel/shoes/accessories. Responsible for developing and managing strategy, assortment plans, vendor relations, retail pricing, merchandise plans, and promotional planning while achieving financial goals. Identifies, recruits, challenges, and develops buying staff.

Job Requirements:

Four-year degree, 25 percent travel, ten plus years' experience in apparel, and excellent established vendor relationships in the apparel industry. Negotiation skills.

Specialty store buying experience preferred.

Other:

Position reports directly to the president. Excellent benefits including life, medical, dental insurance; 529, 401(k), profit sharing plan; and a generous merchandise discount. Relocation assistance will be provided as needed.

are ultimately responsible for overseeing merchandise selection and procurement of goods by the buyers. Box 11.1 is a classified advertisement seeking to fill this position.

Qualifications

What does it take to be at the highest level of the merchandising career ladder? While it takes intelligence, perseverance, and high energy, the retail employer will expect the following educational background, experience, and personal characteristics as well:

▶ **Education:** A bachelor's degree in fashion merchandising, retailing, retail merchandising, business administration, or a related field is necessary. A master's degree in apparel merchandising or business administration may be required.

▶ **Experience:** A minimum of ten years of retail management, divisional merchandise management, or extensive buying experience in a full-line department store or specialty store chain is usually required for this key position. Experience in multilocation retail stores as a merchandiser or with multiple delivery systems (e.g., brick-and-mortar, Internet, and catalog) and product development is preferred.

▶ **Personal characteristics** Strong leadership, communication, and organizational skills are necessary. The ability to change priorities and work topics quickly is a needed personal quality. Being able to manage teams and relate to all levels of employees is important. Effective negotiation skills are critical for the successful GMM, as is being able to plan ahead and be an analytical problem solver.

The number of GMM positions is limited, as these are top leadership slots available in midsize and large retail operations. Annual salaries range from $100,000–$250,000 for GMMs in large retail firms. Some companies offer GMMs supplementary packages, such as bonuses or stock options, based on company sales-volume increases.

Career Challenges

As the leader of the merchandising staff, the GMM must understand and oversee all merchandising personnel and all merchandise classifications. It is an important job to be able to move quickly between buyers and their respective departments and be up-to-date on each of their areas. As a leader, the GMM is challenged to keep all merchandisers on the same path in terms of merchandise selection, price ranges, fashion trends, and similar variables. The GMM needs to know when to push or pull back buyers who are not meeting sales-volume goals or buying into the fashion trend statements that the retailer will feature.

DIVISIONAL MERCHANDISE MANAGER

Once you have mastered the buying side of the fashion world as a fashion merchandiser, you may be ready for advancement. Before becoming a GMM, the next step up the career ladder for a buyer is to the divisional merchandise manager position. A **divisional merchandise manager (DMM)** works under the GMM and provides leadership for the buying staff of a division, or a related group of departments, such as men's wear, women's wear, or home furnishings. DMMs coordinate teamwork among the buyers and delegate responsibilities to the buyers, assistant buyers, and planners. They collaborate with the buyers on future purchases, marketing and promotional efforts, merchandise expenditures, and inventory management. The main objective of DMMs is to keep profits up and losses to a minimum by maximizing sales. They also study the fashion industry through shopping the competition, forecasting trends, attending markets, and working with buyers on the right fashion directions for the upcoming season. Box 11.2 is a classified advertisement seeking a DMM.

In general, DMMs oversee the buyers' merchandise selections and procurement for a particular segment of the business. Specifically, their job responsibilities include the following:

BOX 11.2 • SAMPLE CLASSIFIED ADVERTISEMENT: DIVISIONAL MERCHANDISING MANAGER

Direct report to our merchandising director; you are responsible for the merchandising activities for assigned product lines, managing product integrity, and ensuring compliance with product standards.

Key Responsibilities

- Develop good sourcing and production strategy that aligns with business requirement and departmental goals and objectives
- Responsible for overall product development and production activities
- In charge of all Far East order allocation for assigned product lines
- Provide technical and costing advice to customer at products engineering stage
- Vendor management: responsible for new vendor sourcing, vendor development, and building up a 360-degree view of

vendors by gathering soft and hard data around business to simplify ways of working, reduce costs, and increase efficiency
- Supervise product development and product managers while providing direction and drive for business results

Job Requirements

- University degree with eight to 10 years' experience with fast-growing fashion brands
- Business acumen and good understanding of product development and manufacturing process for both knits and wovens
- Good interpersonal skills and management sense
- Product passionate
- True leader and team player

- ▶ Developing merchandise strategies in support of the total company
- ▶ Managing, coaching, and developing the buying staff
- ▶ Fostering an environment that promotes personal development of buyers and their businesses, resulting in high morale among the entire divisional buying team
- ▶ Personally setting the example for development of associate and assistant buyers
- ▶ Setting the overall strategy and merchandise direction for the division
- ▶ Directing buyers to develop assortments that support the needs of the customer and the financial objectives of the merchandise division
- ▶ Ensuring that pricing, promotional strategies, and marketing support the financial objectives of the merchandise division
- ▶ Working with the planning organization to develop by-store assortment plans that support the overall plan for in-stock positioning of key merchandise categories, selected trends, items, and vendors
- ▶ Working with the buyers to strengthen market relationships and knowledge of market trends
- ▶ Understanding competitors' strengths, weaknesses, and strategies
- ▶ Facilitating and promoting timely communication and cooperation between stores, merchandising functions, and resources

Qualifications

Are you looking for a leadership role in the buying division? What educational background, work experience, and personal characteristics combine to make the best candidate for this position? A list of the qualifications for a top-notch DMM follows.

- ▶ **Education:** A bachelor's degree in fashion merchandising, retailing, retail merchandising, or a related field is necessary. A minor or elective course work in business administration and fashion design is a plus. A master's degree in apparel merchandising or business administration may be required.
- ▶ **Experience:** A minimum of five to 10 years of retail management or buying experience in full-line department stores or specialty store chains is usually required for this key administrative position. Experience in merchandising for multilocation retail stores or in trend forecasting and product development is preferred. The successful DMM will advance to the position of GMM.

▶ **Personal characteristics:** Strong leadership and organizational skills, as well as the ability to adapt to quickly changing priorities, are needed personal qualities. Excellent communication skills, the ability to work well with all levels of management, and effective negotiation skills are critical characteristics of successful DMMs. They should be articulate and enthusiastic, and they must be analytical thinkers and effective problem solvers, particularly in mathematical applications.

Advancement into this career level is good with broad, executive experience and the right credentials. On average, divisional merchandise managers can earn from $80,000 to over $150,000 annually.

Career Challenges

The divisional merchandise manager faces many of the same challenges as the GMM. Leading a group of diverse buyers working with a wide range of merchandise classifications requires a great deal of multitasking and prioritizing. The DMM is often held accountable for the accuracy of the numbers the buyers submit, such as planned sales and inventories. This executive must specialize in a variety of areas—fashion, merchandising mathematics, vendor negotiations, and personnel management. All of these areas are demanding the time and attention of the DMM, who must decide how much time to focus on each and when.

BUYER OR FASHION MERCHANDISER

Are you someone who enjoys the thrill of the shopping hunt? Do you enjoy reading trend forecasts and being involved in product development? Are attending markets and purchasing the newest trends to sell on the retail floor for you? Then you may want to pursue a career as a buyer/fashion merchandiser. **Buyers**, or **fashion merchandisers,** are typically responsible for all of the product purchases for a company or particular department of a company within a certain budget. Buyers monitor the fashion trends and determine which seasonal items their customers will buy. They search for the items (often traveling to do so) that best fit the seasonal theme and their customers' preferences, locate suppliers, and negotiate prices, shipping, and discounts. They sometimes work with other departments in the retail operation on advertising and product placement. The ultimate goal of a buyer is to recognize trends that fit with the target market in terms of taste and price, procure merchandise that reflects these trends, and translate them into a profitable business plan for the retailer. Buyers select and purchase products from designers, manufacturers, or wholesalers for retail sale to their customers. They use their fashion sense, knowledge of trends, and understanding of their target customers' desires to create desirable merchandise assortments for their retail stores (Figure 11.2).

Figure 11.2. A buyer selects merchandise from a showroom.

Due to the length of time it takes for a designer or manufacturer to fill orders, buyers often make their purchases three to six months in advance or longer if they are high-fashion goods. Buyers must be effective at budgeting and planning their assortments so that a good selection of products is always available to the consumer. Buyers for larger retail operations usually specialize in a merchandise classification, such as men's tailored apparel or home tabletop fashions.

A fashion merchandiser may work for a specialty chain (e.g., Gap, The Limited, or Wet Seal), a department store (e.g., Nordstom's, Macy's, or Saks Fifth Avenue), or a privately owned store or boutique. A fashion merchandiser also does extensive research on the department's or store's customers, trying to predict what the customers will want to buy for the upcoming season. To get started, a buyer will develop a buying plan, usually six months to one year before the merchandise can be purchased by customers. The **buying plan**, or *six-month plan*, is a financial plan that takes into account past and projected sales, inventory, markups and markdowns by department, and profit, or **gross margin**. After developing the buying plan, the buyer will track and analyze market trends, calculate how much will be spent on new products, and then go to marts and meet with manufacturers to preview apparel being produced. Once the manufacturers' lines are reviewed, the buyer will place orders for merchandise to arrive in the future, from one month for reorders to as much as one year in advance for new merchandise.

Being a fashion merchandiser or buyer is like being a product developer with a twist. Instead of reinventing the wheel every season, the buyer takes the retailer's best sellers from the previous season or year and finds the item with slight changes. The buyer may locate an item that was a best-seller with an updated color or new styling detail. The result is a new item with a good sales history for the upcoming selling season.

Figure 11.3. Saks Fifth Avenue buyer June Haine and designer Victor Alfera assess the line.

A fashion merchandiser also makes decisions on new, fashion-forward merchandise. The buyer always wants fresh, trendy looks to welcome customers into the department. This career path, however, is not all about shopping. The fashion merchandiser is accountable for the bottom line. The company wants to know whether the merchandise selected for customers to buy has made a profit. Fashion merchandisers are responsible for the financials of their departments and the resulting profit or loss. It is a daily task for fashion merchandisers to track the sales of merchandise and decide whether items need to be reordered or put on sale. They also spend time talking with vendors and negotiating the best wholesale prices so that higher profits can be achieved. Since most fashion merchandisers have worked their way through the ranks, they also know how important it is to communicate with the department and store managers and solicit feedback about what customers are seeking, buying, and rejecting, as in Figure 11.3. A career as fashion merchandiser is a very exciting and rewarding one for a high-energy person. During daily tasks, one can be in the moment, looking at today's sales, and then receive a phone call about next season's merchandise and have to predict the future.

The most important task performed by the buyer is merchandise selection. This responsibility encompasses determining which goods are needed, calculating the size of purchases and from which vendors the goods should be bought, recognizing when merchandise should be ordered for timely delivery, and negotiating the prices and terms of a sale. From a planning perspective, the buyer projects sales and inventory levels by month for each department and, subsequently, determines the amount of funding to be spent on inventory. Another part of the planning process is determining merchandise assortments in terms of color, size, and style. The amount of money allocated for new merchandise purchases each month is referred to as **open-to-buy**. With open-to-buy as the lead factor, the buyer determines which lines will be carried in large quantities and which ones will be stocked in smaller quantities. Those lines of manufacturers featured as the greatest proportion of inventory are called **key vendors**. Lines carried in smaller quantities are referred to as **secondary vendors.**

Buyers have a great number of responsibilities in addition to locating the vendors, selecting and purchasing the right amount of the right merchandise, and setting prices on the merchandise. They also assign floor space for items or lines, select specific merchandise for visual displays and advertisements, and manage or collaborate with personnel in various areas of the business, such as sales, receiving, advertising, and visual merchandising. For example, a buyer may hold training seminars to educate sales staff on the newest trends and product lines. In multiunit retail operations, the buyer advises store personnel on how many units of a product should be transferred to one branch store or another. With the advertising department, the buyer determines marketing plans and promotional calendars for each month. Collaborating with the visual merchandising department, the buyer develops visual presentation guidelines for the stores to support seasonal strategies. For example, the buyer may meet with the director of visual merchandising to discuss color trends, specific manufacturers' lines, and key fashion items that should be featured in windows and interior displays to give the retail operation a strong, fashion-forward look and, ultimately, sell products. Box 11.3 is a resume of a buyer for Hall's in Kansas City, Missouri.

Qualifications

Do you love to travel, enjoy searching for a specific item, and have proficient mathematical and analytical skills? You may consider the career path of buyer. What are the education and work experiences you will need to secure a position in this field? Which personal characteristics are significant to the success of a buyer? The answers to these questions are as follows.

- ▸ **Education:** A bachelor's degree in fashion merchandising, retailing, retail merchandising, or a related field is required. A minor or additional course work in business administration and fashion design is very helpful.
- ▸ **Experience:** Two to five years of work in the apparel industry is required for an assistant buyer, including retail or sales experience. Retail sales experience is very helpful because understanding customer buying behavior is a key part of being a successful buyer. The common step into a buyer position is from assistant buyer. To move up the career ladder, buyers gain experience buying for a variety of departments, usually moving from one department to another of higher sales volume.
- ▸ **Personal characteristics:** Successful buyers love fashion and have knowledge of fashion history and trends, as well as an understanding of the fashion industry as a whole. They have good analytical, mathematical, and computer skills (e.g., Microsoft Excel software), particularly in budgeting, planning, and inventory management. Successful buyers are good negotiators, possess

BOX 11.3 · SAMPLE RESUME OF A FASHION BUYER

JENNIFER M. SMITH
1111 State Line Boulevard
Kansas City, Kansas 66103
913.555.1215
JSmith@gmail.com

Career Experience

Footwear and Hosiery Buyer *(2003-2007)*
Halls, Kansas City, Missouri

- Responsible for buying junior, bridge, and designer footwear
- Increased designer shoe sales by 29 percent
- Managed extensive vendor structure that included 94 ongoing vendors, such as Prada, Rossi Moda, Robert Clerferie, Donald J Pliner, Schwartz and Benjamin, Bennett Footwear, and Aerosoles
- Increased gross margin and overall sales annually
- Traveled for buying trips seven times a year, including New York, Las Vegas, Los Angeles, and Dallas
- Toured footwear factories in such locations as Milan and Florence
- Oversaw billboard advertising, Internet layouts, and organization of seasonal fashion shows
- Managed and trained assistant buyers

Footwear Catalog Creator *(2002-2003)*

- Produced seasonal catalogs four times annually
- Increased sales 60 percent with each catalog
- Selected product mix, directed page layout, and initiated first classification catalog in store history
- Raised all cooperative advertising monies to fund catalogs from Stuart Weitzman, Rossi Moda, Etro, Vera Wang, Schwartz and Benjamin, and others

Department Manager, *Salon Footwear and Hosiery at Halls Plaza (2001-2002)*

- Responsible for sales, merchandising, and maintaining inventory; hiring, training, and scheduling sales associates
- Increased annual sales 30 percent
- Member of Quarter Million Dollar Club for individual sales volume

Assistant Department Manager, *Ladies Shoes at Halls Crown Center (2000-2001)*
Buyer/Assistant Manager/Intern
Vinones, Kansas City, Missouri (1999-2000)

- Interned during summer of junior year in college
- Promoted to assistant manager after graduation
- Promoted to buyer following one year as assistant manager

Education
Bachelor of Science in Fashion Merchandising (2000)
Cumulative Grade Point Average: 3.4/4.0 scale
Fashion University of Design and Merchandising, San Diego, California

Additional Information
Computer skills in STS Merchandising, Microsoft Excel, and Word
Member of Fashion Group International, Inc. (2003 to present)
Board of Directors (2006–07), Co-chair for Career Day (2005)
United Way Campaign (2004) Exceeded Hallmark's goal by 15 percent
References available upon request

excellent communication and organizational skills, are detail-oriented, and are able to deal well with deadlines and stress.

The salary range for a buyer is from $40,000–$100,000 annually. Entry-level pay ranges from $40,000–$50,000, while experienced buyers earn around $60,000–$70,000 a year. Top-level salaries range from $80,000–$100,000 annually. With bonus options, a salary can easily exceed $100,000. The outlook for career opportunities in buying is very good to excellent. The number of new buyer positions available is expected to remain stable, and existing positions will become available because of internal promotions or transitions. One can grow on the job by being promoted to the buyer's position in a larger department with greater sales volume. Prospects for the advancement of buyers are also good.

Career Challenges

There are a good number of buyer positions available in the fashion industry; however, buyers excel by showing maintained profitability and growth within their departments and making good buying decisions for their particular target markets (Figure 11.4). Because the numbers tell the story, buyers are under pressure to reach or surpass sales-volume goals while

Figure 11.4. A career in buying requires knowledge of the customer and good mathematical skills, particularly in planning inventories and making sales projections.

maintaining the planned inventory levels—every single month. If a line does not sell, the buyer is expected to negotiate with the vendor for returns, exchanges, or a reduced price to cover the cost of markdowns. Items planned for advertising can be a source of stress if they are not delivered as planned. The buyer has a multitude to tasks to juggle, and all of them require a high attention to detail and quick turnarounds.

ASSISTANT BUYER

An **assistant buyer** works directly for the buyer of a department or group of related departments. Assistant buyers primarily work with the six-month plan, open-to-buy, and inventory, taking cues from buyers. In some companies, they will accompany buyers to markets. They often work hands-on with the merchandise assortment, transferring items from one retail location to another as needed, and placing special orders. In most companies, the assistant buyer is in training for a buying position in the future.

Qualifications

Following are the education and work experience requirements for assistant buyers, as well as personal characteristics:

- ▶ **Education:** A bachelor's degree in fashion merchandising, retailing, retail merchandising, or a related field is usually required. Some companies will accept an associate's degree in these disciplines. Additional course work in business administration and fashion design is very helpful.
- ▶ **Experience:** Two to three years of apparel industry experience, including retail or sales experience, is required. Experience in accounting and budgeting is extremely helpful. Some companies have an executive training program to prepare entry-level employees for a merchandising career, often beginning as an assistant buyer.
- ▶ **Personal characteristics:** Assistant buyers understand the fashion of today and yesterday—its history and current trends. To move up the career ladder, they must have both a sense of what is fashionable and of who the customer is. Additionally, they should have knowledge of retailing and sales and strong analytical, mathematical, and computer skills (e.g., Microsoft Excel software), as their responsibilities include extensive work in budgeting, planning, and

inventory management. Assistant buyers who are self-directed and motivated will advance quickly. Effective communication and organizational skills, attention to detail, an eye for accuracy, and the ability to work well under pressure are significant attributes.

An assistant buyer in the Midwest is likely to earn between $38,000 and $42,000 annually. College graduates who begin at the assistant buyer level and have the right skills, personal qualities, and ambition have a good chance of becoming full-fledged buyers within three to five years.

Career Challenges

Many assistant buyers describe their job responsibilities as "doing what the buyer does not want to do." The key word in the job title is *assistant*, as this person is employed to help the buyer accomplish all merchandising tasks. Some buyers believe it is a part of their responsibilities to educate assistant buyers on all it takes to become a buyer; others do not. Some buyers do not want to retrain a new assistant and, consequently, prefer to keep their assistant buyers in this position. It can be a challenge for the assistant buyer to learn all of the ropes of merchandising and earn the support of the buyer to move into a buying position, but it can be accomplished. Anticipating what needs to be done and doing it well and independently are keys to succeeding in this position.

PLANNER

In large companies, a **planner** works in collaboration with a buyer to develop sales forecasts, inventory plans, and spending budgets for merchandise to minimize markdowns and achieve the retailer's sales and profit objectives. Using past sales data and sales projections based on fashion trends, planners construct merchandise assortments for specific departments. The merchandise assortment plan can include sizes, colors, styles, price ranges, and classifications. For example, a planner in a junior sportswear department may construct a chart, referred to as a **planning module**, for top-to-bottom ratios. In this planning module, the planner will project how many blouses, T-shirts, and tank tops to purchase and how many pants, shorts, or skirts need to be purchased for a given season. Today's junior customer, for instance, buys two to four times as many tops as she does bottoms. The merchandise assortment needs to reflect this proportion to be profitable. Using the planning module, planners recommend product flow (e.g., tanks, tees, and long-sleeved shirts) by department and by month or season. They also project markdown dollar budgets by month or season, based on actual markdowns during prior seasons, and assist buyers in determining how much money will be available to spend on new merchandise by providing seasonal buying budgets and monthly open-to-buy dollars by department and by season.

In addition to planning at the start of a season, planners in multiunit retail firms review sales and stock performance by retail location as it compares to plans. They also ensure that key vendor plans are in place and that there is adequate inventory for the sales of major lines. Throughout each season, the planner coordinates communication to and from stores with regard to merchandise performance and sales plans. A department manager in the retail store may, for example, contact a planner for additional types of items that have sold out in the store. The planner will transfer the preferred merchandise into this store from a branch store that has not sold the items as well. Box 11.4 is a classified advertisement for a planner.

In partnership with the buying staff, the planner's main goal is to accurately anticipate and control inventories at the retail locations to maximize sales, inventory, and profit. The planner works to keep all store locations in stock of key items by directing the distribution of goods through reorders and transfers of merchandise. If you enjoy working with numbers, are accurate, and want to move into buying, the position of planner is a great place to begin.

Qualifications

A listing of the educational background, experience, and personal characteristics needed for the job of merchandise planner follows.

BOX 11.4 • SAMPLE CLASSIFIED ADVERTISEMENT: PLANNER

Planner

Ya-Ya Brand Inc. is looking for a dedicated, driven individual to work in Los Angeles and/or New York offices. Position responsibilities include product and category reporting and analysis and sales tracking, as well as product assortment planning and merchandising with an emphasis on department stores. Candidate must have extensive experience as a sales analyst, merchandiser/planner, or allocator with a minimum of five to seven years of experience. Experience with visual merchandising is a plus.

- **Education:** A bachelor's degree in fashion merchandising, retailing, accounting, finance, or a related field is a prerequisite. Some companies hire candidates who have completed a two-year associate's degree in one of these fields for the position of assistant planner.
- **Experience:** Gaining retail sales experience is an excellent way for the future planner to start. The person who understands the customer's desires as they pertain to sales and inventory is a step ahead of job candidates without this work experience.
- **Personal characteristics:** Planners must be detail oriented with strong analytical skills. They must be quick, accurate, and able to work with advanced spreadsheet applications (e.g., Microsoft Excel software). Effective interpersonal and communication skills are important in this position, as is the ability to work well with all levels of employees of the organization.

Some larger retail organizations offer the position of planning manager. A **planning manager** provides leadership, direction, and support at the merchandise-division level to plan, distribute, and monitor inventory appropriately within the company's various retail locations to maximize sales. The planning manager supervises planners and partners with the DMM in the financial planning process.

A planning manager working in Ohio earns an average annual salary of $62,000. Planners in this geographic area earn approximately $44,000 annually, while assistant planners receive an annual salary between $32,000 and $38,000.

Career Challenges

The planner is a number cruncher, and this may be a challenging job for the fashion graduate entering the merchandising field. While planner is an excellent entry-level position for the future assistant buyer or buyer, it can be a tough tour of duty for those who are interested in working with the actual merchandise. The important thing to remember is that those numbers represent the merchandise, and there is much to be learned in the planner's position. Accuracy is a critical part of this job, as one decimal point off can equal thousands of the company's dollars.

DISTRIBUTION MANAGER/ALLOCATOR

Have you ever thought about how merchandise gets to the retail floor for customers to purchase? A **distribution manager**, or **allocator**, is responsible for planning and managing merchandise deliveries received from vendors, as ordered by buyers, to the retail locations. In some companies, this position is referred to as *replenishment analyst*. The merchandise is held in a central distribution warehouse to be allotted to the right store, at the right time, and in the right quantities to meet customer demands and maximize sales for the retail stores. Figure 11.5 depicts an allocator assessing inventory of merchandise prior to distribution. Distribution managers oversee merchandise receipts from manufacturers, shipments to the retail stores from the distribution center, and shipments from one store to another via the distribution center. They arrange for the transportation of merchandise to the retail outlet locations and may work for catalog and Internet distribution centers where they are responsible for keeping items in stock in the warehouse. Their main job is to be certain that merchandise is available when a customer orders an item over the phone, by mail, or via the Internet. Distribution managers have some of the responsibilities of buyers. They must study sales and inventory reports and then analyze the needs of each individual retail store to determine the correct quantities to distribute to the stores.

Qualifications

If you are detail oriented and organized, and enjoy working with merchandise and numbers (while not on a sales floor), this career path may be ideal for you, if you meet the following criteria:

Figure 11.5. An allocator tracks merchandise in a central distribution warehouse.

▸ **Education:** A bachelor's degree in fashion merchandising, retailing, business administration, or a related field is usually required. Some firms hire employees with associate degrees in these fields.

▸ **Experience:** One of the most important backgrounds for the distribution manager may be surprising. It is retail experience. Working on the sales floor, observing the flow of merchandise, and getting to know the customer provide a future distribution manager with a solid foundation for this career. An internship in a distribution department is an ideal door-opener. Merchandising experience, such as being an assistant buyer, is another way of going into distribution management.

▸ **Personal characteristics:** Good problem-solving skills, detail and deadline orientation, the ability to coordinate scheduling, and strong math skills are important personal characteristics for distribution managers. Effective communication skills are important as well.

Opportunities for distribution manager positions can be found throughout the industry with major retailers of all kinds. Salaries range from $28,000 (entry-level) to $60,000 (mid-level) a year. For example, a distribution manager working in New York City earns an average annual salary of $61,000. Half of those in this position currently earn between $43,000 and $69,000 annually.

Career Challenges

If merchandise is not on the selling floor, then it will not sell. A distribution manager, or allocator, is under pressure to push products out of the distribution warehouse to the correct retail store quickly and in the right amounts, after it is tagged correctly. During pre-holiday times, when there are huge amounts of merchandise receipts and many buyers calling to check on the distribution of their orders, this is particularly challenging. Speed, organization, and accuracy must go hand in hand in this career track.

MERCHANDISING TRAINEE

One avenue college graduates often choose to move into a merchandising career track is through an executive training program. Many retailers, particularly larger ones, offer these programs, which help graduates work their way up to buying positions. For example, the executive training programs at Neiman Marcus and Bloomingdale's prepare participants for jobs as assistant buyers and, ultimately, buyers for the company.

A **merchandising**, or *merchant*, **executive training program** is designed to prepare new hires, former interns, college recruits, or current employees who have shown skills in merchandising for their first assignments as assistant buyers. Through on-the-job and classroom training, trainees gain the necessary skills needed for analyzing financial data, planning assortment selections, and developing vendor relationships to achieve business goals. The executive training program is a structured development program of classes, guest speakers, and projects. The trainee must show active participation and successfully complete all of the training assignments within the time frame of the program, which can range from six weeks to twelve months. Merchandising trainees may earn an average of $28,000–$32,000 per year.

Qualifications

What do you need to know to become a merchandising trainee?

- ▶ **Education:** A bachelor's degree in fashion merchandising, retail merchandising, retailing, business administration, or a related field is often required.
- ▶ **Experience:** A retail sales position and, possibly, an internship with a retail organization are work experiences that make a potential merchandising executive trainee appealing to a retailer. Many companies require trainee candidates to complete tests that reveal proficiency in the areas of mathematics, case study analysis, writing, and presentation skills.
- ▶ **Personal characteristics:** Merchandising trainees exhibit strong analytical abilities, effective computer skills, organizational skills, and excellent communication skills—written, oral, and visual. Effective time management, flexibility, and the ability to react quickly and calmly to change are also important attributes. Successful merchandise trainees are self-motivated, self-directed, and are able to work effectively as part of a team.

Career Challenges

There are very few career disadvantages when starting as a merchandising trainee with a major company. You select the company of your choice, secure the trainee position, and the company prepares you for an entry-level executive position. These training programs are often referred as a form of "graduate education without the price tag." While you do not earn college credits or pay tuition, you do receive additional education that can be applied directly to the company. Frequently, the tough part is making the cut or securing the position. Company recruiters often interview a thousand candidates for less than one hundred trainee openings. In some firms, trainees complete a general company training program and then are assigned to either the merchandising or management track, based on their performance in the program. For those trainees who have their hearts set on one track or the other, this may be a difficult assignment if it does not match their preference.

SUMMARY

Merchandising encompasses all of the activities involved in the buying and selling of a retailer's products. The major responsibilities of merchandising personnel are to locate and purchase products, with the preferences of the consumer in mind, and then sell these products at a profit. Merchandising career opportunities include the following positions: general merchandising manager; divisional merchandise manager; buyer/fashion merchandiser; assistant buyer; planner; distribution manager; or allocator, and merchandising trainee.

General merchandising managers (GMM) lead and manage the buyers of all divisions in the retail operation. They are the key administrators responsible for setting the overall strategy and merchandise direction of their retail operations. The divisional merchandise manager (DMM) works under the GMM and provides leadership for the buying staff of a division or a related group of departments. Buyers, or fashion merchandisers, are typically responsible for all of the product purchases for a company or particular segment of the company within a certain budget. Buyers monitor fashion trends and determine which seasonal items their customers will purchase. They search for the items at trade marts that best fit the seasonal theme and their customers' preferences and negotiate prices, shipping, and discounts. They then monitor sales and inventory, adjusting the prices of merchandise and the amount of money they spend on new items accordingly. The assistant buyer works directly for the buyer of a department or group of related departments (e.g., handbags, jewelry, and scarves). The assistant buyer helps the buyer with updating the six-month plan, open-to-buy, and inventory. The planner works in collaboration with the buyer and assistant buyer to develop sales forecasts, inventory plans, and spending budgets for merchandise to achieve sales and profit objectives. The distribution manager, or allocator, is responsible for planning and managing the deliveries of goods received from the vendors, as ordered by the buyers, to retail locations. A merchandising, or merchant, executive training program is designed to prepare new hires, former interns, college recruits, or current employees who have shown skills in merchandising for their first assignment in the merchandising division of the retail operation. There are a number of career tracks in merchandising for the retailer, and they have several challenges in common—locating products that appeal to the customer, are priced right, arrive at the right place when needed, and sell!

KEY TERMS

assistant buyer

buyer (fashion merchandiser)

buying plan (six-month plan)

distribution manager (allocator)

divisional merchandise manager (DMM)

general merchandising manager (GMM)

gross margin

inventory (merchandise assortment)

key vendor

merchandising

merchandising (merchant) executive training program

open-to-buy

planner

planning manager

planning module

secondary vendor

Discussion Questions

1. Consider a major department store and construct a diagram separating the departments into divisions that would be headed by three separate divisional merchandise managers. Bracket together the departments that would be covered by an individual buyer.

2. Visit a men's wear store or department in a large retail operation to study how the merchandise may be segmented into classifications. Develop the categories for

the merchandise plan of a men's sportswear department, including merchandise classifications, styles, sizes, colors, and price ranges.

3. What will the buyer of the future need to know? Think ahead to about a decade from now. What will customer trends be, and how will they influence the requirements and knowledge of a fashion merchandiser?

4. Assume that you are the buyer of a large home accessories department. How will you divide the responsibilities of the planner and the assistant buyer assigned to your department? Compare and contrast the duties of each.

CHAPTER 12

Management for the Retailer

You may envision yourself running a specialty store, an exclusive boutique, or a large department store, if you are a person who loves the retail experience. You may be the individual who recognizes that a corporate office is not the place for you. You may be someone who thrives in a retail environment. Do you crave the excitement of the hustle and bustle of holiday shopping, assisting customers with purchases, motivating sales associates, and rearranging the retail floor for new merchandise? If this describes you, a career in retail management may be your path to profit and pleasure. **Management** refers to the organizing and controlling of the affairs of a business or a particular sector of a business. This chapter focuses on management careers in the retail sector of the fashion industry, such as store manager for an apparel firm, customer service manager of an Internet fashion operation, or assistant store manager of a home furnishings retail outlet. There are a number of career tracks in retail management, including the following positions: regional or district manager; operations manager; retail store manager; manager-in-training (MIT); assistant and associate store manager; department manager; security manager; customer service manager; and retail operation owner.

REGIONAL OR DISTRICT MANAGER

Regional, or **district, managers** are responsible for directing the retail stores of a particular company that are located in a particular area of the United States or abroad.

They are responsible for the smooth running of the operation and for the success of employees in the retail outlets located within a specific geographical area, often referred to as a *region* or *territory*. They are the liaisons between the corporate office and the retail store, and they collaborate with store managers within the region by making store visits, communicating through e-mail or telephone, or facilitating conferences, in person or electronically. During these meetings, store managers share their current sales, markdowns, and returns; point out items that are selling well; and identify programs or incentives for employees that are increasing sales or traffic flow into the store. If sales are declining, regional managers work with store managers to stimulate sales by implementing in-store promotions or working with the retail organization's headquarters on promotional campaigns. The four main goals of the regional store manager are to maximize sales at a profit, motivate store employees, share successes from one store with another, and communicate with the corporate office.

Qualifications

If regional store management is your career choice, there are a number of educational goals, work experiences, and personal characteristics that will help you get a foot in the door.

- ▸ **Education:** A bachelor's degree in fashion merchandising, fashion retailing, business administration, retailing, management, or a related field is a requirement.
- ▸ **Experience:** Retail sales and store management experience are mandatory work experiences. Buying, advertising, visual merchandising, human resource development, marketing, inventory control, and customer service knowledge are areas of experience for which a regional manager candidate will receive preference.
- ▸ **Personal characteristics:** Strong communication and leadership skills are required. The ability to speak effectively before groups of customers or employees of the organization is important. Business-accounting skills, human resources knowledge, and an understanding of retail laws are important. Organization, cognitive thinking, and time management are personal skills that support the regional manager's tasks in coordinating stores in a wide geographical area.

The regional manager usually begins with an annual salary of $60,000 and, with a few years of success, can earn much more than $100,000 annually. In large corporations, the regional manager may earn a bonus or commission based on increases in sales in addition to the salary.

Career Challenges

Because they are responsible for a number of retail locations, regional managers' work can be stressful but very rewarding. Regional managers are responsible for not just one store but rather a significant number of retail units in the operation. This means they oversee all of the employees who take care of the customers shopping in each store. It takes a person with abundant fashion and retail knowledge, excellent communication skills, and business savvy to succeed in this career choice. Long hours and frequent travel are realities of the job.

OPERATIONS MANAGER

In major companies, there is an operations manager who reports to the regional manager or, in a very large company, the national director of stores. The **operations manager** works with other administrators in developing visual marketing strategies and plans for merchandising, training management and sales teams, and supervising stock replenishment and inventory controls. The primary objective of the operations manager is to develop and maintain effective sales and operational programs with a focus on superior customer service for all of the retail units in the company or in a region. For example, the operations manager may work to find a faster, less expensive way to move merchandise from the central distribution warehouse to store units scattered about a region. Developing a company-wide training program to help all employees improve customer service may be another task of the operations manager.

Qualifications

Here are the educational background, work experience, and personal characteristics needed to succeed in the position of operations manager.

- ▸ **Education:** A bachelor's degree in business administration, merchandising, operations management, retail management, retailing, or a related discipline is required.
- ▸ **Experience:** A minimum of five years' experience in the operations field is required. Operations managers must have experience in training, motivating, and developing company employees and be knowledgeable about budgets and forecasts. Experience in Microsoft Excel and Word is necessary.

▶ **Personal characteristics:** Excellent organization, communication, and leadership skills are necessary for this position, as are superior analytical and technical skills. Good decision-making and problem-solving abilities are required. The operations manager is expected to travel extensively to store unit locations.

The operations manager for a small company earns approximately $60,000–$80,000 annually. For operation managers of large companies, the annual salary is usually in excess of $100,000 per year. Some operations managers also receive bonuses that may be calculated as a percent of the dollar amount of operational savings or as a percent of sales-volume increases in the region or the company as a whole.

Career Challenges

The disadvantages for an operations manager are similar to those of the regional store manager. Being responsible for the operations and employee performance in a significant number of store units is a large workload. Extensive travel and long hours are common requirements for this position. The operations manager spends much time analyzing sales and inventory of stores and developing ways to save money and improve sales without compromising quality. This requires much attention to detail, strong analytical skills, and the ability to see the big picture that will result when changes are implemented.

RETAIL STORE MANAGER

A **retail store manager** oversees the activities of a retail store's operation, from sales transactions and advertising to special events and the store's people, the customers, and employees including assistant managers, department managers, sales associates, and other staff. The retail manager is responsible for implementing the firm's retail marketing and sales plans, while ensuring the efficient operation of sales, operations, and administration within the assigned retail locations (Figure 12.1). Store managers' primary responsibilities are overseeing sales promotions, placing merchandise on the sales floor, monitoring sales and inventory levels, managing personnel, and generating profits. They oversee the inventory, ensuring that the store has the right quality, type, and amount of merchandise available. They also make sure supplies are reordered on time.

Depending on the store's size, the store manager may be involved in some manner with all of the store's departments, from displays and advertising to merchandising

Figure 12.1. A retail store manager is responsible for all operations of a store.

and human resources. Store managers may have hundreds of employees or just a few sales associates to lead. Either way, they set a tone for the store and share a vision of success and expectations about customer service, promotions, and store goals with all employees. They work with a wide variety of individuals, from executives in the corporate office to the customer who has a complaint. The main objectives of the store manager include ensuring: the sales targets are reached and profits increased; customer service issues and complaints are successfully handled; health, safety, and security regulations are implemented; and strong employees are recruited, interviewed, trained, supervised, motivated, and retained. Following is a detailed listing of the supervisory and administrative responsibilities that the store manager of a large retail operation may have.

Supervisory Tasks

▶ Oversees employees engaged in selling, cleaning and rearranging merchandise, displaying, pricing, taking inventory, and maintaining operations records

▶ Ensures efficient staffing of employees through proper assignments of duties while respecting break periods, work hours, and vacations

▶ Ensures compliance with human resource regulations by implementing established benefits and record-keeping procedures

▶ Trains, supervises, advises, and monitors store employees. Encourages employee advancement if an employee's skills and the organizational structure allow it; may be called on for assistance in preparing or executing training sessions for employees on store policies, procedures, job duties, and customer service

▶ Plans and conducts regular sales meetings for staff to discuss latest sales techniques, new products, overall performance, and other topics the store manager believes will promote high team spirit and company pride

▶ Supervises department managers and sales associates, performs work of subordinates as needed, and assists in completing difficult sales

▶ Plans store layout of fixtures, merchandise, and displays with the regional manager, taking into account special and seasonal promotions as well as store safety and security measures

▶ Inspects merchandise to ensure it is correctly received, priced, and displayed

- Maintains all safety and security policies of the company, including locking and securing of the store at closing time, balancing receipts, and making cash deposits
- Communicates and upholds all company policies, rules, and regulations, while maintaining a productive and pleasant customer and employee environment; recognizes employees positively for achieving the same and initiates disciplinary action where needed
- Answers customer's complaints or inquiries and resolves customer's problems to restore and promote good public relations; makes decisions on returns, adjustments, refunds, customer checks, and customer service, as required
- Coordinates and supervises store housekeeping, maintenance, and repair
- Maintains physical inventory as required
- Assumes general responsibility for the inventory of the store falling at or below the company's shortage percent goal

Administrative Tasks
- Handles staff schedules, sales reports, inventory reports, and personnel reports
- Prepares each employee's appraisal reports and conducts evaluation meetings after input from regional manager and director of the HR department
- Coordinates the store's sales promotion activities and campaigns, in coordination with regional manager and according to established budgets
- Keeps abreast of developments in the retail sales area by studying relevant websites, trade journals, sales and inventory analyses, and all merchandising and sales materials; initiates suggestions for improvement of the business
- Coordinates merchandise and advertisements, and maintains the store's offerings
- Maintains a current knowledge of management principles and has the willingness and ability to make difficult decisions under pressure

Qualifications

Following are the educational goals, work experiences, and personal qualities that enhance one's opportunities to secure a store manager position:

- **Education:** A bachelor's degree in fashion merchandising, fashion retailing, business administration, management, retailing, or a related discipline is a requirement.

- **Experience:** Several years of retail sales and management experience are needed. Additional work experience in buying, advertising, store planning and visual merchandising, human resources management, marketing, inventory control, and customer service areas are helpful in securing prime positions.
- **Personal characteristics:** Store managers must be good team leaders who are self-motivated and adaptable and quick thinkers who are prepared to make and be accountable for decisions. They must enjoy a fast-moving, high-pressure environment. On an interpersonal level, store managers must be able to communicate clearly with a variety of people at all levels and be committed to the needs of the customer. They must understand relevant retailing and human resources laws, business accounting, and computer programs in word processing, spreadsheet development, and inventory control.

Salaries begin at $30,000 and rise to $100,000 annually for a large company. Some firms offer bonuses and commissions for store sales that exceed planned goals. Some store managers advance to the position of regional store manager, then national store director. Others move into related areas such as finance, human resources, or buying.

Career Challenges

Store managers should anticipate a lengthy work schedule, which includes weekends, nights, and holidays. Working six days a week is common. The work includes office work, but managers are expected to spend much of their time on the sales floor. The store manager is head of the day-to-day business in the store with the support of and responsibility to higher management. This means that the store manager must respond to the requests of the regional manager. The store manager who aspires to become a regional manager, the next step up the career ladder, should anticipate relocating a number of times to gain experience in various stores within the company. Moving from one location to another with little advance notice can be a difficult process for some people.

MANAGER-IN-TRAINING

A **manager-in-training (MIT)** is just that: an employee who is being trained to move into a management position. A number of large retail organizations offer a MIT program through which prospective management employees are trained for assistant manager or store manager positions within the company. In Chapter 11, the executive trainee program is examined. The main difference between an executive training program and a MIT program is that most companies train the MIT on-the-job in one of the branch store locations, rather than in a training facility at company headquarters.

Qualifications

Here are the qualifications often required for admittance into a manager-in-training program.

- **Education:** A bachelor's degree in fashion merchandising, fashion retailing, business administration, management, retailing, or a related field is usually required.
- **Experience:** One to three years' experience as an assistant manager or top sales associate with a large retail firm is often required for this position. A college graduate can apply directly for placement in a MIT program, or a company employee may decide to apply for admission into the program.
- **Personal characteristics:** Excellent interpersonal skills that support a team environment are required. Effective oral and written communication skills are needed to work with a wide range of employees. Strong planning and organizational skills with a sense of priority for deadlines and attention to detail are necessary for the successful MIT. Most important, the MIT is dedicated to high levels of customer service and sales productivity.

Career Challenges

As with the executive training program, one of the toughest parts of the MIT position is securing the job. As many as one hundred candidates inside and outside of the retail operation may apply for as few as ten positions. Of those selected for the MIT openings, only a few are promoted to the position of manager. The job is challenging in that it is "trial by fire," learning how to do the job well while on-the-job. Long hours, which are often scheduled on weekends, holidays, and nights, are required for this job. The MIT is often on call and must be ready to go to work if the manager or another key employee is unavailable.

Figure 12.2. A manager and assistant manager working together to calculate inventory.

Assistant and Associate Store Manager

An **assistant store manager** helps the store manager in all of the daily responsibilities of operating a store successfully. The assistant manager takes direction from the store manager and works closely with all of the other departments in assuring the store's mission and financial goals are met. In some companies, assistant store managers have specified responsibilities, such as scheduling employees, supervising sales floor moves, and monitoring sales and inventory levels. In other companies, they may support store managers in all store management duties. Figure 12.2 shows a store manager and assistant store manager working together to assess inventory.

Some companies with large individual store units hire for a position that lies between the assistant store manager and the store manager. This position is called **associate store manager**. There are several prerequisites in education and experience for assistant or associate store managers, as follows:

- ▸ **Education:** A bachelor's degree in fashion merchandising, fashion retailing, business administration, management, retailing, or a related field is usually required.
- ▸ **Experience:** Retail sales experience, managerial experience, or in-house management training is usually required. Work experience in buying, advertising, human resources management, marketing, inventory control, and customer service make the job candidate more appealing to the employer.
- ▸ **Personal characteristics:** Effective interpersonal and communication skills are significant attributes for this position. Assistant store managers also have knowledge of business accounting, personnel, and marketing. They are detail oriented, have strong organizational skills, and are flexible. They must be able to adapt to constantly changing work schedules.

The salary potential for an assistant store manager ranges from $28,000–$65,000 annually, depending on the size of the retail operation and the skills and experience of the job candidate. Box 12.1 is a classified advertisement for an assistant manager.

BOX 12.1 • SAMPLE CLASSIFIED ADVERTISEMENT: ASSISTANT STORE MANAGER

Purpose and Scope

The assistant store manager will ensure a consistently memorable customer shopping experience for the men's department while generating meaningful revenue and positive operating profit for the store.

Responsibilities

- Responsible for sales and profit performance in store. Responsible for achieving store shrinkage goals and for the establishment and implementation of both new and existing loss prevention procedures.
- Work with the general manager to establish and achieve sales and margin goals, develop operating budgets, and monitor employee and store performance. Partner with visual merchandising team in regard to merchandise presentation.
- Responsible for training and supervision of store staff to maximize sales and profit performance

- Direct the execution of promotional strategies and programs, assuring that they support retail sales, marketing, and profit objectives
- Regularly visit relevant competition to maintain an awareness of store-performance issues and market trends

Job Requirements

- Four-year college degree
- Three years of retail management experience
- Strong business acumen and skill set that enables the management and development of staff.
- Strong communication and interpersonal skills.

We are an equal opportunity employer offering dynamic career opportunities with growth potential and a generous company discount.

DEPARTMENT MANAGER

A **department manager** oversees a specific area, or department, within a store. For example, a department manager may be responsible for men's clothing, junior sportswear, or women's accessories. Department managers coordinate the sales associates in their areas, assisting with employee hires, scheduling weekly work hours, handling employee and customer complaints, and monitoring the performance of employees. They schedule regular meetings with the store managers, assistant store managers, and other department managers. During these meetings, department managers report on weekly sales, discuss promotions, and talk about concerns or opportunities in their respective areas. They also stay in close contact with the buying office, as they relay employee and customer feedback on merchandise and advise buyers on reorders or possible promotions to help sell merchandise.

Department managers also maintain the sales floor by setting out new merchandise, adding signage for promotions, recording markdowns, and executing floor sets. Changing **floor sets** refers to moving fixtures and merchandise on the sales floor of the department to create a fresh look and to highlight new or undersold merchandise. Department managers work with sales associates in keeping the department neat and organized so that customers can easily find exactly what they are seeking.

Qualifications

What does it take to become a department manager? It is an excellent starting place for the college graduate. A list of qualifications follows:

- ▸ **Education:** A bachelor's degree in fashion merchandising, fashion retailing, an area of business administration, or a related degree is often required. Some companies accept an associate's degree in these disciplines.
- ▸ **Experience:** Successful retail sales experience is the top requirement for a department manager position. The sales associate who has gained experience in floor sets, personal shopping, exceptional customer service, and visual displays is well qualified for a promotion to department manager.
- ▸ **Personal characteristics:** The department manager is detail oriented, well organized, and an effective problem solver with good interpersonal skills. This position often demands a flexible work schedule, including weekends, nights, and holidays.

The salary potential for a department manager ranges from $20,000 to $45,000 annually.

Career Challenges

The department manager often works long hours for fairly low pay. There are a number of people to whom the department manager reports, including the assistant or associate store manager, store manager, and buyer. Each may have a different perspective on how to run the department. The department manager is challenged with satisfying a number of bosses who may have dissimilar priorities.

SECURITY MANAGER

Security in a retail operation affects the bottom line—profit. **Security** refers to safekeeping of merchandise in the store, as well as the safety of employees and customers. As inadequate lighting, unsafe equipment, and poorly placed fixtures can prove to be safety hazards for people in the store, this is an important focus for the security manager. Without a **security manager** overseeing the safekeeping of merchandise in the retail operation, theft would occur more often in fashion businesses. Currently, losses due to theft or accounting errors make up more than 3 percent of a retail operation's sales volume. The difference between the **physical inventory**, the merchandise actually in the retail operation, and the written inventory, also called the **book inventory**, is referred to as shrinkage or overage. **Shrinkage**, also called **shortage**, refers to losses: merchandise that is not accounted for when transferred, missing, or stolen. **Overage** refers to a higher dollar amount of products on the retail floor than was actually purchased and received. If there is an overage, then there are likely problems in accounting, such as not recording and deducting all transfers, markdowns, or sales transactions. The security manager collaborates with receiving, accounting, and management to be certain that accurate accounting procedures are in place and true losses are identified when the physical inventory is taken, usually biannually.

The security manager determines the equipment that will be used to deter theft, such as tags (Figure 12.3), security cameras, uniformed guards, or inconspicuous security, such as a security employee disguised as a shopper. These barriers help keep potential thieves from making the wrong decision. The security manager not only protects the inventory from outside theft, but also monitors against internal theft or pilferage. **Internal theft** refers to merchandise stolen by employees within the company. Employees may be required to have personal purchases processed through the cash terminal by a store manager, rather than on their own. They may be required to store

Figure 12.3. The security tag is a common theft deterrent provided by manufacturers for use by apparel retailers.

Figure 12.4. Beware of shoplifters! Customer service is often the best way to prevent theft.

their handbags and packages in lockers and use a clear bag on the sales floor. These techniques minimize the opportunity for employees to steal from the retail firm.

Additionally, security managers provide loss training for employees of the company. They hold seminars on how to spot a shoplifter, who to contact, and where to go for assistance when identifying a thief (Figure 12.4). Management employees are educated on opportunities for employee theft and how to minimize these. The security manager is part teacher, part detective, and part store planner when selecting security systems and assisting with creating store layouts that deter theft.

Qualifications

If this sounds like a career path for you, what do you need to know and do? Following is a list of qualifications for a security manager:

- ▸ **Education:** A security manager often holds an associate's or bachelor's degree in business administration, retailing, criminal justice, or a related field. In addition to college course work, the security manager must have a clear understanding of criminal law.
- ▸ **Experience:** Many security managers have little or no experience in the fashion industry. Instead, they often have work experience in criminal justice areas. A number of security managers begin their positions by training on the sales floor, then move to the cash exchange areas, receiving, and other departments to gain an understanding of how the business operates and where the potential for loss exists.
- ▸ **Personal characteristics:** Curiosity and attention to detail are key attributes of the security manager. This person must stay on top of laws relating to theft and be aware of the processes and policies that relate to theft prosecution.

The salary for security manager positions ranges from a starting point of $25,000 to $65,000 and more for an experienced professional in a large company.

Career Challenges

The security manager must oversee that security is implemented in a wide range of areas: customers and employees, equipment and electronic security systems, store layout, and the receiving and accounting divisions. Most important, this person needs to know the law. If a shoplifter is incorrectly stopped and detained for security, a positive court judgment may not be given. Conversely, if a customer is inaccurately accused of theft, the company may face a lawsuit that could cost it both money and positive image.

CUSTOMER SERVICE MANAGER

It is likely that you have heard the saying "The customer is always right," but is this really true? Most retailers have specific policies concerning merchandise returns and exchanges, out-of-stock advertised merchandise, and returned bank checks. With the Internet as an emerging retail channel, e-retailers need another set of policies concerning returns, shipping costs, payment, and security. All retailers want to keep their customers satisfied to establish a loyal customer base, yet policies often have to be implemented to assure a profitable bottom line. A **customer service manager** assists a customer with an issue or complaint and implements the retail operation's policies and procedures for returns, exchanges, out-of-stock merchandise, product warranties, and the like (Figure 12.5). It is the customer service manager's responsibility to maintain company policies, while assuring that customers feel their problems are being heard and taken care of in a professional and timely manner. The customer service manager often trains the sales staff to effectively assist customers with concerns and teaches them the people skills needed to calm irate customers and find win-win solutions for all involved.

Some business operations have an organized, separate department under the customer service manager that has the sole function of servicing the customer. Larger companies separate the customer service responsibilities into several divisions, such as maintenance, credit, and adjustments. Finally, there are retail organizations that handle the customer service

Figure 12.5. A customer service manager assists customers and implements store policies.

Figure 12.6. High-fashion boutiques frequently offer alteration services to customers.

responsibilities informally through management or personnel who have direct contact with the customer.

Which types of services are coordinated by the customer service manager? Businesses offer varying types of services, often reflecting the price ranges of their products. For example, a high-fashion boutique carrying expensive designer garments will usually offer a wide range of customer services from alterations, as shown in Figure 12.6, to home delivery. However, discount retail operations, such as Sam's Wholesale Club, provide minimal customer services in an effort to maintain retail prices that are below those of its competitors. At Sam's, for example, the customer is not provided with dressing room facilities, packaging, or delivery. Types of services the customer service manager may be responsible for vary with the type of company, but may include:

- ▶ Customer product adjustments
- ▶ Delivery service
- ▶ Layaway availability
- ▶ Information on product care
- ▶ Technical advice
- ▶ Discounts
- ▶ After-sales services
- ▶ Replacement guarantees
- ▶ Credit service
- ▶ Alterations
- ▶ Special order availability
- ▶ Reorder availability
- ▶ Maintenance service
- ▶ Training of personnel

Qualifications

Are you an individual who remains calm in any situation? Are you an active listener? Do people find you to be an effective negotiator and a fair decision maker? If so, then the position of customer service manager may be the career option for you. The qualifications of a customer service manager include the following:

- ▸ **Education:** A bachelor's degree in fashion merchandising, fashion retailing, business administration, management, human resources, or a related field is a common requirement.
- ▸ **Experience:** Three to five years of experience in retail sales, preferably management, are required. Evidence of superior customer service through sales awards and customer recommendations is a plus.
- ▸ **Personal characteristics:** The effective customer service manager has exceptional interpersonal and communication skills and is trustworthy, personable, and outgoing. Being a capable negotiator and a good listener are also important skills. The customer service manager must have a thorough understanding of the company and its policies.

The salary for the customer service manager is comparable to similar retail management positions, ranging from a starting point of $25,000 to $65,000 and more for an experienced professional in a large company.

Career Challenges

The customer service manager works with all kinds of people. If you have ever stood in line waiting to return a purchase, you may have seen a few of the types. They can be demanding to the point of unreasonable and rude to the point of unbearable. Regardless of the customer's state of mind, the customer service manager has to remain calm and polite. The hours can be long, and the starting pay can be low.

RETAIL OPERATION OWNER

Perhaps you dream of owning your own retail business. Many aspiring fashion students do. Maybe you love the fashion industry, but working in a corporate setting is not for you. The good news is that a great number of people open their own businesses each year. The bad news is that you must, as a store owner, do everything discussed in this chapter (and several others). The **retail operation owner** is financially responsible for the company and oversees all aspects of the retail business. There are three types of business ownership: sole proprietorship, partnership, and corporation. A business owned by an individual is referred to as a **sole proprietorship**. A **partnership** is owned by two or more people. In a **corporation**, stockholders own the company, which may be run by an individual or a group.

Before opening a business, the prospective owner or ownership group must develop a **business plan**, a document that details plans for the business concept and target market, location and space needs (e.g., building lease, facility purchase, or website), growth and exit strategies, sales and inventory, and financing needs. Whether the prospective business owner is purchasing an existing business or opening a new one, securing funding to own the business is often a critical first step. **Funders**, financing sources such as banks and the Small Business Administration, require a well-written business plan that justifies financing due to a good potential for profit, minimal risk, and a strong long-range plan. Many funders are now working with potential owners of Internet retailing businesses, a new business area for them.

Once the business loan is approved, the owner will often attend to the merchandise selection for the business by identifying the trends customers will want and then buying, or overseeing the buying, of the merchandise that fits the target market. The retail owner is responsible for developing a budget for seasonal purchases to make certain that the company's finances are not overextended. Once merchandise is received, the store owner and employees inventory, price, tag, and place the merchandise on the sales floor. The owner and staff are often responsible for creating and installing window and in-store displays. Straightening the inventory, cleaning the store, and restocking fixtures and shelves are all tasks the store owner handles personally or assigns to employees.

Figure 12.7. This boutique owner and designer sells her custom designs.

A store owner often locates, hires, trains, motivates, and evaluates all employees. In a small business, the owner is a one-person human resources department. Scheduling employees to meet the needs of fluctuating customer traffic and fit within the payroll budget is often a challenge for small business owners. In many small operations, the customer prefers to work with the store owner, valuing the personal attention and expertise. Rather than leaving it to employees, the business owner is also the customer service manager, handling customer returns, exchanges, and complaints. It can be a juggling act for the owner to decide when to be in the business and when to take a break from it. Figure 12.7 depicts a boutique owner working in her store.

In most cases, a store owner does *everything*, including taking the trash out! Being a store owner can be one of the most gratifying experiences, though it can be very stressful at times. Being solely responsible for all the expenses incurred by the business can be overwhelming, but reaping the benefits of individual freedom and profits outweighs the negatives. There is no average salary range for store ownership.

Qualifications

Are you ready to take on an ultimate challenge? Consider the following list of educational backgrounds, work experience, and personal characteristics needed for successful business ownership:

▸ **Education:** A bachelor's degree in fashion merchandising, fashion retailing, business administration, marketing, retailing, entrepreneurship, or a related field is beneficial.

▸ **Experience:** Three to 10 years of experience in the fashion industry, working in as many areas of a fashion business as possible, are critical to the future retail operation owner. An internship with an entrepreneur provides ideal on-the-job education.

▸ **Personal characteristics:** Successful business owners are calculated risk-takers. They are well organized, financially savvy, respectful of money, flexible, responsible, and willing to ask for and accept help.

Career Challenges

Each month, the retail business owner faces the pressure of paying employees, vendors, the landlord, utility companies, and more. It can be a huge burden for some. As there is no way to estimate accurately how much profit the business will generate, it is a risky profession in which one must constantly search for ways to maintain or grow the business. The retail business owner is ultimately responsible for all facets of the business.

SUMMARY

This chapter explores management career options in fashion retailing. It is difficult to envision how many people are required to get a single product from the retail sales floor into the customers' shopping bags. The administrative employees in the industry sector are referred to as retail management. Management is the organization and control of the affairs of a business or a particular sector of a business. There are a number of career tracks in retail management, including the following positions: regional manager, operations manager, store manager, assistant and associate store managers, manager-in-training, department manager, security manager, customer service manager, and retail operation owner.

The regional store manager is responsible for the smooth running and profit of the operation and the success of employees in the retail store outlets located within a specific geographical area. Working with the regional store manager, the operations manager analyzes sales and inventory performance and procedures for general business practices, such as customer service and merchandise distribution. A store manager oversees all aspects of a retail store unit's operation, from advertising and special events to the customers and employees. A number of large retail organizations offer a manager-in-training program in which prospective management employees train for assistant manager or store manager positions within the company. The assistant store manager supports the store manager in all of the daily responsibilities of operating a store successfully. In some companies, there is a step between the assistant store manager and the store manager: the associate store manager. A department manager oversees a specific area, or department, within a store. The security manager selects security systems, trains employees on identifying and minimizing theft, assists with store layout that deters theft, and works with the accounting department to assure accurate inventory figures. The customer service manager assists consumers with their needs and concerns. Finally, retail operation owners are financially responsible for their own companies and oversee all aspects of the retail business. They are the managers of all managers.

KEY TERMS

assistant store manager

associate store manager

book inventory

business plan

corporation

customer service manager

department manager

floor set

funder

internal theft

manager-in-training (MIT)

management

operations manager

overage

partnership

physical inventory

region

regional (district) manager

retail operation owner

retail store manager

security manager

security

shrinkage (shortage)

sole proprietorship

Discussion Questions

1. Using the Internet or interviewing a professional in a regional manager position, investigate the advantages and disadvantages of this career. Find out about the size of the regional manager's territory, the number of management personnel with whom the regional manager interacts, and the prospects for promotion in this field.

2. Investigate one of the job responsibilities of the security manager by exploring the types of security systems that are available to deter theft. Compare and contrast both technological devices and common-sense techniques, such as placing small, easily pocketed items at the cash counter.

3. Using the Internet or your college's career services department, locate four companies with MIT programs and compare them. What are the requirements to enter each of the programs? What is the length of each MIT program? How many participants are in each? What types of training and projects are included in the programs? Which types of positions can one expect after successfully completing MIT training?

4. Assume that you plan to open your own retail business in two years. First, conduct research to identify the type of fashion business that will have the best opportunity for success by identifying market voids and consumer shifts in the location where you would like to work. Next, develop a list of the work experiences that will prepare you for ownership of this retail operation. Finally, construct a chart of the general steps you will need to take to get ready for the business opening.

ancil fact

bus fan heos

ials f s

product retail

Produ

fash

ash ion a

sial

ancialla

business

ashion

UNIT 3

THE ANCILLARY BUSINESSES

There are a vast number of businesses that promote, educate, and provide support to the producers and retailers of fashion goods. Whether working as freelancers or within a company, these ancillary businesspeople frequently offer services rather than tangible products for a fee. The fashion show and event planner or modeling and talent agency director offer assistance with promotional events. The fashion photographer and stylist provide visual communications to promote a business or a product. A costumer may work with the photography, video, film, or television industries or in a museum. Opportunities in a historical costume division of a museum include the museum director, curator, collections manager, conservator, and technician. Another career track within the fashion scholarship segment of the industry is the fashion educator who may work in historical costume or many other facets of the fashion industry from production to design to merchandising.

Another segment of fashion ancillary businesses focuses on environments. In Unit 3, the environments that are examined include websites, architecture, commercial real estate sales and development, commercial interior design, visual merchandising, and mall management. All of these environments represent spaces in which fashion businesses may be located, whether in the production, retail, or ancillary levels of the industry.

The final segment of fashion ancillary businesses explored in Unit 3 is the beauty, spa, and wellness industries. Product development and marketing in cosmetics, skin care, and hair care are growing areas of the fashion industry. Chapter 16 examines the careers of a product developer or technician working in research and development and those of the beauty merchandising and marketing professionals working in the manufacturing and retail levels of the industry. The career of a makeup artist can take this professional to the theater, a film set, a photo shoot, an individual's home, a salon, or a spa. As with the makeup artist, estheticians and hairstylists provide services that are gaining popularity in the beauty industry, particularly in the area of spas and wellness centers. Finally, the career of the director of a spa is explored, as growth is expected to continue in spa and esthetics companies. These ancillary businesses are evolving into full-service facilities that include services for makeup, hair, skin, and body. As we have watched health services integrate medicine and natural homeopathic remedies, we will see beauty services integrated with health and fitness in the future. New careers will evolve for those interested in beauty, health, and longevity.

CHAPTER 13

Fashion Visuals and Media as Ancillary Businesses

You have seen the work of a fashion show and event planner, a modeling and talent agency director, or, perhaps, a fashion photographer, if you have ever been to a fashion show, trunk show, or retailer's grand opening. Did you think all of the products, models, food, entertainment, and workers arrived and knew just what to do and where to be on their own? Fashion show and event planners, modeling and talent agency directors, and fashion photographers work with a wide range of activities, from small boutique and megastore openings to product launches and trade shows. There are lesser known activities that are arranged and implemented by event planners; these include trunk shows, sample sales, and conferences. Whether a fashion show or a conference, it takes a huge amount of advance planning and on-the-job management to make an event a success.

When you think about the tasks involved in planning an event, contemplate the steps you might go through as a member of a committee planning a wonderful party for an organization, such as your senior class. First, you would develop a theme for the party and construct a list of potential guests. Next, you would scout and secure a location for the party. This is the first cost to include in your overall budget, one that you keep in mind throughout the planning process. Later, you would work on securing talent for the event, such as a band or a performer. In the case of a fashion show and event planner, talent includes models, designers, hairstylists and makeup artists, photographers, and videographers. At this point, you may decide to recruit sponsors to help pay for the event and appeal to the party audience. Staging the party is the next job on the list, as you plan the layout of tables, chairs, and the stage and determine lighting and music needs and placement. As a final step in the planning process, you may hire someone to manage the actual party, photograph the event, and, possibly, oversee the mailing of invitations and receipt of replies. The list of jobs is long, and these apply to just the pre-party tasks.

In this chapter, companies that produce **fashion visuals** (e.g., fashion shows, photography, model management, and costumes) are examined as ancillary businesses. Some retail organizations, for example, hire a fashion show coordinator and a fashion photographer as employees. Many, however, go to outside companies to contract out these activities. These companies are what this chapter is all about. The following career paths, as independent businesses, are explored: fashion show and event producer, modeling and talent agency director, fashion photographer, art photographer, stylist, and fashion costumer.

FASHION SHOW AND EVENT PLANNER

In Chapter 5, "Promotion," the job descriptions and responsibilities of the fashion show producer and special events planner were discussed. These functions can be conducted by an auxiliary firm or by freelance personnel. A retailer, a manufacturer, a designer, or an organization may contract an independent firm, the fashion show and event planning company, to do all or part of this work for a fee. In general, the **fashion show and event planner** manages fashion shows and special events for its clients. The company works with the client to determine the intended purpose, designated audience, and type of event. It then directs the advance planning in terms of budget, publicity, and advertising. The company may be contracted to handle part or all of the public relations, which includes contacting the media and writing press kits, biographies, and letters. In addition, the fashion show and event firm may guide the selection process for products and models. For example, a jury of selection may be configured to review fashion products for acceptance into a show. For the apparel industry, the planner may also recruit and select models, fit them in garments, and then

Figure 13.1. Prior to a fashion show, models must be recruited, selected, and fitted into garments and their performances choreographed and rehearsed.

choreograph and rehearse the presentation (Figure 13.1). Company employees are often responsible not only for the site selection but also for the design and installation of staging, dressing rooms, seating, lighting, and music. Preparing and handling a reception following the show may be part of the fashion event company's contract as well.

Many fashion show and event companies do not solely produce fashion shows for their clients. A number of them design, organize, and coordinate other types of events, such as conventions, conferences, corporate meetings, and exhibitions. Fashion show and event planners may be responsible for every aspect of these functions, from marketing, catering, preparing, signage and displays to locating audiovisual equipment, printing sources, and security. They may also be contracted to coordinate participants' registration, accommodations, and travel. Most significantly, they are often responsible for the financial side of events by working with clients to establish realistic budgets and then monitoring expenses and income for the ventures.

What types of activities are assigned to a fashion show and event firm? While conferences and conventions, trade shows, and company training seminars are common events for the manufacturing and retail sectors of the fashion industry, the fashion show and event firm may also be contracted to coordinate company social gatherings and meetings, organize charity fund-raisers, and direct the grand openings of new retail locations or the launches of new product lines. An area of growth in event planning is the wedding-planning field. Today, engaged couples are spending thousands of dollars to hire someone to plan, implement, and manage the wedding event, from the engagement party to the honeymoon, as depicted in Figure 13.2.

What are the typical tasks for a fashion show and event planner? In many ways, event management is similar to advertising and marketing. The fashion show and event planner views the event as a product or brand and then develops and promotes it in creative ways. The ultimate goal is to assure that the attendees (the consumers) have a positive experience that leaves them feeling good about the product and its sponsors, whether the sponsor is a business, a charity, or a club. Organization is critical in the planning process, especially when dealing with the management and coordination of services and supplies. Every physical detail needs to be considered, from the layout and design of the venue to lighting, sound, communications, videography, and other technical concerns. Catering and bar services must be organized, along with less glamorous concerns such as security, parking, and

Figure 13.2. Engaged couples may pay thousands of dollars for a wedding planner to plan, implement, and manage their wedding event, from the engagement party to the honeymoon.

restroom facilities. Promotion, public relations, and advertising must also be planned and executed. Last but not least, the performers, speakers, or participants need to be located, terms negotiated, and plans confirmed.

The fashion show and event planner must anticipate the costs of all of these aspects in advance, continually checking that the budget balances. Finally, the management of the event is an organizational challenge in itself. The degree of the event's success is often a result of the level of planning and organization. Following the conclusion of the event, the fashion show and event planner is responsible for assuring that all income and expenses are reconciled and evaluating the success of the event, noting corrections of errors to implement in the next event.

Qualifications

Is a career in fashion show and event planning for you? If so, you may want to work toward achieving the following educational goals, work experiences, and personal characteristics:

- ▸ **Education:** Top event planners typically have bachelor's degrees in fashion merchandising, business administration, marketing, event management, tourism or hospitality administration, or a similar field.
- ▸ **Experience:** Knowledge of marketing and press relations is invaluable. Work experience as an assistant or an intern in fashion show production or event planning is critical.
- ▸ **Personal characteristics:** An excellent understanding of fashion marketing, a great amount of energy and flexibility, and a high level of organizational and logistical skills are required for successful fashion show and event planners. Their presentation and communication skills should be excellent. Fashion show and event planners need the skills to motivate other people, along with creative abilities to solve problems and make things happen. If you aspire to become a fashion show and event planner, be prepared to put in extra hours to ensure that the job gets done within its budget and on time. This work requires perfection, so the event planner must pay attention to every detail and be capable of handling last-minute disasters that may happen despite superb planning.

The event-planning industry continues to grow rapidly, particularly in the areas of weddings, international conferences, and hospitality. Marketing and public relations are becoming even more important facets of the event-planning business.

The starting annual salary for a fashion show and event planner is $40,000–$50,000. An assistant to the planner will earn between $28,000 and $32,000. Those planners with five to seven years of successful experience can expect to earn $80,000–$100,000 or more annually.

Career Challenges

The fashion show and event planner works in a high-stress environment. Lack of attention to a detail or two, a narrowly missed deadline, or an unexpected emergency can literally annihilate a major fashion show, trade show, or charity ball. If, for example, an event planner remembered everything but forgot to confirm catering arrangements, there may not be food and drinks at a charity ball. Another pressure for fashion show and event companies or freelancers comes with generating regular business events with repeat clientele to assure consistent income.

MODELING AND TALENT AGENCY DIRECTOR

Most models are recruited by modeling scouts or modeling and talent agency directors who travel around the world in a tireless search for fresh faces. Models are often discovered in shopping malls, schools, clubs, concerts, or other obvious places where young people hang out. Some agencies also locate models through photographs sent by "model hopefuls"; another way is through an agency's open casting calls. Most prestigious agencies do not charge upfront fees to join the agency; rather, these agencies are profitable by taking a percent of the models' earnings. Often, fees for administration and training are deducted after the model has found paid assignments. Training can consist of full- or part-time courses that last for a few days to a few months. Topics for courses may include diet, health, image, grooming, runway turns and movements, photographic modeling techniques, and professional conduct with clients. Individual guidance may be provided on such areas as skin care, hairstyling, makeup, and overall appearance when the model first joins the agency. The **modeling and talent agency director** is ultimately responsible for locating and contracting new models, training them, and, later, securing modeling jobs for them.

Modeling agency directors are often very involved with their models at the start of their careers. They will often find newly signed models an apartment and help them get settled into their new lives. Many modeling and talent agency directors have found that the beginning of a modeling career is a very difficult time for a young person. A great number of models are young, far away from home, and often without many modeling jobs at first. The agency director tries to support them through difficult times while teaching them to be safe and disciplined, show up to meetings on time, and treat modeling as a real job.

Modeling agencies hire for a variety of modeling positions. **Fit models**, or *fashion house models,* are used as live models to test how garments fit and for designers to drape, cut, and pin fabric and garments. Some companies rely on fit models to give them feedback on how a garment fits and feels, as well as where it needs adjustments. They also model the finished garments for retail buyers, fashion journalists, and, in the case of couture, individual customers. Box 13.1 is an article about fit models. House models may show the collections at fashion shows or the apparel company may consign an agency to book show models. The modeling agency takes bookings from clients who need **show models** to display clothes at fashion shows. They may also work at fashion exhibitions, or trade markets, modeling apparel and accessories. Show models may also be hired to demonstrate or display nonapparel items, such as cosmetics or furniture, at product launches and exhibitions.

Photographic models are those who are hired to be photographed in a studio or on location. While a select few top models work in the high-fashion magazines, a large number of opportunities exist through mail order catalogs, newspaper advertisements, television, and the Internet.

What is the talent part of the modeling and talent agency director's job? In addition to locating and booking models, the modeling and talent director also finds and hires talent for film and media companies. For example, a movie producer from Los Angeles may choose Seattle as the location for filming. The casting director for the film may contact a modeling and talent agency to locate actors, extras, costumers, or hair and makeup professionals in the Seattle area. The modeling and talent agency director may also commission entertainment for special events, such as conferences, galas, benefits, parties, management and sales meetings, weddings, designer appearances, book signings, and so on.

Qualifications

What are the educational, experiential, and personal characteristics of a successful modeling and talent agency director? The list is as follows.

BOX 13.1 • MORE SURPRISING SIX-FIGURE JOBS: THIS WEEK, WE LOOK AT (UNSUPER) MODELS . . .

by Jeanne Sahadi, CNN/*Money* Senior Writer

NEW YORK (CNN/*Money*)—If you're asked who earns a six-figure income, you're likely to come up with a list of doctors, lawyers, corporate executives, and high-powered salespeople. Plenty of other, less predictable occupations can command big paychecks.

Keep in mind, not everyone in these occupations makes $100,000 or more, but the most skilled and experienced can. If they are freelancers, some of their six figures must be used to pay for taxes, insurance, retirement savings, and business-related expenses, which may include commissions to an agency that sent a job their way. We take a look at the fitting model:

If you are a perfect size fill-in-the-blank and have dimensions that match fashion industry standards—"plus," "petite," and "big and tall" sizes included—you may find work as a fitting model with a clothing company or designer.

The job involves modeling outfits in a manufacturer's showroom and letting the designers, clothes makers, and buyers know what works and what does not about an outfit, for example, how it falls and how it feels, said Darryl Roberts, men's director for modeling agency The Lyons Group.

The most successful fitting models know how clothes are made, know how different fabrics behave, and are very knowledgeable about the line they're modeling. In fact, some have degrees in pattern making, said Susan Levine, owner of Model Service Agency, LLC.

"The model is the one that gives the direction of how to make the garment," Levine said. "The model can make or break your sales."

While you do not need the face or figure of a supermodel, you do have to be attractive and well-groomed. "You need to project a certain image. You have to maintain your size at all times," Roberts noted.

A successful fitting model can earn between $750 and $1,500 a day. On an hourly basis, you might earn between $200 and $275. And you might work three to five days a week, for between five and eight hours a day.

Source: CNN, January 9, 2004: 9:14 AM EST

▶ **Education:** A bachelor's degree in fashion merchandising, marketing, business administration, visual arts, or a related field is a common requirement.

▶ **Experience:** A number of modeling and talent agency directors once worked in the field, either as models or actors. Others gained work experience through employment with this type of company. Employment with a retailer in the fashion coordinator's office will provide excellent opportunities to work with print and runway events. An internship with a modeling and talent agency is an excellent way to determine whether or not this business is for you and get your foot in the door.

▸ **Personal characteristics:** Modeling and talent agency directors are constantly observing those around them, networking with industry professionals, and building relationships. The successful director is truly a "people person." Business skills are critical, as this person often owns the company and must hire the right people to maintain a positive reputation and repeat business.

A modeling and talent agency director earns an average annual salary between $41,000 and $68,000. Owners of successful agencies receive incomes greater than $100,000 a year.

Career Challenges

The modeling and talent agency director is only as lucrative as the people employed by the firm. If the modeling agency and talent director discovers and hires a new model who becomes a supermodel, the director benefits financially from all of the model's jobs. Training, guiding, and managing new and often young talent can be challenging, as is maintaining a positive reputation in an industry not always viewed as having high integrity.

FASHION PHOTOGRAPHER

Thanks to our fashion-conscious society and the Internet, a fashion photographer can live just about anywhere. Fashion photographers used to locate to Paris, Milan, New York, or Los Angeles to earn a good living. As long as you live in a city where there are fashion designers, boutiques, retailers, and manufacturers, this career dream is a possibility. Good **fashion photographers** are more than people who take good pictures. They must also be able to make products and their models look their best artistically. To succeed, a fashion photographer must possess the technical and artistic skills to ensure a professional, eye-catching, and distinctive photograph. Photographers work to develop an individual style of photography to differentiate themselves from their competition.

Fashion photography can be a highly creative and well-paid career. **Fashion photography** is the business of taking pictures of models wearing the latest apparel, accessories, hairstyles, and makeup or highlighting the newest home furnishings and other fashion products, primarily for commercial use (see Box 13.2). The photographs are used in a variety of media, including advertisements, catalogs, billboards, television, websites, and art venues. Photographers create permanent visual images. Often working to meet a client's requests, they control lighting, tone, and perspective in their work, using a range of photographic equipment, accessories, and imaging software. Photographers must have a technical understanding of the medium as well as artistic vision. Key tasks of the fashion photographer include choosing and preparing locations; setting up lighting; selecting the appropriate cameras, lenses, film, and accessories; composing shots; positioning subjects; and instructing assistants. After shooting, they may process and print images or view and manipulate digital images using software such as Adobe Photoshop.

Some fashion photographers may choose exclusive employment with a retailer, a publication (e.g., a magazine or a newspaper), a designer, an advertising company, a manufacturer, or a direct-mail company. Others may choose to freelance, with or without an agent, or open their own studios. These independent photographers are the ones who make up the ancillary segment of the fashion industry. A majority of successful independent photographers develop positive reputations by accumulating considerable work experience in mail order, editorial, or advertising work. Some photographers

BOX 13.2 • THE FASHION PHOTOGRAPHER AND THE PHOTO EDITOR

"Most people who cold call me haven't done their research, which is the world's biggest mistake," says Clio McNicholl, photo editor of *Allure* magazine. "The single biggest thing that people should do is their research. They should know what the magazine does, and see how you can apply that to what you do. And they should at least know the name of the photo editor."

When you submit work to photo editors, remember that you are showing rather than selling. Editors almost never buy the specific image they see before them; they're looking for a photographer who can execute future commissions. You'll need to be persistent in sending out your work, and ruthless in editing what you choose to show.

The best way to grab an editor's attention is to show previously published work, but there is a downside. Because there is such an oversupply of photographers, a number of magazines really take advantage of that fact. Some mags have a decent budget, but many magazines just cover the photographer's expenses. McNicholl says *Allure's* rates start at $350 a day for unknown photographers, up to $130,000 for a fashion spread.

Women's magazines all over the world buy hundreds of stock shots every month—typically young women having fun with their boyfriends, hanging out with friends, or maybe moping home alone with their stuffed toys—all of which express a sentiment commonly dealt with in feature articles. If your work speaks clearly, you will stand a much better chance with picture editors than with vague or ambiguous images.

Source: www.fashion-photographer.net (2007).

enter the field by submitting unsolicited photographs to magazines. There are many avenues for a fashion photographer to break into this business: freelance without an agent, freelance with an agent, or through one's own studio.

Photographers usually specialize in one of the following six areas: general practice, advertising or editorial, fashion, press, corporate, and technical. **General practice**, or *social*, **photography** refers to photographic services for local communities or businesses, with the majority of work in wedding and family photography. **Advertising** or **editorial photography** expresses a product's personality or illustrates a magazine story. It is usually classified as still life, food, transportation, portraiture, or landscape photography. Fashion photographers work with models and art directors in the apparel, accessories, or home products industries. They are often commissioned by art directors of catalogs and magazines. **Press**, or *photojournalism*, **photography** focuses on images directly related to news stories, both events and personalities. **Corporate**, also referred to as *industrial* or *commercial*, **photographers** produce images for promotional materials or annual reports. **Technical photographers** produce photographs for reports or research papers, such as textile durability analyses. Figure 13.3 is an example of technical photography.

In all areas of specialization in photography, the successful photographer has a number of work objectives:

Figure 13.3. An example of a technical photograph, this is a microscopic image of woven polyester.

▸ Maintaining a technical knowledge of cameras and related rapidly changing technologies, as photographers increasingly need to know how to use computer software programs and applications that allow them to prepare and edit images

▸ Developing an artistic understanding of light, distance, and perspective

▸ Cultivating a keen eye for esthetic detail and inventive ways to communicate moods and ideas

▸ Building strong interpersonal skills to work with models and be sensitive to their moods so that they are comfortable in front of the camera

▸ Understanding studio lighting to bring out the best in skin tones and textures and colors of different fabrics

▸ Working well with natural light (or a lack of) for on-location shoots

▸ Establishing good relationships with stylists, art directors, modeling agents, and fashion editors

- Identifying and securing future assignments and clients
- Understanding the roles and responsibilities of an entrepreneur

What are the benefits of a career in fashion photography? The attractions of fashion photography are obvious: exotic locations, plenty of foreign travel, and personal publicity in fashion journals and other magazines. There is also the chance to work within the world of fashion and design and associate with the glamorous people who live there.

Qualifications

What do you need to know and do to secure a position in this field? Following are the qualifications required of a fashion photographer:

- **Education:** A bachelor's degree in photography or visual arts and a strong portfolio are usually essential. Freelance photographers need continuing education in technical proficiency, whether gained through a degree program, vocational training, or extensive work experience.
- **Experience:** Because entry-level positions for a fashion photography firm are rare, gaining a position as a photographer's studio assistant is a common way to enter the field. Some of the entry career paths for fashion photographers interested in freelance work or business ownership include working for periodicals, advertising agencies, retail operations, fashion designers, modeling agencies, catalogs, galleries, or stock photography agencies.
- **Personal characteristics:** Those fashion photographers who succeed in attracting enough work to earn a living are likely to be the most creative and adept at operating a business. They are also excellent at building and retaining relationships with other professionals. The independent fashion photographer needs to be extremely confident and have the persistence to solicit consistent work. Stamina is needed for working long hours, sometimes in uncomfortable conditions. Excellent communication skills and a flexible personality are needed, as the photographer must often have patience: it can take a long time to get the right shot.

The Portfolio

A photographer's most important tool is the portfolio, particularly for beginners who have not established a reputation. A **portfolio**, or *book*, is a collection of work that illustrates the job candidate's range of skills and outcomes. Many photographers find that websites offer an inexpensive way to showcase a relatively large number of their images. Some photographers have found that computer editing is also a method of keeping down retouching and printing costs. Despite the advantages of developing a website, most industry clients will still need to see a traditional portfolio before they hire a photographer. The website makes a great calling card, but fashion photographers need portfolios to show prospective clients when they call for an interview.

As most magazine editors receive a pile of unsolicited portfolios a month, the fashion photographer must develop a portfolio that stands out in a crowd. Many fashion photographers find the sharp, bright imaging of four-by-five transparencies show off their work to best effect. At least 20 of these should be included in the portfolio. As Figure 13.4 shows, a *tearsheet* is a page that has been pulled from a newspaper, model book, or magazine. Tearsheets are excellent to include in the portfolio if the photographer has been published. The photographer should be prepared to leave the portfolio with a potential client for at least a week. The portfolio should exhibit a common thread throughout it to illustrate a photographer's style and personality. The images chosen to be showcased in the portfolio should be thematically linked to the prospective job, such as home interior product shots for an advertising job with a furniture manufacturer. The portfolio should include a few other images to demonstrate the photographer's range. Strong portraits are also a good inclusion, as they tend to stay in the mind of the viewer.

The photographer with several years of experience who is contracted by a fashion firm can expect to earn between \$42,000 and \$64,000 annually. Fashion photographers with reputable industry experience and an extensive portfolio of commercial work can earn much more than this, more than \$100,000 a year.

Figure 13.4. Tearsheet from a photography spread by Mert Alas and Macus Piggot in *W* Magazine.

Career Challenges

This is a tough field to enter, as it takes many years of experience at low pay to find opportunities to build a portfolio of work. Fashion photographers often pay their dues before establishing a strong reputation in the field. Some photographers find it frustrating to be directed by the retailer or designer on who will model or how and where to shoot print work.

Assistant Photographer

Professional photographers often employ assistants to help the business run smoothly. **Assistant photographers** may deal with clients and suppliers; organize estimates, invoices, and payments; arrange props and assist with lighting; communicate with photographic labs and stylists; work with the photographer on shoots; and maintain the photographer's website and portfolio.

ART PHOTOGRAPHER

Once inaccurately viewed as "without artistic value," photographs are now one of the hottest growth areas in the international fine art market. Figure 13.5 is a photograph by Guy Bourdin, well recognized as an **art photographer** whose subjects were fashion related. While gelatin silver prints are the staple of fine art photography, there is a growing consumer interest in contemporary photos using either antique or modern printing methods. Like many artistic undertakings, art photography is unlikely to pay a living wage for many years. Although many artists sell their work directly from the Internet, critical attention and the strongest sales come from a relationship with a gallery. In most major cities, there is now at least one photo gallery, but the headquarters of the world art photography market is New York City, where prices tend to be highest.

Before approaching a gallery with work, the art photographer should contact the gallery to request its submissions policy. Many galleries review new work only at set times of the year, and may require the recommendation of someone known to the gallery directors. If a

Figure 13.5. An image by art photographer Guy Bourdin.

gallery is interested in interviewing a photographer, the gallery director will want to see a representative sampling of the photographer's work to know that there is a substantial body of work with a consistent standard throughout. Photographers may be invited to join a gallery by having their work go into the backroom inventory, where it will be shown to specific collectors, rather than having a public exhibition, as not many photographers are offered a solo show. The most important thing for the photographer to remember about working with a gallery is to maintain a proper business relationship. Every print given to a gallery should be inventoried by the photographer and payment terms should be agreed on. Industry standard is that the artist receives 40 to 50 percent of the selling price of a photograph after it is purchased. Photographers should discuss with gallery directors if they are free to exhibit work in other galleries or if the gallery expects exclusivity. Each relationship between an artist and a gallery is unique.

STYLIST

Fashion stylists are responsible for bringing to life a photographer's or director's vision for a fashion photography shoot, magazine layout, music video, television or film commercial, or print advertisement. Fashion stylists often scout locations and create the mood for a shoot by selecting the appropriate props, fashions, accessories, and even models to fit the theme of the shoot. Every job is different, from catalogs to commercials to movies. Stylists work with teams of people such as photographers, designers, lighting technicians, and set builders. Companies such as magazines, newspapers, retailers, advertising agencies, and music production companies often employ fashion stylists. Many stylists also choose to run their own businesses.

Typical work activities for the stylist are varied, from the shopping time to shooting the photograph or film. Stylists, or assistant stylists, are responsible for contacting public relations companies, manufacturers, and retailers to locate the best assortment of merchandise to be used in a shoot. Next, they will borrow, lease, or purchase garments and props and then arrange to transport the selections to the studio or location to determine which combinations work best. Before the shoot begins, stylists work with hair and makeup personnel and dress the people featured in the shoot, adjusting the fit of apparel and accessories as needed.

Interning or apprenticing with a well-known stylist is an ideal way to learn the business, including inside information such as where the best military uniforms or 1940s evening wear is available, which tailor can do overnight alterations, and who can design and sew a sailor suit for a Chihuahua. Occasionally, a stylist has to deal with big egos, as well

BOX 13.3 • FIELD CALLED ON INFLUENTIAL FRIENDS FOR FASHION FAVORS

Former *Sex and the City* stylist Patricia Field called on some famous friends in the fashion industry to make sure Meryl Streep and Anne Hathaway had the absolute best wardrobe for *The Devil Wears Prada*. Field had a costume budget of only $100,000 for the film shoot, set in the world of high-fashion publishing, but ended up scoring over $1 million worth of clothes. She tells the *New York Post*, "We could never have done it without my friends in the fashion industry helping us along. It would have been impossible. The level of fur coats and designer bags. Oh, my . . . It has to be over 100 designers. We must have used at least $1 million worth of clothing." Field had a say in which designers were mentioned in the film, but insists there was no intentional product placement. She says, "They were going to mention designers no matter what, so I said, 'Let's mention the ones that helped us,' because that's one way of thanking them." Among those designers lending a helping hand was Garavani Valentino, who even scored a cameo in the movie. Field adds, "He helped us so much with Meryl. And then I suggested he be in the movie and he went for it and he came with his entourage. He had fun!"

Source: www.contactmusic.com, 06/25/2006

as big-time constraints; it simply goes with the territory. Stylists have to avoid allowing their egos and tastes to interfere with a director's vision or a client's image. Ultimately, the stylist is not the final decision maker. Box 13.3 is an article about a successful stylist.

Qualifications

If the vision of searching for the right look, pulling together wardrobes, and creating strong visual images sounds ideal to you, then the career of stylist is one to consider. It requires the following education and work experiences, as well as personal characteristics:

- ▶ **Education:** An associate's or bachelor's degree in fashion design, fashion merchandising, visual arts, photography, or visual merchandising, or a related field is often required.
- ▶ **Experience:** Retail sales or management experience is helpful, as are internships with fashion publications or fashion stylists. Stylists may progress from editorial assistant work on fashion magazines where there is constant contact

with public relations companies, manufacturers, and retailers. The career path for a stylist may also begin with an internship or apprenticeship with an experienced stylist before moving into an assistant stylist position, and then to a staff fashion stylist.

▶ **Personal characteristics:** The fashion stylist has an eye for style and upcoming fashion trends, as well as a broad knowledge of historical fashions. Technical knowledge for creating sets and using lighting effectively is important. One needs to be creative, resourceful, persistent, and self-motivated. The fashion stylist should have good interpersonal, presentation, and communication skills. The ability to market one's self is critical. Aspiring fashion stylists should have the perseverance to work their way to the top. The most successful fashion stylists have extensive networks of contacts within the fashion industry to get the job done quickly and within budget.

With the influence of movies, television, and the Internet on the consumer, it is no surprise that stylists are often credited with setting fashion trends around the globe. A stylist may dress an actress in a funky retro gown or an amazing necklace to wear to a premiere. Once the image is splashed across the pages of fashion magazines and featured on television and the Internet, it can become a trend and put the stylist's name in the spotlight around the world.

In terms of salary, there is a downside to the job. It is often freelance, and as such offers no job security. Daily pay rates, however, usually range from $600 to $1,000, in part to compensate for the on-again, off-again nature of the job. Often, benefits are paid through a theater workers' union. Box 13.4 is a classified advertisement for a stylist.

Career Challenges

The stylist may find this career filled with irregular work, long hours, limited budgets, and clients with conflicting personal tastes. It can be difficult to work for a number of bosses, from the client to the photographer or film director. This is a career track in which there is growing interest and strong competition for the minimal number of jobs that currently exist. It is challenging to get your foot in the door, and when you do, you have to be great. For those who are great, excellent remuneration, job satisfaction, and the opportunity to build a reputation are quite possible.

BOX 13.4 • SAMPLE CLASSIFIED ADVERTISEMENT: STYLIST

Stylist for the Gap
Full-time employee
San Francisco, California

Major Responsibilities

- Manage styling direction
- Responsible for executing each website's styling point of view for all in-house photography to include product laydown and on-figure photography, and special laydown and marketing photography
- Responsible for understanding the marketing and merchandising seasonal objectives and executing site features based on those objectives
- Establish partnership with brand-styling team to promote styling and product consistency from the stores to the websites
- Responsible for obtaining appropriate approvals from cross-functional partners to ensure consistency and translate the brand point of view appropriately for each website
- Responsible for creating/managing a product style guide of all e-commerce sites
- Partner with creative team to colead and drive the styling direction for all e-commerce sites

- Accountable for creating a relationship between the photography, stylist, and assistant stylist team to provide team synergy
- Manage operating practices
- Responsible for driving photography work flow by assessing the volume and photography set requirements
- Responsible for identifying/documenting/presenting process efficiencies within the photography floor

Minimum Qualifications

- Minimum four years of experience with fashion styling and/or visual fashion retail experience.
- Bachelor's of art or science degree
- Ability to balance creative with strategic deliverables
- Strong collaboration skills and ability to form effective partnerships across cross-functional team: photo studio, creative, merchandising, and marketing teams
- Extremely flexible, detail-oriented, organized, and self-motivated with leadership skills
- Comfortable in a fast-paced environment
- Comfort level working with Excel, Filemaker, and databases in general
- Experience in managing others

FASHION COSTUMER

A **fashion costumer** collaborates with film and video directors to design, consign, or construct apparel and accessories that fit with the mood, time frame, and image of the visual. Depending on style and complexity, costumes may be rented, made, bought, or revamped out of existing stock. The costumer's designs need to reflect faithfully the personalities of the characters in the script. Stage costumes can provide audiences with information about a character's occupation, social status, gender, age, sense of style, and personality. Costumes have the ability to reinforce the mood and style of a production and distinguish between major and minor characters. Costumes may also be used to change an actor's appearance or be objects of beauty in their own right.

The shapes, colors, and textures that a costumer chooses make an immediate and powerful visual statement to the audience. Creative collaboration between the costumer, production director, and set and lighting designers ensures that the costumes are smoothly integrated into a production as a whole. Costuming also includes any accessories needed to project a character, such as canes, hats, gloves, shoes, jewelry, or masks. These costume props add a great deal of visual interest to the overall costume design. The costumer may also collaborate with a hair and wig master, hairstylist, and makeup artist. In European theater productions, these are often the items that truly distinguish one character from another.

Costumers begin their work by reading the script to be produced. If the production is set in a specific historical era, the fashions of this period need to be researched. To stimulate the flow of ideas at the first meeting with the director and design team (e.g., set, costume, lighting, and sound designers), the costumer may choose to present a few rough costume sketches. This is also an appropriate time to check with the director on the exact number of characters who need costumes, as any nonspeaking characters the director plans to include may not have been listed in the script.

It is the costumer's responsibility to draw up the costume plan, or plot. The **costume plot** is a list or chart that shows which characters appear in each scene, what they are wearing, and what their overall movements are throughout the play. This helps track the specific costume needs of every single character. It can also identify any potential costume challenges, such as very quick changes between scenes. Following the director and production team's approval of the preliminary sketches, the costumer draws up the final costume designs. The final designs are done in full color and show the style, silhouette, textures, accessories, and unique features of each costume.

Costuming may also include creating masks, makeup, or other unusual forms, such as the full-body animal suits shown in Figure 13.6 and worn in the musical *Cats*, designed by John Napier, winner of the 1983 Tony Award for Best Costume Design. Costume designers typically work to enhance a character's personality through the way that character is dressed, while at the same time allowing the actor to move freely and perform actions as required by the script. The designer needs to possess strong artistic capabilities, a thorough familiarity with fashion history, as well as knowledge of clothing construction and fit.

Professional costumers generally fall into three classifications: freelance, residential, and academic. **Freelance costumers** are hired for a specific production by theater companies or production studios. A freelance costumer is traditionally paid in three installments: at hiring, on the delivery of final renderings, and on the opening night of the production. Freelancers are usually not obligated to any exclusivity in projects they are working on and may be designing for several theaters concurrently. A **residential costumer** is hired by a specific theater for an extended series of productions. This can be as short as a summer

Figure 13.6. Andrew Lloyd Webber, creator of *Cats*, and a feline mannequin wearing a costume from the production.

stock contract or as long as many years. A residential costumer's contract may limit the amount of freelance work the costumer is permitted to accept. Unlike the freelancer, a residential costumer is consistently on location at the theater and is readily at hand to work with the costume studio and other collaborators. Residential costumers are more likely to be associated with a union than freelancers, as most theaters that can retain such a position have agreements with such organizations as the Actors' Equity Association. An **academic costume designer** is one who holds a teaching position with a college or university. This costumer is primarily an instructor who may also act as a residential designer for productions of the university theater. Designers or costumers with academic careers are often free to freelance as their schedules allow. In the past, college instructors of costume design were mostly experienced professionals who may not have had formal post-graduate education, but it has now become increasingly common to require a professor to have at least a master of fine arts degree to secure employment with an accredited university.

Qualifications

If the career of a costumer appeals to you, following is a list of educational credentials and work experiences that will contribute to your success and the personal characteristics you should acquire.

- ▶ **Education:** A bachelor's degree in theater costuming, historical costume, visual arts, fashion design, or a similar field is required.
- ▶ **Experience:** A number of successful costumers begin in the career field through an internship with an experienced costume designer. Others gain work experience as assistant fashion designers or fashion stylists before moving into the film and theater industry. Interning in summer stock productions, volunteering to assist in off-Broadway or local theater productions, and working or volunteering at a costume rental agency are excellent ways for college students to acquire work experience in this field. High school and college students can gain experience through costume, hair, or makeup work in school theater productions.
- ▶ **Personal characteristics:** A creative and resourceful personality is a plus. An understanding of historical fashion, clothing construction, and fit are necessities. Many fashion costumers find that the ability to sketch well is essential to communicating their ideas to directors and producers.

The salary range for a costumer is wide, with assistant costumers often starting at a wage of $12–$15 per hour. Beginning costumers can expect to start at $28,000–$32,000 annually, while those with several years' experience and a portfolio of work earn $40,000–$60,000 per year. Established costumers working on a notable stage, television, or film production can earn between $120,000 and $200,000 annually.

Career Challenges

The costumer is challenged with accurately interpreting the words and vision of the writer, director, or producer. In some cases, such as productions set in a different time or unique location, this takes a great deal of research. The costumer often works on a tight budget and an even tighter timeline. Costumes may require alterations, repairs, or replacement during the production. As costumers often work on several projects simultaneously, this career fits a person who can effectively multitask. Low pay and long hours should be expected at the start of this career track.

SUMMARY

Fashion visuals include such activities as fashion shows, photography shoots, and films or videos wardrobed by fashion costumers. These career tracks have been examined as ancillary fashion businesses. Some retail organizations, for example, hire fashion show coordinators and fashion photographers as employees. Many, however, go to outside companies to contract out these activities. These career paths, as independent businesses, include the fashion show and event planner, modeling and talent agency director, fashion photographer, fashion stylist, and fashion costumer.

The fashion show and event planner manages fashion shows and special events for its clients for a fee. Special events include, but are not limited to, trunk shows, sample sales, weddings, meetings, conferences, training seminars, and trade markets. The modeling and talent agency director is ultimately responsible for locating and contracting new models, training them, and, later, securing modeling jobs for them. Fashion photographers take photographs of models wearing the latest apparel, accessories, hairstyles, and makeup or highlighting the newest home furnishings and other fashion products, primarily for commercial use. The photographs are used in a variety of media, including advertisements, catalogs, billboards, television, websites, and art galleries. Fashion stylists are responsible for bringing to life a photographer or director's vision for a fashion shoot, magazine layout, music video or film, television commercial, or print advertisement. The fashion costumer collaborates with stage, film, and video directors to design, consign, or construct costumes that fit with the mood, time frame, and image of the visual.

All in all, fashion media and visual career options are creative and growing entrepreneurial paths. As diverse as the careers of the freelance fashion show and event planner, modeling and talent agency director, photographer, stylist, and costumer are, they have something major in common. They are all entrepreneurs—owners of their own futures. As such, they require the business skills needed to estimate expenses and labor accurately, sell and market their services, and maintain and grow a client base. It is a creative, independent, and self-directed lifestyle that combines creativity with passion.

KEY TERMS

academic costume designer
advertising or editorial photography
art photographer

assistant photographer

corporate photographer (industrial or technical)

costume plot

fashion costumer

fashion photographer

fashion photography

fashion show and event planner

fashion stylist

fashion visuals

fit model

freelance costumer

general practice

model and talent agency director

photographic model

portfolio

press photography (photojournalism)

residential costumer

show model

technical photographer

Discussion Questions

1. By surfing the Internet and perusing trade publications, develop a list of fashion show and event planning firms that are available to fashion retailers and manufacturers for contract. In what areas do these firms specialize? What career opportunities are available?

2. What are the requirements for a costumer designer who wants to secure clients in the entertainment industry? Compare and contrast the licenses, union memberships, or other credentials that are required or are helpful.

3. What are the sign-on requirements for a major modeling agency? How does the director determine who receives a contract and who does not?

4. Select a costume designer for a well-known period film and describe this costumer's research and outcomes for the film's characters' costumes.

CHAPTER 14

Fashion Scholarship

There are many different kinds of museums, museum centers, and historic sites throughout the world, and they hold a vast treasure trove of history. Museums can be large or small, public or private, and operated by the government, a community, a foundation, or a college. For example, the Fashion Institute of Technology (FIT) and Kent State University present excellent fashion-related exhibitions in their museum facilities. Museums are not only sites of exhibitions for public view but they are also centers of research and conservation. Within large museums like Victoria and Albert Museum (V&A) in London and smaller ones in towns around the world, there is also a variety of career options, many that are lesser known to the general public. The work is interdisciplinary, combining the study of fashion and textile history with hands-on skills in analysis, conservation, storage, and exhibition of textile and costume materials.

The following fashion careers in museums are examined in this chapter: museum director, museum curator, assistant curator, collections manager, museum archivist, museum conservator, and museum technician. There is another career path that may be related to those in museums, that of the educator. Fashion educators often study, research, and teach in the specialization of historical costume, as well as other areas of fashion. They are included in this chapter. In addition to these positions, there are similar jobs, though with a commercial component, in private galleries and auction houses that sell the works of fashion and textile designers. There are additional museum positions that are not examined in this chapter. These include the development associate, who is in charge of generating revenue for the museum; the membership associate, who is responsible for increasing the number of members; the education specialist, who

BOX 14.1 • FASHION MUSEUMS AND GALLERIES IN PARIS

Paris's lifelong affair with fashion lives on in the Musée de la Mode et du Textile, which houses a vast retrospective of costumes, style, and dress design since the 16th century. Palais Galliéra is yet another Parisian museum; this one featuring costumes from the 18th century to the present. Additionally, the designs and inspirations of the renowned contemporary fashion designer Yves Saint Laurent are now the focus of Paris's exhibition gallery of the Fondation Pierre Bergé—Yves Saint Laurent (YSL).

Hundreds of thousands of fabrics in the collection of the Musée de la Mode et du Textile chronicle the history of textiles. Of special interest are a seventh-century Coptic tunic, court costumes from the era of Louis XIV, the Sun King (1638-1715), and crinolines made with iron hoops. Of more recent vintage are designs by such 20th-century couturiers as Chanel, Dior, Guy Laroche, and Balenciaga. With over 80,000 items, only a fraction of the collection can be exhibited at any one time. As a result, exhibits are changed annually, and the museum kicks off each year with a different theme. Although special homage is paid to the Parisian couture legends, young designers' work is also featured in temporary exhibitions. Located aside the Louvre, the street address of Musée de la Mode et du Textile is 107, rue de Rivoli, Palais du Louvre, 75001 Paris.

French fashion and costume from the 18th century to the present; etchings, engravings, and fashion photographs are presented in the Palais Galliéra, with architecture inspired by the Italian Renaissance. There are thematic exhibitions, a library that may be visited by appointment, and a fashion-oriented bookstore and gift shop featuring items inspired by the museum's exhibitions. The Palais Galliéra is located at 10, ave. Pierre Ier de Serbie, 75116 Paris.

The exhibition gallery of the Fondation Pierre Bergé—Yves Saint Laurent is located in the former ateliers of Yves Saint Laurent. Pierre Bergé has been Yves Saint Laurent's partner since the conception of the business. In the gallery's debut exhibition, the relationship between art and fashion designer was visually communicated. Forty-two different haute couture outfits by YSL created between 1965 and 1988 were displayed in conjunction with five paintings that inspired YSL. The artists included Picasso, Mondrian, Matisse, and Warhol. The gallery currently houses 5,000 garments and over 15,000 accessories, illustrations, patterns, and miscellaneous items by YSL, all stored in state-of-the-art archival conditions. In the future, the foundation intends to expand its boundaries past YSL and fashion to include other exhibitions of paintings, photography, and drawings. The gallery is located at 3, Rue Léonce Reynaud/angle 5, Avenue Marceau, Paris. The gallery's Web address is www.fondation-pb-ysl.net.

develops educational programs for visitors; the docent, who presents lectures or conducts educational tours of exhibitions; and the exhibit designer, who creates and installs displays. These positions are limited to large and prestigious museums.

An example of a large and prestigious museum with a significant fashion collection is V&A in London, which has collected both dress and textiles since its earliest days. The collections cover fashionable dress from the 17th century to the present day, with an emphasis on progressive and influential designs from the major fashion centers of Europe. The V&A collections also include accessories such as jewelry, gloves, millinery and handbags. Research is a core activity of V&A and is carried out in all of its departments. Some research concerns the identification and interpretation of individual objects, while other studies contribute to systematic research. This helps develop the public understanding of the art and artifacts of many of the great cultures of the world, past and present. The conservation department of V&A is primarily responsible for the long-term preservation of its collections. At the core of the V&A conservator's work is the development and implementation of storage, mounting, and handling procedures that reduce the risk of damage during movement and display. Additional examples of museums and galleries in Paris are described in Box 14.1.

Most towns and cities have museums, and staffing of the museums depend on their size. Larger museums employ a director and a team of curators, assistants, and technicians. In a small museum, the curator may take on the responsibilities of a museum director. Large or small, museums offer many career opportunities that fill the needs of a fashion student who enjoys learning about, sharing with others, and preserving cultural references in history through costumes and interiors. We begin our study of careers in museums with the lead position, that of the museum director.

MUSEUM DIRECTOR

Museum directors are responsible for managing collections of artistic, scientific, historical, and general interest artifacts. In large facilities, **museum directors** manage the general operations and staffing of the institution and coordinate the public affairs mission of the museum (Figure 14.1). They literally run the business of the museum, being responsible for the human resources, public relations, budget development, and management of the facility. They work closely with

Figure 14.1. Museum Director Dr. Anan Ameri gives a tour at the opening of the Arab American National Museum.

Figure 14.2. The Getty Center, at the billion-dollar Getty Museum, has special events and programs designed to attract families.

assistants, curators, and staff to fulfill the mission of the organization. Foremost, the museum director is a steward of the artifacts held by the museum.

Increasing areas of focus for the museum director include public affairs, marketing, and development. **Public affairs** work includes collaborating with the community, the government, the industry, and social and academic organizations to develop exhibitions and collections that appeal to and educate the community and its visitors. Often, the museum director is a guide for groups viewing the exhibitions, answering visitors' questions and giving talks in the museum to local organizations or school groups. Outside of the museum, directors may also be invited speakers at clubs or universities to present on the museum's collections or a specific installation. They may be asked to cochair a gala or work with an outside sponsor on a public event planned to raise awareness or funds for the institution, as in Figure 14.2.

A leading museum can influence not only the educational and civic well-being of a community but also it can affect its fiscal health through revenue generated by tourists coming to see the museum. When visitors travel to a city to view its museum, they often spend money in the local restaurants, hotels, and stores in addition to the museum admission fee and, possibly, its gift shop. While directors work to attract visitors to a museum, they may also be asked to seek out and secure funding for the museum through national and state grants. Today, a significant part of a director's duties, and perhaps that of assistants, involves fund-raising and promotion, which may include researching, writing, and reviewing grant proposals, journal articles, and publicity materials. Fund-raising and promotional activities may also include attending meetings, conventions, and civic events.

Qualifications

The position of museum director requires knowledge and experience in diverse areas: museum studies, public relations, marketing, and human resources, to name a few. Following is a list of the educational qualifications, work experience, and personal characteristics that are needed for a museum director:

▶ **Education:** A bachelor's degree in fashion design, textiles, historical costume, museum curatorship, museum studies, heritage studies, art history, history, archaeology, or a related field is expected. Many museums require that the director have a master's of arts or fine arts or a master's of science degree in one of these fields. Candidates with a doctoral degree in a related discipline have an edge in the job search.

▶ **Experience:** Applicants for the position of director must have experience in museum work, preferably as a museum curator or the director of a smaller museum. Management experience is essential, particularly in the areas of human resources and budget development and control. Many museums require that the prospective museum director have public relations and marketing experience; some view experience in the tourism and hospitality industries as a plus. Fund-raising experience may be required or preferred. Computer skills are needed for information retrieval, maintaining the inventory of artifacts, and imaging of collection items.

▶ **Personal Characteristics:** Museum directors are often passionate about history, community affairs, and education. The effective museum director is a strong leader and a visionary who is committed to generating public interest, and possibly funding, for the museum. The work requires a range of skills, including organizational abilities, time-management skills, and paying attention to detail. The successful director has strong oral and written communication skills, a heightened esthetic sense, and excellent presentation skills.

Museum director positions are limited, particularly in some geographic areas where the number of museums is few. The average annual salary for a museum director in a midsize museum is $64,000–$85,000. In a large museum, the director can earn a six-figure salary annually.

Career Challenges

The museum director carries the weight of many responsibilities from budget development and management of the facility to human resources and public relations. In human resources, the director supervises assistants, curators, and all other staff in the museum. In public relations, the director must find innovative and inexpensive ways to promote the museum and generate funding through events and programs. It is challenging to "sell" an institution and its services, rather than a tangible product. The museum director has the role of being a jack-of-all-trades, a role that often takes long hours and much multitasking.

MUSEUM CURATOR

In large museums, **museum curators,** referred to as *museum keepers* in some countries, work under the supervision of the museum director. Curators direct the accession, deaccession, storage, and exhibition of collections (Figure 14.3). While **accession** refers to receiving new items and adding them to the collection, **deaccession** refers to removing items from a collection because of repetition of artifacts, the receipt of better examples, loss, or decay. Sometimes, museums sell valuable pieces (often, duplicates in the collection) to raise money to buy items that they want more than the deaccessioned pieces to build collections. Curators negotiate and authorize the purchase, sale, exchange, or loan of collection items. They may be responsible for authenticating, evaluating, and categorizing the items in a collection. Curators also oversee and help conduct the museum's research projects and related educational programs.

When there is a team of curators, each may be involved in one area of specialization, such as 18th-century fashions or Gothic furnishings. A large historical costume museum, for example, may employ different curators for its collections of textiles, accessories, men's wear garments, and women's apparel. Some curators maintain their collections, some conduct research, and others perform administrative tasks. In small institutions with only one or a few curators, a curator may be responsible for a number of tasks, from maintaining collections to directing the affairs of the museum. The main role of the curator is to acquire objects and research, identify, and catalog them, usually on a computer. Curators in large and small museums are also responsible for ensuring correct storage conditions. Other duties that they may be assigned include overseeing security and insurance and developing policies and procedures for the collections in collaboration with the museum director if there is one.

Figure 14.3. A museum curator.

Providing information to the public is an important part of the museum curator's job. This is accomplished through written reports, presentations, and exhibitions to the public. When assigned the task of a public exhibition, the curator either identifies or assists the museum director in identifying topics for public exhibitions (e.g., wedding gowns through the ages, 1940s costumes of women in film, Amish quilts, or men's wear of the 18th century). After the subject of the exhibition is determined, the curator plans and designs the exhibition and selects the items to be displayed. In selecting items for display, the delicacy and rarity of some items will keep them from being included. If a museum collection does not contain all of the artifacts needed to implement the theme of the exhibition, the curator may decide to borrow items from other establishments, companies, or private individuals. After the items to be displayed are confirmed, the artifacts are installed and correctly labeled, and related publications are developed. The curator may be responsible for writing signage copy and working with other departments in the museum to publicize the showing and writing a program for viewers to follow. A trend in museum exhibitions is the interactive display, in which viewers can press a button to run a video or actively participate in the exhibition's subject matter. For example, a textile exhibition may include an instructional video and work area where the viewer can weave a piece of fabric. Museums have added entertainment to their educational goals to engage the public. With such large undertakings, the curator often works with a staff of assistants and technicians.

While the range of museums has expanded enormously from large museums with full-scale models being prepared for the public to visit and recapture past ages and small museums specializing in specific artifact categories (e.g., Victorian decor, or 19th-century apparel and accessories), the curator's role has also expanded. Granted, most curators have the primary responsibility of collecting and displaying objects of historical, cultural, and scientific interest to inform and instruct. However, on a regular basis, the majority of curators' work also includes establishing policies and procedures to protect artifacts in their care. Most curators are called on to talk to museum visitors and answer their questions and give lectures and visual presentations to local groups. Now, there is a new addition to the curator's job: fund-raising and development. Writing grants and other publications, soliciting donors for gifts, locating sponsors for exhibitions, and attending conferences—with or without a museum director—help stretch limited museum budgets.

Museum curatorial training covers three main areas: academic, museological, and managerial. **Academic curator training** refers to how to study and understand collections. **Museological training** for the museum curator covers how to care for and interpret collections. **Managerial training** for the curator focuses on how to run a museum, from personnel to finances to operations. Some large museums offer a type of internship or apprenticeship for the prospective curator, often referred to as the **curatorial traineeship**. If you do not secure one of these prestigious and limited positions, how can you open the door to a career as a museum curator?

Qualifications

Here is a list of educational goals, work experience, and personal characteristics you will need.

- **Education:** A bachelor's degree in fashion design, textiles, historical costume, museum curatorship, museum studies, heritage studies, art history, history, archaeology, or a related field is required. Many top museums require that the curator have a master's of art or fine arts or a master's of science degree in one of these fields. Candidates with a doctoral degree have an advantage, particularly in museums with a widespread reputation for their collections or exhibitions.

- **Experience:** Preference is usually given to applicants with experience in museum work, which may be obtained on a voluntary basis. An internship in a museum, usually unpaid, is an excellent way to gain experience and, perhaps, college credit. Computer skills are needed for information retrieval, inventory of artifacts, and imaging of collection items. Promotion will probably be from a small museum to a larger one that will be more specialized. From there, curators can progress to directors. There are career opportunities for curators within private or national collections.

- **Personal characteristics:** Curators show a deep interest in the past and heritage and a commitment to education. In addition to an intellectual curiosity, they often have high levels of sensitivity and patience. The work is often time consuming and methodical, requiring strong organizational skills and attention to detail. The successful curator has strong oral and written communication skills, an eye for esthetically pleasing displays, and managerial abilities that include human resources, as well as budget development and management.

Curators work closely with technicians, conservation officers, and restoration personnel who care for a wide range of artifacts and exhibits, from Egyptian jewelry to centuries-old pictures and wallpaper to costumes and accessories. The curator may work with assistants, as well as the conservation and restoration staff, to research and identify the source, material, and time period of artifacts. Establishing authenticity, providing as much information as possible about museum artifacts, soliciting new items, and clearing out unwanted items are key parts of the curator's job. In Box 14.2, an article about the Metropolitan Museum of Art's task of clearing out its closets illustrates a part of the curator's job.

BOX 14.2 • FASHION MUSEUMS BULGING AT THE SEAMS: METROPOLITAN MUSEUM OF ART AND THE BROOKLYN MUSEUM OF ART ARE REVIEWING AND DOCUMENTING THEIR COLLECTIONS

By Eric Wilson

NEW YORK—Clearing out the closets is a tough process for most people, so just imagine how tough it is for the Metropolitan Museum of Art and the Brooklyn Museum of Art.

In surveys of their fashion holdings, curators and officials at the Met's Costume Institute and the Brooklyn Museum's costume and textile collections have initiated systematic reviews of the thousands of stored historical garments and accessories.

The crux of the issue is space and how much room a museum should be able to dedicate to the storage of its holdings within a particular discipline, in this case fashion.

> "Nobody wants their collections to be deaccessed. It's the last thing you ever want to do."
> —Harold Koda, Costume Institute

The Met's Costume Institute has swelled from about 30,000 pieces under the eye of Diana Vreeland in the eighties to more than 80,000, a collection that far exceeds the museum's ability to properly archive. Removing some of its lesser holdings would be an obvious solution, but one museums consider with varying perspectives—from utter distaste to a necessary means to finance new and presumably better acquisitions.

It is coincidental that the city's two most significant centers of fashion history are reviewing and documenting their holdings at the same time, museum officials said. Both institutions acknowledged that the process is a likely precursor to removing a significant amount of their inventories judged to be of lower quality than their overall collections.

At the Brooklyn Museum, which includes an acclaimed representation of 19th-century American and English costumes and fare pieces from Charles Worth and Charles James among its holdings, there has been a proposal to donate its entire collection to another institution. Sally Williams, public information officer for the museum, dismissed speculation in the curatorial community that disposal of the clothing is imminent, but acknowledged that long-term plans are "under consideration."

In curatorial speak, the process—which, depending on the institution, can take several years and requires meticulous documentation with a lengthy approval process—is known as "deaccessioning."

"Nobody wants their collections to be deaccessed," said Harold Koda, chief curator of the Costume Institute. "It's the last thing you ever want to do."

Bringing the debate to the costume departments raises another set of issues beyond the merit of Christian Dior versus Galliano for Dior, given the personal nature of many donations to museums by collectors or individuals.

(continued)

There is also the historic perception within museums that fashion is an inferior art form to painting or sculpture and less deserving of expansive space. Apart from the Met's unfortunate headquarters for its Costume Institute in its basement, the possibility of pruning its fashion collection comes at the same time the museum has proposed an expansion plan with a major capital campaign. In what would appear to be a similar twist of fortunes, the Brooklyn Museum unveiled only last month its new $63 million front entrance and plaza.

The Brooklyn Museum intends to survey its fashion collection in the near future, a process that would take at least two years. The museum's fashion and textiles collection, housed within its department of decorative arts, exceeds 300,000 pieces, according to published reports.

"This is not something you wake up one morning and say, 'We're going to remove our costume collection,'" Williams said.

The possibility, however, has piqued the interest of other institutions, most notably the Museum at the Fashion Institute of Technology here. The Museum at FIT is curated by Valerie Steele, who, according to her colleagues, aspires to build the collection as a competing force to the Met.

"If the Brooklyn Museum decided the right place for the collection was the Museum at FIT, we would be thrilled," [a] spokeswoman said. "We agree it's a totally appropriate place. The museum is the only one dedicated solely to the world of fashion."

Koda was less enthusiastic about the prospect of the Met as a potential repository, considering the Costume Institute has its own survey to face.

"We are trying to get a handle on a collection that is much too big for its space," Koda said. "We really are trying to fit into the museum in a way that does validate us as an art collection. We are like the rest of the museum—encyclopedic in our scope. Our collection has a lot of great names, but not always the best pieces from those collections. They may be the most wearable, the most elegant, but they are not always the most artistic."

Koda blames the sensitivity for popular culture for a spate of acquisitions in the nineties that valued fashion from social history on the same par as that from the great masters of design.

His approach to the survey is to determine the value of each piece to the overall collection, based on the history of the garment and who wore it, and then based on who designed it and when. So far, curators have gone through about 20,000 pieces stored in a hodgepodge of crates in subterranean vaults, some forgotten and unopened for years—and marked fewer than 800 for possible deaccession, although there is the potential to reduce as much as a quarter of the collection.

The Costume Institute has also changed its strategy in terms of current acquisitions, appealing directly to designers for pieces from their runway shows rather than waiting for customers who purchase variations of the original at retail, potentially alter them and then, after considerable wear, offer them to the museum. Koda's intent is to ultimately create a collection reflective of fashion as it first appears from the creator, citing Japan's Kyoto Costume Institute as a model, and thereby reinforce the notion of the medium as art.

Source: *Women's Wear Daily*, May 28, 2004,
copyright 2004 Fairchild Publications, Inc.

ASSISTANT CURATOR

In mid- to large-sized museums, the curator may supervise one or more assistant curators. An **assistant curator** often serves as the registrar of the collection by coordinating the collection's accessions. Once the items are correctly identified, they are accurately labeled, properly catalogued, safely stored, and maintained. This task has a technical side, as the assistant curator has the responsibilities of cataloging artifacts, entering related data into a computer, and processing collection imaging including photography, digitizing, slide labeling, and responding by e-mail to requests for images. Some of these images may be used in the publication of collection materials, such as catalogs, postcards, and exhibition programs. The assistant also works with the curator to organize and present lectures and host outside groups. If the museum has an organized membership of donors and public attendees, the assistant curator also works on a computer to maintain a member database. A number of assistant curators are assigned the responsibility of coordinating and managing student and volunteer staffs, as well as working with faculty and students on class activities and projects.

Qualifications

The assistant curator position has a number of educational and work experience requirements in addition to preferred personal characteristics as follows.

- ▸ **Education:** While a bachelor's degree in fashion, textiles, museum studies, archaeology, history, art history, or a related field is required, a master's degree in one of these areas may be preferred.
- ▸ **Experience:** Work experience, volunteer or paid, in curatorial activities is required. Computer skills are needed for information retrieval, cataloging of acquisitions, and imaging of the collection inventory.
- ▸ **Personal characteristics:** Successful experience and a commitment to team-based activities is needed, especially when working with the public and volunteers. Communication and marketing skills are a must, as the successful assistant curator needs a good understanding of how to make information accessible to the public, including tourists, people with disabilities, and educational groups and schools. Assistant curators must be organized and effective managers who are capable of running a department or team and overseeing a budget. They must have a strong attention to detail for accuracy

in cataloging objects. Finally, a creative flair for devising displays and exhibitions is needed.

It is significant to note that museums are a growing part of the leisure and hospitality industry. The information museums provide to the public must combine entertainment and education and present these in creative, appealing, and accessible ways. Attracting visitors is a key part of the curator's and assistant curator's work.

A museum curator in the Washington, D.C., area can expect to earn a starting salary of $38,000 annually. For a museum curator with a master's degree and several years' experience working in this geographic location, a salary of $68,000 can be expected. An assistant curator in this area can expect to earn between $28,000 and $36,000 annually.

Career Challenges

The museum curator works with creative projects, a detailed inventory, and budget management. It can be difficult for a creative person to work on projects that require a high level of accuracy, such as recording descriptions of new items in the collection, and quantitative analysis, such as overseeing the collection's budget. However, it can be a struggle for the analytical person to construct an artistic display. The museum curator, however, must work in both areas. It is not easy to develop and install exciting and attractive exhibits with limited resources, but the curator must manage to stretch the museum's budget.

COLLECTIONS MANAGER

Collections managers provide front-line supervision of specific museum collections. A collections manager usually takes one of two tracks to move up in the museum world: the curator or conservator track. Occasionally, the collections manager may prefer to take the archivist track. Collections managers are responsible for preparing, managing, and supervising the collections records; processing and cataloging items in the museum collections; and maintaining and entering data into a computerized collections management system. They maintain and supervise the organization of artifacts in storage, making sure everything possible is being done to keep items safely preserved. They also supervise artifact cataloging, keeping in mind that systems must provide access to the collections by the public, staff, researchers, and other museums. Collections managers work with volunteers in the collections department by preparing instructions, assembling needed materials, training them in tasks, and reviewing their work. Additional duties may include overseeing the photography of the collection, handling the preservation of the collection, conducting research, and participating in exhibit development.

Qualifications

In the job search, there are a number of educational requirements, work experiences, and personal characteristics that the collections manager candidate is expected to have. An overview of these expectations follows.

- ▶ **Education:** A bachelor's degree in fashion, textiles, museum studies, archaeology, history, art history, or a related field is required. Some museums require or prefer the candidate with a master's degree in fine arts or museum studies for this position.
- ▶ **Experience:** Work experience, volunteer or paid, in museum activities is required. College students may want to secure an internship in a museum to gain experience. Some collections managers gain paid work experience as a museum technician. Computer skills are needed for information retrieval, cataloging of acquisitions, and imaging of collection inventory.
- ▶ **Personal characteristics:** Strong written, oral, and visual communication skills are needed. Collections managers must be organized and effective managers who are capable of leading and motivating a staff or team of volunteers. They must have a strong attention to detail and accuracy, as well as knowledge of history, for cataloging artifacts. An eye for effective displays and exhibitions is also needed.

The collections manager can earn an annual salary of between $42,000 and $64,000 annually in a midsize to large museum.

Career Challenges

Working with volunteers requires the abilities to schedule, train, and motivate workers who are not being paid for the jobs they do. This can be a tough way to acquire the workforce that you need to get the job done. The collections manager is also challenged

Figure 14.4. An archivist works in the archive of the Historic Museum in Sarajevo.

with maintaining high levels of accuracy and organization when dealing with collection artifacts. At any time, the collections manager should be able to quickly locate a single item in the collection.

MUSEUM ARCHIVIST

With the curator's busy roles in accessing and displaying historical artifacts, public relations, and marketing, the position of museum archivist has become more important and prevalent in today's museums. Although some duties of archivists and curators are similar, the types of items they deal with are different. Curators usually handle objects with cultural, biological, or historical significance, such as sculptures, textiles and textile-related items, and paintings. **Archivists** mainly handle records and documents that are retained because of their importance and potential value in the future (Figure 14.4). Archivists analyze, describe, catalog, and exhibit these important records for the benefit of researchers and the public. They preserve important records and photographs that document the conception, history, use, and ownership of artifacts.

Archivists are responsible for collecting and maintaining control over a wide range of information deemed important enough for permanent safekeeping. This information takes many forms: photographs, films, video and sound recordings, computer tapes, and video and image disks, as well as more traditional paper records, illustrations, letters, and documents. Archivists also solicit, inventory, and save records and reports generated by corporations, government agencies, and educational institutions that may be of great potential value to researchers, exhibitors, genealogists, and others who would benefit from having access to original source material.

Archivists maintain and save records according to standards and practices that ensure the long-term preservation and easy retrieval of the documents. Records may be saved on any medium, including paper, film, videotape, audiotape, computerized disk. They also may be copied onto some other format to protect the original and make the records more accessible to researchers who use them. Some archivists work with the originals of specialized forms of records, such as manuscripts, electronic records, photographs, motion pictures, and sound recordings and determine the best ways of creating copies and saving the originals of these works. As various storage media evolve, archivists must keep abreast of technological advances in electronic information storage.

Computers are increasingly being used to generate and maintain archival records. Professional standards for the use of computers in handling archival records are evolving with technology. Expanding computer capabilities that allow more records to be stored and exhibited electronically have transformed and are expected to continue to transform many aspects of archival collections. Some archivists specialize in a specific area of technology so they can more accurately determine how records should be stored. Others specialize in a particular area of history to determine which items qualify for retention and should become part of the archives. Archive technicians help archivists organize, maintain, and provide access to historical documentary materials.

Qualifications

If working with history and preserving it for the future sounds like a fascinating and fulfilling career, here is what you need to do and know to become a museum archivist.

- ▸ **Education:** A bachelor's degree in textiles; museum studies; costume and textiles; fashion and textile studies: history, theory, and museum practice; art history; or a related discipline is required.
- ▸ **Experience:** Archivists may gain work experience in a variety of organizations, including government agencies, museums, historical societies, and educational institutions. An internship or work experience as an archive technician is an ideal way to open the door to this career path. Experience in computer imaging, including photographs, illustrations, and films, is a plus.
- ▸ **Personal characteristics:** Archivists are methodical, detail oriented, and well organized. They often have inquisitive natures. They work to stay up-to-date on evolving restoration and preservation techniques.

The annual salary for an archivist ranges between $40,000 and $58,000 for a mid-size museum in a midsize city.

Career Challenges

Education is never ending for the museum archivist. This person must constantly learn about the latest techniques to restore and preserve artifacts. Technological advances and new types of cleaning and restoration equipment help the archivist maintain collection

Figure 14.5. A conservator from Sotheby's prepares a cinnibar lacquer box for auction at Easton Neston House near Towcester in Northamptonshire in central England.

items for longer periods of time. The archivist is always working with details and must work methodically and with focus.

MUSEUM CONSERVATOR

Museum conservators manage, care for, preserve, treat, and document works of art, artifacts, and specimens (Figure 14.5). Museum conservators are also referred to as *restoration and preservation specialists.* With regard to fashions or costumes, conservators acquire and preserve important visuals (e.g., photographs, illustrations, or sketches), costumes, accessories, furnishings, and other valuable items for permanent storage or display. Much of their work requires substantial historical, scientific, and archaeological research. Conservators use X-rays, chemical testing, microscopes, special lights, and other laboratory equipment and techniques to examine objects. Conservators' objectives are to determine the artifacts' conditions, their need for treatment or restoration, the best way to repair worn or damaged items, and the appropriate methods for preserving items. Many institutions prefer not to repair but to preserve artifacts to minimize damage and deterioration by effectively maintaining items. The conservator's work is performed under close supervision with an emphasis on saving and maintaining, or **stabilizing**, artifacts while developing the studies of historical preservation. Conservators may specialize in a particular material or group of objects, such as documents and books, paintings, decorative arts, textiles, metals, or architectural materials.

Qualifications

Qualifications for the museum conservator include the following educational goals, work experiences, and personal characteristics:

> ▸ **Education:** A bachelor's degree in museum studies, archaeology, textile science, art history, or a related field is a requirement. Larger, more prestigious museums require a master's degree in one of these areas.
> ▸ **Experience:** Museum conservators must have the knowledge, skills, and abilities required to perform basic preservation maintenance, repair, and treatment

BOX 14.3 • THE CONSERVATION DEPARTMENT OF THE VICTORIA AND ALBERT MUSEUM

The conservation department of the Victoria and Albert Museum in London is primarily responsible for the long-term preservation of the collections. The department conserves all of the collections held by the V&A and its branches, the Theatre Museum, and the Museum of Childhood. The conservators specialize in particular areas of conservation, which reflect the collections held by the museum. The core of the conservator's work is the care and understanding of the V&A's collections. This is achieved not only through surveys, assessments, and hands-on treatment of objects but also through the provision of advice from professional conservators from around the world.

Correct packaging, mounting, and handling procedures reduce the risk of damage during movement and display, and conservators frequently act as couriers when V&A objects are loaned to other institutions. These aspects of conservation work are known as preventive conservation. They include activities such as controlling the museum environment (e.g., temperature and light) and preventing pests (e.g., insects) from entering the museum. This type of conservation helps to slow down rates of deterioration. Other treatments come into the category of interventive conservation. They include cleaning and reintegration to strengthen fragile objects, reveal original surface decoration or technology, and restore shape. Interventive treatment makes the object more stable but also more attractive and comprehensible to the viewer. It is usually undertaken on items that are to go on public display. Before embarking on any interventive treatment, the conservator carefully examines the object and records evidence of use, manufacture, materials, techniques, or design.

Through their research into the deterioration and preservation of the collections, their development of new conservation processes, and their knowledge of original technology, the V&A's conservation staff members have become leading experts in their fields. This knowledge is passed to others through publications and involvement with training and education programs.

Source: www.vam.ac.uk/res_cons/conservation/index.html

of historical artifacts. Consequently, training, course work, or an internship with a museum or educational institution can provide the opportunity to learn these skills and remain up-to-date on the latest technology and restoration techniques.

▶ **Personal characteristics:** Museum conservators must have the patience and organizational skills to work methodically. They have the curiosity and ability of an investigator to piece information together. They are interested in science and keep current with restoration and preservation techniques.

The challenges of a museum conservator's career are similar to those of the archivist as previously described. Box 14.3 illustrates the mission and duties of the conservator department in the Victoria and Albert Museum. It also describes the work of a museum technician, next on the list of career options in museum organizations.

MUSEUM TECHNICIAN

Museum technicians assist curators by performing various preparatory and maintenance tasks on museum items. Some museum technicians assist curators with research. As a result of their close collaboration with collections managers and curators, museum technicians often move to the position of collections manager. Most technicians work to preserve, maintain, and repair artifacts. They perform their work with an emphasis on safety, of the items and themselves because of the use of chemicals, and have an understanding of historic preservation treatment techniques. Museum technicians have the ability to differentiate contemporary and period fabrication and construction and take appropriate steps to protect artifacts. Working from blueprints, sketches, shop lists, and written and oral instructions, museum technicians procure equipment and materials for project work. Next, they recommend treatments for the items. After implementing restoration and preservation treatments, they accurately and completely document project work through photography, drawings, and written narratives.

Qualifications

Technicians need the skills and knowledge of environmental legislation to assess material, environmental, and other workplace hazard potential and develop safety programs. Educational requirements, work experience, and preferred personal characteristics for museum technicians include the following:

▸ **Education:** While an associate's or a bachelor's degree in textiles, museum studies, history, visual arts, or a related field is required by most museums, some technicians enter the career path by acquiring knowledge and abilities in a specific skill area. Technicians, for example, may have hands-on expertise in knitting, lace making, couture sewing techniques, wool tailoring, weaving, fabric dying, or other skill areas.

▸ **Experience:** An applicant may enter the museum as a technician with no formal qualifications required; however, some kind of applied skill, such as pattern making or embroidery, is usually required. Some technicians gain training and experience by working as a volunteer with the technicians in a museum.

▶ **Personal characteristics:** Technicians have the patience and focus to work with great care and precision. They are planners, as artifacts must be thoroughly reviewed and restoration techniques thoroughly detailed before restoration begins. Often, the best technicians are those who are perfectionists in their areas of expertise.

Museum technicians can expect to earn between $34,000 and $47,000 annually, depending on the amount of experience they have, as well as the geographic location of and the size of the museum for which they work.

Career Challenges

Technicians must come up with the techniques, products, and equipment to restore and preserve artifacts. While they may have an interest in fashion, it is more important that they have an understanding of chemistry, textile science, and technology. They are challenged to work methodically and accurately with safety and preservation of artifacts as key pressures.

FASHION EDUCATOR

Middle and high school teachers in the area of apparel and textiles often graduate from college and university programs with a bachelor's or master's degree in **Family and Consumer Science Education (FCSEd)**. They may be asked to teach courses in textiles, fashion, clothing selection and apparel care, clothing construction, interior design, fiber arts, consumer education, personal financial literacy, and careers in the fashion industry. Some FCSEd graduates choose employment with high school or **vocational schools**, providing training for students who elect not to participate in a four-year college degree program after high school graduation. In these programs, they teach a range of courses, such as commercial clothing construction, apparel alteration, pattern making, and retailing. Upon completion of these programs, the student may earn an associate's degree. There is also the opportunity for employment as a teacher in a **trade school**. These institutions may offer fashion programs and provide certificates, rather than degrees, once the student

Figure 14.6. A fashion educator works in the classroom.

completes the program. Trade schools offer programs in such areas as fashion design, illustration, retailing, and fashion merchandising.

Regardless of the type of school, educators in fashion programs are professionals who have many roles in addition to classroom instruction. Many make purchasing decisions about textbooks, supplies, and equipment such as sewing machines, sergers, and dress forms. Some conduct research, write about their findings, and submit their reports for publication. Others seek out funding sources for their programs in the schools, sourcing and writing grants and soliciting sponsors from the government or industry. Many participate in organizations and on committees that focus on pedagogical issues, curricula in schools and colleges, instructional methods, and job outlooks in fashion industry professions, among other topics. A great number of fashion educators include **professional development** on their to-do lists. This includes continuing education, often toward a higher degree; internships in the field; conference participation; and memberships in trade and educational organizations. Figure 14.6 shows a fashion educator at work.

Educators in colleges and universities often have the **terminal degree**, or highest degree available, or its equivalent in fashion, business administration, higher education, or a related field—with specializations in their areas of instruction. For example, a fashion design professor may have a doctorate in the field, industry experience as a designer, and a broad knowledge of fashion design. In addition to a general knowledge of the field, it is expected that the professor have technical expertise in specialized areas such as computer-aided design, draping, pattern making, or garment construction. In addition, many universities require college-level teaching experience, often not only in the classroom but also through other delivery methods, such as guided studies and online courses, also referred to **e-learning courses**.

If the college-level teaching position includes responsibilities for advising and instructing graduate students, the faculty member must hold a terminal degree and be approved as a member of the graduate faculty. Experience in research and publication is preferred to demonstrate professional potential in scholarly work. Terms of appointment for college faculty range between nine and 12 months. They may be tenure track, instructor, or lecturer positions. With prior experience, tenure track positions can be secured at the levels of assistant or associate professor. Many colleges and universities specify the proportion of teaching and research that a position will hold, such as 50 percent research and 50 percent teaching.

Qualifications

The following is a list of the educational goals, work experiences, and personal characteristics that will assist the person seeking a career in fashion education:

- ▸ **Education:** Fashion teachers in middle and high schools need at least a bachelor's degree and teaching certification. Their majors in college may include FCSEd, education, fashion design, textiles, interior design, fashion merchandising, and similar degree programs. Many of these teachers choose to complete a master's degree in the field to attain a higher knowledge level and a higher salary. For the college or university educator, a master's degree in an appropriate discipline (e.g., fashion design, fashion merchandising, education, or business administration) is minimally required. Most colleges and universities prefer a teaching candidate with a doctoral degree in a related field; some require this.

- ▸ **Experience:** For many college and university teaching positions, the candidate must have a minimum of five years of professional industry experience. College teaching experience in specific areas (e.g., fashion design, fashion merchandising, or product development) may also be required by certain colleges or universities. In some cases, a record of juried, scholarly publications is either required or preferred. Prospective employers may require a portfolio that includes examples of one's own work and examples of students' work.

- ▸ **Personal characteristics:** Flexibility, creativity, and a passion for lifelong learning are qualities of the successful educator. The ability to work as a team member is critical, as is the ability to develop and maintain collegial and industry relationships. The effective teacher is often a constant student, participating in professional development activities to stay abreast of industry trends and career opportunities.

The fashion educator with a terminal degree and some teaching experience earns between $44,000 and $65,000 on an average for a nine-month appointment. Educators who carry administrative 12 month appointments in addition to teaching or research duties earn approximately between $65,000 and $85,000 annually.

Career Challenges

Staying up-to-date on industry trends while staying on top of teaching responsibilities, such as preparing lectures and grading assignments, is a challenge. Many universities also require faculty to maintain a program of research, one that results in creative exhibits or publications, and serve on college or community committees. This requires time management, organization, balance, and devotion to one's profession. Many fashion educators must wear a number of hats, from teacher and author to advisor and recruiter.

SUMMARY

Museums offer a wide range of career opportunities, including that of museum director, curator, assistant curator, collections manager, archivist, conservator, and technician. Curators administer the affairs of museum centers and historic sites. The head curator of a museum is usually called the museum director. Depending on the size of the museum, the curator may supervise one or more assistants. While curators usually handle objects of historical significance, archivists handle mainly records and documents that are retained because of their importance and potential value in the future. The collections manager is responsible for preparing, managing, and supervising one or more specific groupings of artifacts in the museum. Museum conservators manage, preserve, treat, and document works of art and artifacts. Technicians perform various preparatory and maintenance tasks on museum items to restore and preserve artifacts. On a related yet different career track, fashion educators teach, research, and contribute to the fashion industry through career instruction and further studies.

KEY TERMS

academic curator training
accession
archivist
assistant curator
collections manager
curatorial traineeship

deaccession

e-learning course

Family and Consumer Science Education (FCSEd)

managerial training

museological training

museum conservator (restoration and preservation specialist)

museum curator (museum keeper)

museum director

museum technician

professional development

public affairs

stabilizing

terminal degree

trade school

vocational school

Discussion Questions

1. Compare and contrast the work responsibilities of the museum conservator with those of technician. Using the Internet, research and report on the types of technological advances that may affect conservation and restoration of historic textiles.

2. After perusing classified advertisements online (e.g., www.HigherEd.com and www.itaaonline.org) for clothing and textile educators in colleges and universities, list the differences in education and work experience requirements for the following types of educator positions: tenure track, lecturer, and instructor.

3. Locate and list descriptions of six lesser-known museums around the world that specialize in decorative arts, apparel, accessories, and interior furnishing and accessories. What are their missions, educational programs, and preservation strategies?

4. Many fashion designers visit museums for design inspiration, construction ideas, and color ideas. Identify three well-known designers who use historical costume as a source on inspiration. Provide illustrations, such as magazine clippings, of current garments the designers have created that were inspired by historical costumes. Identify the time periods and designers of these historical costumes.

CHAPTER 15

Environments: Websites, Exteriors, and Interiors

Envision a fashion business as a jewel, think of its environment as a jewelry box with a strong, good-looking leather exterior and a beautiful velvet interior. A building, the kiosk in a mall, a boutique in a strip center, and even a website can function as the "boxes" that house various types of fashion businesses. Someone locates the right building or storefront for the retailer; if the right facility cannot be found, it may be built to order. Others design and install the interior—from the ceiling and lights to the floor coverings and furnishings. When viewing a retailer in e-commerce, the website *is* the store exterior and interior, with its visuals, links, sound, and motion.

The fashion industry is a visual one. As a result, the way a fashion business's building, website, and interior look can affect the business's profitability and image. Website developers, architects, and real estate professionals work to create or locate the right exterior for a fashion business. Combining knowledge with esthetic vision, the interior designer often collaborates with the architect and visual merchandising professional to develop interior environments that are safe, functional, and attractive while meeting the needs of the people using the space. Once the space design is complete in a mall, the mall manager works to keep the interior environment looking fresh and appealing for consumers. Careers involved in developing the environments of fashion businesses (and other retail businesses) are examined in this chapter and categorized as websites, exteriors, and interiors. They include the following: website developer, architect, commercial broker and real estate agent, commercial real estate developer, interior designer, visual merchandising professional, and mall manager.

WEBSITES

We begin our exploration of careers that relate to the sites of fashion businesses with the newest career path, that of the website developer.

Website Developer

Website development, or design, a relatively new field in design and fashion, is concerned with constructing Web pages and sites from both esthetic and marketing perspectives (Figure 15.1). The titles used to describe positions in website construction are not standard by any means, and often the terms *website designer* and *website developer* are used interchangeably. **Website developers** are responsible for everything from designing a website's look and feel to incorporating features such as e-commerce, online community, animations, interactive applications, and advertising hosting into the site—all while ensuring that the site's design is optimized for the specific technologies supporting it. While many website developers are salaried employees (e.g., in advertising, marketing, or design agencies or at web consulting firms, which build and manage websites for client organizations), there are a large number of freelance website developers in the industry, and they are who this chapter is about. These professionals need general design skills (e.g., an understanding of drawing and a knack for creating attractive combinations of color and form) and knowledge of web-specific design factors (e.g., screen resolution, image compression, accessibility, and website architecture). A career as a website developer requires a combination of visual skills and proficiency in technology.

The success of website developers determines whether people stay on a site or leave and whether they do what the site wants them to do while they are there. If the website's purpose is to generate e-commerce, sales results ultimately provide the measure of the success of the website developer's work. If the website depends on advertising or subscriptions for its revenue, then calculations such as online advertisement click-throughs and new subscribers will provide the measure of success. If the website's primary purpose is to increase brand value or product value to the consumer, then its effectiveness is more difficult to

Figure 15.1. Successful website developers are design-savvy and proficient in technology.

measure. Website developers create the look, feel, and navigation for websites. Their work includes defining the **user interface (UI)**, the visuals people see and interact with when they view a website and the navigation by which they move through the site. The developers create catchy graphics or animated images and choose the style, fonts, and other visual elements that make a site appealing and help a company advance its business goals. Because Web surfers are increasingly accessing the Internet via wireless devices, whether they are WiFis or Bluetooth-enabled computers, cell phones, or personal digital assistants, website developers are increasingly facing the need to equip the pages they design for wireless devices.

A good website can be many times more effective than a print brochure by delivering the exact type and amount of information that a consumer desires. The successful website allows clients to order without filling out a print form or dialing a phone number. Along with orders, a site captures relevant user data, such as pages viewed, time spent at the site, and other information that can allow for targeted marketing, thus improving a company's business. As with design in general, a website developer's job is to make the product (i.e, the website) functional and entertaining for the user. For example, some apparel websites allow customers to "try on" clothing selections in different colors and combinations on body forms that resembles theirs. A corporate website should help sell or market whatever business is promotion as an institution. A website developer working on a corporate intranet site, for instance, will want to ensure easy access to relevant information. A website developer working at an e-commerce site will want to make sure users recognize what the company is selling and help make the process of buying it as easy as possible. The website developer interacts with clients or other departments; takes other forms of information, such as brochures, slide presentations, print advertisements, or other documents, and turns them into multimedia experiences; and incorporates user data to help define and shape a website that people enjoy visiting and helps the sponsoring company achieve its goals.

The interactive and highly integrated nature of a website means that there is a constant cycle of creating, troubleshooting, and publishing involved. Companies may give a website developer raw information or documents to publish. While web developers may attend organizational or departmental meetings on a regular basis, the largest portion of their workdays is spent on computers—creating new graphics and scripts, experimenting with animation, implementing new navigational techniques, or hunting down broken or expired hyperlinks. Website development is a high-profile role, as this work is viewed and assessed by thousands of people every day. The downside to this high visibility is that a mistake can affect the entire company. Still, for artists and techies at heart with a perfectionist streak and the desire to have their work presented around the world, website development may be the ideal profession.

Qualifications

What do you need to learn to become a website developer? The list of educational requirements, work experiences, and personal characteristics follows.

- ▸ **Education:** A bachelor's degree in graphic design, computer information science, visual arts, fine arts, or similar fields is required. Some fashion design majors complete a minor in graphic design or computer information technologies to make them marketable in this career track. Increasingly, universities are offering, and employers are requesting, specialized degrees in such areas as user interface design and information design.

- ▸ **Experience:** Minimally, website developers need to be familiar with HTML and JavaScript and understand the way Web graphics, such as JPEGs and GIFs, work. The website developer should also be proficient with industry-standard graphic-design software, such as Adobe Photoshop and Illustrator, and Web layout tools, such as Microsoft FrontPage and Adobe's (formerly Macromedia's) Dreamweaver. The multimedia design field includes many companies that are developing new and better design tools all of the time, but the industry is dominated by applications from Adobe, including Director, Shockwave, and Flash. Web graphic designer is an entry-level position that requires as much knowledge of design-tool software as it does creative energy. A person can move into the website development field after working as a website graphic designer, creating the graphic elements for websites, including banner ads, buttons, and other navigational elements.

- ▸ **Personal characteristics:** The website developer must be open to learning new skills on an ongoing basis. Designing pages is not simply creative, though artistic talent is required for a successful career; it also supports a business goal. The website developer needs an understanding of business and marketing concepts. Good people skills and imagination complement the mastery of the design tools.

As with many positions, salaries for website developers vary according to location and the size of employer. Following are some typical annual salary ranges: starting website developer, $25,000–$60,000; senior website developer, $50,000–$80,000; creative director, $65,000–$100,000; interface developer, $65,000–$85,000, and interface development director, $120,000–$140,000.

Career Challenges

The website developer must work with creativity and a strong attention to detail. It can be a stressful job to stay on top of technology, troubleshoot problems, and interpret people's requests for website additions. The website developer is challenged with being a perpetual student of the craft. As the Internet and technology evolve and the needs of Internet users change, there is a continual need for new skills among website developers.

EXTERIORS

There are several careers that relate to the exteriors of fashion businesses. These include architect, commercial broker and real estate agent, and commercial real estate developer, among others. While these careers do not require education in a fashion-related discipline, professionals in these careers may find it profitable and interesting to choose fashion businesses as a specialization.

Figure 15.2. Exterior of the new Tokyo Prada store, at night. The building took years to finish and is quite famous for its architecture. It is located in one of Tokyo's prime shopping areas, the Aoyama district. The architects are Herzog and de Meuron.

Architect

An **architect** is a building designer who may work with a wide variety of structures. Those who specialize in serving retail clients have opportunities for projects ranging from small freestanding retail stores to large malls. Architecture is the creative blend of art and science in the design of environments for people. The plans for a building ultimately focus on the needs of the people who use them, to include esthetic, safety, and environmental factors. The architect and client first collaborate on the client's vision. They discuss options, costs, and materials. Architects also communicate with builders, contractors, plumbers, painters, carpenters, and air-conditioning and heating specialists, those who will make the spaces that satisfy those needs. Most commercial work has strict budgets and practical limitations. In contrast, Figure 15.2 is an example of an elaborate architectural creation with few limitations, the Prada retail store in Tokyo.

The architect creates concept drawings, often on the computer, for the client to review. When the concepts are approved by the client, the architect draws up plans that illustrate not only how the building will look but also how to build it. The drawings show the beams that hold up the building; heating, air-conditioning, and ventilation; electrical and plumbing systems; and so on.

Most architects enter the field with a vision, desire to build, and prediscovered engineering ability; unfortunately, most architects do not exercise these skills until many years after entering the profession. Beginning architects research zoning, building codes, and legal filings; draft plans from others' designs; and build models at the side of a more experienced architect. Accomplished architects may not spend as much time as they would like designing. Often, they spend it consulting closely with their clients and builders, selling or explaining concepts.

Qualifications

The profession of architect requires the following educational goals, experiences, and personal characteristics:

- ▶ **Education:** Becoming an architect is a long process. A prospective architect must complete an academic degree specifically focused on architecture. This can be a five-year bachelor's of architecture program, an affiliated two-year master's of architecture program, or, for those whose undergraduate degrees were in a field unassociated with architecture, a three- to four-year master's of architecture program. Many students also prepare for a career in architecture with a four-year (undergraduate) liberal arts degree followed by a three- to four-year (graduate) master's of architecture degree. To be called an architect, it is necessary to be licensed in the state where one works. Most states require a candidate with an accredited **National Architectural Accrediting Board Inc. (NAAB)** first-professional degree. Candidates are expected to have completed an internship period of, typically, three years with an architecture firm. All states require applicants to pass a rigorous, eight-part **Architect Registration Examination (ARE).** Employers now place greater emphasis on applicants who have mastered computer-aided design programs, which promise to become required knowledge for any architect as technology continues to develop.
- ▶ **Experience:** Many college students gain work experience through an internship with an architect, required by some colleges and universities. Most new

architects begin in an assistant position, working with an experienced architect in an area of specialization in which they plan to build a career. Once experienced, architects move into a variety of employment venues and often develop an area of specialization. Some move to universities, public design firms, or private design companies, including product design in home fashions. Some architects work as consultants for projects under construction, advising on such details as materials, construction, and scheduling.

▸ **Personal characteristics:** Architects must be able to visualize projects and communicate these visions through drawing or computer-generated images. Presentation skills, effective writing, and public speaking are also important. Decision making, team leadership, and creativity are key attributes of the successful architect. The architect must have a high attention to detail and strong time-management skills.

The new architect with three or four years of experience as an assistant can expect to earn between $60,000 and $70,000 annually. Experienced architects who have established a strong reputation in a specialty area, such as retail store development, will earn in excess of $150,000 annually.

Career Challenges

The first career disadvantage for an architect is how long and how much effort it takes to arrive at the start of this career track. Many years and much money must be invested in education and licensing. It takes a great deal of perseverance and dedication to complete a degree successfully and become certified in architecture. Once in the field, the architect faces daily challenges of constant revision of plans based on client needs, contractor issues, and budget restrictions. Plans and priorities have to be reevaluated regularly and revised accordingly. Additionally, there are legal aspects of the architect's career as the architect must stay on top of building codes, safety requirements, and legal filings.

Commercial Broker and Real Estate Agent

Commercial brokers and **real estate agents** specialize in income-producing properties, such as office buildings, retail stores, warehouses, shopping centers, and industrial parks. Commercial brokers and real estate agents are independent businesspeople who sell real estate owned by others; they also may lease or manage other properties for a fee. Brokers supervise agents who may have many of the same job duties. Brokers may also manage their own or others' offices, advertise properties, and handle other business matters. In many states, commercial real estate agents are required to be licensed for up to a year before they can take the additional training and testing to be licensed as a commercial broker.

To understand and explain why properties are good investments, commercial brokers and real estate agents need to be aware of the growth possibilities of the area where the property is located, current income tax regulations, and purchasing arrangements that give the buyer a greater return on investment. They are familiar with local zoning and business tax laws. They also act as intermediaries in price negotiations between buyers and sellers. The commercial broker or real estate agent may negotiate sales or leases, representing both landlords looking to market retail space and tenants looking to open, relocate, or expand a retail business.

When selling real estate, commercial brokers or real estate agents arrange meetings between buyers and sellers during which the details of the transactions are negotiated to be agreed on and allow the new owners to take possession of the property. Commercial brokers or real estate agents may help to arrange favorable financing from a lender for the prospective buyer; often, this makes the difference between success and failure in closing a sale. In some cases, commercial brokers assume primary responsibility for closing sales; in others, lawyers or title companies do.

To make sales, commercial brokers and real estate agents must have properties to sell. Consequently, they spend a significant amount of time finding and securing **listings**, agreements by owners to place properties for sale with them. When listing a property for sale, the commercial broker or real estate agent uses three approaches to determine a **competitive market price**, a fair and competitive selling price, for a property.

1. The **comparative market approach** compares the listed property with similar properties that have recently sold.
2. The **cost approach** looks at the new construction costs of similar types and styles of buildings.
3. The **income approach** examines return-on-investment ratios known as *CAP rates*.

Once the price is determined and the listing is developed, the broker works to market the property. In some cases, brokers use computers to give buyers virtual tours of properties in which they are interested. With a computer, buyers can view interior and exterior images or floor plans from their homes or offices. Once the property is sold, both the agent who sold it and the agent who obtained the listing receive a portion of the commission. As a result, agents who sell properties that they themselves have listed can increase their commissions. The managing broker of an office often receives a commission percent on every sale made through the office.

Box 15.1 is an interview with a successful commercial real estate broker.

BOX 15.1 • INTERVIEW WITH A COMMERCIAL REAL ESTATE BROKER

Interviewee: Scott T. Axon, CBI

Job Title: Commercial Real Estate Broker/Business Intermediary

Background (education and experience) to move into this career track:

Most commercial real estate brokers begin with a bachelor's degree; finance or marketing is often most related. Previous business ownership or experience is helpful but not necessary. Successful brokers often engage in continuing education and professional credentialing from trade associations, such as Certified Commercial Investment Member (CCIM) from the CCIM Institute or Certified Business Intermediary (CBI) from the International Business Brokers Association, Inc. (IBBA). This field requires a professional to have an in-depth knowledge of finance as well as marketing and sales.

If you were hiring someone to work for you, these are the personal characteristics in the job candidate that you would look for:

Success as a commercial real estate broker requires a blend of self-motivation and strong people skills. A candidate should possess a firm command of many legal and finance issues while being able to motivate and manage clients. To excel in this career, an individual must have many of the characteristics of a lawyer, accountant, salesperson, and senior-level consultant.

What do you enjoy most about the job:

I enjoy helping people, being part of a team that equips professional investors and business principals to make strategic decisions that impact their bottom line for years. I like the challenge of problem solving, working with many diverse people, and coming back years after a project is complete, knowing that I was able to be a small part of something permanent. I also like the fact that the income potential is limited only by my own abilities.

What do you like the least:

It is possible to invest a significant amount of work, time, and effort in a project and not get paid.

Industry trends that you believe will affect what you are doing or will be doing in the next five to ten years:

This is a dynamic market. I think there will be regions of the country that have seen speculative land investment (e.g., Phoenix, areas of Southern California, and others) that will see a decrease in real estate values. The professionals in these markets might experience a softening in demand, resulting in a reduction in their income-producing ability. In regions outside of these pockets of speculation, the real estate market should experience stable, strong growth for years to come. Opportunities in this field are significantly impacted by interest rates. If the federal government chooses to raise rates significantly in the coming years, real estate transactions will slow significantly.

Advice to people interested in entering this career field:

Take a hard look at yourself. If you are strongly self-motivated and work well with people, this is a great career path. If you are security oriented and like working with facts and figures more than conducting a meeting or talking on the phone, this may not be the place for you.

Anything else you want to add:

A career in commercial real estate requires strong self-confidence and leadership skills. For the right person, it is one of the few careers requiring little financial investment that has an income potential that matches or exceeds that of a top surgeon.

Qualifications

The qualifications for this career follow:

▸ **Education:** A bachelor's degree in real estate, finance, accounting, or a similar field is a minimal requirement. Some universities offer graduate-level courses, particularly important for those interested in analysis and property acquisition. As with other professions, licensing is required. Licensing requirements vary from state to state, but all require prospective real estate agents and brokers to pass written exams. Continuing education is required to maintain a commercial broker's license.

▸ **Experience:** Some states allow students to take pre-licensing educational courses accredited by the state licensing agency before they qualify to sit for the exam. In other states, students can take these educational courses within a specified time after being licensed. The realtor must first earn a real estate license and then sign on with a brokerage. Other career entry options include office assistant, listing or rental agent, or assistant in the mortgage division of a bank. With more experience and on passing of an additional exam, becoming a commercial broker is the next step. Commercial brokers often own their own businesses and employ a team of commercial real estate agents.

▸ **Personal characteristics:** Successful people in commercial real estate are goal oriented, positive, persevering, self-motivated, ambitious, and people oriented. The real estate professional must be adaptable, have a good sense of timing, and know when to say "no." The rewards of a career in commercial real estate are a potential for high earnings, autonomy, an intellectual challenge, and a never-dull environment. The commercial broker with a good balance of industry knowledge and entrepreneurial spirit can have a profitable and fulfilling career.

Commercial Real Estate Developer

Among the most entrepreneurial of the real estate career paths, **commercial real estate developers** acquire land, prepare it for development, and, sometimes, oversee the construction process. Commercial developers specialize in business-related land and building developments, and within one of these areas, they focus on geographic location, property size, and types of property. A developer who decides to focus on a geographic location identifies areas with strong population growth that will see increased retail and investor demand. Currently, such areas include California, Florida, Texas, Arizona, and other Sun Belt states. Some commercial developers may specialize in the development of specific types of retail space. Some of these commercial developers focus on building enclosed malls in metropolitan areas, yet others may concentrate on building shopping centers near high-income residential areas.

Commercial retail space includes malls, business districts, and shopping centers. **Shopping centers** are distinctly different from downtown and local business districts. The shopping center building is preplanned as a merchandising unit for interplay among tenants. Its site is deliberately selected by the developer for easy access to pull customers from a trade area. Figure 15.3 shows the first shopping center in the United States, Country Club Plaza on the outskirts of Kansas City, Missouri. An important attribute of shopping center layouts is on-site parking. Many customers enjoy this convenience as they are able to drive in, park, and walk to their destination with relative safety and speed. Some shopping centers provide weather protection with canopies and interior corridors, while a mall provides a fully enclosed shopping environment.

Figure 15.3. In 1922, J. C. Nichols created Country Club Plaza on the outskirts of Kansas City, Missouri, as an automobile-centered plaza built according to a unified plan and owned and operated by a single entity who leases space to tenants, rather than as a random group of stores.

Retail space development is one of the most important and challenging specialties in real estate today. For a commercial real estate developer to turn land into profitable and marketable commercial development, site selection is the critical first decision. Planning and layout are begun only after the developer determines the need for a project. Before the actual building begins, developers first analyze all costs and arrange the financing. Next, they contract for the physical structures and may supervise construction. Finally, commercial real estate developers promote the finished development to the retail prospects for whom it was planned. The commercial real estate developer has educational requirements, work experiences, and personality traits similar to those of the commercial broker.

A commercial real estate broker or developer with four or five years of experience can expect to earn between $70,000 and $100,000 annually. Successful brokers and developers with several additional years of experience often earn over $200,000 annually, depending on the geographic location. Commercial real estate agents can earn between $40,000 and more than $100,000, depending on their experience and location. Box 15.2 discusses the training and other qualifications for a career in commercial real estate.

BOX 15.2 • TRAINING AND OTHER QUALIFICATIONS FOR REAL ESTATE

In every state, real estate brokers and sales agents must be licensed. Prospective agents must be high school graduates, be at least 18 years old, and pass a written test. The examination, which is more comprehensive for brokers than for agents, includes questions on basic real estate transactions and laws affecting the sale of property. Most states require candidates for the general sales license to complete between 30 and 90 hours of classroom instruction. Those seeking a broker's license need between 60 and 90 hours of formal training and work experience selling real estate, usually one to three years. Some states waive the experience requirements for the broker's license for applicants who have a bachelor's degree in real estate. State licenses typically must be renewed every one or two years, usually without an examination. Many states require continuing education for license renewals. Prospective agents and brokers should contact the real estate licensing commission of the state in which they wish to work to verify the exact licensing requirements.

As real estate transactions have become more legally complex, many firms have turned to college graduates to fill positions. A large number of agents and brokers have some college training. College courses in real estate, finance, business administration, statistics, economics, law, and English are helpful. For those who intend to start their own company, business courses in areas such as marketing and accounting are as significant as courses in real estate and finance.

Many firms offer formal training programs for both beginners and experienced agents. Larger firms usually offer more extensive programs than smaller firms. More than a thousand universities, colleges, and junior colleges offer courses in real

(*continued*)

estate. At some, a student can earn an associate's or bachelor's degree with a major in real estate; several offer advanced degrees. Many local real estate associations that are members of the National Association of Realtors sponsor courses that cover the fundamentals and legal aspects of the field. Advanced courses in mortgage financing, property development and management, and other subjects also are available.

Advancement opportunities for agents may take the form of higher rates of commission. As agents gain knowledge and expertise, they become more efficient in closing a greater number of trans- actions and increase their earnings. In many large firms, experienced agents can advance to sales manager or general manager. Persons who have received their broker's license may open their own offices. Others with experience and training in esti- mating property value may become real estate appraisers, and people familiar with operating and maintaining rental properties may become prop- erty managers. Experienced agents and brokers with a thorough knowledge of business conditions and property values in their localities may enter mortgage financing or real estate investment coun- seling.

Career Challenges

Professionals in the real estate careers of agent, commercial broker, and commercial devel- oper share similar challenges in their careers. They do not know when the next paycheck will arrive. Most work on commission and are paid only after a sale is closed. Sometimes, the real estate professional is at the closing table when a detail in the transaction or the per- sonality of one of the players in the negotiation will kill the sale at the last minute. After spending days, weeks, or even months on this deal, the real estate professional now must start all over. Working with bankers, lawyers, buyer representatives, and inspectors, among others, the commercial real estate professional is constantly negotiating and collab- orating with experts in related fields. In many cases, it takes a team to close a sale.

INTERIORS

We now shift our focus indoors to explore the auxiliary career options of interior designer, visual merchandising professional, mall manager, and assistant mall manager.

Interior Designer

Interior designers work in a wide range of environments, including homes and busi- nesses. They can work alone, as is often the case in residential interiors, as part of a team of professionals, or in collaboration with other professionals in related careers, as with the interior designer and the architect. Some interior designers work primarily in **residential design**, focusing on home environments. These interior designers function as fashion service providers for residential clients. Others function as ancillary fashion providers for retail clients or businesses. They may work with architects and other designers to provide fashion services for public structures. A number of architectural firms include an interior design department. Referred to as **commercial,** or **contract, designers,** these interior designers concentrate on public spaces including such projects such as retail stores; hotels, motels, and restaurants; office buildings; and institutions, including hospitals and other health-care sites, schools, and government facilities. Some commercial designers work with the visual merchandising divisions of retail operations, whether planning a store's layout, locating furnishings and props, or designing major visual displays.

Interior designers often specialize in an area within either residential or contract interior design. For example, a residential designer may build a reputation and clientele through working exclusively with high-end homes. Commercial designers may specialize in retail operations or, even more specifically, high-fashion boutiques. Yet another commercial designer may earn a good living through work with the hospitality industry in the design of restaurants and clubs, hotels (Figure 15.4), or museums. As designers gain work experience, they often identify an area of particular interest, one that uses their skills and pays well and in which they build industry contacts and a positive reputation. Box 15.3 is an interview with an interior design entrepreneur.

Successful interior designers know how to plan a space and how to present that plan visually so that it can be communicated to the client. Interior designers must also know about the materials and products that will be used to create and furnish the space. These materials are constantly changing, as new products are introduced daily. The effective designer knows how texture, color, lighting, and other factors combine and interact in a space. On a more technical level, interior designers understand the structural requirements of their plans, the health and safety issues, building codes, electrical and plumbing requirements, and many other practical aspects.

Figure 15.4. A guest sits and reads in a stylish armchair at the Art'otel Berlin Mitte. The hotel resembles an art museum, designed with paintings, sculpture, and unique furniture throughout.

BOX 15.3 • INTERVIEW WITH A BUSINESS OWNER

Interviewee: Marciann Patton

Job Title: Business Owner Wee Design, manufacturer and designer of original children's playthings, play areas, and bedroom designs, and wholesale, retail, and contract sewing.

Education:

Bachelor's of science degree in interior design with a minor in business; master's degree in education and human services

Experience:

Freelance interior designer Business owner—Wee Design College educator in interior design and clothing and textiles

Necessary characteristics for the person looking at this type of career

- Be flexible in regard to diverse job responsibilities
- Approach job assignments with originality and creativity
- Maintain a positive attitude and diplomacy when working with the public, as well as professionalism in demeanor, attitude, dress, and job performance
- Engage in problem solving and accept it as a natural element in conducting business.

What do you enjoy most about the job: Diversity in duties and responsibilities and meeting the ever-present and changing business challenges.

What do you like the least: Paperwork and accounting.

Industry trends that you believe will affect what you are doing or will be doing in the next five to 10 years: Greater influence of the world's markets and continued increase in the importation of products and materials; explosion of cultural interchange; and the fluctuating economy and rapid changes in consumer preferences and purchases.

Advice to people interested in entering this career field: Constantly look to the future and update knowledge; continue to refine skills; and keep abreast of current trends, styles, materials, and new products. Give 110 percent to your job and career, and you will be rewarded a hundredfold. Approach problems with the attitude that they provide opportunities for creative thinking and creative solutions, a valuable commodity in today's competitive world.

What exactly do interior designers learn to do the job effectively? They must be knowledgeable in the areas of building construction, building materials, specification writing, building codes, technical drawing, and business practices. Interior designers analyze the client's needs and problems, develop detailed design solutions to present to

BOX 15.4 · A TASK LISTING FOR AN INTERIOR DESIGNER'S TYPICAL PROJECT

1. Research and analysis of the client's goals and requirements and development of documents, drawings, and diagrams that reflect those needs
2. Formulation of preliminary space plans and two- and three-dimensional design concept studies and sketches that integrate the client's program needs and are based on knowledge of the principles of interior design and human behavior
3. Confirmation that preliminary space plans and design concepts are safe, functional, and esthetically appropriate and meet all public health, safety, and welfare requirements, including code, accessibility, environmental, and sustainability issues
4. Selection of colors, materials, and finishes to appropriately portray the design concept and meet functional, maintenance, life-cycle performance, environmental, and safety requirements
5. Selection, specification, and documentation of furniture, furnishings, equipment, and trim work, including layout drawings and detailed product description; and contract documentation to facilitate pricing, shipping, and installation of new furnishings
6. Provision of project management services, including preparation of project budgets and schedules
7. Preparation of construction documents, consisting of plans, elevations, details, and specifications to illustrate nonstructural and/or nonseismic partition layouts, power and communications locations, reflected ceiling plans and lighting designs, materials and finishes, and furniture layouts
8. Confirmation that construction documents adhere to regional building and fire codes, municipal codes, and any other jurisdictional statutes, regulations, and guidelines that are applicable to the interior space
9. Coordination and collaboration with other allied design professionals who may be retained to provide consulting services, including but not limited to architects; structural, mechanical, and electrical engineers; and various specialty consultants
10. Confirmation that construction documents for nonstructural and/or nonseismic construction are signed and sealed by the responsible interior designer and are filed with code-enforcement officials
11. Administration of contract documents, bids, and negotiations as the client's agent
12. Review and reporting on the implementation of projects while in progress and upon completion

Source: www.asid.org

the client, then organize and supervise projects to full completion while being attentive to the client's desires and resources. Interior designers collaborate with suppliers and other building specialists throughout the process. Box 15.4 provides a listing of the tasks that may be required of an interior designer. Many people assume that the work of interior designers is all glamour; however, interior design is a discipline that demands research, analytical skills, a command of technology, and knowledge of products.

Qualifications

A list of the education, experience, and personal characteristics of a successful interior designer follows.

- ▸ **Education:** A bachelor's degree in interior design, housing and interior design, visual arts, or a related field is a minimal requirement.
- ▸ **Experience:** Many college students must complete an internship or two before graduation. This experience, especially for students with internships in more than one area, opens the door to contacts and knowledge within the interior design field. Retail sales or visual merchandising work with a home fashions retailer, a do-it-yourself building firm, or a textile store provides a strong background for the prospective interior designer.
- ▸ **Personal characteristics:** Interior designers are creative, imaginative, and artistic, yet they also need to be disciplined and organized businesspeople. As members of a service profession, interior designers depend on their ability to satisfy clients. The top interior designers know how to sell their ideas to clients, create informative and persuasive presentations, and maintain good client relationships. They must understand the artistic and technical requirements of a project, interpersonal communication, and management strategies. In terms of interpersonal skills, most interior designers are comfortable meeting and dealing with many kinds of people. They communicate clearly and effectively and are attentive listeners. Because they often must work with architects, contractors, and other service providers, interior designers are constantly working as part of a team. Negotiation and problem solving are parts of their daily routines. Box 15.5 details the earnings of an interior designer, and Box 15.6 discusses accreditation requirements in the interior design field.

BOX 15.5 • INTERIOR DESIGNER WORK SETTINGS AND EARNINGS

According to the U.S. Bureau of Labor Statistics, interior designers of all types are nearly four times as likely to be self-employed, often as residential interior designers, as are other specialty professionals. Many work in small firms of one to five employees. Earnings for interior designers vary widely depending on the type of design they do, whether they are self-employed or salaried, and their years of experience, reputation, demand, regional differences, and other factors. As in many other professions, entry-level salaries are low, and senior practitioners and firm principals or partners often earn several times that of junior staff.

Recent surveys indicate that, on average, beginning interior designers earn about $30,000 a year. Mid-level interior designers, those with three or more years' experience, make slightly more, around $35,000–$40,000 annually. Interior designers who also demonstrate good project and/or people-management skills can command substantially higher salaries ($50,000–$55,000) as managers. Principals or partners in well-to-do firms may receive $75,000–$100,000 or more. The demand for design services tends to reflect the fortunes of the economy at large. In a strong economy, demand is high, and design firms will find it difficult to attract and retain talented and experienced employees, especially at the junior level. In a downturn economy, the opposite will occur, with jobs harder to come by and interior designers tending to stay in a position rather than transferring to another firm. The Bureau of Labor Statistics projects that employment of interior designers of all types is likely to grow faster than the average for all other occupations through the year 2008. Nonetheless, competition for better-paying design jobs will be keen. Interior designers who are better educated and have strong business skills, as well as talent and perseverance, are likely to fare best.

Source: U.S. Department of Labor, *Occupational Outlook Handbook* (2006), http://www.bls.gov/emp

Career Challenges

Succeeding at interior design requires energy, technical proficiency, vision, and, often, entrepreneurial knowledge. Many interior designers own their businesses and must have the skills to run a business. Watching expenses, working with vendors, meeting deadlines, and managing projects can be huge undertakings. Working on more than one project at a time under demanding deadlines is part of the job. Within each project, there are bound to be changes along the way. Clients change their minds, and suppliers no longer have products available. The interior designer is challenged with keeping the client, vendors, contractors, and builders on the same track.

BOX 15.6 · ACCREDITATION IN INTERIOR DESIGN

The Council for Interior Design Accreditation (formerly FIDER) (www.accredit-id.org) sets specific standards for interior design education. These standards describe what students must learn to become professional interior designers. The standards also address curriculum structure, faculty, facilities, and other important elements necessary in interior design learning environments. While council accreditation is not the only measure of quality for an interior design education, it is a reliable indicator for the programs that go through the voluntary evaluation process and become accredited.

Your career as a professional interior designer will be built on three major steps. Following formal education, the next step is entry-level work experience, which is then followed by a qualifying examination administered by the National Council for Interior Design Qualification (NCIDQ).

An internship or other structured mentoring program can supplement your university degree. The quality of this practical experience complements your academic work and enhances your development as a professional.

A special program has been developed to help entry-level interior designers get a broad range of work experience in interior design. The Interior Design Experience Program provides guidance and a structure for getting the most out of initial work experiences. IDEP gives both the employer and the employee useful tools for keeping records of various professional assignments and can be a very effective transition between formal education and professional practice.

There is a qualifying examination for interior design just as there is for law, accounting, architecture, and many of the health professions. The interior design exam provides a method for identifying interior designers who have met the minimum standards for professional practice, and it is a formal way of making certain an individual is qualified in terms of particular knowledge or skills. The exam protects the public by assuring competent professionals.

NCIDQ is the organization responsible for certifying individuals as competent in interior design through an examination administered twice annually throughout the United States and Canada. The organization conducts regularly scheduled research and uses the information gathered to update the examination.

Successful completion of the NCIDQ examination is required for professional registration in those states and provinces that have enacted licensing or certification statutes to protect the health, safety, and welfare of the public.

To be eligible to take the NCIDQ examination, you must have an interior design education background and actual full-time interior design experience as required by NCIDQ or as required by a United States or Canadian regulatory board.

Learn more about the work experience and eligiblity requirements for the NCIDQ qualifying examination by visiting www.ncidq.org/exam/examreq.htm.

Twenty-five states and jurisdictions have enacted some type of interior design legislation. Of these, 16 have title acts, and six have practice acts. California has adopted self-certification law, and Colorado has a permitting statute. In Canada, one province has a practice act and six provinces have titles acts.

It is important to check the province or state requirements, as they are not necessarily all the same.

Visual Merchandising Professional

The job of visual merchandiser was examined in Chapter 10. In Chapter 10, the visual merchandiser is also discussed as a position that may be freelance or one of employment with a firm that is not a traditional retailer. In this chapter, you will see how visual merchandising has grown as a career area that is a spin-off of the tremendous growth of interiors businesses.

There are many auxiliary businesses that have developed from the increasing emphasis on the importance of visual merchandising; all hire visual merchandising professionals. Mannequin manufacturers offer a range of choices and now can design and produce mannequins to resemble a specific celebrity or person. **Prop houses** are gaining market share. These firms rent furniture, fixtures, mannequins, and decor accessories to visual merchandisers, saving the company money on limited-use display pieces while reducing the amount of warehouse space and labor needed to inventory and store visual merchandising props. Another area of employment in visual merchandising is with the equipment and fixture supplier.

These companies sell all that one needs to outfit a store. Fixtures, such as T-stands, rounders, and four-ways, are offered; wall slats and hanging bars provide additional merchandise displays. The visual merchandising professional working for one of these interior-related firms is, in essence, responsible for in-house promotion that will be seen by the company's clients. These visual merchandising professionals design spaces and often sell the merchandise or services. Most interior businesses believe that image and presentation are the most critical areas through which a company can distinguish itself from its competition.

Some fixture and equipment companies hire visual merchandising professionals to work with their clients, retailers, and manufacturers on efficient and attractive space usage. Often using a computer-aided design system, the visual

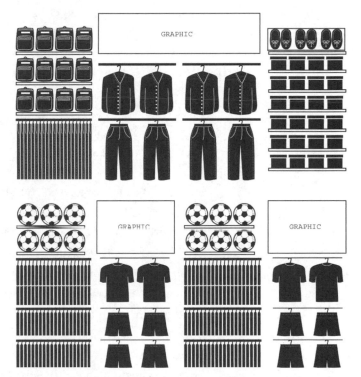

Figure 15.5. A plan-o-gram is a floor map that indicates the placement and types of racks, fixtures, display units, and merchandise needed to create an easy flow of traffic and present the merchandise most effectively.

Figure 15.6. A manufacturer's showroom featuring a designer's collection on display.

merchandising professional will develop plan-o-grams, also referred to as prototypes. As depicted in Figure 15.5, a **plan-o-gram** is a floor plan on which the placement and types of racks, fixtures, display units, and merchandise should be placed to create an easy flow of traffic and to present the merchandise most effectively. The plan-o-gram is used as an effective selling tool to show the retailer or manufacturer how many different types of fixtures will be needed and what the interior of the business will look like when it is furnished.

Take, for example, a manufacturer's showroom on Broadway in the Fashion District of Manhattan. The manufacturer may hire a visual merchandising company to design and install displays in the showroom and store windows with every seasonal line change, as shown in Figure 15.6.

Qualifications

Successful visual merchandising professionals working in the interiors industry are likely to possess the following qualities:

- ▶ **Education:** A bachelor's degree in fashion design, fashion merchandising, interior design, retail planning and design, visual arts, or a related field is a minimal requirement.
- ▶ **Experience:** Many visual display professionals begin as a member of the visual merchandising team for a retailer, installing windows and interior displays. Others may come from the fields of interior design, fashion styling, or store planning. Through a variety of visual merchandising work experiences, sales training, and a solid portfolio of work, these professionals may be hired by a mannequin or fixture retailer, prop house, or manufacturer in apparel or home furnishings.
- ▶ **Personal characteristics:** The visual merchandising professional must understand design, marketing, and merchandising. A high-esthetic sense, computer-aided design skills, and an understanding of visual art principles are keys to securing a position in this area. The ability to create effective displays using props, mannequins, and other display components is critical.

A visual merchandising professional working for a fixture and equipment company installing displays and selling products in a showroom can expect to earn about $45,000 annually. A visual merchandising professional working for a major home furnishings company and developing room displays that are featured in sales catalogs and copied on the firm's retail store floors can earn over $100,000 annually.

Figure 15.7. Shoppers on the walkways and escalator inside the Pacific Place shopping mall in the Central District of Hong Kong Island.

Career Challenges

Beginning a career in visual merchandising is not easy. The jobs are available in many sectors of the fashion industry, including retail stores, manufacturers' showrooms, and visual merchandising companies; however, not everyone is interested in making the sacrifices often required to get started in this field. Low pay, hard work, and long hours, including nights and weekends, describe the start of many visual merchandising careers.

Mall Manager

A **mall manager** is responsible for everything in the mall, from planning its budget and promotional activities to developing its mix of tenants and building community relations. On a given day, the mall manager is involved with marketing, tenant leasing, increasing capital, building improvement, construction, and security, a very important issue. What makes a mall successful is often the mix of stores available to the customer (Figure 15.7). The mall manager examines the mall's retail mix to determine its strengths and weaknesses. Incorporating interesting stores and concepts that are unique to the area, as well as balancing the number of apparel, home, and food retailers, are keys to a mall's success. Mall managers calculate customer demand into the equation, striving to meet the needs of the current demographic segment and anticipate through research what the future demographics may be. They look at home ownership, income, and customer profiles within the community to understand what the customer is looking for and who that customer is. The ultimate goals of the mall manager are to grow the value of the property itself and at the same time improve tenant listings and leasing capacity. "100 percent filled" is the dream, as are finding ways to complement the already integrated mix of stores.

Qualifications

A list of the educational requirements, work experiences, and personal characteristics for the successful mall manager follows.

- ▸ **Education:** A bachelor's degree in management, marketing, retailing, business administration, or a related field is a minimal requirement.
- ▸ **Experience:** Retail sales experience with a variety of retail operations is a must, even through summer or part-time employment during college. An internship with a mall management firm is an excellent way to gain experience in this career path. Many mall managers also secure store management experience so they can understand the needs and concerns of their mall tenants. Property management is yet another path to enter the career of mall manager.
- ▸ **Personal characteristics:** The mall manager must be a strong leader who knows what needs to be done. Because multiple tasks arise daily, the mall manager must be a self-motivated individual who is able to work independently. Working in a mall with staff, tenants, and consumers demands being a good listener and an effective problem-solver.

Assistant Mall Manager

In larger malls, the mall manager may supervise one or more assistants. An **assistant mall manager** is responsible for administering mall programs under the supervision of the property's mall manager. This person is critical in communicating operational issues to tenants, contractors, and staff.

Qualifications

The person who fills this role needs the following attributes:

- ▸ **Education:** A bachelor's degree in management, marketing, business administration, retailing, or a related field is required.
- ▸ **Experience:** Ideally, two to three years of work experience in business administration, property management, or retail management is needed to open the

door to this career path. Assistant mall managers usually work a minimum of three to five years before moving up to mall manager.

▸ **Personal characteristics:** Effective oral and written communication abilities and organizational and management skills are needed. Proficiency in computers and a good working knowledge of budgeting, accounting, and financial analysis are necessary, as are strong human relation skills. The assistant mall manager must be able to adapt to a changing work environment and be a self-motivated individual who is able to work independently and multitask under pressure.

The mall manager of a large facility in a metropolitan area will earn approximately $100,000 annually. In smaller cities and smaller malls, the mall manager can expect an annual income of $45,000–$80,000, depending on the manager's qualifications and the revenues of the mall. The assistant mall manager can expect to earn between $32,000 and $38,000 annually for this entry-level position.

Career Challenges

The mall manager and assistant mall manager have a team of bosses, all of the tenants in the mall. It is not easy to please a group of employers with different needs, expectations, and lease costs. Communicating with a group of this size is another challenge. Mall management reports to yet another audience, the mall's customers. It can be stressful to strive for a leasing level of full capacity, particularly when existing tenants and customers have specific ideas on which retailers will complement the current tenant mix. For example, the owner of an athletic footwear store that has made its home in the mall for years may be extremely dissatisfied to find that the mall manager has leased space to a similar retail operation. Keeping tenants and customers happy and encouraging growth in the mall are two key objectives that may be tough for mall management to accomplish.

SUMMARY

Digital, exterior, and interior environments profoundly influence image and profitability of all types of businesses in the fashion industry. Pursuit of a career in environments demands both technical and esthetic know-how. Website developers must have a strong grasp of Web design applications and programming, understand the process of Web formatting, and possess the design sense to put it all together in a user-friendly format. Similarly, a career in architecture requires education and accreditation to ensure awareness of safety and environmental factors, in addition to drafting skills and ingenuity in building design. Real estate firms that specialize in commercial property rely on brokers and agents to sell the retail operations, and commercial real estate developers to build new spaces. The best commercial realtors research and analyze regional market conditions to give investors the best information possible in choosing real estate. Once the facility is located, the commercial interior designer works with clients and other design professionals to develop inside spaces that are functional and attractive and meet the needs of the people using the space. Because of the growth of commercial interior design, visual merchandising professionals now work with such companies as mannequin manufacturers, prop houses, home furnishings manufacturers, and equipment and fixture vendors. They are responsible for presenting an esthetically appealing environment that reflects the company's image and sells merchandise. The mall manager and assistant mall manager are responsible for everything in the mall from planning its budget and creating promotional activities to developing its mix of tenants and building community relations.

Physical and virtual spaces are continually in demand to create, buy, sell, and transform. As with many careers, the key to success in these fields is to satisfy the client. If you have strong technical, visual, and communication skills, consider a future in environments.

KEY TERMS

architect
Architect Registration Examination (ARE)
assistant mall manager
commercial broker
commercial real estate developer
commercial retail space
comparative market approach
competitive market price
commercial designer (contract)
cost approach
income approach
interior designer
listing
mall manager

National Architectural Accrediting Board Inc. (NAAB)
plan-o-gram
prop house
real estate agent
realtor
residential design
shopping center
user interface (UI)
website developer (website designer)
website development

Discussion Questions

1. Compare and contrast the careers of architect, interior designer, and website developer. Examine the education and licensing requirements common to these three professions.

2. Consider a shopping district the area in which you live. What types of businesses stand out? How do the exteriors, interiors, and websites relate to one another within each business? Evaluate how well the sum of the business's environments creates a successful entity.

3. Visit a mall or other type of shopping center and consider the tenants (e.g., types of businesses, including retail, restaurant, and entertainment), their adjacencies, and any voids in types of tenants that would draw customers to the facility. Describe the lifestyle approach the shopping facility represents. Identify the most desirable location in the facility based on customer traffic, proximity to parking, and proximity to the most desirable stores.

CHAPTER 16

Beauty, Spa, and Wellness

There is a sector of the fashion industry that is dramatically affected by evolving fashion trends, particularly in the area of color; shifts in environmental esthetics; the changing customer; *and* science, medicine, psychology, physiology, and technology. Fashion as a lifestyle includes personal beauty, health, and body image choices. As there are changing trends in the fabrics, colors, forms, and themes of apparel and home fashions, there are shifts in "what is in fashion" in the areas of personal care, interpretations of beauty, and wellness strategies. Aerobics and jogging are being replaced by Hatha yoga and Pilates. Plastic surgery is being augmented by microfacials, collagen, and Botox. If you think of fashion as a way for people and their homes to look good and stay current, then choices in how to spend personal time and money on looking and feeling good fits into the fashion industry. Concentrating on these lifestyle preferences, the **beauty and wellness industries** focus on cosmetics, fragrances, hair and skin care, as well as spa, fitness, or wellness centers and their services. As a consumer, you contribute financially to this sector every day. When you wash your hair and style it, put on your makeup, take your vitamins, apply sunscreen, go to the fitness center, and head to your pedicure and massage appointments at the spa, you are adding to the increasing revenues of the beauty and wellness industries. The beauty and wellness industries are growing fields with a wide range of career tracks that require fashion and nonfashion training. If you have an interest in fitness and health and enjoy the image changes that hair and makeup can create, then the beauty and wellness sectors of the fashion industry can offer you a variety of career options. In this chapter, the following career paths are explored: product developer, or technician; beauty merchandising and marketing professionals; makeup artist; esthetician; hairstylist; and director of a spa or wellness center.

To begin, the **beauty industry**, the producers of cosmetics, fragrances, hair and skin care products, is examined. There are a number of well-known mass marketing companies in this field: Esteé Lauder, Lancome, Olay, and L'Oreal, to name just a few. There are two classifications of beauty industry corporations: mass market and prestige market. **Mass market** beauty companies, such as Cover Girl and Revlon, distribute their product lines through a wide variety of retailers, including drugstores, discount merchants, and mass merchandising retailers. **Prestige market** beauty companies, such as Prescriptives and MAC, distribute their product lines through better department and specialty store retailers, primarily in leased departments. Within these corporations, there are many subsidiaries through which a number of product lines are developed, marketed, and sold to the retail operations that offer them to the consumer. Some employees work with the creation of products, while others assist with promoting the product lines or selling them to the retailers and customers. The product developer/technician starts the product cycle through the creation of new and innovative products that customers may not even know they want and need until hearing about them (see Box 16.1).

PRODUCT DEVELOPER OR TECHNICIAN

Product research and development (R and D) is the technical area that creates products that meet the manufacturer's standards of performance and safety by continually conducting research on existing products, as well as new and innovative products. In the cosmetics, skin care, and fragrance industry, the marketing and research and development areas work closely together on a common goal, developing products that fulfill consumer needs and desires.

The idea for a new product or product modification may emerge in a variety of ways. Often, the **technician** is assigned an existing product in the line for which changes are needed. The technician works to develop new features for the product, often using consumer research studies in the process to clarify the direction of and predict the consumer response to the changes. In contrast, the product developer may be asked by the marketing director of the company to create a completely new product that will meet unfulfilled consumer needs (Figure 16.1). Frequently,

Figure 16.1. In the cosmetic, skin care, and fragrance industry, the marketing and research development areas work closely with each other on a common goal: developing products that fulfill consumer needs.

BOX 16.1 • SOIL ASSOCIATION "OSCARS" FOR NEW BEAUTY PRODUCT

The Soil Association, Britain's esteemed charity promoting organic farming, has announced its 2006 organic industry awards—akin to the Oscars—and the winner is Spiezia Organics. This small Cornish company has won the certified organic beauty product award for its organic lemon and marigold soap. The business was started by an Italian doctor turned naturopath, who moved from Italy to Cornwall and began farming organically. The products are 100 percent organic and made by hand. The lemon and marigold soap uses only the purest of oils and herbs grown on the farm. The soaps are "made with passion, and respect for people and nature." The prize for best large store went to Oliver's Wholefoods & Natural Remedies. This charming shop, with a villagelike atmosphere, is impeccably stocked with every organic food, cosmetic, and vitamin imaginable. The owners are dedicated to community involvement and have food tastings in-house, speakers on relevant topics, and a clinic. Best organic restaurant, should you be in the Yorkshire Dales: the Austwick Traddock. And best name (best small store): Pillars of Hercules (in Fife).

Source: Soil Association

product developers and technicians work independently to create a new product without initial marketing specifications and then submit the product to marketing to determine whether it will meet a consumer need.

Qualifications

A list of the educational requirements, experience, and personal characteristics needed in the career track of a R and D product developer or technician follows.

- ▸ **Education:** Typically, positions in R and D are available to persons with bachelor's degrees in chemistry, engineering, biology, or other related sciences; however, some firms are hiring candidates with esthetician licenses.
- ▸ **Experience:** Working as an intern in the R and D division of a beauty industry firm is an excellent way to enter this career track. A number of companies hire students directly out of college and train them in this area. Creative and resourceful individuals who acquire an expertise in cosmetic chemistry or product development may become eligible for promotion to a project manager, with their being responsible for a single product or groups of products.

▸ **Personal characteristics:** Product developers and technicians are, first and foremost, scientists with high levels of curiosity and an understanding of the customer. They are methodical problem solvers with a strong attention to detail.

The salary range is $42,000–$52,000 annually for an R and D product developer or technician with two to three years' experience working for a midsize firm or brand.

Career Challenges

The R and D product developer and technician need skills in chemistry or a related science discipline. As the technician often works alone on a project, taking it from start to finish, this is not the job for someone who is motivated by being part of a team. The work takes a great deal of concentration and often must be completed in a limited amount of time.

BEAUTY MERCHANDISING AND MARKETING PROFESSIONAL

A **beauty merchandising and marketing professional** is involved in the promotion and sales of cosmetic, fragrance, and skin care products. Beauty merchandising and marketing professionals include the account coordinator, trainer, account executive, and counter or line manager. An **account coordinator** organizes special events and promotions for a cosmetic, fragrance, or skin care line, traveling to different retail locations. The account coordinator develops and implements marketing programs that perpetuate the image of the brand, introduce new products, and generate customer traffic and press for the retail accounts. A *trainer* works for the cosmetic, fragrance, or skin care line by educating sales and marketing employees on the company's product line and how to sell it. The trainer directs seminars on new products, how they are to be used, and the results the consumer can expect. An account executive can work in two main areas: retailing and public relations. The **retail**, or *sales*, account executive sells the line to retail accounts and oversees the sales performance of the line in large retail accounts. The retail account executive works with retailers that carry the line by providing marketing and merchandising suggestions to maximize consumer sell-through. This account representative assists store accounts with inventory management, making recommendations to increase sales. On-site staff training, incentives to motivate sales personnel, and assistance with consumer promotional events are parts of the retail account executive's job. The **public relations account executive** works with beauty media contacts, such as fashion publications like *Marie Claire*, *Vogue*, *Allure*, *Elle*, *W*, and *InStyle*, to promote the line in magazine editorials and feature stories. Box 16.2 is classified advertisement for an online marketing manager of a beauty and fashion house.

In the retail operation, the **counter**, or **line**, **manager** coordinates special events and promotions in the retail operation, manages employees, and works closely with buyers. Selling the product line and servicing the customer are key objectives for the counter manager. Counter managers are constantly acquiring product knowledge through

BOX 16.2 • SAMPLE CLASSIFIED ADVERTISEMENT: ONLINE MARKETING MANAGER WITH A BEAUTY AND FASHION HOUSE

Location: U.S.—New York City, Midtown
Salary: $35,000–$40,000, commensurate with qualifications and experience
Start Date: Open
Job Description:
Do you love beauty, fashion, and online marketing? We have the perfect fit . . . Prestigious fashion and beauty house seeks an online marketing manager to lead the e-commerce and Internet marketing initiatives. This is a temporary to permanent opportunity. You will work with the director to actively manage the overall distributor relationship and online partnership projects and search marketing campaign activity. Additionally, you will conduct in-depth analysis and reporting by developing and maintaining sales reports and operational metrics for online marketing. You will track trends to identify and capitalize on Internet marketing developments to protect and grow the brand online.
Other Requirements:

- Six years' work experience in management, Internet consulting, investment banking, advertising agency, or corporate marketing
- Developed analytical and problem-solving skills
- Skill set to contribute in-depth reporting
- Strong attention to detail; ability to prioritize
- Experience in management of others, with demonstrated success at building and mentoring a team
- Ability to handle multiple tasks in a fast-paced environment
- Must have a good understanding of online production technologies, plus an enthusiasm for keeping abreast of emerging initiatives
- Strong proofreading and editing abilities
- Appreciation for fine fashion

Please apply online. Thank you for your interest.

corporate training materials and seminars to educate sales associates and customers. They also develop merchandise displays and demonstrate products to staff and clients (Figure 16.2). They coach and develop a sales staff to achieve their personal productivity and company sales goals, often through building a **client registry file**, a computerized or print record of the names and contact information of the line's customers. The counter manager is also responsible for replenishing inventory through back stock or reorders. Finally, counter managers also develop and participate in special events that will increase business. For most mass market brands, counter managers are employed by the retailer; in prestige market brands, they usually work directly for the cosmetic, fragrance, hair, or skin care lines.

Figure 16.2. A counter manager stocks and displays cosmetics at L'Oreal Paris's counter at a department store in Tokyo.

Qualifications

Account representatives, trainers, and counter managers have similar requirements in education, work experience, and personal characteristics, as follows:

- ▶ **Education:** A bachelor's degree in fashion design, fashion merchandising, communications, marketing, journalism, or a related field is a minimal requirement.
- ▶ **Experience:** Sales experience, especially in the cosmetic, fragrance, and skin care areas, is preferred. An internship in the beauty division of a department store is an excellent way to gain work experience. Several years of work experience in the beauty industry are minimal requirements. Some large companies prefer a candidate who also holds esthetics certification or has training and experience as a makeup artist. A strong knowledge of the beauty industry is expected. The candidate who can show successful sales experience through awards, a client listing, and so on, moves ahead of the competition. Evidence of exceptional customer service skills and the abilities to multitask, lead, and coach teams are also helpful.
- ▶ **Personal characteristics:** Great people skills and a love of travel are important in this career field. Common skills of beauty merchandising and marketing

professionals include the ability to be energetic and articulate in conversation and writing. They are often ambitious self-starters, competitive spirits, and have creative and optimistic attitudes. In the beauty business, an image that exudes professionalism and a sense of style that fits with the employer's image is essential.

Career Challenges

Beauty merchandising and marketing professionals have a variety of job challenges. The account coordinator works under the pressure of coming up with innovative special events and promotions for the company every season. The trainer must continually find ways to educate employees on the company's new products and how to sell them. The retail account executive must meet or surpass sales goals in selling the line to retail accounts. The counter manager has the same goal, exceeding the sales goal set by the retailer. Persons in both of these positions have to balance sales and inventory so that both the retailers and the beauty product manufacturer are satisfied and making a profit. Extensive travel to different retail locations is often part of these jobs. Finally, the public relations account executive needs to persuade beauty media contacts to feature new product lines. All of these jobs have the following in common: the possibility of high stress, involvement in a fast-paced environment, and the need to sell one's self and the product line.

MAKEUP ARTIST

The person interested in working with cosmetics is not limited to working as an account executive or a counter manager for a single cosmetics firm. The makeup artist works hands-on with a variety of product lines and has a variety of employment opportunities (Figure 16.3). **Makeup artists** work with cosmetics, wigs, and other costuming materials to color and enhance a client's face and body. Working in television, film, music videos, commercials, and print ads, they use makeup to improve or alter actors' and models' appearances. Other makeup artists work at the retail level, applying lipstick and mascara on customers at store cosmetic counters. Some makeup artists work on photo shoots and runway shows for designers and magazines or cosmetic companies as consultants or sales representatives. Makeup artists also provide their services as independent contractors in beauty salons, retail stores, large hotels and resorts, spas, or the medical profession, where they provide camouflage techniques to help clients following injuries or surgeries. It is also possible to become a makeup adviser or lecturer.

What is the work of makeup artists in the video, media, television, film, and theater industries? They apply makeup for presenters, performers, and others appearing on screen. Some have completed training in both makeup and hair techniques (e.g., styling, cutting, and coloring) to prepare and work on the makeup and hair design required for each individual production. Makeup artists skilled in both makeup application and hairstyling have better job prospects. Makeup designers and chief makeup artists research and design the makeup required for a production. The style of makeup and hair depends on the type of production. It varies from straightforward, contemporary makeup and hairdressing (e.g., for news broadcasters and presenters in conservative, public settings) to more creative, specialized techniques (e.g., varying historical periods, different nationalities, aging, or special effects). This may entail researching the looks and learning the techniques for elaborate makeup and wigs needed for period films, such as *Marie Antoinette*. It may also require using materials to change the shape of a face or creating scars and wounds for films, such as *Pirates of the Caribbean: Dead Man's Chest.* The makeup artist or assistant makeup artist must ensure the availability of materials, such as the correct colors and brands of various cosmetics, period makeup, prosthetics like false noses and scars, as well as wigs and hair decorations. The makeup artist is expected to own an extensive kit of cosmetics to take to each job, though larger productions like films and ongoing television series usually provide a makeup budget. Some makeup artists specialize in a medium, such as theater, film, runway, or photography, while others work in all of these areas.

Figure 16.3. A makeup artist applies makeup to a model backstage prior to a runway show (left) and to customers at the manufacturer's counter in a department store (right).

Makeup artists in the entertainment industries collaborate closely with producers, directors, costume designers, hairdressers, and performers. Together, they develop and design the characters' looks, evaluating the length of time and cost required to complete each character. Most of these makeup artists are freelance and are engaged for each film production, television series, fashion season, or other project. As such, they are paid set or negotiated fees for each project. Some trade organizations in the media industries set minimum rates for independent productions and require membership in a trade union.

Training and educational requirements for makeup artists vary; there are a number of cosmetology schools that specialize in makeup studies. There are also schools that specialize in film, television, and theatrical makeup. The demand for these specialists is expected to grow about 10 to 20 percent over the next decade. Box 16.3 is a career profile of a successful makeup artist.

BOX 16.3 · INTERVIEW WITH A MAKEUP ARTIST

Ever wanted to work in fashion, television, or the movies? Laney Maiai is a freelance makeup artist who has worked in all areas of the fashion and entertainment industry.

Name: Laney Maiai

Age: 31

Location: New Zealand

Job: Freelance makeup artist

Salary range: Varies from job to job as I am a freelance makeup artist

Dress code: Casual but smart.

A typical day at work: Usually bright and early! Apart from being a makeup artist, my role is also to make the models and work area feel relaxed and stress-free. I always have a brief meeting with the directors or photographers to get an idea of what look they're after. Sometimes this is the hardest part. Their ideas for fresh and natural might be completely different from mine, so we usually look at some pictures to get a better feel for the look. Depending on the job, location, and number of models, it can be a very long and tiring day! But if you love what you do, it makes it so much easier.

Best perks of the job: Each job I do has its own perks. Getting freebies is always good. I never get sick of trying new makeup (what girl wouldn't?). I love seeing a whole day's work come together and seeing the client happy. I worked at L'Oreal Fashion Week, and I got to meet lots of celebs.I must admit that was awesome!

Mundane aspects of the job: Waiting. Doing a TV ad or a photo shoot is not as easy as it seems. There is a lot of waiting around at times, but because I am mad, I usually find something crazy to do!

Most memorable moment since getting the job: I suppose I have a few, but working at L'Oreal Fashion Week has got to be a highlight. Seeing my makeup on television was a buzz. I also just recently did a wedding that was very cool. They liked me so much they made me part of the wedding party!

What do you enjoy about your job most of all: Everything! Meeting people, being creative, getting paid for something that I love doing. Each job is different, and being a freelance artist, no two makeups are the same.

Qualifications and previous experience: I had my kiddies, Jimmie and KDee, when I was in my early 20s and spent those years being a mom. I had a really good job, but then one day, I decided I needed to do something that I wanted, so I gave up my job and went to the Cut Above Academy to become a makeup artist. I will never forget my first day. My kids packed me a lunch box and hoped that my teacher was nice! I have never looked back. You have to get out there and chase your dreams, even if it is playing with lipstick and mascara. If I can do it at 31, anyone can!

Personality traits/skills/attributes that help a person to get a job like yours: First, you have to be passionate about what you do. Being a makeup artist means dealing with all sorts of people, not just the drop-dead gorgeous. It is definitely a people-oriented career, so good people skills are a must (being able to get up at 4:00 A.M. and looking alive also helps). Also, being confident in yourself is important. I am forever learning new tricks, and being able to apply that to a job is sometimes a bit scary.

Advice for people wanting to get into your industry: There are plenty of makeup schools out there, but before you go out and spend loads of money, try and get some work experience first just to see how it feels. Local theater companies and high school plays are a great place to start. Practice looks you see in a magazine on your friends and take pictures. It is a fun career but hard to get into, so you have to start somewhere. If it is what you really want to do, go to school, get qualified, and be prepared to work.

What sort of job could you go to from here: Now, this is the hardest question of all. New Zealand is such a small market as far as my profession is concerned. But New Zealand is getting a high profile with all the movies being filmed here, so I suppose working on one of the big budget movies would be nice. I love teaching young girls (15–25; remember, I am ancient!) all the new tricks and tips of wearing makeup. I have heaps of them, and you do not need hundreds of dollars to look good!

Qualifications

If you love color, makeup, and drama and if you are willing to start out at a low salary in a career area of growth with high earning potential, this may be the career path for you. Education requirements, work experience, and key personal characteristics for the career of a makeup artist are as follows:

▸ **Education:** The common educational requirements are a one-year vocational program or a two-year associate's degree. After completing educational programs, the makeup artist often trains on-the-job in retail, television, or film, by assisting experienced makeup artists. Some industries, such as filmmaking, require that the makeup artist have specific certifications and union membership.

▸ **Experience:** An internship or apprenticeship with an established makeup artist is a great way to get through the career door. Sales experience in the cosmetics department of a retail store provides additional knowledge and on-the-job experience. Volunteering as a makeup artist with a local theatrical production company provides excellent additional work experience.

▸ **Personal characteristics:** The successful makeup artist enjoys working with people and communicates well at all levels, including listening and empathizing. A strong visual sense and a creative imagination are a makeup artist's most important traits. The ability to look at a face and picture what it will look like with makeup and under specific lighting is a great talent. An awareness of health and safety and sanitation procedures is also necessary. A makeup artist must be organized and able to work well under pressure while paying attention to detail and as part of a team of often diverse colleagues.

Of all the jobs discussed in this chapter, the career of makeup artist has the greatest variance in salary. Some makeup artists earn $100,000 a year; some make $15,000 a year. Self-employed makeup artists usually earn between $25,000 and $50,000 per year, depending on the number of hours they work. On film and photo shoots, the day rate for an experienced makeup artist is between $450 and $650 a day. The outlook for makeup artists is good, as the number of employees in this occupation is expected to increase over the next two to three years. It is becoming more common for people to have their makeup done professionally for job interviews, school dances, weddings, or other special occasions. Another trend is for makeup artists to work alongside hairstylists in salons, applying clients' makeup after they have their hair done.

Career Challenges

Starting out, the makeup artist usually earns low pay and works long and unusual hours. If a film director or photographer decides to shoot a scene at sunrise, then the makeup artist must be ready to go before dawn. Extensive travel with little downtime during a project can be exhausting. Setting one's ideas of the best makeup approach aside to defer to those of the producer can be challenging. The makeup artist needs the confidence and tact to suggest changes to accomplish the goal in an individual's appearance. For these reasons, flexibility is key. Building up a business of regular clients can be difficult, and work may be irregular initially; however, once established, makeup artists often remain in this industry for a long time.

Some makeup artists choose to work in a spa, either as an independent contractor or as an employee. As the spa industry grows, so do the opportunities for makeup artists to work as part of a team of esthetics professionals.

WELLNESS AND ESTHETICS

Wellness and personal care are topics of keen interest in today's beauty industry as it prepares for the future. As baby boomers become youthful seniors, there is an increasing consumer interest in slowing down or reversing the aging process and preventing health problems. Additionally, consumers are seeking a higher quality of life through reduced stress; greater self-care; and safer, healthier food and product choices (see Box 16.4). They are beginning to view services like massages and facials as ongoing necessities, rather than occasional luxuries. The increasing customer interest in health, youth, and longevity has attracted new participants to the wellness industry. They include alternative medicine providers, pharmaceutical firms, energy drink and food supplement producers, full-service beauty salons, fitness and nutrition centers, and spas. Trends in the wellness industry include antiaging and protection through skin care (Figure 16.4), relaxation and rejuvenation, facial treatments and body sculpting, stress management, and health concerns management.

Esthetics, or *aesthetics*, is a relatively new field that combines wellness, science, and beauty. The field views the client as a whole person by providing integrated esthetic services through comprehensive makeovers and beauty-enhancement treatments that combine medical, beauty, and spa treatments for men and women in safe and comfortable environments. Many of these spas employ nail manicurists and pedicurists, masseuses, makeup artists, and facial technicians. An **esthetician** is a licensed professional who provides services such as facials, makeup, and hair removal to improve one's physical appearance.

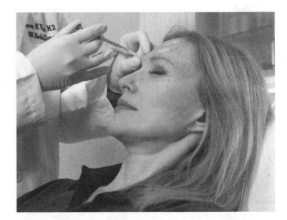

Qualifications

Here are the educational and experience requirements, as well as personal characteristics, for a successful career as an esthetician.

Figure 16.4. A growing customer interest in prolonging youthful beauty promotes skin care treatments such as Botox.

BOX 16.4 • MARKETING BEAUTY PRODUCTS FROM THE INSIDE OUT

By Dale Buss

For centuries, skin care manufacturers have primarily dealt with beauty from the outside. But now a growing number of cosmetic brands, including Olay and Avon are rolling out new products promoting the idea that what consumers ingest can have just as big an effect on the healthfulness of their skin and the luster of their appearance as anything external they may apply. Simultaneously, more food and beverage companies like Snapple are investing in products that use green-tea extract and other nutrients as the basis for a brand extension into skin care. The upshot: These brand owners are betting that outer and inner beauty are more connected than previously explored.

"There are certain compounds that you can ingest that help your skin become more taut; they're nutrients for skin regeneration," says Peter Leighton, vice president of marketing and product development for Natrol Inc., a California-based manufacturer of dietary supplements and nutritional products. "There's actually good sci-ence behind that," Leighton continues. Adds Gordon Tareta, director of spas for Chicago-based Hyatt Hotels, which provides a number of treatments that are based on dessert ingredients: "There's a lot of realization nowadays stemming from general awareness of health that the outside is a mirror of what's within."

The merging of skin care between nutrients that are topically applied and those that are ingested is as old as the admonition that drinking cola and eating chocolate will promote acne or as venerable as the milk bath. Some experts are dubious about the overall benefits of products such as Olay Vitamins and SkinCola. "Some things are potentially helpful, such as green tea, which studies show may inhibit chemical carcinogenesis and aging caused by the sun," says Dr. Joshua Fox, a dermatologist in New York. "But the vast majority of these products don't show you research." If the inner-beauty category does continue to grow, Fox and others maintain that the U.S. Food and Drug Administration should begin to regulate it.

Source: www.brandchannel.com, August 11, 2003

▸ **Education:** In most cities, there are vocational schools that offer a program based on a curriculum, up to two years, covering the following subjects: anatomy, physiology, hygiene, skin disorders and diseases, skin analysis, massage, makeup application, hair removal, basic medical terminology, professional ethics, the business of esthetics, retailing, marketing and promotion, customer service, interpersonal skills, salon administration, as well as salon layout and design.

▸ **Experience:** After completion of an esthetics program and becoming licensed (requirements vary from state to state), many graduates opt to practice esthetics in a salon or spa or open their own businesses. Others may also be employed by a makeup artist or an image consultant. Some work in medical practices such as dermatology, plastic surgery, oncology, or burn treatment centers. Additional opportunities include work as a product developer in cosmetic R and D or as a manufacturer's representative in the beauty and skin care industry.

▸ **Personal characteristics:** The esthetician has good manual dexterity, a high energy level, effective communication skills, and a high level of sensitivity. The ability to work with different types of people and to build relationships with clients are important attributes of the successful esthetician.

There are four factors that determine an income for the esthetician, as well as most of the careers examined in this chapter. They are location; quality and reputation of the employer (e.g., the salon or spa); whether the candidate is launching an esthetic department, taking over an experienced person's established clientele, or starting a new clientele base; and the candidate's skills and references. Some spas pay a salary; others pay commission. The commission on services may start at 40 percent and increase gradually as one gains experience. Additional money can be made through tips and commission on products sold. Some estheticians start off with a salary as low as $28,000 per year, and a good experienced esthetician makes $65,000 or more per year. Some employers offer benefits.

Career Challenges

The esthetician must have an understanding and interest in the three Ss: science, sanitation, and safety. Working with the human body requires a sensitive approach with a strong attention to detail and methodical procedure. As estheticians need to stay up-to-date on skin care products, technology, and services, continuing education is an integral part of the job.

HAIRSTYLIST

Hairstyling is a profession of tremendous growth all over the world. As with apparel and accessories, hairstyles change with fashion. People are now realizing that it is not simply clothing, shoes, and jewelry that express their personalities. It is also their hair, a reason customers are becoming more experimental and open to change. **Hairstylists** not only work in hair salons but also in the film and television industry, for fashion houses, for magazines, for photo studios, and for special events firms. Hairstyling is a creative art, and a good hairstylist is a valuable commodity (ask anyone who has had a bad hair day).

Qualifications

The professional hairstylist is trained in the areas of hair and scalp care, cutting, styling, and coloring and has the following credentials, background, and personal attributes:

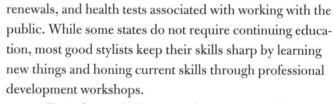

- **Education:** Most cities offer an array of vocational schools that specialize in hair and cosmetics training, which may take up to a year or two. Once a hairstylist has earned a license, the next step is often to apprentice under an established stylist before working solo to build a clientele. Different states have different rules governing hairstylists. Some simply require a onetime test to keep the license current, while others require continuing education, license renewals, and health tests associated with working with the public. While some states do not require continuing education, most good stylists keep their skills sharp by learning new things and honing current skills through professional development workshops.

  - **Experience:** Stylists can often secure positions as soon as they complete training and receive a license; however, they often begin in an assistant capacity working with an established stylist.

  - **Personal characteristics:** Creativity, imagination, and continual training are necessary parts of the hairstylist's profession. Dealing effectively with people is critical. Hairstylists need effective communication skills to talk to clients and build good relationships. They should have an attractive presence, a friendly manner, and good listening skills. As it is a physically demanding job, the stylist must have good stamina. Figure 16.5 shows a hairstylist working on a model backstage before a fashion show.

Figure 16.5. A hairstylist prepares a model backstage at a fashion show.

In terms of remuneration, hairstylists working in salons or spas may be paid on commission; the more clients they have, the more money they make. Many stylists earn additional money through tips from clients and commission on products they sell. Some firms pay stylists a salary, believing the guaranteed paycheck creates a team atmosphere. A newer approach to the hair salon is leasing space to the stylist. The stylist pays a monthly fee for the use of a booth, often also paying a portion of the receptionist's salary so that appointments can be made at all times. The income range for a hairstylist is between $17,000 and $38,000 annually. Hairstylists who have training and certification in additional fields such as a makeup artist, nail technician, or facial technician have greater career and salary advancement opportunities.

Career Challenges

There is a great deal of competition in hairstyling. Think about how many hair salons exist in a midsize city. The number is often large enough that the competition is intense and salons go out of business regularly. Finding an employer who has a solid base of repeat clientele and long-term stylists and is willing to take on a new hairstylist is a challenge. Skill and personality are critical factors in making it in this business. Continuing education is essential as products, techniques, equipment, and looks change frequently in this industry.

DIRECTOR OF A SPA OR WELLNESS CENTER

Resort and hotel spas originally began to make headway as a leisure time amenity and were not often thought of as profit centers for the beauty, health, and wellness industries. That has changed; now spas and medi-spas are prospering because of consumer lifestyle shifts, efficacy of treatments, and education. **Medi-spas** combine traditional spa services with those that must be offered by a physician, such as health screenings and minor surgery. The day spa may eventually offer all services, making the idea of a separate hair salon somewhat obsolete as spas incorporate hair and makeup services, massages, hair removal, skin rejuvenation, and other esthetic services. In fact, the term *day spa* may eventually be replaced by **wellness center**, or a similar term. Even the athletic center and spa may become a place of treatment and education through well-designed nutrition and exercise programs, such as Hatha yoga and Pilates. Whether referred to as a spa today or a wellness center tomorrow, the operation must be guided by an efficient and effective manager, the director.

The **director of a spa or wellness center** is responsible for keeping the spa running smoothly by managing customer service, budgets, marketing plans, and environment and staff appearance standards. In terms of human resources, the director ensures that employees have the training needed to perform their jobs and the knowledge they need to sell the retail product lines. Spa directors assure the staff operates with peak efficiency through coordination, communication, and cooperation. They schedule, plan, and facilitate team meetings. Personnel duties include directing the recruitment, interviews, selection, and training of new employees. They mediate problems, organize and set work schedules, and effectively communicate and enforce company and health rules. Finally, directors are responsible for maintaining an inventory of supplies and purchasing new products. In essence, the spa director manages all of the personnel and services that make the organization a success.

Qualifications

Here are the educational, experience, and personal characteristics needed to be a successful spa director.

- ▶ **Education:** A bachelor's degree in management, hospitality, marketing, business administration, or a related field is a minimal requirement. CPR and first aid training are often required.
- ▶ **Experience:** The director position usually requires a minimum of three to five years of experience in spa or salon management. It is desirable to have training, certification, and licenses in spa-related services. The position requires a working knowledge of computers, in particular, computer spa software skills.
- ▶ **Personal characteristics:** Spa or wellness center directors must have strong leadership skills, the ability to motivate others, excellent organizational and communication skills, and the ability to multitask. Their approach to work must be customer-service oriented, diplomatic, and composed. Excellent problem-solving skills are essential.

The salary range for a spa director with two to three years of experience is wide, $33,000–$77,000 annually, and varies greatly with geographic location. Areas with a high level of tourism, such as California and Florida, offer the high end of the range.

Career Challenges

In managing all of the personnel and services that make the organization, the spa director may work long hours, including weekends. This is a position that requires many skills; chief among them are scheduling and motivating employees and creating a peaceful and immaculate environment. The successful spa director is highly attuned to image and ambiance, as well as a high level of customer service. Day after day, it can be challenging to work with personnel, customers, and vendors concurrently in a calm and controlled manner. The spa director sets the tone for the wellness center.

THE FUTURE OF SPAS AND WELLNESS CENTERS

What does the future look like for the wellness industry? The wellness center will focus on physiological relief of fatigue and stress, while functioning as a haven for rest and relaxation. It will also be a source of education for the customer on antiaging and protection, as well as holistic principles of health. There will be developments in hair and scalp care through nourishing masks and treatments. For nails and hands, treatment will focus on protection and antiaging through depigmentation treatments and sun protection. We may even see driving gloves again, but designed to cover and protect the backs of the hands from sun damage. Waxing will continue to be a common part of the spa service but, as the technology of laser hair removal advances, more clients will choose semipermanent or permanent laser hair removal technology. Natural botanical ingredients in skin care products will drive the new trend of caring and soothing sensitive skin. The products and treatments of the future will continue to concentrate on antiaging and protection but will also heavily involve increasing the immune system. While body treatments and products now take second place to the face in the spa, body skin care may be the greatest growing segment in the beauty and wellness industries of tomorrow. After all, if technology can improve the tone and texture of the face, why not use it for the entire body? As stress levels and fast-paced lifestyles continue to increase, there will be a natural need for the consumer to explore the value of detoxification for overall energy and wellness. The key to growing the beauty, health, and wellness industries lies in educating the consumer on the physical and psychological benefits of self-care as a necessity, not a luxury (Figure 16.6).

SUMMARY

The product cycle of the beauty industry begins in research and development with the creation of innovative products by product developers and technicians who often have backgrounds in science. After the cosmetics, fragrance, and skin care products are developed and produced, beauty product merchandising and marketing professionals promote and sell them. The account coordinator organizes special events and promotions for product lines, traveling to different retail locations. A trainer works to educate employees and directs seminars on new products—how they are to be used and how to sell them. The retail account executive works to sell the line to retailers carrying the product line, and the public relations account executive works with beauty media contacts to solicit promotion in consumer publications. The counter manager's key objectives are to sell the product line at the retail store and service the customer through product knowledge and special promotions in the retail operation.

The creative talents in the beauty industry are makeup artists, who work with cosmetics, wigs, and other costuming materials, to color and enhance the client's face and body, and hairstylists, who are trained in the areas of hair and scalp care, cutting, styling, and coloring. Makeup artists and hairstylists may provide their services as independent contractors in beauty salons, retail stores, large hotels and resorts, or spas. They may also work for runway productions, as well as the video, media, television, film, and theater industries.

However, the beauty industry is no longer just concerned with hair and makeup. The popularity of alternative physical treatments has broadened concepts of personal care and the career options within the beauty and wellness industries. Spas, or wellness centers, offer a variety of treatments and services, including antiaging and protection through skin care, relaxation and rejuvenation, facial treatments and body sculpting, stress management, and health concerns management, and services provided by estheticians. A spin on the traditional spa, the medi-spa combines long-offered spa services with those that must be offered by a physician. The director of a spa or wellness center is responsible for keeping the spa running smoothly by managing customer service, budgets, marketing plans, and environment and staff appearance standards.

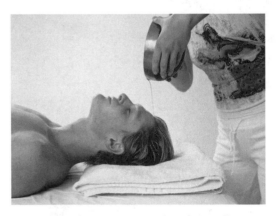

Figure 16.6. A young man receives Ayurvedic treatment in a spa and wellness center

Beauty, health, and wellness businesses are rapidly growing sectors of the fashion lifestyle industry.

Career opportunities are flourishing with new ones developing as innovative products and techniques are introduced. Increasing consumer interest and awareness in the well-being, longevity, and beauty that results from self-care indicates that this area will be one to watch in the future.

KEY TERMS

account coordinator

account executive

beauty industry

beauty and wellness industries

beauty merchandising and marketing professional

client registry file

counter manager

esthetician

esthetics (aesthetics)

hairstylist

makeup artist

mass market

medi-spa

prestige market

product developer

public relations account executive

retail (sales) account executive

technician

wellness center

Discussion Questions

1. Which beauty products and treatments do you incorporate into your lifestyle? Describe what the future of these and new products and treatments may be in response to the growth of the wellness industry.

2. Are department-store-branded beauty products superior to generics and drug-store lines? Compare and contrast the differences in product development, merchandising, and promotion.

3. Many of the job descriptions in the beauty and wellness industry compare to those of positions discussed earlier in the chapters on product development, marketing, merchandising, and management. Compare and contrast three positions in this chapter with those requiring similar backgrounds and skills in three other chapters. What would it take for a professional to move from the primary or retail level of the industry into beauty and wellness?

4. Search the Internet to find out who the major manufacturers of cosmetics and beauty products are. Construct a four-column chart of 10 beauty product corporations, listing the name of the corporation in the first column and the brand names in the second column. In column three, indicate whether the brands are mass or prestige market; in the fourth, list examples of retailers that sell each brand.

GLOSSARY

academic costume designer One who holds a teaching or staff position with a college or university; this type of designer is often primarily an instructor who may also act as a residential designer for college theater productions. (CH 13)

academic curator training Instruction on how to collect, preserve, store, and exhibit museum collections. (CH 14)

accession Artifact added to a museum collection. (CH 14)

account coordinator Organizes special events and promotions for a cosmetic, fragrance, or skin care line, while traveling to different retail locations; develops and implements marketing programs that perpetuate the image of the company; introduces new products; and generates customer traffic and press for retail accounts. (CH 16)

account executive Sells to and manages accounts for a manufacturer. See also *manufacturer's representative* and *sales representative*. (CH 2)

accounts payable Monies owed to creditors for goods and services; it is the amount owed by a business to its suppliers or vendors. (CH 7)

accounts payable clerk Reviews invoices for accuracy and completeness, sorts documents by account name or number, and processes invoices for payment. (CH 7)

accounts payable manager Directs the accounts payable division of a company under the organization's established policies and monitors monies owed to creditors. (CH 7)

accounts payable supervisor Oversees accounts payable record keeping by supervising the recording of amounts due, verification of invoices, and calculation of discounts. (CH 7)

accounts receivable Amounts of money owed to a business that it expects to receive for goods furnished and services rendered, including sales made on credit, reimbursements earned, and refunds due. (CH 7)

accounts receivable clerk Verifies and posts transactions related to money owed to the business to journals, ledgers, and other records. (CH 7)

accounts receivable manager Supervises the accounts receivable function that oversees monies owed to the business within an organization's established policies. (CH 7)

accounts receivable supervisor Oversees record keeping in the accounts receivable department and ensures that cash receipts, claims, or unpaid invoices are accounted for properly. (CH 7)

advertising A type of promotion that is a paid for, nonpersonal communication delivered through mass media. Designed to serve different purposes, there are five primary types of advertising: institutional, brand, sales, classified, and advocacy. (CH 10)

advertising agency An outside firm that may be contracted by a retail organization to help choose the right media types to reach the retailer's target market and maximize its promotional budget. (CH 10)

advertising director Develops and implements a company's paid promotional strategy for the purpose of increasing sales. (CH 10)

advertising/editorial photography Expresses a product's personality or illustrates a magazine story and is usually classified as still life, food, transportation, portraiture, or landscape. (CH 13)

advertising promotion staff Develops presentations to help the sales representatives of print and electronic media firms sell advertising to new and existing accounts. (CH 5)

advertising research assistant Helps sales representatives sell advertising space, in a publication for example, by supplying facts that an advertiser will want to know, such as the number of issues sold and top locations in terms of sales volume, or the profile and buying power of the publication's readers. (CH 5)

advocacy advertising Supports a particular cause; e.g., a home building retailer may run a newspaper advertisement featuring green design merchandise in support of environmental awareness. (CH 10)

allocator See *distribution manager*. (CH 11)

apparel mart Houses temporary sales booths and permanent showrooms leased either by sales representatives or manufacturers; holds scheduled markets for buyers. (CH 6)

architect Building designer who works with a wide range of structures that may range from small freestanding retail stores to large malls. (CH 15)

Architect Registration Examination (ARE) Professional licensure examination for architects in the United States and Canada. (CH 15)

archivist Analyzes, describes, catalogs, and exhibits records and documents that are retained by museums because of their importance and potential value, benefiting researchers and the public. (CH 14)

art director Develops and implements the creative concepts for advertising, catalogs, mailers, and signage; this person provides an overall and consistent visual view of the manufacturing or retailing company, including signage, photography, direct mail, and packaging. (CH 10)

art photographer Specializes in photography as a fine arts media, rather than a commercial product. (CH 13)

assistant buyer Primarily works with the six-month plan, open-to-buy, inventory, and vendor follow-up, taking direction from the buyer. (CH 11)

assistant controller Supports the company's controller in directing budget and cost controls, financial analysis, and accounting procedures. (CH 9)

assistant curator Often serves as the registrar of museum collections by coordinating the collections' accessions. (CH 14)

assistant human resources manager Responsible for maintaining records and files on all injuries, illness, and safety programs. This person ensures that all reports are maintained to meet regulatory requirements and corporate policies and often keeps records of hired employee characteristics for governmental reporting. (CH 8)

assistant importer Works for the import production coordinator and follows up on orders with overseas suppliers. He or she also communicates with freight companies and customs agents, processes documents, and checks pricing agreements. (CH 3)

assistant mall manager Responsible for administering mall programs under the supervision of the property's general manager. This position is critical in communicating operational issues to tenants, contractors, and staff. (CH 15)

assistant photographer Works with clients and suppliers; organizes estimates, invoices, and payments; arranges props and assists with lighting; communicates with photographic labs and stylists; works with the photographer on shoots; and maintains the photographer's website and portfolio. (CH 13)

assistant piece goods buyer Often works with the piece goods buyer to calculate quantities of fabrics needed, to follow up on deliveries, and to locate fabric sources, while training for a buying position in the future. (CH 3)

assistant store manager A store manager-in-training, this position assists the store manager in scheduling employees, overseeing sales performance in the store, planning promotions, etc.—all of the daily responsibilities of operating a store successfully. (CH 12)

assistant textile designer Works under the direction of the textile designer in developing new fabric prints and colorways, sourcing new patterns for fabrics, and modifying successful fabric prints and patterns. (CH 2)

associate store manager This is a position that lies between the assistant store manager and the store manager; assists with employee hires, personnel scheduling, promotional activities, employee training, and other responsibilities assigned by the store manager. (CH 12)

base pay Set wage calculation based on an employee's role within an organization and the market for the expertise required to fulfill that role. (CH 8)

base salary plus commission Remuneration for an employee that is determined by the established monthly wage plus a percent of sales for products or services the employee sells. (CH 6)

beauty and wellness industries Focus on cosmetics, fragrances, hair and skin care, as well as spa, fitness, or wellness centers and their services. (CH 16)

beauty industry The producers of cosmetics, fragrances, and hair and skin care products. (CH 16)

beauty merchandising/marketing professional Involved in the marketing of cosmetics, fragrances, and skin care products. (CH 16)

benchmarking The activity of identifying competitors with features or skills in areas that a given company does not currently possess yet desires. (CH 8)

benefits coordinator *See benefits manager.* (CH 8)

benefits manager Part of the human resources division of a company, this position's responsibilities may include handling tax and legal aspects of benefits providers, overseeing payments to providers, finding the right vendors or administrators, and implementing mandated benefits. (CH 8)

block A basic flat pattern that is used as a starting place for pattern modifications. (CH 4)

body scanning Use of light beams to accurately measure the human body. (CH 4)

bonus A form of variable pay or employee benefit. (CH 8)

book inventory Written dollar amount of merchandise assortment. (CH 12)

bookkeeper Records the organization's business transactions and retains all accounting records. (CH 7)

bookkeeping manager Supervises the accounting record keepers in a firm. (CH 7)

book signing Beauty or fashion writer signs copies of his or her latest publication in a book, specialty, or department store. (CH 5)

brand advertising Promotes a particular label or manufacturer and is one of the five primary types of advertising. (CH 10)

breakdown The segmenting of a purchase order into quantities by sizes and colors to prepare for shipping from the manufacturer or retailer's warehouse to specific branch stores. (CH 3)

brick-and-click store A retail business that offers its products to consumers through a store facility and the Internet.

brick-and-mortar-store A retail business that has a physical appearance, as opposed to an Internet-based company (e.g., department stores, mass merchants, specialty stores, boutiques, discount stores, and outlet stores located in buildings). (CH 9)

bridal show Bridal wear manufacturers and retailers team up with auxiliary businesses, such as wedding planners, caterers, florists, and travel agents, to present a fashion presentation of the season's offerings for brides-to-be, their friends, and their families. (CH 5)

business plan A document used to solicit business funding that details strategies for the business concept and target market, location and space needs (e.g., building lease, facility purchase, or website), growth and exit strategies, sales and inventory levels, and financing needs. (CH 12)

buyer Typically responsible for all of the product purchases and inventories for a company or particular department of a company, within a certain budget; this position is also referred to as a *fashion merchandiser*. (CH 11)

buying plan A financial plan that takes into account past and projected sales, inventory, markups, and markdowns by department; it is also referred to as a *six-month plan*. (CH 11)

cafeteria plan See *flexible compensation*. (CH 8)

carryover A best selling item from one season that is featured again with minor modifications in the next season. (CH 9)

chargeback Credits to a vendor for damaged merchandise and returns on defective goods. (CH 3)

charity group fashion show A fashion show with ticket sales that benefit a nonprofit or charitable organization. (CH 5)

chief financial officer Top Director of the overall financial plans and accounting practices of an organization. (CH 7)

classified advertising Disseminates information about a sale, service, opportunity, or event. These are usually presented as small advertisements in specific sections of print publications. (CH 10)

client registry file A computerized or print record of the names and contact information of the retailer's or the line's customers. (CH 16)

cold calling Contacting businesses or people without a personal contact. (CH 8)

collection Groupings of related styles. (CH 3)

collections manager Supervises museum personnel working in a specific area within a museum classification, such as historical textiles, 18th-century millinery, or Egyptian jewelry. (CH 14)

color integrity Refers to the hue of the original color sample as it compares to the final manufactured product. The higher the color integrity, the closer the sample matches the actual product. (CH 2)

color palette A group of colors. (CH 2)

colorist Chooses the color palette or color combinations that will be used in creating product lines. (CH 9)

colorway Color selections for a particular pattern or print. (CH 2)

commercial broker Independent businessperson who secures buyers and sellers of public real estate and facilitates sales transactions; may specialize in income-producing properties, such as office buildings, retail stores, warehouses, shopping centers, and industrial parks. (CH 15)

commercial designer Interior designers who concentrate on public spaces, including projects for retail stores, hotels, motels, schools, etc. (CH 15)

commercial real estate developer Among the most entreprencurial of the real estate career paths, they acquire land, prepare it for development, may oversee the construction process, and often sell the real estate at a profit. (CH 15)

commercial retail space Public properties that include malls, business districts, and shopping centers. (CH 15)

commission Percent of the sales volume on merchandise paid to a sales representative based on the goods sold that are shipped and accepted by the retailer. (CH 6)

communications training Human Resources instruction that has become a need as a result of the increasing diversity of today's workforce, it encompasses an understanding of how to speak and listen effectively with those of other languages, ethics, and customs. (CH 8)

company salesperson Sales representative employed directly by a particular firm. (CH 6)

comparative market approach To establish a commercial real estate value, new construction costs of similar types and styles of buildings are compared to the purchase price of the property. (CH 15)

competition A manufacturer producing a similar product to another manufacturer at roughly the same price point, targeted toward the same customer or market niche. (CH 9)

competitive market price A rate for a property that lies within the average list price for properties of similar value. (CH 15)

complimentary service Features offered by a retail operation, such as alterations, delivery, and gift wrap, with the intent of drawing in and keeping customers. (CH 5)

computer-aided design (CAD) The process of developing garments, prints, and patterns on a computer screen; this is an important trend in textile design. (CH 2)

computer-aided pattern making Manipulation of the components of pattern pieces on a computer screen. (CH 4)

computer-integrated manufacturing (CIM) Computers are tied together to communicate throughout the entire product development and manufacturing processes, from design to distribution. (CH 4)

computer skills training Educational programs on computer skills needed for conducting administrative and office tasks and for communicating with other departments in the company. (CH 8)

comptroller *See controller.*(CH 7)

consumer publication Magazine or newsletter that is written for and made readily available to the general consumer. (CH 5)

consumer tracking information Information from sales data and credit card applications that is focused on demographics and psychographics. (CH 1)

contract designer Concentrates on the design of retail, office, and health environments, such as stores, health clinics, and government facilities. Also see commercial designer. (CH 15)

contractor Can either be a factory that makes and finishes goods or a firm that is hired to manufacture a product line domestically or abroad. (CH 2, CH 3)

controller Responsible for a company's financial plans and policies, its accounting practices, its relationships with lending institutions and the financial community, the maintenance of its fiscal records, and the preparation of its financial reports. (CH 7)

cooperative advertising Also referred to as *co-op advertising*, this form of advertising involves a manufacturer contributing to the cost of advertisements paid for by the retailer. (CH 6)

corporate photographer Also referred to as an *industrial* or *commercial photographer*, this person produces images for promotional materials or annual reports. (CH 13)

corporation Stockholders own the company, which may be run by an individual or a group. (CH 12)

cost approach A return-on-investment ratio for real property that is used in pricing real estate. (CH 15)

cost price (cost) Wholesale price. (CH 6)

costume plot A list or chart that shows characters as they appear in each scene, what they are wearing, and what their overall movements are throughout a play. (CH 13)

counter/line manager In the beauty industry, this person coordinates special events and promotions within the retail operation, manages employees, and works closely with buyers. (CH 16)

counterfeit merchandise An imitation of a product, usually one with a designer name, that is intended to fool the customer into thinking it is the real deal. (CH 9)

country of origin The nation in which goods are primarily manufactured. (CH 3)

creative director Person who identifies the apparel, accessories, and lifestyle trends in various merchandise classifications. (CH 1)

croquis A rendering or miniature visual of a textile pattern or print. (CH 2)

cross-shopping A customer's inclination to purchase a wide variety of products in an array of brands and prices from any number of providers—directly from the manufacturer, in a resale store, at a flea market, or through a couturier. (CH 9)

curatorial traineeship Internship or apprenticeship for the prospective museum curator. (CH 14)

customer service manager Assists customers with issues or complaints and implements the retail operation's policies and procedures for returns, exchanges, out-of-stock merchandise, product warranties, and the like. (CH 12)

customer service training Human Resources instruction to help a company's employees understand and meet the needs of customers. (CH 8)

cut Fabric yardage amount. (CH 6)

cutter Uses electronic machines, knives, or scissors to precisely cut around the pattern pieces through layers of fabric, often several inches in thickness. (CH 4)

cutting for approval (CFA) Also referred to as *memo;* this refers to a fabric swatch ordered by an interior designer. (CH 6)

cut-to-order Considered the safest method of projecting manufacturing needs, this refers to making the quantity of products specified on orders received. (CH 4)

cut-to-stock Involves purchasing fabrics and other product components before orders are secured. (CH 4)

deaccession The removal of items from a museum collection because of repetition of artifacts, the receipt of better examples, loss, or decay. (CH 14)

decentralized buying Individual stores or groups of stores within a retail chain that have a buyer who selects from the company's primary buyer's purchases. (CH 9)

demographics Consumer data that can be interpreted as numbers (i.e., age, income, education attained, and number of family members). (CH 1)

department manager Oversees a specific area or department within a store and maintains the sales floor by superrising sales associates, placing new merchandise on the sales floor, adding signage for promotions, recording markdowns, and executing floor sets. (CH 12)

design-driven brand A brand that is led by a designer expressing a personal artistic vision and sense of taste. (CH 9)

design process The conception of a style to include its inspiration or theme, the color palette, fabric selection, form, and fit. (CH 9)

development An ongoing, multifaceted set of activities created to bring an employee or an organization up to another threshold of performance, often to perform a higher-level job or new role in the future. (CH 8)

digitizer An electronic tool that is used to manipulate the size and shape of pattern pieces. (CH 4)

direct market brand Describes a brand that often includes the name of the retailer and the name of the manufacturer on the label. Often, this is carried by a specialty store chain, such as Ann Taylor, IKEA, and Banana Republic. (CH 9)

director of product development Ultimately responsible for strategic planning of the division, this person specifies exactly what the company will make and market, as well as when it will do this. (CH 9)

director of a spa or wellness center Responsible for keeping the spa running smoothly by managing customer service, budgets, marketing plans, and environment and staff appearance standards. (CH 16)

distribution manager Also referred to as an *allocator* or a *replenishment analyst*, this position is responsible for planning and managing the flow of goods received from the vendors, as ordered by the buyers, to the retail locations. (CH 11)

district manager See *regional manager*. (CH 12)

diversity training Explanation from Human Resources of how people of different cultures, races, and religions, for example, may have different perspectives and views. It includes techniques to value and expand diversity in the workplace. (CH 8)

divisional merchandise manager (DMM) Works under the general merchandising manager and provides leadership for the buying staff of a division or a related group of departments, such as men's wear, women's wear, or home furnishings. (CH 11)

draping Process in which a pattern maker shapes and cuts muslin or the garment fabric on a dress form or a live model to create a pattern. (CH 4)

dye lot A quantity of fabric colored at one specific time so that color matches are most accurate. (CH 6)

educational event A fashion event planner, a manufacturer's representative, or an employee hired by the planner educates an audience about a product. (CH 5)

e-learning course Online delivery method for teaching students outside a traditional classroom environment. (CH 14)

electronic data interchange (EDI) Refers to the transfer of computer-generated information between one company's computer system and another's. (CH 4)

employee benefits Forms of value, other than financial compensation, that are provided to personnel in return for their contribution to the organization. Examples are vacation pay, health insurance, and merchandise discounts. (CH 8)

employee compensation The amount of money paid to personnel in exchange for the work they do for the company. (CH 8)

end product The final product to be purchased by the customer. (CH 4)

entry-level accountant Maintains records of routine accounting transactions. (CH 7)

equipment Fixtures, furnishings, and machinery purchased for long-term use by a company, such as cash terminals, T-stands, mannequins, and track lights. (CH 10)

esthetician A licensed professional who provides services such as facials, makeup application, and hair removal to aid in improving someone's physical appearance. (CH 16)

esthetics Also referred to as *aesthetics*, this is a relatively new field that combines wellness, science, and beauty. The field views the client as a whole person by providing services through comprehensive makeovers and beauty-enhancement treatments that combine medical, beauty, and spa treatments. (CH 16)

exclusive An item that only one retailer carries. In some cases, a retailer may negotiate to be the only one in a geographic region to carry a particular item or the only one in the country to carry a particular color. For example, the label may read: "Burberry Exclusively for Neiman Marcus." (CH 9)

exempt Professional, management, and other types of skilled jobs are considered exempt. Employees in these jobs receive a salary, that is, a fixed amount of money per time interval, usually a set amount per month. (CH 8)

export A product that is bought by an overseas company from a vendor in the United States and sent out of the country. (CH 3)

Family and Consumer Science Education (FCSEd) Certification for an instructor who teaches high school, vocational, or college courses in textiles, fashion, interior design, consumer education, personal financial literacy, clothing construction, and careers in the fashion industry. (CH 14)

fashion costumer Collaborates with film and video directors to design, consign, or construct apparel and accessories that fit within the mood, time frame, and image of the film or video. (CH 13)

fashion director This position in the textile industry is responsible for determining the trends, colors, themes, and textures for piece goods or fabrics that the firm will feature for a specific season. In retailing, this position is responsible for designating the trends, themes, colors, and fabrics that the buyers will purchase for the retail operation. (CH 2)

fashion editor Supervises the process of creating and presenting content for fashion-specific magazines, websites, newspaper sections, or television shows. (CH 5)

fashion event planner Someone who increases the visibility of a design house, organization, brand, product, or fabric by coordinating special events, such as fashion shows and seminars, that provide exposure for these products. (CH 5)

fashion exclusivity Refers to merchandise that is unique to a particular company. (CH 9)

fashion forecaster Continually monitors the consumer and the industry through traveling, reading, networking, and, most important, observing. (CH 1)

fashion house model See *fit model*. (CH 13)

fashion importer Sources products from overseas locations to sell domestically. (CH 3)

fashion merchandiser See *buyer*. (CH 11)

fashion photographer Works with models and art directors in apparel, accessories, or home products and is often commissioned by the art directors of catalogs and magazines. (CH 13)

fashion photography Photographs of models wearing the latest apparel, accessories, hairstyles, and makeup or highlighting the newest home furnishings and other fashion products, primarily for commercial use. (CH 13)

fashion production planner Projects timelines for manufacturing the products in a line. (CH 3)

fashion show/event planner Responsible for developing and implementing a variety of promotional activities for a designer, manufacturer, or retailer, such as a fashion show, party, or conference. Works with budgets, media, and customers in producing cost-effective and high-profile events. (CH 13)

fashion stylist Responsible for bringing to life a photographer's or director's vision for a fashion photography shoot, magazine layout, music video, television or film commercial, or print advertisement. (CH 5, CH 13)

fashion visuals Refers to the images used in the fashion industry, such as photographs, trend boards, and magazine clippings. (CH 13)

findings Functional product components that may not be visible when viewing the final product; they include zippers, thread, linings, and interfacings. (CH 3)

findings buyer Responsible for purchasing zippers, threads, linings, and such for a manufacturer. (CH 3)

first cost Price of making an item. (CH 3)

first pattern Used to cut and sew the prototype. (CH 4)

fit model Also referred to as the *fashion house model,* this is a live model on whom a designer may drape, cut, and pin fabric and on whom the designer will check the sizing and proportion of garments. (CH 13)

flat pattern Method that uses angles, rulers, and curves to create patterns. (CH 4)

flexible compensation Also known as a *cafeteria plan*, this allows an employee to plan for tax-exempt expenses as a fringe benefit by projecting medical and dental expenses, for example. (CH 8)

floor set The arrangement of fixtures and merchandise on the sales floor to create a fresh look and highlight brand-new or undersold merchandise. (CH 12)

freelance costumer Hired for a specific production by a theater company or production studio and may or may not actually be local to the theater for which he or she is designing. (CH 13)

fringe benefits Tangible employee benefits such as health insurance, tuition reimbursement, and family leave. (CH 8)

foreign commissionaires Also known as *foreign-owned independent agents*, they usually have offices located in key buying cities overseas and assist with the purchase of goods for a fee. (CH 3)

funder Financing source, such as a bank or the Small Business Administration, used by a prospective business owner with a well-written business plan that justifies financing due to a good potential for profit, minimized risk, and a strong long-range plan. (CH 12)

general merchandising manager (GMM) Leads and manages the buyers of all divisions in a retail operation. (CH 11)

general practice photography Also referred to as *social photography*, this refers to photographic services for local communities or businesses, with the majority of work completed in wedding and family photography. (CH 13)

globalization The process of interlinking nations of the world with one another; this is a growing trend in the fashion industry. (CH 3)

global sourcing Refers to the process of locating, purchasing, and importing or exporting goods and services from around the world. (CH 3)

gross margin Actual profit after cost of goods, markdowns, and other expenses are deducted. (CH 11)

hairstylist Person specializing in hair design, color, and care. (CH 16)

hiring manager Responsible for locating and employing personnel for the various positions within a company. (CH 8)

human relations training Focuses on helping people get along with one another in the workplace. Conflict management is often part of this training seminar. (CH 8)

human resources (HR) Refers to the function in charge of an organization's employees, which includes finding and hiring employees, helping them grow and learn in the organization, and managing the process when an employee leaves. (CH 8)

human resources development (HRD) Professionals who work in the field of business concerned with recruiting, training, maintaining, motivating, and managing personnel. (CH 8)

human resources director See *human resources manager*. (CH 8)

human resources management (HRM) Key activities include the following: determining staffing needs; recruiting, training, and providing support to employees; dealing with performance issues; ensuring that personnel and management practices conform to various regulations; and overseeing the management of employee benefits and compensation, as well as maintaining employee records and personnel policies. (CH 8)

human resources manager Also known as a *director*, this person plays a leadership role in the business and people issues of the company. He or she identifies the human relations and work-related issues in the workplace and meets with supervisors and managers to determine effective solutions. (CH 8)

illustrator Works freelance or within the advertising divisions of major retailers, designers, or manufacturers to sketch garments for print advertisements. (CH 10)

image Refers to the way the product developer wants the brand to be perceived and the way that will best attract the target customer or the way the retailer wants the store to be perceived by the customer. (CH 9)

import A good or service that is brought into a country. (CH 3)

import production coordinator Liaison between the domestic apparel or home furnishings company and the overseas manufacturer or contractor. (CH 3)

incentive plan A form of variable pay such as a bonus for exceptional work submitted early. (CH 8)

income approach A method used to price commercial real estate, the property's value is determined by the income or money it can make through leases, percent of tenants' sales volume, and such. (CH 15)

institutional advertisement Promotional activity that sells an organization as a fashion leader, a community supporter, or a provider of the best value for the dollar, among other images. (CH 10)

institutional advertising Intended to build an organization's image and create community goodwill; one of the five primary types of advertising. (CH 10)

interior designer Often working with either homes (i.e., residential) or businesses (i.e., commercial or contract), this person is responsible for creating the facility's inner environment with attention to esthetics, safety, and well-being of those using the space. (CH 15)

intermediate/mid-level accountant Prepares and maintains accounting records that may include general accounting, costing, or budget data. (CH 7)

internal theft Refers to merchandise stolen by employees within the company. (CH 12)

inventory The selection of products available for sale in a fashion operation; this is also referred to as *merchandise assortment*. (CH 11)

inventory replenishment Reorders and stock placement on the sales floor. (CH 6)

key account For a manufacturer, this term refers to a large retailer, in terms of sales volume, that carries the manufacturer's line consistently and in depth. (CH 6)

key vendor Manufacturers' lines featured as the greatest proportion of inventory in a retail operation. (CH 11)

knockoff A copy of another style, often with minor modifications and being of lesser quality. (CH 9)

labdip A swatch of dyed fabric sent by mills to the product development team for color approval prior to dyeing large yardages of fabric. (CH 9)

landed costs The actual price of goods after taxes, tariffs, handling, and shipping fees are added to the cost of imported goods. (CH 3)

lead time Number of days, weeks, or months needed for the intricate planning and production steps that are implemented before fashion products actually arrive at the retail store; it is also considered the amount of time needed between placing a production order and receiving the shipment of products. (CH 1, CH 4)

letter of credit A document issued by a bank authorizing the bearer to draw a specific amount of money from the bank, its branches, or associated banks and agencies. (CH 3)

license An agreement in which a manufacturer is given exclusive rights to produce and market goods that carry the registered name and brandmark of a designer, celebrity, character, or product line. (CH 3)

licensee The manufacturer of a licensed product. (CH 3)

licensing director Responsible for overseeing the look, quality, labeling, delivery, and distribution of the company's licensed product lines. (CH 3)

licensor The owner of the name or brandmark who receives a percent of wholesale sales or some form of compensation based on a licensing agreement. (CH 3)

line plan Shows the number of styles in the line, the number and general types of fabrics and yarns to be used, colors per style, anticipated stock keeping units (SKU), and approximate preferred costs. (CH 9)

listing An agreement between the owner and the agent or broker to place a property for sale. (CH 15)

lookbook A publication that contains photographs or illustrations of a designer's newest collections for a given season. (CH 5)

makeup artist Works with cosmetics, wigs, and other costuming materials to color and enhance the client's face and body. (CH 16)

mall manager Responsible for everything in the mall from formulating its budget and planning promotional activities to developing its mix of tenants and building community relations. (CH 15)

management The process of organizing and controlling the affairs of a business or a particular sector of a business. (CH 12)

manager-in-training (MIT) An employee who is being trained to move into a management position. (CH 12)

managerial training An educational program offered by a retailer to develop management employees. (CH 14)

mandated benefits An employer is required by law to provide full-time employees with government benefits such as Social Security, unemployment insurance, and workers' compensation. (CH 8)

mannequin modeling Refers to live models standing motionless in the place of regular mannequins in windows or on showroom or retail floors. (CH 5)

manufacturer A company that produces, markets, and distributes product lines on a continual basis. (CH 9)

manufacturer's representative Also referred to as a *manufacturer's rep*, this person is a wholesale salesperson who is often independent. See also *account executive* and *sales representative*. (CH 2)

marker The layout of pattern pieces on the fabric from which the pieces will be cut. (CH 4)

marker maker Tracing of pattern pieces by hand or by computer into the tightest possible layout, while keeping the integrity of the design in mind. (CH 4)

market representative A specialized buyer of individual merchandise classifications who works closely with his or her client stores, keeping them up-to-date on new product offerings in the marketplace, recommending new vendors, and assisting them in locating needed goods. (CH 3)

market week Scheduled at the apparel and trade marts throughout the year in conjunction with the introduction of the new, seasonal lines presented by manufacturers. (CH 6)

mass customization Strategy that allows a manufacturer or retailer to provide individualized products to a consumer. (CH 4)

mass market Distribution of a product line through a wide variety of retailers. (CH 16)

master pattern Final pattern; often evolved from adjusting and perfecting a sample pattern. (CH 4)

media form Type of promotion that includes magazines and newspapers, television and radio, Internet outdoor displays, direct mail, novelties (e.g., calendars, pencils, and memo tablets), catalogs, directories, and circulars. (CH 10)

media planner Determines prices, including quantity discounts, for a media buy that may include several venues, such as radio, television, and newspaper. The media planner determines how the advertising budget is best spent to generate the most exposure and sales. (CH 5)

medi-spa Combines traditional spa services with those that must be offered by a physician, such as health screenings and minor surgery. (CH 16)

merchandise coordinator Employed by a manufacturer and works within retail stores carrying the manufacturer's line, restocking products, installing displays, reordering top-selling styles, and educating sales staff and customers on the product line. (CH 6)

merchandiser Collaborates with the director of product development to decide what to produce and organizes and manages the entire product development process; this person is responsible for the development of a balanced, marketable, profitable, and timely line. (CH 9)

merchandising Refers to all of the activities involved in the buying and selling of a product line. (CH 11)

merchandising calendar The product development team's schedule, created to deliver the right product (e.g., style, quality, and price) at the right time. (CH 9)

merchandising-driven brand "Void-filling" brand; a market-based brand designed to fill a void in a market (i.e., an underserved customer) and create a product to appeal to a distinct customer. (CH 9)

merchandising executive training program Designed to prepare new hires, former interns, college recruits, or current employees who have shown skills in merchandising for their first assignment as assistant buyers; also referred to as *merchant executive training program*. (CH 11)

modeling/talent agency director Ultimately responsible for locating and contracting new models, training them, and, later, securing modeling jobs for them. (CH 13)

multiline rep A manufacturer's salesperson who carries a number of lines, often working with noncompetitive product lines and manufacturers. (CH 6)

museological training For the curator, this covers how to preserve, maintain, and interpret museum collections. (CH 14)

museum conservator Manages, cares for, preserves, treats, and documents works of art, artifacts, and specimens; with regard to fashions or costumes, conservators acquire and preserve important visuals (e.g., photographs, illustrations, or sketches), costumes, accessories, furnishings, and other valuable items for permanent storage or display; this position may be referred to as a *restoration and preservation specialist.* (CH 14)

museum curator Works under the supervision of the museum director. A curator directs the accession, deaccession, storage, and exhibition of collections. This position may also be referred to as a *museum keeper.* (CH 14)

museum director Runs the business of the museum; manages the general operations and staffing of the organization, and coordinates the public affairs mission of the museum. (CH 14)

museum technician Assists the curator by performing various preparatory and maintenance tasks on museum items. Most technicians work to preserve, maintain, repair, and treat historic structures and may assist curators with research. (CH 14)

National Architectural Accrediting Board Inc. (NAAB) Develops standards and procedures to verify that each accredited program in the United States meets standards for the education of architects. (CH 15)

news release See *press release.* (CH 10)

nonexempt Employees who receive additional payment for overtime, that is, extra pay for hours worked over 40 hours a week or on certain days of the week or holidays. (CH 8)

open-to-buy The amount of money allocated for the buyer to make new merchandise purchases each month, based on sales and inventory amounts. (CH 11)

operations manager Develops and maintains effective sales and operational programs with a focus on superior customer service for all of the retail units in the company or for units in a region. (CH 12)

outsourcing Manufacturing a product abroad that was developed domestically. (CH 2)

overage A higher dollar amount of products on the retail floor than was actually purchased and received. (CH 12)

overtime Extra pay for hours worked over 40 per week or on certain holidays. (CH 8)

partnership A business owned by two or more people. (CH 12)

party planning Putting together a party event to include budget planning, location selection, decor, theme, and guest list. (CH 5)

pattern grader Cuts a pattern in the full range of sizes offered by the manufacturer. (CH 4)

pattern maker Translates the design concept into a flat pattern to create an actual garment. (CH 4)

payroll manager Responsible for employee compensation. (CH 8)

personal shopper Assists an individual in selecting an entire season's wardrobe or an outfit for a specific occasion, based on the needs of the customer, including his or her budget, activities, and personal style; a personal shopper may be employed by an individual, boutique, upscale department store, or specialty store. (CH 10)

personnel The employees of an organization. (CH 8)

photographer Freelance or employed by large retailers in the promotion division to photograph the visual components of promotions. (CH 10)

photographic model Hired to be photographed in the studio or on location. While a select few top models work in high-fashion magazines, a large number of opportunities exist through mail order catalogs, newspaper advertisements, and television. (CH 13)

physical inventory The merchandise actually in the retail or manufacturing operation. (CH 12)

piece goods Fabrics or materials, such as leather, used to create products. (CH 2)

piece goods buyer Purchases the textiles used in the production of final products. (CH 3)

planner Works in collaboration with the buyer to develop sales forecasts, inventory plans, and spending budgets for merchandise to achieve the retailer's sales and profit objectives. (CH 11)

planning manager Provides leadership, direction, and support at the merchandise division level to plan appropriately; this person also distributes and monitors inventory within a company's various retail locations to maximize sales. (CH 11)

planning module A chart constructed by a planner that details inventory ratios, such as top-to-bottom ratios of junior sportswear. (CH 11)

plan-o-gram Floor plan on which the placement and types of racks, fixtures, display units, and merchandise should be placed to create an easy flow of traffic and present the merchandise most effectively. (CH 15)

point-of-sale Analysis of transactions as they are processed through a retailer's cash registers or computer terminals. (CH 1)

portfolio A collection of work that illustrates a job candidate's range of skills and outcomes. This also referred to as a *book*. (CH 13)

press package Also referred to as *press kit*, this is a parcel containing photographs and related information, such as news articles from similar events in other cities or background information, included with a press release. (CH 10)

press photography Also known as *photojournalism*, this focuses on images directly related to news stories, both events and personalities. (CH 13)

press release A summary of the important facts relating to a company event, formatted specifically for the media and sent directly to them by the publicity director; this is also known as a *news release*. (CH 10)

prestige market Product lines that are distributed through high-end department and specialty store retailers. (CH 16)

primary level Fashion industry segment that includes fiber and fabric producers and trade organizations, designers and product developers who create for manufacturers, and the manufacturers with their brand names and images. (CH 5)

print service Company that sells print designs to mills, wholesalers, product developers, and retailers. (CH 2)

private brand A name owned exclusively by a particular store that is extensively marketed with a definite image, such as Target's Mossimo and Isaac Mizrahi brands. (CH 9)

private label A line name or brand that the retailer develops and assigns to a collection of products and is owned exclusively by a particular retailer, such as Antonio Melani at Dillard's. (CH 9)

product developer/technician Assigned to modify an existing product in a line and works to develop new features for the product. (CH 16)

product development Creating and making a product such as a dress, belt, or chair from start to finish. (CH 9)

product development designer The creator of a product line; he or she is a trend forecaster in his or her own right by determining what the customer will be ready for next. Going through the design process with each new season, this person in a retail firm is also referred to as a *private label designer*. (CH 9)

product development pattern maker Takes accurate measurements and develops a pattern, either by using draping or flat pattern methods, to create a pattern that, if correctly written, ensures that the designer's vision will be implemented. (CH 9)

product manager Responsible for all products within a company's product lines or for a specific product category within the line. (CH 4)

product research and development (R and D) The technical division of a company that creates products that meet the manufacturer's standards of performance and safety by continually conducting research on existing products, as well as developing new and innovative products. (CH 16)

product void Merchandise categories in which there are few, if any, items to fill consumer needs and desires. (CH 4)

production assistant Supports the production manager with detail work and record keeping. This person may track deliveries, assist development of production schedules, and communicate the work flow of the factory to the production manager. (CH 4)

production authorization The process of selecting and quantifying styles that will be manufactured. (CH 9)

production efficiency manager Responsible for monitoring the speed and output of a manufacturing facility and for managing waste. (CH 4)

production manager Also referred to as a *plant manager*, this person is responsible for all operations at the manufacturing plant, whether it is a domestic or overseas location and contracted or company-owned. Job responsibilities of a production manager include supervising or completing the estimation of production costs, scheduling work flow in the factory, and hiring and training production employees. (CH 3)

production planner Estimates the amount and types of products a company will manufacture, either based on previous seasonal sales or on orders being received from the sales representatives on the road and in the showroom. (CH 4)

professional development Includes continuing education, often toward a higher degree; internships within a field; conference participation; and memberships in trade and educational organizations. (CH 14)

promotion The endorsement of a person, a product, a cause, an idea, or an organization (CH 5); these activities communicate a company's or product's attributes to the target consumers using two primary tools: publicity and advertising. (CH 10)

promotion director Guides the marketing activities of a fashion operation. (CH 10)

prop house Firms that rent furniture, fixtures, mannequins, and decor accessories to visual merchandisers, saving the company money on limited-use display pieces while reducing the amount of warehouse space and labor needed to inventory and store visual merchandising props. (CH 15)

prototype First sample garment, accessory, or home product. (CH 4)

psychographics Refer to lifestyle choices, values, and emotions of a population. (CH 1)

public affairs As a mission in museums, this refers to collaborating with the community and government and industry, social, and academic organizations to develop exhibitions and collections that appeal to and educate the community and its visitors. (CH 14)

public relations Promotional activities for a business or organization. (CH 10)

public relations account executive Works with media contacts such as fashion publications like *Vogue*, *Elle*, *W*, and *InStyle* to promote the line in magazine editorials and feature stories. (CH 16)

public relations director Responsible for finding cost-effective ways to promote the company he or she represents. (CH 5)

publicity The dissemination of information about people, places, special events, or other newsworthy topics through a variety of communications media—in essence, free press: the mention of a company or its merchandise in the media for which the company does not pay a fee. (CH 10)

publicity director Responsible for securing publicity for the retail operation. This person may collaborate with other departments to create events such as fashion show productions or celebrity personal appearances to secure publicity. (CH 10)

purchase order (PO) A contract for merchandise between the buyer, as a representative of his or her firm, and the vendor. (CH 3)

quality control manager Also known as the *quality control engineer*, this person develops specifications for the products that will be manufactured and is responsible for the final inspection for garments from the manufacturer, checking fabric, fit, construction for quality and adherence to product specification guidelines (CH 4).

quality initiatives training Examines such programs as total quality management (TQM), quality circles, and benchmarking. (CH 8)

quick response (QR) Decreasing the amount of time required between design and the purchase of raw materials to production and distribution of the final product. (CH 4)

quota plus commission Form of remuneration in which the manufacturer's representative is paid commission on sales he or she has procured over a specific amount or baseline. (CH 6)

raw materials buyer This person planns and purchases all of the parts needed to make the final product. (CH 3)

real estate agent See *commercial broker*. (CH 15)

realtor An intermediary who puts the buyer and seller of real property together and facilitates the sales transaction. (CH 15)

recruiter Company representative who locates and encourages job candidates to join the firm as hires. (CH 18)

regional manager Responsible for the retail stores of a particular company that are located in a segregated area of the United States and/or overseas; this position is also referred to as a *district manager*. (CH 12)

reorder Fill-in on merchandise that is selling well. (CH 6)

residential costumer Hired by a specific theater to design and develop costumes for an extended series of productions. (CH 13)

residential designer Interior designer who focuses on home environments. (CH 15)

resource room director/reference librarian Responsible for managing the inventory of books, fabrics, garments, and resources and for procuring new ones for a fashion library or resource room. (CH 2)

restoration and preservation specialist See *museum conservator*. (CH 14)

retail account executive Also referred to as a *retail sales account executive*, this person sells a product line to retail accounts and oversees the sales performance of the line in large retail accounts. (CH 16)

retailer A business that sells products to the ultimate consumer and can include the vast range of brick-and-mortar stores (e.g., department stores, mass merchants, specialty stores, boutiques, discount stores, and outlet stores), as well as catalog and on-line stores. (CH 9)

retail label A brand with the retailer's name on it, such as Neiman Marcus, Custom Interiors, or Saks Fifth Avenue. A retailer may negotiate with a manufacturer to put its label on a group of items instead of or in addition to the manufacturer's label, though the retailer may not have anything to do with the design or development of the items. (CH 9)

retail operation owner Financially responsible for the company and oversees all aspects of the retail business. (CH 12)

retail store manager Oversees all aspects of a retail store's operation, from advertising and special events to the customers and employees, often consisting of assistant managers, department managers, sales associates, and staff. (CH 12)

retail trend forecaster Researches many sources to create formal reports that summarize important fashion trends in a particular season that will appeal to the retailer's clientele. (CH 9)

safety training Educating employees on safety precautions; this is critical where there are employees working with heavy equipment, hazardous chemicals, and repetitive activities, such as in an apparel factory or textile mill. (CH 8)

salaried An employee is paid a set amount every month. (CH 6)

salary A fixed amount of money per time interval, usually a set amount per month. (CH 8)

sales advertising Announces specific value items; it is one of the five primary types of advertising. (CH 10)

sales forecast Includes projections of sales by category, style, color, and size based on historical data and statistical analysis. This information may be used to place preliminary fabric and trim orders and block out production time in factories. (CH 9)

sales promotion Activities designed to sell products; often feature short-term incentives that encourage the sale of the product (i.e., samples, coupons, gift-with-purchase giveaways, point-of-purchase displays, and contests). (CH 10)

sales representative A wholesale salesperson who is often independent, also called a *sales rep*. See also *account executive* and *manufacturer's representative*. (CH 2)

sample A prototype of a product that will be reproduced in quantity if selected to be in the final line. (CH 2)

sample line Line that includes a prototype of every style available in the final line. (CH 6)

sample size Used for testing fit and appearance in addition to selling purposes. (CH 4)

secondary vendor Line carried by a retailer in small quantities. (CH 11)

security Refers to the safekeeping of the merchandise in the store. (CH 12)

security manager Works to prevent merchandise theft; collaborates with receiving, accounting, and management to be certain that accurate accounting procedures are in place and true losses are identified when the physical inventory is taken. (CH 12)

senior accountant Responsible for establishing, interpreting, and analyzing complex accounting records or financial statements for management. (CH 7)

sexual harassment training Usually includes careful description of the organization's policies about sexual harassment: what are inappropriate behaviors and what to do about them. (CH 8)

shopping center Distinctly different from downtown and local business districts, the shopping center building is preplanned as a merchandising unit for interplay among tenants. (CH 15)

shortage See *shrinkage*. (CH 12)

short-run production Planned manufacture of select merchandise for a short period of time. (CH 2)

show model Employed by a modeling agency that takes bookings from clients who need to display clothes at fashion shows, exhibitions, or trade markets. (CH 13)

showroom A place where product lines are displayed; usually caters only to the trade. (CH 6)

showroom representative See *showroom salesperson*. (CH 6)

showroom salesperson Also referred to as a *showroom representative*, this person works at a manufacturer's and/or designer's place of business, where he or she meets with visiting retail buyers and presents the latest product line to them. (CH 6)

shrinkage Merchandise that is missing or stolen; it also known as *shortage*. (CH 12)

single-line rep Manufacturer's representative who prefers to sell solely one manufacturer's line as an independent, rather than as a company employee. (CH 6)

sloper Flat pattern method that uses angles, rulers, and curves to alter existing basic patterns. (CH 4)

sole proprietorship A business owned by an individual. (CH 12)

sourcing The activities of determining which vendor can provide the amount of product needed, negotiating the best possible price and discounts, scheduling deliveries, and following up on actual shipments to make certain due dates are met and that quality control is maintained. (CH 3)

sourcing manager Director of the activities related to locating goods and producers of goods. (CH 3)

spec sheets Specification lists; they typically provide detailed measurements and construction guidelines. (CH 9)

special events Designed occurrences, such as model searches, designer visits, and charity events, that are intended to communicate particular messages to target audiences. (CH 10)

special events coordinator Develops and executes events that are fashion related, such as fashion and trunk shows, as well as fashion presentations at clubs and for organizations. Additionally, the special events coordinator creates and directs activities that are not fashion related, yet put the company in the public eye in a favorable light. (CH 5)

spreader Lays out the selected fabric for cutting. (CH 4)

stabilizing Saving and maintaining museum artifacts. A museum curator stabilizes artifacts when preparing them for storage or an exhibition. (CH 14)

store-planning director Develops a plan that details fixture placement, lighting, dressing rooms, restrooms, windows, aisles, and cash and wrap areas of a retail department. Objectives include aesthetic appeal, image consistency, visibility and security of merchandise, comfort and ease of staff and consumers in moving within the facility, and merchandising flexibility. (CH 10)

strikeoff A few yards of fabric printed by a mill and sent to the product developer (e.g., colorist, designer, and sample maker) to be made into a sample. (CH 9)

supplies Replenishable materials purchased and used by a company, such as hangers, trash bags, tissue paper, and lightbulbs. (CH 10)

stylis A computerized pen. (CH 4)

tearoom modeling An informal fashion show, often taking place in a hotel or restaurant, in which models circulate among the tables as the meal is being served. (CH 5)

tearsheet A page that has been pulled from a newspaper, model book, or magazine. (CH 6)

technical photographer Produces photographs for reports or research papers, such as textile durability analyses. (CH 13)

technician Develops new features for products. (CH 16)

terminal degree Highest educational degree available in a particular field. (CH 14)

territory The specific geographical area within which a retail store outlet is located or in which a sales representative sells the line. (CH 12)

textile colorist Chooses the colors or color combinations that will be used in creating each textile design. (CH 2)

textile design The print, pattern, texture, and finish of fabrics. (CH 2)

textile designer Creates original patterns, prints, and textures for the fabrics used in many types of industry, from fashion to interiors. (CH 2)

textile engineer Works with designers to determine how a design can be applied to a fabric in terms of more practical variables, such as durability, washability, and colorfastness. (CH 2)

textile librarian Responsible for organizing and collecting fabric and print samples for a fabric firm, a textile manufacturer, an apparel or accessory manufacturer. (CH 2)

textile stylist The creative person who modifies existing textile goods, altering patterns or prints that have been successful on the retail floor to turn them into fresh, new products. (CH 2)

textile technical designer Creates new textile designs or modifies existing fabric goods, altering patterns or prints that have been successful on the retail floor to turn them into fresh, new products. (CH 9)

textile technician Works with the issues that are directly related to the production of textiles, such as care factors, finishing techniques, and durability. (CH 2)

trade mart Houses temporary sales booths and permanent showrooms leased either by sales representatives or manufacturers. (CH 6)

trade publication Periodical designed for specific professions, vocations, or merchandise classifications. (CH 5)

trade school An institution that may offer fashion programs and provide certificates, rather than degrees, upon the student's completion of the program, including programs in such areas as fashion design, illustration, retailing, photography, and merchandising. (CH 14)

trade show Scheduled at the apparel and trade marts throughout the year in conjunction with the introduction of the new, seasonal lines presented by manufacturers. (CH 6)

traffic manager Supervises work flow on the factory floor, monitoring the product from start to finish. (CH 4)

trainer An educator who works with employees to provide them with certain knowledge or skills to improve performance in their current jobs. (CH 8)

trend book Design resource publication intended to assist creative teams and manufacturers in developing future product lines. Trend books may include photos, fabric swatches, materials, color ranges, drawings of prints, product sketches, silhouettes, commentaries, and related materials. (CH 1)

trend forecaster Continually monitors the consumer and the industry through traveling, reading, networking, and, most important, observing; this person creates formal reports that summarize important fashion trends with seasonal themes. The trend forecaster in the product development division of a retailer identifies the fashion trends and then interprets them for the retailer's particular customer or market. (CH 1)

trendspotter A person located at universities and other locations worldwide who provides information to WGSN on the latest trends in the locale. (CH 1)

trimmings Decorative components designed to be seen as part of the final product (e.g., buttons, appliqués, and beltings). (CH 3)

trimmings buyer Person who is responsible for ordering decorative components for products. (CH 3)

trunk show Consists of a fashion event planner and/or a manufacturer's representative bringing a manufacturer's full seasonal line to a retail store that carries this manufacturer. (CH 5)

user interface (UI) The visuals people see and interact with when they view a website and the navigation by which they move through the site. (CH 15)

variable pay Salary that is based on the performance of the individual employee. (CH 8)

vendor The person selling a product or service, or a manufacturer or distributor from whom a company purchases products or production processes. (CH 3)

visual merchandiser Responsible for the window installations, displays, signage, fixtures, mannequins, and decorations that give a retail operation esthetic appeal and a distinct image. This position is also known as a *visual merchandising director*. (CH 10)

visual merchandising Design, development, procurement, and installation of merchandise displays and the ambiance of the environment in which the displays are shown. (CH 6, CH 10)

vocational school Training for students who elect not to participate in a four-year college degree program upon high school graduation. Courses taught include commercial clothing construction, apparel alteration, pattern making, and retailing. (CH 14)

wage The amount of money workers earn per hour. (CH 8)

website designer Constructs, maintains, and builds on a company's website; this person must possess general design skills and knowledge of Web-specific design factors (e.g., screen resolution and accessibility). He or she designs a website's look and feel, incorporating features such as e-commerce, online community, animations, and interactive applications into the site. This position is also referred to as a *website developer*. (CH 10, CH 15)

website development A relatively new field in design and fashion concerned with constructing web pages and sites from technological, aesthetic, and marketing perspectives. (CH 15)

website developer See *website designer*. (CH 10, 15)

wellness center A type of spa that often incorporates health programs, such as exercise (e.g., yoga and Pilates) and nutrition. (CH 16)

window trimmer An assistant in visual merchandising who works with the installation of displays in retail store windows and interiors. (CH 10)

written inventory Merchandise documented as existing within the retail operation. The difference between written, or book, inventory is referred to as *shrinkage* or *over-age*. (CH 12)

yardage A given amount of fabric, based on its length in yards. (CH 3)

CREDITS

Chapter 1

1.1 Courtesy of Fairchild Publications, Inc., 1.2 Photo by Steve Griffen; 1.3 Courtesy of Expofil; 1.4 © Atlantide Phototravel/Corbis; 1.5 © the Baltimore Museum of Art: the Cone Collection, formed by Dr. Claribel Cone and Miss Etta Cone of Baltimore, Maryland BMA 1950.261; 1.6 Courtesy of Fairchild Publications, Inc.; 1.7 Photo by Donato Sardello/Courtesy of Fairchild Publications, Inc.; 1.8 Photo by Thomas Iannaccone/Courtesy of Fairchild Publications, Inc.; 1.9 © B.S.P.I./Corbis; 1.10 © Royalty-Free/Corbis; Box 1.1 © Anna Clopet/Corbis; Box 1.2 Photo by Joel Niedfeldt/Courtesy of Josh Rubin; Box 1.3 Courtesy of Li Edelkoort

Chapter 2

2.1 Reprinted with permission of Lectra. All rights reserved.; 2.2 (top) Courtesy of Zakee Shariff; 2.2 (bottom) Courtesy of Zakee Shariff; 2.3 Reprinted with permission of Lectra; 2.4 © Bob Krist/Corbis; Box 2.1 Reprinted with permission of Lectra; 2.5 Designed by Prof. Simon Frostick and Dr. Alan McLeod; textile designed by Peter Butcher (2003); developed by Ellis Developments Ltd.; manufactured by Pearsalls Ltd. (2004); copyright Nuvasive Inv and Ellis Developments Ltd.; machine-embroidered polyester (base cloth dissolved); longest diameter: 14.6 (5 3/4 in.). Cooper-Hewitt, National Design Museum, Smithsonian Institution. Gift of Ellis Developments Ltd., 2004-15-1. Photo by Matt Flynn; 2.5 (bottom) Manufactured and designed by Sakase Adtech Co., LTD, Fukui, Japan; designed 1991, manufactured 2002; Triaxially woven carbon fiber; 497.2 x 155.6 cm (16 ft 3 3/4 in x 5 ft. 1 1/4 in.). Cooper-Hewitt, National Design Museum, Smithsonian Institution. Gift of The Museum of Modern Art. Courtesy of the designer, 2002-28-1. Photo by Matt Flynn; Logos: Courtesy of Cotton Incorporated; Courtesy of Woolmark Co.; Courtesy of the Fur Council of

Canada; Courtesy of NAFFEM; Courtesy of Mohair; Courtesy of Springs Global; The DuPont Oval Logo is a trademark of DuPont or its affiliates.

Chapter 3

3.1 (left) © Patrick Robert/Sygma/Corbis; 3.1 (right) © Patrick Robert/Sygma/Corbis; 3.2 Photo by Erin Fitzsimmons; 3.3 © Jason Bleibtreu/Corbis Sygma; 3.4 (top) © Ed Kashi/ Corbis; 3.4 (bottom) ML Sinibaldi/Corbis; 3.5 Courtesy of Fairchild Publications, Inc.

Chapter 4

Box 4.1 Photo by Colleen McNiff Photography; 4.1 © Brownie Harris/Corbis; 4.2 (top) Photo by Jennifer McKelvie; 4.2 (bottom) © Ute Kaiser/zefa/Corbis; 4.2 (middle) Reprinted with permission of Lectra. All rights reserved; 4.3 Reprinted with permission of Lectra. All rights reserved; 4.4 (bottom) Reprinted with permission of Lectra. All rights reserved; 4.5 Reprinted with permission of Lectra. All rights reserved; 4.6 Reprinted with permission of Lectra. All rights reserved; 4.7 Courtesy of Fairchild Publications, Inc.; 4.8 (top left) © Mark Peterson/ Corbis; 4.8 (top right) © Mark Peterson/Corbis; 4.8 (bottom) © Mark Peterson/Corbis

Chapter 5

5.1 Courtesy of Fairchild Publications, Inc.; 5.2 Photo by Fairchild Publications, Inc.; 5.3 Courtesy of Fairchild Publication, Inc.; 5.4 Photo by Marquita Sayres; 5.5 Courtesy of Fairchild Publications, Inc.; 5.6 Courtesy of Fairchild Publication, Inc.; 5.7 Courtesy of Fairchild Publications, Inc.; 5.8 Courtesy of Fairchild Publication, Inc.; 5.9 © Toby Melville/Reuters/Corbis

Chapter 6

6.1 © Royalty-Free/Corbis; 6.2 © Chris Farina/Corbis; 6.3 Courtesy of Showroom Seven; 6.4 Courtesy of Springfield Town & Country; 6.5 Photo by Shari Smith Dunaif, High Noon Productions

Chapter 7

7.1 © Randy Faris/Corbis; Box 7.1 Courtesy of Fairchild Publications, Inc.; 7.2 © JLP/Jose L. Pelaez/Corbis; 7.3 © Guntmar Fritz/zefa/Corbis; 7.4 © Paul Hardy/Corbis; 7.5 © Royalty-Free/Corbis

Chapter 8

8.1 © P. Winbladh/zefa/Corbis; 8.2 © JLP/Jose L. Pelaez/Corbis; 8.3 © Royalty-Free/Corbis; 8.4 © Richard Townshend/Corbis; 8.5 © Royalty-Free/Corbis; 8.6 © Royalty-Free/Corbis

Chapter 9

9.1 © Kim Kulish/Corbis; 9.2 (top) Courtesy of Fairchild Publications, Inc.; 9.2 (bottom) Courtesy of Yoox.com; 9.3 Photo by Thomas Iannaccone/Courtesy of Fairchild Publications, Inc.; 9.4 Courtesy of Fairchild Publications, Inc.; 9.5 © Jerry Arcieri/Corbis; 9.6 Courtesy of Fairchild Publications, Inc.; 9.7 Photo by John Aquino/Courtesy of Fairchild Publications, Inc.; 9.8 © Gareth Brown/Corbis

Chapter 10

10.1 © Reuters/Corbis; 10.2 © Bernard Annebicque/Corbis Sygma; 10.3 © Julio Donoso/ Corbis Sygma; 10.4 Courtesy of Fairchild Publications, Inc.; 10.5 Photo by Marquita Sayres; 10.6 Bravo TV/Courtesy Everett Collection

Chapter 11

11.1 © Royalty-Free/Corbis; 11.2 © Zhuang Jin/Xinhua Press/Corbis; 11.3 © Mark Peterson/ Corbis; 11.4 © Satchan/zefa/Corbis; 11.5 © Yang Liu/Corbis

Chapter 12

12.1 © Royalty-Free/Corbis; 12.2 © Chuck Savage/Corbis; 12.3 © Royalty-Free/Corbis; 12.4 © Pinto/Corbis; 12.5 © LWA-Dann Tardif/Corbis; 12.6 © Anna Peisl/zefa/Corbis; 12.7 © Peter Beck/Corbis

Chapter 13

13.1 © Mark Savage/Corbis; 13.2 Photo by Chris Bickford/Courtesy of Jessica and Duncan; 13.3 © Micro Discovery/Corbis; 13.4 Courtesy of Fairchild Publications, Inc.; 13.5 Courtesy of Fairchild Publications, Inc.; 13.6 © Jens Kalaene/dpa/Corbis

Chapter 14

Box 14.1 Reprinted with permission of the Victoria & Albert Museum; 14.1 © Jeff Kowalsky/EPA/Corbis; 14.2 © David Butow/Corbis Saba; 14.3 Courtesy of Fairchild Publications, Inc.; 14.4 © Danilo Krstanovic/Corbis; 14.5 © Mike Finn-Kelcey/Reuters/Corbis; 14.6 Photo by Ed Diamante

Chapter 15

15.1 Courtesy of Fairchild Publications, Inc.; 15.2 Courtesy of Fairchild Publications, Inc.; 15.3 Courtesy of Jennifer McKelvie; 15.4 © Ludovic Maisant/Corbis; 15.5 Courtesy of Fairchild Publications, Inc.; 15.6 Courtesy of Jillian Lemaster; 15.7 Photo by Talaya

Centeno/Courtesy of Fairchild Publications, Inc.; Box 15.1 Courtesy of Michele Granger; Box 15.3 (top) Photo by Jennifer McKelvie; Box 15.3 (bottom) Courtesy of Marciann Patton

Chapter 16

16.1 Courtesy of Fairchild Publications, Inc.; 16.2 © Yuriko Nakao/Reuters/Corbis; 16.3 (left) Courtesy of Fairchild Publications, Inc.; 16.3 (right) Courtesy of Fairchild Publications, Inc.; 16.4 © Reuters/Corbis; 16.5 Courtesy of Fairchild Publications, Inc.; 16.6 © Holger Winkler/zefa/Corbis

INDEX